The Language of
Turn and Sequence

The Language of
Turn and Sequence

Edited by
Cecilia E. Ford
Barbara A. Fox
Sandra A. Thompson

OXFORD
UNIVERSITY PRESS

2002

OXFORD
UNIVERSITY PRESS

Oxford   New York
Athens   Auckland   Bangkok   Bogotá   Buenos Aires   Cape Town
Chennai   Dar es Salaam   Delhi   Florence   Hong Kong   Istanbul   Karachi
Kolkata   Kuala Lumpur   Madrid   Melbourne   Mexico City   Mumbai   Nairobi
Paris   São Paulo   Shanghai   Singapore   Taipei   Tokyo   Toronto   Warsaw

and associated companies in
Berlin   Ibadan

Library of Congress Cataloging-in-Publication Data
The language of turn and sequence / edited by Cecilia E. Ford, Barbara A. Fox, and
Sandra A. Thompson.
    p.   cm.—(Oxford studies in sociolinguistics)
Includes bibliographical references and index.
ISBN 0-19-512489-8
1. Conversation analysis.   I. Ford, Cecilia E.   II. Fox, Barbara A.
   III. Thompson, Sandra A.   IV. Series
P95.45 .L29   2001
302.3'46—dc21   00-058896

9 8 7 6 5 4 3 2 1

Printed in the United States of America
on acid-free paper

This volume is dedicated to
Emanuel A. Schegloff

ACKNOWLEDGMENTS

We thank Douglas Maynard for helpful comments on our proposal and Edward Finegan for feedback and support in all stages of the production of this volume. We gratefully acknowledge Makoto Hayashi for his special contribution to this volume; Makoto gave us invaluable editorial support and intellectual stimulation throughout this project. Finally, we are deeply indebted to Peter Ohlin and Cynthia Garver at Oxford and copyeditor Barbara Wild for their careful treatment of a manuscript filled with special characters, symbols, figures, and language.

CONTENTS

*The Language of
Turn and Sequence*

1

Introduction

CECILIA E. FORD, BARBARA A. FOX,
& SANDRA A. THOMPSON

Consider . . . the philologist or historical linguist of the distant or proximate future who treats as the linguistic remains of contemporary society not scrolls, books, or memoranda but film and video/audio tape of everyday, spontaneous interaction in the lives people live. Imagine as well that such a linguist is not committed to a theoretical set and to terms of analysis like those currently familiar but is prepared to derive the appropriate terms of analysis from the materials under investigation. What understanding of the English language might result if not only the analyses but also the very terms of analysis were formed on the basis of such materials?   —Emanuel A. Schegloff, 1979

In "The Relevance of Repair to Syntax-for-Conversation," Emanuel Schegloff (1979) offered discourse-functional linguists the opportunity to imagine the kind of linguistics that could emerge as a result of modern data-recording technology. He pointed to the profound reworking of linguistic methods and terms of analysis that such new forms of data might demand.

While some discourse-oriented linguists continue to work with written data, a number of scholars who work at the intersections of linguistics, anthropology, sociology, psychology, and education have taken seriously the challenge presented to discourse linguistics by the kinds of data available through new technologies, especially with reference to our ability to document the interactional nature of language. These scholars have begun to develop the new analytical terms that such data require of us. Now, twenty years after the publication of Schegloff's study of repair and syntax, the contributors to the current collection are working within an expanded conceptualization of discourse-functional linguistics, one informed by the availability of videotaped face-to-face conversational data.

In our experience, the greatest aids to working with such conversational data are the methods and findings of Conversation Analysis (CA). Conversation Analytic research draws attention to the temporal, spatial, and interactional character of naturally occurring talk. Within this temporal, spatial, and interactional matrix, it appears that two of the main functions of language are the actions of building turns and sequences; thus, turn and sequence are core concepts for a functional linguistic perspective on talk-in-interaction. Because the goal of the current volume is to bring the frameworks of discourse-functional linguistics and CA to bear on one another, we have chosen to focus on turn and sequence.

The studies in this volume explore the systematic nature of talk-in-interaction, employing units of analysis that are explicitly reflective of what interactants treat as real. The studies collected here have in common their foundations in seminal work in CA, documenting the provisional yet recurrent and predictable patterns of turn-taking and action sequencing in conversational interaction (e.g., Sacks, Schegloff, and Jefferson 1974; Schegloff and Sacks 1973; Schegloff, Jefferson, and Sacks 1977; Jefferson 1978).

In this introduction we briefly outline a perspective on the intellectual context of research on interaction. We then preview the chapters in the volume, discussing subsets of the studies in light of their treatment of issues of turn construction and the centrality of practices in sequence organization in the analyses they present.

The Intellectual Context

For many linguistic theories, social interaction—the phylogenetic and ontogenetic habitat of natural language—continues to be viewed as a messy, derivative, and flawed form of language (either explicitly or implicitly). Taken in the context of these theories of language, the scholarship that has grown from the influence of CA presents a sharp contrast. For more than thirty years, CA has offered to a broad interdisciplinary community, with interests in language use, a theoretical and methodological foundation for documenting the interactional construction of social orders. Social order, from this perspective, is understood as practice, an order created by participants in talk-in-interaction—jointly, contingently, and always locally. From an originally nonlinguistic perspective, Harvey Sacks, Emanuel Schegloff, and Gail Jefferson, the founders of the field, developed this theory and method to account in a detailed, data-driven manner for the resources and practices used in creating social orders through situated language use.

This volume brings together current research that is strongly influenced by the Conversation Analytic approach to understanding language use, with a special emphasis on what the methods and findings of CA can offer to discourse-functional linguistics (see Cumming and Ono 1997 for a review of discourse-functional linguistics). We use the term "discourse-functional linguistics" here to cover a wide range of research methods and findings. Under this umbrella we mean to include researchers such as Dwight Bolinger, Joan Bybee, Wallace L. Chafe, Susanna Cumming, John Du Bois, Talmy Givón, John Haiman, M.A.K. Halliday, Paul Hopper, Robert Longacre, Doris Payne, and Sandra Thompson, to name a few, who have examined the recurrence of forms and structures in language use, uncovering functional motivations for such patterns. This research tradition is notable in tying together discourse structures, cognitive mechanisms, and patterns of grammar. The work of William Labov and Deborah Schiffrin can also be considered discourse-functional, cutting as it does across linguistics and sociology in unique ways.

We would also include within the subfield of discourse-functional linguistics the groundbreaking work of Erving Goffman, Dell Hymes, John Gumperz, and Frederick Erickson. While these scholars are distinct from one another in many ways, their collective contributions have given impetus to a broad area of inquiry sometimes referred to as interactional sociolinguistics (see Schiffrin 1994 for distinctions between the ethnography of communication and interactional sociolinguistics). The work of Gumperz and Deborah Tannen has elucidated contextualization and framing practices of diverse speakers, who often come together in the complex and rapidly changing settings of social interaction (Gumperz 1982). While these researchers are largely committed to exploring issues of language and social equity, much scholarship in this area contributes to the discourse-functional enterprise as well. Indeed, researchers such as Peter Auer, Susanne Günthner, Margret Selting, and Elizabeth Couper-Kuhlen make use of the contextualization framework in their linguistic analyses (see Auer and di Luzio 1992).

Included within our use of the term "discourse-functional linguistics" are a number of researchers with intellectual roots in linguistics and anthropology and also influenced by Goffman, who have for many years been pointing to the intersection of grammar and social interaction. Elinor Ochs, Bambi B. Schieffelin, and Alessandro Duranti are prominent among these pioneers. In a 1976 paper, Ochs Keenan and Schieffelin took issue with the syntactic notion of "left-dislocation" as one that missed the obvious point that referents introduced before propositions about them were clearly tied to interactional sequences and gained their function as much from their placement in emergent talk as from their relation to a subsequent sentence. Duranti (1984) demonstrated the analytic leverage one gains by looking at turn-initial forms from the point of view of their functions in interactional sequences.

Given this characterization of discourse-functional linguistics, it is reasonable to ask what CA can offer to such a diverse community of scholars. A look at current and past issues of such journals as *TEXT, Language in Society, Journal of Pragmatics, Research on Language and Social Interaction,* and *Pragmatics* provides a daunting picture of the vastness and variety of methods and findings on language in interaction. However, we believe that the methods and findings of CA show particular promise for providing a strong empirical framework for accounts of linguistic structures.

CA emerged from ethnomethodology, a subdiscipline of sociology (see Heritage 1984, Maynard and Clayman 1991). From this sociological perspective, the original impetus for the study of conversation was an interest in documenting the ongoing collaborative creation of social structure through interaction. The early work in CA grew from a dissatisfaction with what these researchers viewed as an undisciplined and unmotivated positing of social categories by sociologists. One goal, then, has been to ground social practices and conceptions of social context in the empirical study of human interactions, an approach that looks for social categories as they are oriented to by participants in social activities. Thus, social context is treated in a rigorous way by examining the social displays of interactants. Through the close examination of taped and transcribed talk, CA researchers have discovered highly predictable patterns: turn-construction practices along with principles that guide the joint construction of action sequences carried out through those turns.

The focus on the moment-by-moment indexing by participants of what is relevant for them has led to a set of fundamental but powerful concepts, principles, and structures used in CA. Indeed, CA findings are being borrowed and adapted by scholars who study interaction from diverse theoretical perspectives. Among the systems that have been particularly well documented are turn taking (including turn projection), sequence organization, and the intersection of turn and sequence in the differential organization of affiliative and nonaffiliative talk (preference organization). It is this set of principles and patterns that the contributors to this volume have found to provide particularly relevant social-interactional grounding to the enterprise of understanding the functional bases of language use.

While a number of other useful frameworks exist that document structures in conversational interaction (e.g., the systemic account represented in Eggins and Slade 1997), the CA approach is distinct in its goal of basing observations, claims, and generalizations on the close analysis of specific cases from naturally occurring talk. The principles of turn taking and sequence organization that are fundamental to the CA enterprise are explicitly referenced in accounts for particular collections of new cases; thus, generalizations, while presented as strong claims for particular data sets, are always to be taken as provisional, testable, and revisable as further empirical research, with new data, provides convergent or divergent cases.

In 1979, with the publication of Schegloff's study of repair within a volume dedicated to discourse and syntax, the path was laid for a line of Conversation Analytic research to contribute to the growth of discourse-functional linguistics. In the years since, CA scholarship has converged with discourse-functional linguistics in two ways:

1. CA researchers have produced studies that in themselves constitute functional accounts of language use. For example, Goodwin (1979) describes the contingent and joint achievement of a single sentence, Heritage and Roth (1995) provide an account for turns that function as questions in news interviews, and Lerner (1991) examines collaborative turn sequences in relation to grammatical structures.
2. Discourse-functional linguists have begun to adopt CA methods in order to expand our understanding of grammar as an interactionally shaped phenomenon. For example, Fox (1987) finds the notion of sequence to be fundamental to an understanding of anaphora in American English conversations, and Ford (1993) uses CA, in combination with the more cognitively motivated insights of Chafe (1984), to document the interactional uses of adverbial clauses (also in American English data). Houtkoop and Mazeland (1985) and Selting (1998) have addressed issues related to turn taking and units of turn construction in longer stretches of single-speaker talk. In fact, several recent collections serve as evidence for the coming together of discourse-functional linguists and scholars who concentrate on the study of social interaction. (Auer and di Luzio 1992; Couper-Kuhlen and Selting

1996; Ford and Wagner 1996; Ochs, Schegloff, and Thompson 1996; Couper-Kuhlen and Selting 2001).

While CA has a great deal to contribute to discourse-functional linguistics, it also has much to offer to contemporary research in anthropology, sociology, literary studies, and education. Such scholarship regularly cites theories of language and action that emphasize the normative and yet provisional and socially or dialogically mediated nature of social orders. Researchers in these fields find compelling the social and dialogic theories of Mikhail M. Bakhtin, Alexei Leont'ev, and Pierre Bourdieu, among others. What CA offers, however, is a rigorous analytical framework for detailing the practices and resources social actors use to collaboratively create and index the "habitus" (Bourdieu 1990), the socially constituted interactional matrices for cooperation and resistance in social life.

Key to the CA enterprise is the close analysis of the interactional construction of turns and attention to action sequencing in the production and interpretation of interactional meanings and in the collaborative creation of local social structures. CA offers a powerful set of basic principles, accounting for recognizable and recurrent social practices and representing one important level of structure creation and renewal in human interaction. Using the findings of CA as points of departure and specifically working with the emergent linguistic/social structures of turns and sequences, the contributors to this volume explore the complex practices through which interactants create meaning through even the smallest of gestures and tokens of talk.

The Studies

This volume offers contributions by researchers who address gaps in discourse-functional linguistics and the sociolinguistic enterprise of CA, the former having yet to truly address social-interactional foundations of language and the latter often lacking linguistic sophistication. The unifying theme for the chapters in this volume is the intersection of interactional practices and language practices in the contexts of, and through the joint construction of, turns and sequences (Sacks, Schegloff, and Jefferson 1974; Schegloff and Sacks 1973; Sacks 1987; Schegloff forthcoming). The contributors focus on the interwoven systems of turns and sequences as central practices in context creation and renewal to which participants in talk must be answerable in an interactionally contingent and constantly revisable manner.

The choice of theme—the language of turn and sequence—grows out of several convergent research traditions, primarily within linguistics, anthropology, and sociology but also within communication studies, applied linguistics, and cognitive science. In conjunction with expanding the terrain of discourse-functional linguistics to include the matrix of interactional practices in which language arises, the contributions to this volume deal in particular with these two basic systems of practice. While the systems of turn and sequence are ultimately intertwined, we will discuss them with a degree of separation.

Functions of Turns

The turn is a much researched and contested unit; what is not contested, however, is the fact that participants in interaction recurrently treat as relevant, real, and consequential an individual's speaking time/space. This claim is often misinterpreted as implying that speakers never overlap or that turns are always or "ideally" coherent, complete, and produced by single speakers, in the clear. However, much work on turn-taking, beginning with Sacks, Schegloff, and Jefferson (1974), has documented both the fact and the ways that simultaneous talk regularly occurs, as well as the organization of simultaneous gesture, gaze, and talk (Goodwin 1981). Research further demonstrates that speakers' production of simultaneous talk is ordered, consequential, and functional, precisely in relation to the projectable linguistic and social unfolding of turns (Jefferson 1973, 1983; Lerner 1993, 1996; Ford and Thompson 1996:157–164; Schegloff 1995).

The study of turns at talk and participants' orientations to their structures are points of obvious intersection between the goals of CA and those of discourse-functional linguistics. If, as Cumming and Ono have stated, one of the goals of discourse-functional linguistics is to explain why grammars "have the resources they have" (1997:112), then discourse-oriented linguists need to include in the scope of their explanations the ways that interactants themselves deploy and act upon units of talk-in-interaction. All the studies in this volume address the structure, placement, and function of turns, but in particular the chapters of Ford, Fox, and Thompson, Hayashi, Mori, and Takagi, Jasperson, Sorjonen, Heritage, and Lerner deepen our sense of the interactionally adapted shaping of turns.

The chapter by Cecilia Ford, Barbara Fox, and Sandra Thompson stands at the intersection of linguistics and CA, addressing the issues of turn construction by examining the grammatical resources involved in the same-speaker extension of a turn. Such extensions have been noted in the CA literature as "add-ons," "extensions," and "increments." What Ford, Fox, and Thompson suggest is that certain systematic interactional practices associated with turn increments can be usefully understood in relation to the traditional linguistic notion of "constituency"; their findings point to grammatical and interactional distinctions between increments that are produced as continuations of possibly complete turns and increments that are produced as other than continuations (typically "free Noun Phrases"). This study affirms the value of approaching the understanding of turns in talk-in-interaction with an eye toward both the organization of conversation and the adaptive patterns of language use we call grammar.

Makoto Hayashi, Junko Mori, and Tomoyo Takagi employ a high level of linguistic sophistication in revealing, among other phenomena, the close connection between linguistic structures and social actions, as they document how "co-tellership" is achieved in a multiparty conversation. Their study includes attention to such traditional linguistic notions as zero-anaphora, sentence-final particles, and verb-final typology in Japanese; but, critically, they tie these structural aspects of the language into an examination of the contingencies of social interaction, including fine-grained attention to gesture and gaze. The coordination of these nonvocal aspects of talk-in-

interaction with the more familiar verbal components challenges us to reexamine long-held views of the nature of language.

The chapter by Robert Jasperson presents an exquisitely detailed phonetic description of and phonological account for "closure cut-off," that technique by which speakers of English stop "a next sound due" (Schegloff 1979). Because cut-off is one of the major resources by which self-initiated same-turn repair is initiated, its properties are fundamental to the study of repair. Jasperson's study is a crucial contribution to our understanding of repair initiation in that it is the first in-depth documentation of the articulatory characteristics of cut-off as they specifically accomplish cut-off and provides a critical link between those articulatory characteristics and the function of initiating repair.

Marja-Leena Sorjonen's contribution also demonstrates the value in expanding the empirical base of functionally oriented linguistic research. The subject of her investigation, a particle used by recipients of longer turns in Finnish talk-in-interaction, can only be understood in relation to a matrix of interactional practices. The minimal particle *no* in Finnish may constitute a turn in itself, and an action it regularly serves is to show its producer's alignment as an ongoing recipient to the longer turn of a prior speaker. However, after certain types of prior turns, this minimal particle displays not just alignment as a recipient but also a particular stance toward what is being reported in the prior speaker's continuing turn. While the particles that have traditionally interested linguists are ones that are integrated into sentences, Sorjonen's study shows the effects of these minimal linguistic units as turns in themselves, taken in their interactional contexts.

The contributions of John Heritage and Gene Lerner, both sociologists, offer a sense of what the accumulated findings from CA have to offer to functionally oriented linguists. In common with Jasperson's study, Lerner's chapter documents patterns in the real-time unfolding of turns. Lerner shows us just how mistaken it can be to assume a one-at-a-time ordering of turns. As Lerner has demonstrated in prior research, participants in conversations show complex syntactic coordination in their collaborative production of turns; here he documents the choral co-production of turns as a formal practice that is well adapted to a variety of interactional functions. Lerner's investigation also stretches our conceptions of co-production by attending to interactionally consequential practices of gestural coordination.

John Heritage's work also bridges the gap between linguistic and Conversation Analytic research. Like Sorjonen, Heritage investigates a linguistic particle, expanding his long-term study of the different functions of English *oh* deployed as a turn preface. As does Sorjonen, Heritage connects practices of turn construction and turn placement, showing how, in conjunction, these systems provide resources for local displays of interactional stance in relation to the judgments and assessments. Where more mainstream approaches to discourse concentrate on correlations between forms of reference and the cognitive status of information as new or familiar, Heritage's work focuses attention on the interactionally contestable nature of stances taken toward an interlocutor as knowing or unknowing relative to the content of a turn.

While these studies give us insights into the structure of turns and the work that turns do, in these chapters and the others in the volume the matrix of interactional activity, the sequence, is also integral.

The Matrix of Sequence

As units, turns are deployed as actions in sequences. As a dynamic matrix of activity, sequence organization involves two or more individuals in a focused manner. In documenting such organization, the analyst is observing the obvious and yet complex fact that there is a temporal and progressive ordering of actions in interaction. The production of a turn involves an ordered progression through a verbally structured action, and the operation of turn taking depends on an ordering of speaking opportunities. Another obvious fact, though a fact not easily accounted for, is that certain actions are treated as relevant after certain other actions. This observation has led Conversation Analysts to document specific sequence types. Sequence structure has been revealed through research on paired utterances (adjacency pairs), preferred response types and shapes, and the interactional emergence of special speaking roles such as those manifested in story sequences. What is common in this research is that it has been arrived at through methodological reliance on participants' displays that certain specific action types are relevant at specific points in recognizably unfolding sequence types (Schegloff and Sacks 1973; Schegloff forthcoming). That is, though it is clearly the case that answers do not always follow questions, for example, one observes that when an answer does not come in such an interactional slot, whatever *does* come is treated as in some way related to the relevance of an answer.

In the research reported in this volume, the functions of verbal and nonverbal contributions are integrally related to specific sequential contexts. These studies point in a variety of ways to the relationship between what is produced in and across turns and what joint activity is being contingently and collaboratively constructed. Thus, the chapters by Heritage and Sorjonen both treat turn types and the work that these turns do as tightly tied to the sequences in which they are deployed. Likewise, Lerner's analysis, while complicating the notion of sequence in addressing simultaneous talk, is critically dependent on an explication of the work of turns in sequence. Ford, Fox, and Thompson's analysis of increments to possibly complete turns and Hayashi, Mori, and Takagi's treatment of "co-tellership" rely crucially on an understanding of the actions done by turns in their sequential environments.

Charles Goodwin, Marjorie Harness Goodwin, and David Olsher's study is perhaps the most striking with regard to the context of sequence, demonstrating the capacity for sequence structure—in conjunction with resources of prosody, gaze, and gesture—to provide for meaning making. These scholars examine the artful co-participation that characterizes interactions of a severely aphasic man and his interlocutors. While Chil, the participant with severe aphasia, commands only a very limited productive vocabulary, his command of sequence organization and his lived role in his family allow him to interact remarkably well. This study underscores the social nature of language impairments, and in addition to showing the impressive interactional work that goes on to make meaning in this special circumstance, the study challenges us to consider more fully the roles of the body and the setting of action in giving meaning to spoken turns.

Sally Jacoby and Patrick Gonzales's chapter on the functions of negative observations delivered by a senior scientist to his advanced students underscores how the work of a turn type is related to its occurrence in a particular sequence type. Systematic linkages are found among linguistic structure, turn design, and sequential deployment in the practice of the senior scientist commenting on "what wasn't said" during student rehearsals of academic presentations. This research has relevance both to a favorite concern of linguists, reported speech, and to a particularly rich Conversation Analytic topic, the explication of complaint sequences.

Lisa Capps and Elinor Ochs bring a respectful precision to their analysis of the interactional genre of shared, public prayer. They not only show how prayer is different from mundane, nonsacred communication, but they also show that while one can call prayer a genre, it remains an interactional achievement, involving inflections of language and of the body. By attending to children's difficulties in maintaining the "prayerful attitude" over the time of a prayer and the adults' efforts to corral them in, through, and out of the activity, Capps and Ochs draw striking attention to the sequential organization of prayer as a matrix for collective participation.

The chapters in this volume all deal with talk in naturally occurring activities, and three typologically and genetically distinct languages are represented: English, Japanese, and Finnish. While the contributors come from applied linguistics, anthropology, psychology, sociology, and linguistics, they share an intellectual home territory in the work they present here, as well as in the fact that all have been profoundly influenced and informed by the terms and methods developed through CA and, in particular, in Emanuel Schegloff's fine-grained study of turns and sequences. We are his colleagues, students, and the students of his students, and in celebration of his infectious joy in continuing to discover ways in which people live their lives in terms of the language of turn and sequence, we have dedicated this volume to him.

REFERENCES

Auer, Peter, and Aldo di Luzio (eds.). 1992. *The Contextualization of Language*. Amsterdam: John Benjamins.

Bourdieu, Pierre. 1990. *The Logic of Practice*. Trans. Richard Nice. Stanford: Stanford University Press.

Chafe, Wallace. 1984. How people use adverbial clauses. In *Proceedings of the Tenth Annual Meeting of the Berkeley Linguistics Society*, 437–449. Berkeley: Berkeley Linguistics Society.

Couper-Kuhlen, Elizabeth, and Margret Selting (eds.). 1996. *Prosody in Conversation: Interactional Studies*. Cambridge: Cambridge University Press.

Couper-Kuhlen, Elizabeth, and Margret Selting (eds.). 2001. *Studies in Interactional Linguistics*. Amsterdam: John Benjamins.

Cumming, Susanna, and Tsuyoshi Ono. 1997. Discourse and grammar. In Teun A. van Dijk (ed.), *Discourse as Structure and Process*, 112–137. London: Sage.

Duranti, Alessandro. 1984. Referential and social meaning of subject pronouns in Italian. *TEXT* 4:277–311.

Eggins, Suzanne, and Diana Slade. 1997. *Analysing Casual Conversation.* London: Cassell.

Ford, Cecilia E. 1993. *Grammar in Interaction: Adverbial Clauses in American English Conversations.* Cambridge: Cambridge University Press.

Ford, Cecilia E., and Sandra A. Thompson. (1996). Interactional units in conversation: Syntactic, intonational, and pragmatic resources for the management of turns. In Elinor Ochs, Emanuel A. Schegloff, and Sandra A. Thompson (eds.), *Interaction and Grammar,* 134–184. Cambridge: Cambridge University Press.

Ford, Cecilia E., and Johannes Wagner (eds.). 1996. Interaction-based studies of language. Special Issue of *Pragmatics* 6(3): 277–456.

Fox, Barbara. 1987. *Discourse Structure and Anaphora.* Cambridge: Cambridge University Press.

Goodwin, Charles. 1979. The interactive construction of a sentence in natural conversation. In George Psathas (ed.), *Everyday Language: Studies in Ethnomethodology,* 97–121. New York: Irvington.

Goodwin, Charles. 1981. *Conversational Organization: Interactions between Speakers and Hearers.* New York: Academic Press.

Gumperz, John J. 1982. *Discourse Strategies.* Cambridge: Cambridge University Press.

Heritage, John C. 1984. *Garfinkel and Ethnomethodology.* Cambridge: Polity Press.

Heritage, John C., and Andrew L. Roth. 1995. Grammar and institution: Questions and questioning in broadcast news interviews. *Research on Language and Social Interaction* 28(1): 1–60.

Houtkoop, Hanneke, and Harrie Mazeland. 1985. Turns and discourse units in everyday conversation. *Journal of Pragmatics* 9:595–619.

Jefferson, Gail. 1973. A case of precision timing in ordinary conversation: Overlapped tag-positioned address terms in closing sequences. *Semiotica* 9:47–96.

Jefferson, Gail. 1978. Sequential aspects of storytelling in conversation. In Jim Schenkein (ed.), *Studies in the Organization of Conversational Interaction,* 219–248. New York: Academic Press.

Jefferson, Gail. 1983. Notes on some orderlinesses of overlap onset. In V. d'Urso and P. Leonardi (eds.), *Discourse Analysis and Natural Rhetoric,* 11–38. Padua, Italy: Cleup.

Keenan, Elinor Ochs, and Bambi B. Schieffelin. 1976. Foregrounding referents: A reconsideration of left-dislocation in discourse. *Proceedings of the Second Annual Meeting of the Berkeley Linguistics Society,* 240–257. Berkeley: Berkeley Linguistics Society.

Lerner, Gene H. 1991. On the syntax of sentences-in-progress. *Language in Society* 20:441–458.

Lerner, Gene H. 1993. Collectivities in action: Establishing the relevance of conjoined participation in conversation. *TEXT* 13(2): 213–245.

Lerner, Gene H. 1996. On the "semi-permeable" character of grammatical units in conversation: Conditional entry into the turn space of another speaker. In Elinor Ochs, Emanuel A. Schegloff, and Sandra A. Thompson (eds.), *Interaction and Grammar,* 238–276. Cambridge: Cambridge University Press.

Maynard, Douglas W., and Steven E. Clayman. 1991. The diversity of ethnomethodology. *Annual Review of Sociology* 17:385–418.

Ochs, Elinor, Emanuel A. Schegloff, and Sandra A. Thompson (eds.). 1996. *Interaction and Grammar.* Cambridge: Cambridge University Press.

Sacks, Harvey. 1987. On the preferences for agreement and contiguity in sequences in conversation. In Graham Button and John R. E. Lee (eds.), *Talk and Social Organisation,* 54–69. Philadelphia: Multilingual Matters.

Sacks, Harvey, Emanuel A. Schegloff, and Gail Jefferson. 1974. A simplest systematics for the organization of turn-taking in conversation. *Language* 50(4): 696–735.

Schegloff, Emanuel A. 1979. The relevance of repair to syntax-for-conversation. In *Syntax and Semantics*, vol. 12: *Discourse and Syntax*, edited by Talmy Givón, 261–286. New York: Academic Press.

Schegloff, Emanuel A. 1995. Parties and talking together: Two ways in which numbers are significant for talk-in-interaction. In P. ten Have and G. Psathas (eds.), *Situated Order: Studies in the Social Organization of Talk and Embodied Activities*, 31–42. Washington, DC: University Press of America.

Schegloff, Emanuel A. Forthcoming. Sequence organization. *Talking in Interaction: An Introduction to Conversation Analysis*.

Schegloff, Emanuel A., Gail Jefferson, and Harvey Sacks. 1977. The preference for self-correction in the organization of repair in conversation. *Language* 53(2): 361–382.

Schegloff, Emanuel A., and Harvey Sacks. 1973. Opening up closings. *Semiotica* 7:289–327.

Schiffrin, Deborah. 1994. *Approaches to Discourse*. Cambridge, MA: Basil Blackwell.

Selting, Margret. 1998. *TCUs and TRPs: The Construction of Units in Conversational Talk*. Interaction and Linguistic Structures (InLiSt) 4. University of Konstanz, Germany.

2

Constituency and the Grammar of Turn Increments

CECILIA E. FORD, BARBARA A. FOX,
& SANDRA A. THOMPSON

Much work in linguistics of the last fifty years has relied on the notion of grammatical "constituents," hierarchically organized groups of words and phrases. Since the 1930s, "constituent" has generally been understood as a schematic group of words which is:

1. identifiable in terms of characteristic distributional properties as a recurrent part of a larger unit
2. identifiable as a coherent unit in terms of three types of groupings: syntactic, semantic, and prosodic.

This two-part understanding of constituent incorporates both the insight that a "constituent" is a *part of* a larger element (1) and the insight that it has *internal* coherence (2). The notion of "constituent" has proven itself to be valuable to analysts, both within the generative paradigm (see, e.g., Radford 1988, 1997) as well as within a discourse-functional framework (see, e.g., Givón 1995; Nichols 1986; Payne 1990). Langacker (1995, 1997) notes that syntactic distributional criteria for grouping clusters of words may not always coincide with semantic and/or prosodic groupings. He proposes the term *classic constituent* for a cluster of words in an utterance in which all three groupings coincide. We will also find this concept useful in our analysis.

Moreover, studies from within the Conversation Analysis (CA) tradition have provided evidence for how such "classic constituents" might actually be oriented to by participants as a resources for social action in a conversation. That is, CA studies have shown that what linguists would label grammatical constituents can be formats for strategic interactional functions. Turn taking is a closely monitored and coordinated joint activity, with many turn transitions achieved without any overlap or silence; when overlaps or gaps emerge, they are patterned and accountable. Thus, gap-free turn transition and turn changes that involve overlaps or gaps are all interactionally exploited alternatives.

What conversation analysts, beginning with Sacks, Schegloff, and Jefferson (1974), have suggested is that grammatical constituency (though they have not used this linguistic terminology) is central to the projection of points of possible turn completion (see also Ford and Thompson 1996; Selting 1996). In two influential contributions, C. Goodwin (1979, 1981) demonstrates the variety of interactional factors at work in projecting the ends of syntactic units and in extending a turn beyond the first location of potential turn change ("transition relevance place" [Sacks et al. 1974]). Goodwin's research suggests that turn completion and turn extension are coordinated through at least a combination of gaze and syntax in face-to-face interaction. Some of his key examples of "added segments" are, in fact, "classic constituents," such as Noun Phrases (NPs) and adverbials.

Similar patterns of constituents as added segments are evident in the examples cited by M. Goodwin (1980). In that article, she examines the ways that speakers and recipients mutually coordinate their contributions to description sequences, with speakers adding segments to their assessment turns so as to arrive at completion while their recipients are making appreciative contributions. Lerner (1987, 1989, 1991, 1992, 1996a, 1996b) shows how collaborative turn sequences, turn units produced by two or more speakers, provide evidence for the role of syntactic units in projecting completion points. The collaborative turns he analyzes include units whose structures are projected beyond the first point of syntactic completion, such as adverbial clauses. Ford (1993) points to the work of adverbial clause turn extensions as resources for managing emergent disagreement, while Couper-Kuhlen (1996) looks at the complex manner in which prosody contextualizes *because*-clause constituents coming after main clauses in English conversations. Mori (1999) and Tanaka (1999) analyze interactional functions of additions to turns in Japanese conversations, and Auer (1996) examines the information management aspects of turn continuations in German. Fox and Jasperson (1995) and Fox, Hayashi, and Jasperson (1996) offer evidence that "classic constituency" is relevant in analyzing the way English interactants organize repair. And Ford, Fox, and Thompson (1996) explore the relationship among possible turn completion, constituency, and features of prosody, gaze, and sequential action.

Against the backdrop of this research in linguistics and CA, in this chapter we provide further evidence that constituency is functionally exploited by participants in naturally occurring American English conversations; that is, we will suggest that participants in a conversation use constituency (or nonconstituency) as an interactional resource.

The constituents we will be exploring all occur as what Schegloff (1996) terms "increments," constituents that are added to turns that, at a just prior point, are interpretable as possibly complete syntactically and prosodically and as possibly complete actions in a local interactional sequence (Ford and Thompson 1996; Tanaka 1999). As noted earlier in this chapter, upcoming points of possible completion are carefully constructed and monitored by interactants. Social meaning is attached to turn transitions; the "meaning" of a turn can depend on whether the speaker begins just at the termination of the previous turn, in overlap with that turn, or only after a pause. A consequence of this split-second timing (Jefferson 1973) is that a speaker will listen and watch for cues as to whether a recipient is about to begin a turn, and if such immediate uptake does not seem imminent, the speaker may add a unit, thereby producing a new point of completion.

In this chapter, we examine the interactional use of increments and suggest that the way these increments are used by speakers tells us much about the motivations for the sorts of groupings that linguists call (classic) constituents as well as about how speakers exploit grammatical resources in the systematic way they add more talk to what is hearably an already-complete utterance.

Let us now turn to a consideration of what constitutes an "increment."

What Are Increments?

For the purposes of this work, we define an increment as a nonmain-clause continuation after a possible point of turn completion. That is, an increment will be defined here as any nonmain-clause continuation of a speaker's turn after that speaker has come to what could have been a completion point, or a "transition-relevance place," based on prosody, syntax, and sequential action (see Sacks et al. 1974; Oreström 1983; Ford and Thompson 1996; Tanaka 1999). In English such added increments may take the form of simple NPs; they may be prepositional phrases, signaled at their beginnings with a preposition; or they may be subordinate clauses, often introduced by a subordinating morpheme.

In this chapter we will be more concerned with portion (1) of the characterization of "constituent" given earlier: the way in which "constituents" emerge as recurrent portions of material in larger units. By focusing on this aspect of "constituent," we can distinguish two kinds of increments in our data. The first are what C. Goodwin (1981: chap. 4) and M. H. Goodwin (1980) have termed "added segments" and Schegloff (1996) has termed "extensions." Following Schegloff, we will call these Extensions as well. They are increments that are interpretable as continuations of the immediately prior possibly completed turn. That is, they can be heard as syntactically and semantically coherent with what has come before. In example (1) the extension is in boldface:

(1)

> Bill said that he was at le̲a̲st goin' e̲i̲ghty miles an ho̲u̲r.
> ⇒   **with the _two_ of 'em on it.**

In this example, the speaker comes to a place of possible completion at the end of *hour*. At this juncture, the utterance is hearably complete syntactically (a complete clause), prosodically (low falling intonation), and pragmatically. Nonetheless, the speaker speaks again. Crucially, when he speaks, he does so not with a syntactically independent unit but rather with what can be heard as a syntactic continuation of what had looked like a syntactically complete turn. He produces *with the two of 'em on it,* which can be interpreted as an adverbial continuation of *he was at least goin' eighty miles an hour.* For our analysis, then, Extensions can be thought of as *constituents of* prior turn units.

Compare example (1) with our second kind of increment. In these contrasting cases, as with Extensions, the speaker comes to a place of possible completion and speaks again. However, in the second type of increment what is added is not interpretable as a constituent of the possibly completed turn. While there is a range of grammatical types that can occur in this environment, we will focus on what appears to be the largest subclass of these syntactically independent constituents, those that Ono and Thompson (1994) have called "Unattached NPs."[1] These are NPs that occur as increments after a place of possible completion but that are *not* interpretable as syntactic constituents, or syntactically integrated continuations, of that immediately prior turn.[2] Consider example (2):

(2)

> Curt: °(Oh Christ)° fifteen thousand dollars wouldn't <u>tou</u>ch a Co:rd,
>   (0.7)
> Curt: That guy was (dreaming).
>   **<u>fif</u>teen thousand dollars** [**for an original Co:rd,**
> Gary: [<u>Fi</u>gured he'd imp<u>re</u>ss him,

Although *That guy was dreaming.* is possibly complete in terms of syntax, prosody, and sequential action, the speaker adds an increment. In this example the increment is not a possible syntactic constituent of *That guy was dreaming.* Rather than being a continuation of the prior clause, or what we term an Extension, the increment in example (2) is an Unattached NP.

Figure 2.1 summarizes the distinction we have made. To roughly determine the relative frequencies of the types of increments we are discussing, we used a separate and previously coded audio data base from Ono and Thompson (1995). In that data base, out of a total of sixty-four increments, forty-five were Extensions and nineteen were Free Constituents, and of Free Constituents, a great majority (fifteen) were Unattached NPs.

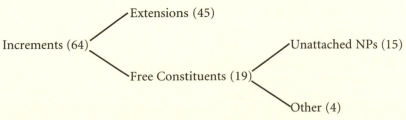

Figure 2.1   Types of increments.

In looking closely at constituents added past points of possible completion in the current data, we have found systematic interactional tasks that correspond to the formal and semantic dichotomy of Extensions and Unattached-NP increments. Our collection of cases offers support for the claim that speakers use the structural resources of English to perform different interactional tasks, making use of Extension increments and Unattached NP increments in documentably distinct ways.

In terms of function, what the two types of increments have in common is that they emerge in environments where *recipiency* is a particular issue; that is, increments are added where there are identifiable problems faced by the speaker in pursuing uptake from a recipient (Heath 1984; Pomerantz 1984). Our data suggest, however, that speakers exploit the formal distinction between Extensions and Unattached NPs for interactional ends. Neither type of increment is interpretable as standing on its own; that is, neither can be taken in context as the beginning of a new and independent clause; but what we have found and will attempt to illustrate here is that Extension increments, as *constituents of* the preceding clause, continue the action of that turn, while Unattached NP increments, though not new turns, do the functionally separate action of assessing or commenting on the prior turn material.

The next section ("Increments as Extensions") examines some of the interactional work accomplished by increments as Extensions, and "Increments as Unattached NPs" examines the interactional work done by Unattached-NP increments. In "A Comparison of Increments as Extensions and Unattached NPs" we point to the importance of semantic properties for the notion "Extension." "Prosody and Increments" briefly considers prosody. In the final section, we discuss some implications of our findings.

The data for this study consisted of five videotaped conversations and one audiotaped telephone conversation among friends speaking American English.[3] The speakers are all in their twenties or thirties.

Increments as Extensions

Extensions turn out to be relatively common; we were able to make a collection of forty Extensions, culled from our conversational data base. While all of our Extensions fit the definition given earlier—that is, they are increments that can be heard as syntactic constituents of the immediately prior turn—the Extensions themselves are of a variety of syntactic types, including NPs, adverbs, adverbial phrases, prepositional phrases, relative clauses, and adverbial clauses. Some further examples from our collection follow (the Extensions themselves are given in boldface):

(3)

> Have you been to New Orleans?
> **ever?**

(4)

> We could'a used a little marijuana.
> **to get through the weekend.**

While our instances of Extensions are heterogeneous in terms of their internal makeup, they are quite homogeneous in their ability to serve as what Tanaka (1999:87) calls "recompleters"; that is, units that are added after a turn has passed through a possible transition-relevance place and "recomplete" that turn. So our Extensions can all be heard as "constituents of" the preceding utterance.[4]

We would like to emphasize that Extensions appear to be interactionally homogeneous as well: The one kind of interactional work they all seem to be engaged in is pursuing uptake by continuing the action of the just possibly-completed turn. In other words, they are attempted solutions to a lack of displayed recipiency. The speaker may be pursuing acknowledgment of or uptake to his/her utterance, pursuing a gazing recipient, or dealing with some other kind of "trouble" with the way the utterance so far is being treated by the addressees. For example, Goodwin (1979) provides illustrations of Extensions being related to the pursuit of a gazing recipient, and Ford (1993: chap. 5) discusses the ways in which adverbial clause Extensions are used when there is some perceived trouble with recipiency, such as lack of uptake, which provides an interactional warrant for further elaboration. In example (5), for instance, S adds an *if*-clause after failing to receive any acknowledgment or uptake from the recipient (taken from Ford 1993: 108; see appendix at end of chapter for transcription symbols):

(5)

      S: Ya know when it- (.) came from the:: I think air conditioning system, it drips
           on the front of the cars?
                     (.)
⇒   S: **If you park in a certain place?**
      R: Mm hmm

Ford argues against the notion of "afterthought," a term that draws attention away from the interactional factors involved in turn construction; she suggests that researchers need to consider how such increments could be "products of speaker–recipient negotiation specifically aimed at achieving interactional ends" (ibid.: 102). And one of those interactional ends is clearly pursuing uptake.

Let us now turn to a discussion of some of the Extensions in the current data to see in more detail the recipiency work that is being accomplished here.

Example (6) comes from a videotaped conversation known as "Chinese Dinner," so named because in it two heterosexual couples and two children are eating takeout food from a Chinese restaurant. These are data shared with us by Charles and Marjorie Goodwin, and our thinking about this example is entirely based on the groundbreaking interactional analysis in Goodwin 1981: 134–135 (also discussed in Goodwin 1989, 1995). The meal takes place at the home of John and Beth; the other couple, Ann and Don, are guests. Ann is visibly pregnant. In the fragment we will be concerned with, Ann is holding her hands to her waist; John is asking her a question and by doing so is proffering a topic for further talk[5]:

(6)

> John: An' how are you feeling?
>   (0.4)
>   **these days,**
> Ann: <u>Fa</u>:t. I can't- I don't have a waist anymore,

In this example, John comes to a place of possible completion at the end of *feeling*. At this juncture, the utterance is possibly complete syntactically (a complete clause), prosodically (high rising intonation), and pragmatically (the first part of an adjacency pair, a fundamental interactional sequence (Schegloff and Sacks 1973)). After a pause, John adds *these days*, which can be retroactively integrated into the previous clause as a temporal adverbial.

Just prior to this fragment, one of the children present has been talking. Ann and Don have been attending to the child. Ann leans back and touches her waist, and John begins a new sequence with his question. As John's turn reaches possible completion after *feeling*, Ann, the intended recipient, is looking down at her plate. Thus, John has come to a place of possible completion without a gazing recipient, a condition that is regularly oriented to by speakers as problematic (see Goodwin 1979, 1981). Moreover, there is no uptake or response from the recipient (Figure 2.2).

This utterance is a wonderful example of the extent to which speakers will go in order to correct such problems. As John comes to the end of *feeling*, he starts to put a piece of food into his open mouth. Finding that he does not have a gazing or responding recipient, he removes the food from his still-open mouth and continues the utterance, using the Extension *these days*. It is possible that the movement of the food serves as a "hitch," a momentary break in the progressivity of an action (Goodwin 1979, 1981), which attracts Ann's gaze.[6] In fact, Ann brings her gaze to John just as he begins the Extension.

Figure 2.2.   Ann (*far left*) looking down as John (*middle*) completes *feeling*.

Because speakers regularly treat the lack of gazing recipient as problematic, any Extension of the turn here would deal in some minimal way with the possible problem, offering a renewed point of possible completion, where the recipient might now meet the gaze of the speaker. The Extension in example (6), however, is designed to elicit the recipiency of Ann in an interesting manner. The question *An' how are you feeling?*, on the one hand, could have been meaningfully addressed to either Don or Ann; hence it is possible that Ann, hearing that particular question without seeing John's gaze direction, might not have found herself to be the intended recipient. *These days*, on the other hand, clearly specifies Ann as the recipient—Ann is pregnant, and it is a commonly held belief among members of this culture that a pregnant woman may feel many different ways in the course of her pregnancy. Thus, time (*these days*) and feelings changing over small periods of time may be relevant topics of discussion to direct toward a pregnant woman, in contrast to, for example, a (nonpregnant) man. And Ann apparently hears the Extension in just this way—she hears it as about her pregnancy, which she demonstrates with her answer (*Fat*).

A similar but alternative analysis is also available. Since Ann's gaze has already been secured by the beginning of the Extension, it is possible that John's Extension serves not to specify Ann as the recipient but to further specify the topic that is being proffered. *These days*, in this interpretation, could thus serve to further specify the question/topic proffer.

Whatever the best analysis for the Extension is, it is clear that John produces an Extension to his turn because of lack of displayed recipiency or uptake from Ann. Moreover, John can be heard to be continuing the same turn as before *and* continuing the same action as before, namely, a question/topic proffer. A continuation of the same action is done through the resource of syntactic Extension; continued action is done in the form of a constituent of the prior syntactic unit. This is a pattern we find throughout the data—continued action done with continuing syntax. We thus see that "constituency" can be usefully viewed as arising from interactional work that speakers do in real time and that is expandable in real time.

While the Extension in example (6) is in the form of an NP, it is not interpretable as an Unattached NP, since it provides a temporal adjunct in a syntactically integral manner for English. This case provides us with an opportunity to underscore the importance of both semantics and syntax for interpreting increments. While NPs may be Unattached (see "A Comparison of Increments as Extensions and Unattached NPs," below), the NP in example (6) is an Extension, a "continuation of," because it relates back to the previous turn unit as a temporal adverbial. Temporal adverbials are regularly included at the ends of intonationally and syntactically coherent units, that is, units without possibly complete subcomponents as marked by prosody. Consider example (7), in which temporal adverbials are, in fact, produced as parts of single syntactic and prosodic units, without gaps and, in one case (a), with the rest of the clause "wrapped around" the adjunct:

(7)

    Adverbial NPs
    (a) they went **the next day** to find (0.2) what room I lived in (SN4:311)

(b) I only went out **one ni:ght.**   (SN4:387)
(c) I've been thinking 'bout it **everyda:y.**   (AR:192)

It is precisely the recurrence of adverbial NPs as fully integrated constituents of larger utterances that makes them useful formats for adding increments as Extensions of prior actions. In contrast, in the case of Unattached NP increments ("A Comparison of Increments as Extensions and Unattached NPs"), there is no possibility of syntactic integration with the prior turn material.

Our next Extension, in example (8), was introduced as example (1) and comes from the videotape known as "Auto Discussion," also provided to us by the Goodwins. This tape was made in the seventies at a backyard picnic in central Ohio. When the tape begins there are three heterosexual couples present; the women gradually remove themselves from the picnic table, leaving behind the three men. The men's conversation revolves for the most part around cars and the "guys" who build and race them. Just prior to the following fragment they have been discussing one such guy, a guy by the name of Little. Little owns a snowmobile, and Gary has just told a story about how Little with his snowmobile raced some other guy with a motorcycle, on dry land, and Little *beat his ass!* In the interactional moment, Gary has not been very successful in securing enthusiastic recipiency from his interlocutors, but Curt eventually displays appreciation for Gary's story with *Those snowmobiles are fast.* Gary now offers another story:

(8)

> AD: 36
> Gary: Well he took Bill (Silvio). a good friend of mine, he weighs about two
>   hunderd'n s::(0.5) two hunderd (fifty)-five pounds I think he weighs. Took
>   him for a ride on that'n Bill said that he was at least goin' eighty miles an
>   hour.
>   with the ↑ two of 'em on it.

As noted, Gary was faced with a lack of displayed appreciation and uptake at crucial points in his earlier story about Little and the guy with the motorcycle. In the fragment given in example (8), Gary is again faced with problems in recipiency: the two other men present, Curt and Mike, are not looking at Gary at all until the turn comes to a place of possible completion (at *hour*), at which point only Curt looks over to Gary. But at this point Gary is looking toward Mike; thus, Gary has the problem of reaching a point of possible completion while directing his gaze toward a nongazing recipient (Figure 2.3). Gary has thus not yet secured an appropriately appreciative audience.

Gary then adds an Extension, *With the two of 'em on it,* an increment in pursuit of an appropriately appreciative audience. This Extension emphasizes what Gary is treating as the remarkable aspect of the event he is sharing—that a snowmobile could go that fast even with so much weight on it. Gary withdraws his gaze from Mike while producing the Extension, approximately at the word *'em* (*them*), and finds Curt as a gazing recipient (Figure 2.4). The Extension thus continues the action of the previous turn unit and provides a new place of possible completion,

Figure 2.3.   Gary directing his gaze at Mike, a non-gazing recipient (*left to right: Curt, Gary, Mike*).

where appropriate recipiency could be displayed (and, in fact, is displayed, albeit by a different recipient).

The intonational and gestural components of Gary's Extension can be interpreted as indicating salience. The Extension reaches its highest pitch on the word *two*, while the hand configuration that accompanies the Extension is iconic (McNeill 1992), being two fingers pointed downward and slightly apart, like two men on a snowmobile. The gesture also has a "beat" component to it, an up-and-

Figure 2.4.   Gary gazes toward Curt, a gazing recipient (*left to right: Curt, Gary, and Mike*).

down motion with the hand configuration maintained, which McNeill would analyze as a speaker-indication of importance. So Gary has built this Extension to draw attention and to elicit recipiency. These gestural features of the Extension enable it to do the work of pursuing recipiency in a fashion specifically tailored to prompting the actions relevant on completion of a story: assessment, appreciation, and displays of understanding (Jefferson 1978).

In this case, then, as in example (6), an Extension increment is used in order to address the problem of lack of appropriate recipiency; the Extension addresses the recipiency problems by continuing the action of the turn and providing a second place of possible completion, where another speaker could offer a show of alignment with the unfolding story. Gary's Extension thus provides another location at which he might secure an appreciative response from one of his recipients.

Our last example of an Extension increment, (9), comes from a videotaped interaction known as "Game Night." This tape was made in 1995, at the home of two of the participants, Terry and Pam, a lesbian couple. During this interaction, Terry, Pam, and three other women friends are playing a game of Pictionary. In the fragment we will be examining, the group is taking a break from the game because Pam is talking on the phone and one of the other participants, Cindy, is leaving to get ice cream. Three participants remain seated at the game table (Terry, Rachel, and Abbie); Cindy is off-camera, preparing to leave. The participants have been discussing a picture on the wall, drawn by the ten-year-old nephew of Pam and done in the style of Toulouse-Lautrec. The question of whether the boy copied a real Toulouse-Lautrec drawing or did an original drawing in the style of Toulouse-Lautrec has come up. Terry has suggested that he was studying Toulouse-Lautrec in school, and the talk continues:

(9)

```
        Cindy:   But still to be able to pr- reproduce it like that
        Rachel:  [Wow.
        Terry:   [It was cool. (.) We were very impressed. (.) He's an artistic little guy.
                     (0.2)
        Rachel:  I should say so.
                     (2.2)
        Rachel:  Is that his name? John Holms? ((reading from picture))
                     (0.2)
        Terry:   Yup.
                     (0.8)
        Abbie:   [Ah:
  ⇒    Terry:   [We had him, (.) this summer, (1.5) for f:i:ve weeks.
  ⇒                 (0.8)
  ⇒             when we were out at the campground?
        Rachel:  Oh really.
                     (0.4)
        Rachel:  Where.
```

At the first arrowed line, Terry starts to tell a piece of news about this young nephew, possibly prefacing a story. The turn is not possibly complete at *him*, since pragmatically that would not be a complete action at this sequential location; the turn is ambivalent as to whether or not it is possibly complete at *summer*, since prosodically *summer* does not come to a terminal rise or fall (it also has the same rise-fall profile as *had him* but does not come down as low as *him*, creating, to our ears, the perception of it being a next but not the last part of a list). Furthermore, just at the completion of *summer*, Terry withdraws her gaze to look upward, displaying a search or calculation of some kind (Goodwin 1981:79; Argyle and Cook 1976:122). She thus treats this turn space as her own and not as a transition-relevance place. After the production of *weeks*, Terry brings the turn to a place of possible completion, with her gaze toward Rachel (first arrow). But Rachel, the recipient whose gaze Terry has secured, produces only a slight lateral head movement and no other uptake at this point. After a fairly long silence (second arrow), Terry adds the Extension increment *when we were out at the campground?*, which ends with the rising intonation characteristic of "try-marked" (Sacks and Schegloff 1979) turns, turns that are built to elicit at least minimal tokens of uptake. Immediately upon completion of this Extension, Terry receives a more aligned uptake from Rachel (*Oh really*). In this example, then, as in the other cases, the speaker comes to a place of possible completion, receives no uptake from the intended recipient, and produces an Extension to the possibly completed turn. The Extension is syntactically continuous with the prior turn unit, treating it as still ongoing in syntax and in action. Terry's Extension provides a second transition-relevance place and thus a second opportunity for her recipient to offer a response.

To summarize the discussion so far, we have found the following interactional features in all of our examples of Extension increments:

- They occur in the environment of lack of uptake at a transition-relevance place.
- They provide a second transition-relevance place, at which the recipient could display recipiency.
- Rather than doing a new action, they continue the action of the extended turn, often by further specifying when, where, or with whom the event being related took place.

Grammatically, we find that adjuncts—prepositional phrases, adverbial NPs, and adverbial clauses—that *could* have occurred as *constituents*, as integral parts, of clauses (as shown in example (7)) are used by speakers as Extensions. Through this grammatical and interactional practice, speakers display that what they are doing with the Extension is not to be heard as "starting something new" but rather as a continuation of what they had just been saying.

Increments as Unattached NPs

The examples we have been examining are instances of increments that could serve as grammatical constituents of a turn in progress; such increments work retroactively on the previous turn unit, the one that was possibly complete, reinterpreting that unit as still in progress. In contrast, the next set of examples illustrates a different kind of increment. While they pursue uptake from a recipient, Unattached-NP increments do not do so by extending the syntax or the action of the previous turn segment. In these cases, the speaker comes to a place of possible completion and then adds an NP that cannot be interpreted as a syntactic part of the just possibly-completed turn; that is, the NP is not a syntactic "constituent of" that turn. In our data, we have found that Unattached-NP increments do a distinct kind of interactional work: in addition to providing an additional transition-relevance place, a new point at which a recipient could display appropriate responsiveness (after lack of uptake), Unattached-NP increments also display a stance toward what has just been said or an assessment of a referent from the previous unit. This stance display serves as a standard or model of alignment for the recipient, a model for the kind of response the speaker may be pursuing from the recipient.

Our first example of an Unattached-NP increment, (10), previewed in example (2), comes from "Auto Discussion." Mike has just told a story about a guy with two original Cords (a valued car from the 1930s). In the story, a guy from California comes to Ohio with $15,000 cash in hand to buy one of those Cords, in spite of the prior warning from the owner of the Cords that such an offer would be a waste of time. As predicted, the owner rejects the offer of $15,000. Although it is not possible from the video to see to whom Mike's gaze is directed during the story, both Curt and Gary are acting as engaged recipients during the course of the story:

(10)

    Mike: The guy ended up turnin' around'n goin <u>ba</u>ck 'cause [he wasn' a<u>bout</u> to
          sell it.
    Curt: [°(Oh Christ). fifteen
          thousand dollars wouldn't <u>tou</u>ch a Co:rd,

                                                  (0.7)

⇒   Curt: That guy was (dreaming).
          <u>fif</u>teen thousand dollars [for an original Co:rd,
    Gary: [<u>Fi</u>gured he'd imp<u>re</u>ss him,

In this excerpt, Mike comes to a place of possible completion not only of a turn but also of his story. As Jefferson (1978) and others have noted, possible ends of stories are interactionally delicate spaces; appreciation of the story is relevant, as is a return to turn-by-turn talk. In this fragment, Curt provides an appreciation of the story by showing that he understands the significance of it (*Oh Christ. fifteen thousand dollars wouldn't touch a Cord*). But Mike does not acknowledge or second Curt's displayed understanding (perhaps because Curt's appreciation ends up in overlap with the completion of Mike's turn). Curt thus tries again, at the arrowed line; he again offers an understanding and stance toward the story just told (with *That guy was (dreaming)*), possibly in pursuit of a second appreciation or assessment from Mike. But Curt's turn also gets no ratification or second from Mike. Curt then adds an Unattached-NP increment—*fifteen thousand dollars for an original Cord*. Curt produces this Unattached NP in a scornful tone, and it provides yet another display of Curt's assessment of and stance toward the "antago-nist" of the story, a display that can be seen as a prompt for the sort of action the recipient might take at this point. Notice that there is no syntactic integrity be-tween this increment and the clause that Curt has just completed.

Why does Curt use an Unattached-NP increment here? In English conversa-tions, as pointed out in Ono and Thompson (1994), Unattached NPs at the ends of turns tend to be used for assessing, evaluating, summarizing, labeling, and clas-sifying. As we have suggested, Curt's Unattached-NP increment, *fifteen thousand dollars for an original Cord*, can be seen as a display of specific appreciation for the outlandishness of the antagonist's actions; Curt's Unattached NP is indeed serv-ing to summarize, evaluate, and assess the absurdity of anyone thinking they could get a Cord for fifteen thousand dollars. Given that the NP increment is produced in the context of Mike's lack of uptake of Curt's first appreciation display, we can see this upgrade of assessment and stance being used as a strategy for attracting and even modeling recipiency action

Example (11) comes from an audiotaped conversation known as "Two Girls." In this conversation, two women, who used to be friends but who have not been in touch for a while, are talking on the telephone. In example (11), Bee begins with an announcement that is also a topic proffer:

(11)   (*bo:way* in Bee's first turn is a marked pronunciation of *boy*)
    1 Bee: Oh Sibbie's sistuh ['sister'] had a <u>ba</u>:by <u>bo</u>:way.
    2 Ava: Who?
    3 Bee: Sibbie's sister.
    4 Ava: Oh really?
    5 Bee: Myeah,
    6 Ava: [° (That's nice) °
⇒   7 Bee: [She had it <u>yes</u>terday.
⇒   8   <u>Ten</u>:: pou:nds.
    9 Ava: °Je:sus Christ. °
   10 Bee: She had a ho:(hh)rse hh .hh

As an announcement sequence, this fragment is problematic from beginning to end. It is common for announcements to be done in an expanded sequence type, starting with a pre-announcement (such as *Guess what.*). A pre-announcement is itself a first pair part, which makes relevant a second pair part from the recipient, namely a go-ahead (or pre-emption of the prefaced news, in case the recipient has already heard it). It is generally after such a go-ahead that the announcement itself is produced (cf. Terasaki 1976; Levinson 1983; Schegloff 1996). Notice that in this example the announcement (*Oh Sibbie's sistuh had a baby boway*) is done without being heralded by a pre-announcement; this may partially account for the prob-lems of recipiency that ensue.

Now it has been argued (Terasaki 1976) that an announcement or a piece of news is also a first pair part, which makes relevant as a second pair part an assess-ment (e.g., *that's great*) or a display of appreciation or interest (e.g., *oh really?*) with respect to the news. Whether or not we make this argument, notice that in example (11) the response from Ava at line 2 (*Who?*) is not an assessment but is rather that ever-possible but dispreferred response, the Next Turn Repair Initiator (NTRI) (Schegloff, Jefferson, and Sacks 1977). An NTRI indicates trouble with the preceding turn and requests that the next turn be taken up with addressing the trouble. Because it is concerned with initiating repair rather than with doing the next expected action, it temporarily delays the progress of the sequence.

Thus line 3 provides a redoing of the problematic reference (*Sibbie's sister*[7]) rather than a further action in the announcement sequence. With the redoing of the reference, the announcement's sequential relevance is reinstated, and at line 4 we might expect Ava to produce the now-delayed appreciation/assessment. Ava's *Oh really?* is a display of interest, a kind of appreciation to the degree that it orients to the newsworthiness of the announcement. However, this response is of such an undifferentiated sort that it indicates no clear stance toward the event—it is not possible to tell if Ava finds the event positive or negative, a joy or a misfortune. This may be because Bee did not indicate what stance *she* was going to take toward the news, a framing that often takes place in the pre-announcement.[8] After responding to Ava at line 5, Bee then speaks again at line 7 (overlapping a contribution from Ava that is extremely difficult to hear but sounds like *That's nice*, an even less appreciative response to the news than her earlier *oh really?*) with *She had it yesterday*. There is no uptake from Ava here, and Bee speaks again (line 8) with an Unattached-NP increment, *Ten:: pou:nds*. This NP qualifies as Unattached in that there is no way to interpret it as a syntactic continuation of the prior turn segment. The phonological prominence given to this NP—created by the steep increase in pitch on *ten* and the sound stretches on both *ten* and *pounds*—is indicative of assessment activity (see Goodwin and Goodwin 1987, 1992), and it is clear that the baby's weight is being constructed as worthy of note. Thus, although it remains somewhat unclear what stance Bee is taking to the birth in general, we now have a clear affective stance toward the size of the baby: he is remarkably big. And this finally gets an appreciation from Ava, who produces a very quiet *Jesus Christ*, acknowledging the remarkableness of the size.

In this example, then, we see an Unattached-NP increment that provides another place of possible uptake after a noticeable lack of uptake from the recipient. This NP increment can again be seen as a comment and display of the stance that the recipient might take toward the speaker's turn. The Unattached NP, produced with a markedly high pitch, works nicely to prompt an affective display from the recipient.

Example (12) is from the "Game Night" conversation. This fragment comes from earlier in the discussion about the artistic young nephew of Pam:

(12)   Rachel: The Cafe de Yin Yang? When he was tw- te:n?
        Terry: Yeah.
                        (0.8)
        Rachel: [That is really something.
        Terry: [An' an' no:te the uh
                        (0.5)
        Rachel: Is that [a real feather on there?
        Terry: [Y'see on the dress? the yin yang? symbols?

```
         Rachel: Oh my go:sh.
    ⇒    Terry:  I was so impressed.
    ⇒            (I mean) this kid.
                 (1.2)
         Rachel: Ten years old.
         Terry:  °Yeah. °
```

Just prior to this fragment, the participants have been talking about the dust on Cindy's coat (Cindy is the participant in the process of leaving to get ice cream). There is a slight "lull" in the conversation after that, and then Rachel, settling into a position looking at the remarkable drawing on the wall, asks a question that is also a topic proffer—*The Cafe de Yin Yang? When he was tw- ten?* Her question and gaze draw the attention of the other two participants at the table to the drawing on the wall. In fact, during *An' an' note* Terry starts to get up from her chair to go over to the drawing to point out something she too finds remarkable about the drawing. While Terry is doing that, Rachel seems to guess at what that remarkable thing might be—*a real feather* is suggested. But Terry goes on to bring attention to the *yin yang* symbols drawn on the figure's dress (and does not explicitly answer Rachel's question about the feather). Rachel displays appreciation for this detail with *Oh my gosh.* Terry gives the upshot of her noticing with *I was so impressed,* delivered at a much higher pitch register than her previous utterance, and she starts to return to her chair. Rachel gives no verbal response to this but does an appreciative wrinkling of the eyebrows and lateral head shake. While it is unclear from the video exactly what Rachel's gaze is focused on during that head shake, it seems that she is still looking at the drawing on the wall while Terry is talking. If this is true, then Terry has reached a point of possible completion without a gaze-secured recipient.

So there are potentially two dimensions along which Terry could view Rachel's response as not entirely satisfactory. First, Terry may view the bit of appreciative behavior from Rachel as inadequate to the "impressiveness" that has just been displayed. And second, Rachel may be gazing at the drawing rather than at Terry. What is clear is that the end of Terry's turn (at the first arrow) is not immediately met with a next verbal turn. This places special responsibilities on Terry for engendering continued talk; that is, her turn has failed to be sequentially implicative (Schegloff and Sacks 1973).

In the environment of no immediate next turn, Terry produces the Unattached-NP increment we are interested in—(*I mean) this kid.* We take the possible occurrence of *I mean* before the NP (parentheses indicating uncertainty of hearing) to be an epistemic "discourse marker" rather than being interpretable compositionally as a subject and main verb (Schiffrin 1987; Redeker 1991). The NP *this kid* cannot be interpreted as a continuation of the prior turn segment, nor can it be seen as a repair replacement of any syntactic constituent of the prior unit, which is a possible interpretation of an NP that follows *I mean.* This Unattached NP is produced at the same high pitch as the segment before it and with gaze toward Rachel. With this particular pitch pattern, it serves to provide a further stance display toward the referent (how amazing and impressive this child is). It displays

Terry's stance and may thus serve as a standard toward which the recipient should orient in producing her response.

What we have seen so far suggests that Unattached-NP increments have the following features in common with Extension increments:

- They occur in the environment of lack of uptake at a transition-relevance place.
- They provide a second transition-relevance place, at which the recipient could display recipiency.

But unlike the Extension increments, these Unattached-NP increments seem to be recurrently used for an additional purpose:

- They display an assessment and stance with respect to the referent. They offer a standard toward which the recipient could orient in producing a response, a display of the sort of response the speaker is pursuing.

A Comparison of Increments as Extensions and Unattached NPs

From the preceding discussion it can be seen that increments as Extensions and Unattached NPs are similar in certain facets of the interactional work they do, and yet they also differ in interactionally consequential ways. They are both used in the environment of problems with recipient uptake, and they both provide for another place of possible completion, a new location at which the recipient could produce a responsive turn. This is the turn-taking work that they both accomplish. But why might speakers use one or the other of these two kinds of increments? How are these resources distinct with respect to how they function in their sequential environments?

We propose that the format of an increment is iconic with the interactional work that increment does. A speaker comes to a point when his/her recipient could, but does not immediately, begin a responsive turn. This presents a problem to which there is more than a single solution. The Extension format embodies continuation of a same action rather than the performance of a new, next, or even repeated action. As "continuations of," Extensions created *renewed points of possible completion* without producing new actions. Just as they are syntactically done as constituents, or continuations, of the "same" turn, so are they interactionally heard as part of the "same" turn. In fact, it is possible that, interactionally, adding an Extension retroactively "deletes" the last place of possible completion and makes the end of the Extension hearable as the "first" real place of possible completion for the turn, thereby masking the interactional trouble that the lack of uptake could represent.

In contrast, Unattached-NP increments are not constituents, or continuations of, their prior turns; they are not syntactically integrated into the prior segment, and they do not necessarily continue the action of the possibly completed turn. In our data, Unattached-NP increments embody the performance of a new action, one of assessing and stance-taking toward a referent. Even if the possibly completed prior turn is an assessment and the Unattached-NP increment may in some sense do the same action, it is nonetheless presented as a further assessment rather than as a continuation of the first assessment. The syntactic form of an Unattached NP, a unit not integrated into the prior turn unit, is well tailored to its interactional function. That is, a less syntactically integrated form does a less interactionally integrated action. Whereas Extension increments add more of the same form and action, Unattached-NP increments are not formally connected to the prior turn segment, but they do function as continuations in pursuit of uptake by modeling the type of stance or assessment that the speaker is pursuing from his/her recipient.

Another dimension of this form–action relationship can be found if we look in greater detail at the kinds of phrases that occur as Extensions and as Unattached-NP increments. Extensions are done as prototypical "endings" of a turn, prototypical "completions." We would then expect them to be done with semantico-syntactic items that can be easily interpreted as "endings" or "completions." And this is in fact what we have found: Extensions are regularly done with prepositional phrases, temporal or locative adverbials, infinitival clauses, relative clauses, and other subordinate clauses—all of which regularly occur at the ends of turns in utterances in general. This is in keeping with our observation that Extensions often further specify where, when, or with whom the event being related took place. Even when simple NPs are interpretable as Extensions, as with *these days* in example (6), they are regularly temporal phrases.[9] Consider the following examples of temporal NPs that serve as Extensions in example (13):

(13)

    (a) Ah, John wz determining that.
        a minute ago.
    (b) I gave, I gave up smoking cigarettes::.
        l-uh one-one week ago t'day.
        actually.[10]
    (c) Mm, tch! I wz gonnuh call you.
        last week someti(h)me .hhhhh!

As we have attempted to underscore in this discussion, Unattached-NP increments in our collection are not possible constituents of their prior turn segments, and they are never temporal or locative phrases. They are either NPs that express a stance or attitude (often with prosodic salience), as with *this kid* (example [12]), or NPs that express degree or amount, as with *ten pounds* (example [11]) or *fifteen thousand dollars for an original Cord* (example [10]). Both are often found in assessments (Goodwin and Goodwin 1987, 1992; Pomerantz 1984); how good or impressive something is can be indicated by an epithet NP or by an expression of its quantity or size. It is thus clear that, even if we compare only NPs in the two collections, there is an important difference in the semantic classes exhibited in them.

In this semantic sense, then, an interaction-based understanding of added constituents requires more than an analysis of the internal syntactic structure of an increment. For example, in order to account for the fact that *these days* is a constituent of its immediately prior turn while *ten pounds* is not, we need to recognize that *these days* is a temporal phrase, while *ten pounds* is a term of degree or amount. We cannot rely entirely on the fact that both are NPs to help us decide if they are continuations of the prior turn or not.

Prosody and Increments

For another perspective on the cases in our collection, we can explore the Extension versus Unattached NP distinction further by examining the prosodic formats of each increment type. Based on important research on prosody and turn completion (especially Auer 1996; Couper-Kuhlen 1996; Ford 1993; Ford and Thompson 1996; Ford et al. 1996; Local 1992), we would expect there to be prosodic correlates to the distinction we are proposing between Extensions and Unattached NPs. In particular, Extensions and Unattached NPs may differ in terms of pitch reset. The Extensions, which are syntactic continuations of the immediately prior possibly completed turn, would be uttered with the pitch of the first accented syllable at the same pitch as, or lower than, the last accented syllable of the just-completed turn. In contrast, the Unattached NPs, which are not syntactic continuations and which, we have argued, can be interpreted as new conversational actions, may be uttered with pitch reset (cf. Couper-Kuhlen 1996 for pitch reset in two types of conversational actions in *because*-clauses; we are grateful to her for valuable discussion of this point).

In the cases we have examined, there is indeed some support for these expectations. For example, the pitch patterns in four of the six cases we have closely examined here are in line with these predictions. The two exceptions are both Extensions (examples [6] and [8]). Unfortunately, in both of these the sound quality does not allow us to extract a pitch trace (an acoustic measurement of fundamental frequency), but auditorily they appear to be counterexamples. In one of these two, namely example (6), with *these days*, testing our predictions is complicated by the overall pitch rise in this utterance (see note 4). The other problematic instance is example (8), with *with the two of 'em on it*, where *two* sounds distinctly higher in pitch than the preceding accented syllable. This example, repeated here, is especially interesting because it is a kind of "blend" of our two types of increments: the increment is a prepositional phrase, which is a canonical example of an Extension, but it contains a numeral which forms part of an expression of stance, as we have argued that our Unattached NPs do.

(8)

> Gary: Well he took Bill (Silvio). a good friend of mine, he weighs about two hunderd'n
> s::(0.5) two hunderd (fifty)-five pounds I think he weighs. Took him for a ride
> on that'n Bill said that he was at least goin' eighty miles an hour.
> with the ↑ two of 'em on it.

We surmise that the pitch reset could be related to the stance-expressing function, which "overrides" the continuation-of-same-action function that we have suggested Extensions usually have.

At this point, then, we take the existence of prosodic correlates to be worth pursuing further, but with our current data base we are not able to make a case for a clear correlation. We keenly anticipate future research that will shed additional light on this question.

Conclusions

In this chapter we have examined a common occurrence in conversation, the addition of more talk by a single speaker in the interactionally sensitive and consequential location of a just possibly-completed turn. As Sacks et al. suggest in their 1974 account of turn-taking, one important functional component of a turn at talk, a central concern for a speaker in producing a turn, is that there be a subsequent and responsive turn by a recipient. Increments added past points of possible turn completion offer one way of dealing with the interactional contingency that emerges when uptake is not immediately forthcoming upon possible turn completion. Not surprisingly, given the manifold sequential contexts for turns and the manifold actions that can be taken in turns, increments are not homogeneous in form or function.

In this study, we have explored some of the ways that increments are used in a sample of American English interactions. We have found interactional consequences for variation in the form of increments and in their relationships with just-completed turn units. Looking at the classic constituents that are used as increments, we have found that while they always address problems of recipiency and uptake, they deal with such problems in distinct and iconic ways. Specifically, increments that are syntactic Extensions of prior turn segments function as action continuations, adding more to the same turn action. As integrated continuations of syntactic structures, Extensions produce renewed opportunities for recipient uptake, but they do not produce new or different actions. In contrast, when speakers produce Unattached NP increments, the actions characteristically involve stance displays or assessments. Thus, these nonintegrated increments are vehicles for accomplishing separate actions, actions such as assessing or displaying a stance that can provide recipients with a model or standard for the type of response the speaker is pursuing.

We have emphasized that the way in which Extension increments can do their interactional work is related to the recurrent use of these same types of phrases and clauses as integrated parts of larger utterances. This is clearly a language-specific matter. Work on grammar and interaction in Japanese has suggested a radically different way of using "added segments" for interactional goals, given the radically different way in which Japanese grammar emerges from interactional patterns (see especially Hayashi 2000, 2001; Mori 1999; and Tanaka 1999 for insightful discussions). We look forward to much more research on conversation in a wide range of languages to uncover the way in which grammatical resources and interactional patterns work together to allow speakers to accomplish their interpersonal goals.

Our work here has been in the spirit of seeking functional contexts and sources for recurrent linguistic resources. We have provided support for the interactional relevance of the classic notion of constituent and for the distinction between Extensions and Unattached NPs in English, in the interactionally salient context of increments to possibly completed turns. To the degree that we have been able to show the interactional relevance of the analytic category of constituent, one dear to us as linguists, we hope to have contributed to the enterprise of building a truly functional account for recurrent linguistic patterns, an account that we believe should be well grounded in the natural social-interactional habitat of language use.

Appendix: Transcription Symbols

Symbol	Interpretation
(.)	A short, untimed pause
(0.3)	A timed pause
hhh	Audible breath
thi-	Hyphen indicates a sound cut off
[	The onset of overlap
she	Underscore indicates prominent stress
°she°	Degree signs indicate lower volume than surrounding talk
she:	Colon indicates sound stretch
.	Low falling intonation
?	High rising intonation
,	Intermediate intonation contours: level, slight rise, slight fall
Bold	Bold type highlights increments in the examples

NOTES

We are grateful to Joan Bybee, Elizabeth Couper-Kuhlen, Susanna Cumming, Pamela Downing, Charles Goodwin, Marja-Liisa Helasvuo, Nikolaus Himmelmann, Shoichi Iwasaki, Gene Lerner, Edith Moravcsik, Tsuyoshi Ono, Emanuel Schegloff, and especially Junko Mori for valuable discussion of the issues in this chapter. Responsibility for any remaining errors remains with us.

1. For Unattached NPs in Mandarin and Finnish conversation, see Tao (1996) and Helasvuo (2001), respectively.

2. Ono and Thompson (1994) actually use the term *unattached NP* to cover all NPs that are produced without a predicate (except, for example, in answers to questions where the predicate is clearly recoverable from the question). In the current study, we are looking only at a subclass of their unattached NPs, namely those that occur as increments, interpretable as additions to a prior possibly completed turn, though syntactically unintegrated.

3. Supplementing our own data, we are grateful to Charles and Marjorie Goodwin, Robert Jasperson, and Emanuel Schegloff for generously sharing their data with us.

4. Tanaka (1999), however, does use the term *extension* in a slightly different way from the way we are using it here.

5. While rising intonation is not usually associated with Wh-questions such as John's in this example, there is indeed a rise in the pitch contour at the end of this turn. We do not have an explanation for the use of this intonation in this instance. We have omitted a simultaneous conversation between Beth and one of her children.

6. We are used to thinking of verbal repair when we think of "hitches." But it is possible that a body movement repair could also accomplish the work of a hitch.

7. This redoing of reference provides a natural example of the phenomenon observed by Labov (1966) in his famous study of r-lessness in New York City. In our example, we can see that the first reference formulation is r-less, while the second, done in response to an NTRI, is r-ful.

8. It is possible that the unusual phonetic production of *ba:by bo:way* is also some clue to Bee's stance toward the event, but it is unclear at least to us as analysts exactly what that stance might be.

9. In our audio increment data base, out of forty-five extensions, seven are NPs, and four of these seven NPs are temporal phrases such as *these days* or *ten years*.

10. See Goodwin (1979, 1981) for the groundbreaking analysis of this example, which provided the stimulus for much of the research into "added segments" and grammatical resources.

REFERENCES

Argyle, Michael, and Mark Cook. 1976. *Gaze and Mutual Gaze*. Cambridge: Cambridge University Press.

Auer, Peter. 1992. The neverending sentence: Rightward expansion in spoken language. In Miklós Kontra and Tamás Váradi, eds., *Studies in Spoken Languages: English, German, Finno-Ugric*, 41–59. Budapest: Linguistics Institute, Hungarian Academy of Sciences.

Auer, Peter. 1996. On the prosody and syntax of turn-continuations. In E. Couper-Kuhlen and M. Selting, eds., *Prosody in Conversation*, 57–100. Cambridge: Cambridge University Press.

Couper-Kuhlen, Elizabeth. 1996. Intonation and clause combining in discourse: The case of *because*. *Pragmatics* 6(3): 389–426.

Du Bois, John W., and Stephan Schuetze-Coburn. 1993. Representing hierarchy: Constituent structure for discourse databases. In Jane A. Edwards and Martin D. Lampert, eds., *Talking Data: Transcription and Coding Methods for Language Research*, 221–260. Hillsdale, NJ: Lawrence Erlbaum.

Ford, Cecilia E. 1993. *Grammar in Interaction: Adverbial Clauses in American English Conversations*. Cambridge: Cambridge University Press.

Ford, Cecilia E., Barbara A. Fox, and Sandra A. Thompson. 1996. Practices in the construction of turns: The "TCU" revisited. *Pragmatics* 6(3): 427–454.

Ford, Cecilia E., and Sandra A. Thompson. 1996. Interactional units in conversation: Syntactic, intonational, and pragmatic resources for turn management. In Elinor Ochs, Emanuel Schegloff, and Sandra A. Thompson, eds., *Interaction and Grammar*, 134–184. Cambridge: Cambridge University Press.

Fox, Barbara, Makoto Hayashi, and Robert Jasperson. 1996. Resources and repair: A crosslinguistic study of syntax and repair. In Elinor Ochs, Emanuel Schegloff, and Sandra A. Thompson, eds., *Interaction and Grammar*, 185–237. Cambridge: Cambridge University Press.

Fox, Barbara, and Robert Jasperson. 1995. A syntactic exploration of repair in English conversation. In P. Davis, ed., *Alternative Linguistics: Descriptive and Theoretical Modes*, 77–134. Amsterdam: John Benjamins.

Givón, T. 1995. *Functionalism and Grammar*. Amsterdam: John Benjamins.

Goodwin, Charles. 1979. The interactive construction of a sentence in natural conversation. In George Psathas, ed., *Everyday Language: Studies in Ethnomethodology*. New York: Irvington.

Goodwin, Charles. 1981. *Conversational Organization: Interaction between Speakers and Hearers.* New York: Academic Press.

Goodwin, Charles. 1989. Turn construction and conversational organization. In Brenda Dervin, Lawrence Grossberg, Barbara J. O'Keefe, and Ellen Wartella, eds., *Rethinking Communication*, Vol. 2: *Paradigm Exemplars*, 88–102. Newbury Park, CA: Sage Publications.

Goodwin, Charles. 1995. Sentence construction within interaction. In Uta M. Quasthoff, ed., *Aspects of Oral Communication*, 198–219. Berlin: Walter de Gruyter.

Goodwin, Charles, and Marjorie H. Goodwin. 1987. Concurrent operations on talk: Notes on the interactive organization of assessments. *IPRA Papers in Pragmatics* 1(1): 1–54.

Goodwin, Charles, and Marjorie H. Goodwin. 1992. Assessments and the construction of context. In Alessandro Duranti and Charles Goodwin, eds., *Rethinking Context*, 147–190. Cambridge: Cambridge University Press.

Goodwin, Marjorie Harness. 1980. Processes of mutual monitoring implicated in the production of description sequences. *Sociological Inquiry*, 50(3–4): 303–317.

Hayashi, Makoto. 2000. Practices in joint utterance construction in Japanese conversation. Ph.D. dissertation, University of Colorado, Department of Linguistics.

Hayashi, Makoto. 2001. Postposition-initiated utterances in Japanese conversation: An interactional account of a grammatical practice. In Elizabeth Couper-Kuhlen and Margret Selting, eds., *Interactional Linguistics.* Amsterdam: Benjamins.

Heath, Christian. 1984. Talk and recipiency: Sequential organization in speech and body movement. In J. Maxwell Atkinson and John Heritage, eds., *Structures of Social Action*, 247–265. Cambridge: Cambridge University Press.

Helasvuo, Marja-Liisa. 2001. *Syntax in the Making: The Emergence of Syntactic Units in Finnish Conversation.* Amsterdam: John Benjamins.

Hopper, Paul J. 1987a. *Emergent Grammar.* Berkeley, CA: Berkeley Linguistics Society 13.

Hopper, Paul J. 1987b. Emergent grammar and the a priori grammar postulate. In Deborah Tannen, ed., *Linguistics in Context.* Norwood, NJ: Ablex.

Jefferson, Gail. 1973. A case of precision timing in ordinary conversation: Overlapped tag-positioned address terms in closing sequences. *Semiotica* 9:47–96.

Jefferson, Gail. 1978. Sequential aspects of story-telling in conversation. In J. Schenkein, ed., *Studies in the Organization of Conversational Interaction.* New York: Academic Press.

Labov, William. 1966. *The Social Stratification of English in New York City.* Washington, D.C.: Center for Applied Linguistics.

Langacker, Ronald. 1987. *Foundations of Cognitive Grammar.* Stanford: Stanford University Press.

Langacker, Ronald. 1995. Conceptual grouping and constituency in cognitive grammar. In Linguistic Society of Korea, ed., *Linguistics in the Morning Calm*, 149–172. Seoul: Hanshin.

Langacker, Ronald. 1997. Constituency, dependency, and conceptual grouping. *Cognitive Linguistics* 8:1–32.

Lerner, Gene H. 1987. Collaborative turn sequences: Sentence construction and social action. Ph.D. diss., University of California, Irvine.

Lerner, Gene H. 1989. Notes on overlap management in conversation: The case of delayed completion. *Western Journal of Speech Communication* 53:167–177.

Lerner, Gene H. 1991. On the syntax of sentences-in-progress. *Language in Society* 20(3): 441–458.

Lerner, Gene H. 1992. Assisted storytelling: Deploying shared knowledge as a practical matter. *Qualitative Sociology* 15(3): 247–271.

Lerner, Gene H. 1996a. Finding "face" in the preference structures of talk-in-interaction. *Social Psychology Quarterly* 59(4): 303–321.

Lerner, Gene H. 1996b. On the "semi-permeable" character of grammatical units in conversation: Conditional entry into the turn space of another speaker. In Elinor Ochs, Emanuel Schegloff, and Sandra A. Thompson, eds., *Interaction and Grammar*, 238–276. Cambridge: Cambridge University Press.

Levinson, Stephen C. 1983. *Pragmatics.* Cambridge: Cambridge University Press.

Local, J. K. 1992. Continuing and restarting. In Peter Auer and Aldo di Luzio, eds., *The Contextualization of Language*, 272–296. Amsterdam: John Benjamins.

McNeill, David. 1992. *Hand and Mind: What Gestures Reveal about Thought.* Chicago: University of Chicago Press.

Mori, Junko. 1999. *Negotiating Agreement and Disagreement: A Study of Connective Expressions and Turn Construction in Japanese Conversations.* Amsterdam: John Benjamins.

Nichols, Johanna. 1986. Head marking and dependent-marking languages. *Language* 62: 56–120.

Ono, Tsuyoshi, and Sandra A. Thompson. 1994. Unattached NPs in English conversation. *Berkeley Linguistics Society* 20:402–419.

Ono, Tsuyoshi, and Sandra A. Thompson. 1995. What can conversation tell us about syntax? In Philip W. Davis, ed., *Descriptive and Theoretical Modes in Alternative Linguistics*, 213–271. Amsterdam: John Benjamins.

Ono, Tsuyoshi, and Sandra A. Thompson. 1996a. The dynamic nature of conceptual structure building: Evidence from conversation. In Adele Goldberg, ed., *Conceptual Structure, Discourse and Language*, 391–399. Stanford: Center for the Study of Language and Information.

Ono, Tsuyoshi, and Sandra A. Thompson. 1996b. Interaction and syntax in the structure of conversational discourse. In Eduard Hovy and Donia Scott, eds., *Discourse Processing: An Interdisciplinary Perspective*, 67–96. Heidelberg: Springer-Verlag.

Oreström, Bengt. 1983. *Turn-Taking in English Conversation.* Lund Studies in English 66. Lund: CWK Gleerup.

Payne, Doris. 1990. *The Pragmatics of Word Order: Typological Dimensions of Verb-Initial Languages.* Berlin: Mouton.

Pomerantz, Anita. 1984. Pursuing a response. In J. Maxwell Atkinson and John Heritage, eds., *Structures of Social Action*, 152–163. Cambridge: Cambridge University Press.

Radford, Andrew. 1988. *Transformational Grammar.* Chapter 2. Cambridge: Cambridge University Press.

Radford, Andrew. 1997. *Syntactic Theory and the Structure of English.* Cambridge: Cambridge University Press.

Redeker, Gisela. 1991. Linguistic markers of discourse structure. *Linguistics* 29:1139–1172.

Sacks, Harvey, and Emanuel A. Schegloff. 1979. Two preferences in the organization of reference to persons in conversation and their interaction. In George Psathas, ed., *Everyday Language: Studies in Ethnomethodology*, 15–21. New York: Irvington.

Sacks, Harvey, Emanuel A. Schegloff, and Gail Jefferson. 1974. A simplest systematics for the organization of turn-taking for conversation. *Language* 50(4): 696–735.

Schegloff, Emanuel A. 1996. Turn organization: one intersection of grammar an interaction. In Elinor Ochs, Emanuel Schegloff, and Sandra A. Thompson, eds., *Interaction and Grammar*, 52–133. Cambridge: Cambridge University Press.

Schegloff, Emanuel A., Gail Jefferson, and Harvey Sacks. 1977. The preference for self-correction in the organization of repair in conversation. *Language* 53:361–382.

Schegloff, Emanuel A., and Harvey Sacks. 1973. Opening up closings. *Semiotica* 8:289–327.

Schiffrin, Deborah. 1987. *Discourse Markers.* Cambridge: Cambridge University Press.

Selting, Margret. 1996. On the interplay of syntax and prosody in the constitution of turn-constructional units and turns in conversation. *Pragmatics* 6(3): 371–388.

Tanaka, Hiroko. 1999. *Turn-Taking in Japanese: A Study in Grammar and Interaction.* Amsterdam: John Benjamins.

Tao, Hongyin. 1996. *Units in Mandarin Conversation: Prosody, Discourse, and Grammar.* Amsterdam: John Benjamins.

Terasaki, A. 1976. *Pre-announcement Sequences in Conversation.* Social Sciences Working Papers No. 99. Irvine: University of California.

3

Cultivating Prayer

LISA CAPPS & ELINOR OCHS

A central function of language is to establish and maintain a sense of continuity and well-being throughout the life course. Language provides a medium for making sense out of past events and coping with the unpredictability of the future. This endeavor involves sorting out temporal-causal orderings of events (i.e., what did/ did not or will/will not happen) and imbuing them with moral castings (i.e., what should/should not have happened or should/should not happen). All levels of language are recruited to this end, including genre (Bakhtin 1981, 1986). Every community has a repertoire of genres that organize particular events and trajectories in terms of conventional structurings, understandings, and sentiments. These communally sanctioned templates can be soothing to those who are working through disarming events. Beyond offering structural containment, genres facilitate collective involvement in grappling with events remembered and anticipated.

Distinct from other genres, public prayer offers a template for recruiting support from the Divine as well as from community members. Prayer is a form of communication in which there is a conscious and active attempt to enter into dialogue with higher powers. In its ideal form, "prayer is religion in act . . . no vain exercise of words, no mere repetition of certain sacred formulae, but the very movement itself of the soul, putting itself in a personal relation of contact with the mysterious power" (James 1902/1982:361). While in that quote William James emphasizes the personal relation of contact, communities the world over attend closely to the conventional form and content of prayer. In particular, prayer is expected to be inflected as sacred communication, thus differentiating it from more mundane interactions. Further, especially in public settings, adherence to prayer formats is often considered a requirement for collective participation.

This research examines children's entry into the genre of prayer. While the focus is prayer, it offers a more general perspective on genre: First, we consider genre as encompassing a *range* of semiotic expression, not only language but also bodily comportment. We illuminate how spirituality is conventionally actualized through assumption of bodily postures, gestures, linguistic forms, and regulation of voice. Second, in keeping with Schegloff (1995), we consider genre to be an *interactional* achievement. As demonstrated here in relation to prayer, this achievement includes transitioning into prayer, maintaining the requirements of the genre, and transitioning out of prayer into other forms of communication. The interactional underpinnings of prayer are particularly salient in instances of collective prayer that involve children praying, because of the demonstrated need to corral their attention and monitor their conduct. Third, genre is not a type of interactionally achieved linguistic and kinesic text but rather a *perspective* on a text. That is, any single stretch of spoken (or written) text may contain features of more than one genre, given that the co-producers of such texts may be engaged in more than one activity, for example, giving thanks, petitioning, confessing, and/or telling a story (Ochs 1994).

The focus of this analysis is the cultivation of a *prayerful attitude* in children. Again according to James (1902/1982:463): "Prayer is the very soul and essence of religion, for it helps us to cultivate the appropriate attitudes toward the world around us. The prayerful attitude cultivates the continuous sense of our connection with the power that made things as they are, so that we are tempered more towardly for their reception." In this perspective, the adopting of a "prayerful attitude" enables one to communicate with God and be in a position to receive Grace. Attitude is a frame of heart and mind, which itself requires work to achieve. In many communities, this attitude is facilitated by assuming a conventional demeanor, for example, postures, words, and voices that display reverence, openness, and humility.

Children's participation in prayer underscores the centrality of the body in accomplishing prayerful attitude. In the material presented here, socialization into prayer concentrates upon the positioning of children's hands, arms, legs, heads, eye gaze, and torso as a means of positioning their minds and souls. Socialization into this kinesic footing is integrated with attention to reverent voice quality, honorific titles for deities, archaic and formal lexicon, formulaic expressions, and conventional predicates for petitioning, interceding, praising, giving thanks, and confessing sins, among other prayerful acts.

Children's participation in prayer also demonstrates the difficulty of maintaining a consistently inflected genre over interactional time. The children observed in this study were constantly breaking out of language and conduct inflected for the sacred into mundane modes of communicating. We argue that such interpenetration of sacred and mundane is grounded in both developmental and situational considerations. Attention span and competence in the register of prayer create discontinuities; however, praying can touch off rememberings and anticipations, in which the child orients to parents, teachers, or classmates at hand as well as to the Divine.

Database

This analysis draws upon three principal corpora of prayerful activity that involve children from Euro-American Christian families: (1) family dinner graces; (2) petitions, blessings, and prayers of thanksgiving offered in an Episcopal Sunday school class for three-to-five-year-old children; and (3) bedtime prayers of a child two years and nine months old.

Socialization into Prayer: Readiness

Praying involves assuming a psychological position of readiness. That is, prayer requires transitioning out of daily life activity into a state of spiritual receptivity (Cavalletti 1992; Scheff 1977; Duranti 1991; James 1902/1982). This state is marked by the display of a distinct set of bodily postures and practices. Here we consider how children's transition to prayerful readiness is interactionally accomplished at the family dinner table and in Sunday school.

Family Grace

In the family dinner graces observed, a state of readiness was signaled through the following body positionings:

- being seated
- heads bowed
- eyes closed
- hands either clasped together or extended to others around the table
- sign of the cross

The overall criterion for collective grace is that *everyone* present display this stance of readiness for prayer. The following dinnertime interaction, for example, evidences the expectation that all family members be seated before anyone invokes God's presence. In this excerpt, Laurie (5;7 years) makes a bid to say grace, displays her own readiness by folding her hands, then summons Jesus:

```
Laurie:  I wanna pray
         ((clasps hands))
         . . .
         Jesus?
```

Laurie, however, fails to recognize that her mother is not yet seated at the dinner table, a point her mother makes clear:

```
Mother: [Wait a minute Laurie
Laurie: [ ((irritated, throwing arms up in semi-despair))
Mother: I'm not sitting down
        ((sits down))
        please - um - help us to love
        and .hh um - Thank you for letting it be a n:ice day
        . . .
```

At another dinner, a Catholic family (Mother, Father, and children Dick, 8;7 years; Janie 5;11 years; and Evan, 3;7 years) is seated, but this kinesic posture alone is not considered a sufficient display of prayerful readiness. Rather, family members are prompted to cross themselves, fold their hands, and be silent:

```
      Mother: Are we gonna (say grace)?
      Janie:  Yes =
→     Father: =I:s everybody ready?
      Dick:   (finally)
              (1.0)
              ((Dick vaguely crosses himself; Janie folds hands in prayer; Father and
              Dick interlace hands and rest them in front of their foreheads; sudden
              quiet.))
      Father: In the name of the Father and of the Son and of the Holy Spirit
              (0.6) . . .
```

Here Mother's initial query signals that it is time to say grace. Although Janie responds, "*Yes,*" Father does not begin. Rather, he produces a follow-up query, "I:s everybody ready?," which serves to prompt kinesic and vocal displays of readiness. Only when Dick produces a verbal acknowledgment and the children cross themselves and assume the requisite body alignment does Father invoke the presence of the three deities in the Trinity ("In the name of the Father and of the Son and of the Holy Spirit").

Evidence that small children have knowledge of the signals of prayerful readiness and the necessity of displaying them comes from a dinnertime interaction that involves a three-and-a-half-year-old, Brandon. In Brandon's family, each child gets a turn at saying grace:

```
Brandon: ((arms outstretched))
         HOLD HA::NDS -
         (I'M MAKING MY TU::R[N -
         HOLD HA::NDS
         ((waves hands))
         I'M [MAKING MY TU:RN
Mom:        [(          ?          )   -     SSSHHH!
         ((Brandon's nine-year-old sister, Joanne, takes his hand, and then the
         entire family instantaneously holds hands in one large circle around table.))
```

Here Brandon is able to initiate the round of grace turns through a variety of strategies for securing prayerful readiness: He displays the family's conventional body comportment, namely, stretching his arms in a move to hold hands; he issues a readiness directive in the form of an imperative to hold hands; and he announces that he is "making" his turn. These strategies receive the desired uptake in that the other family members join Brandon in a collective positioning of bodies for praying.

In some families, a state of readiness for grace can be achieved through *alternative* practices. For example, in the following interaction three-and-a-half-year-old David is presented with two kinesic options, "hold hands or fold hands," before beginning grace, which in this case takes the form of a song family members refer to as "Johnny Appleseed":

Mom:	David, ready to say our <u>prayer</u>↑
Dad:	Hold hands or fold hands?
David:	Fold hands.
	((*folds hands in prayer position*))
	I mean <u>hold</u> hands.
	((*grabs Mom's and Dad's hands; Mom and Dad hold each other's hands*))
Dad:	↑O:: ↓kay
David:	OH↑, OH↑, OH↓ [OH:::: OH ((*singing*))
Dad:	[OH::: the Lord is good to me
	((*singing*))
Mom:	[OH::: [the Lord ((*singing*))
David:	[NOT YET! ((*frees hand*))
Dad:	You're not ready for Johnny Appleseed, David?
David:	No, I mean <u>fold</u> hands.
	((*folds hands in prayer position*))
	[Now I'm ready.
	[((*Mom and Dad fold hands in prayer position.*))
Mom:	Okay, you start.

In this rather jocular interaction, the option leads to prayerful mayhem rather than a smooth transition into readiness for grace. David first chooses "fold hands" and actually positions his hands accordingly. But then he changes his mind to "hold hands" and proceeds to link hands with his parents. Dad takes this as a sign of readiness and prompts David to start grace ("↑O:: ↓kay"). David then launches the grace song, and his parents chime in. But all is not well, for David halts the incipient grace, bellowing out, "NOT YET!" and frees his hands. He has decided to return to the option to fold hands: "No, I mean <u>fold</u> hands." He folds his hands and only then declares his readiness. His parents follow suit and bid him to begin again.

In addition to the management of body orientation, children display that they have assumed a prayerful attitude through their language and tone of voice. A common violation committed by younger children is failure to modulate the loudness of their voice. This is the case in the interaction excerpted earlier in which Brandon's mother admonished him for shouting by saying, "SSSHHH!" In addition, young children may start the vocal prayer with an inappropriate phrase or routine. In the family dinner with little David, for example, after he changes his mind about folding hands and holding hands, he appears to begin singing the words and tune of the usual Johnny Appleseed grace song. Indeed, he reiterates the opening frame he produced a minute earlier:

> Dad: You're not ready for Johnny Appleseed, David?
> David: No, I mean <u>fold</u> hands.
> ((*folds hands in prayer position*))
> [Now I'm ready.
> [(((*Mom and Dad fold hands in prayer position.*))
> Mom: Okay, you start.
> → David: OH↑, OH↑, OH↓

However, rather than continue with the grace, David transitions straight into another favorite Beatles song:

> David: Bang, Bang, Maxwell's sil↑ver↓ hammer
> ((*singing, then laughs, unfolding hands*))

That David laughs after singing about Maxwell's silver hammer and unfolds his hands suggests that mischief rather than development is at the bottom of this shifting of "footing" (Goffman 1979) from the sacred to the profane. David's parents then attempt to derail this shift and return to the opening of the prayer:

> → Dad: ↑Da:::: ↓ vid, are we singing our <u>prayer</u>
> or are we singing Maxwell?
> David: But I LIKE Maxwell AND I like JOHNNY!
> → Mom: How about <u>first</u> prayer singing, and <u>then</u> Maxwell.
> → Dad: Fold your hands, David.
> David: Okay. ((*folds hands, closes eyes*))
> OH, OH, OH! [OH::::: the Lord is good to me:::::::

Mom and Dad endeavor to realign David's demeanor first by pointing out the discrepancy between singing prayers and singing songs, then by proposing that David sing about Maxwell *after* praying, and finally by instructing him to resume the language and bodily comportment of grace. David acquiesces verbally ("Okay"), assumes the appropriate kinesic alignment (folds hands, closes eyes), and begins to sing the proper grace.

Sunday School Prayers

In the Sunday school setting, readiness for a range of prayers (e.g., petitions, thanksgivings, praises) is displayed by:

- either kneeling at the "prayer table" or sitting on a blue mat
- folding hands
- closing eyes
- using "Atrium voices," that is, hushed, slow-paced speech

In the following excerpt, the Sunday school class has just entered the room using "Atrium walking," a quiet, deliberate walk they routinely practice. The students are seated on blue mats, which are arranged in a circle on the floor when Terry, the teacher, invites them to pray:

> Terry: Let's pray together.
> Remember our praying hands and Atrium voices?
> ((*exhales loudly, raises her folded hands, and extends them toward the center of the circle, eyes closed*))

As illustrated earlier, in the Sunday school classroom the teacher socializes readiness for prayer by verbally reminding the children to fold their hands and speak in a reverent tone of voice ("Remember our praying hands and Atrium voices?") and by modeling the appropriate position: she closes her eyes, exhales loudly to mark what on other occasions she refers to as "a quiet way of being," and raises and extends her folded hands for all to see. In addition, teachers and more expert members of the class scaffold kinesic markers of prayerful readiness by physically molding children's bodies into appropriate prayer posture. Following Terry's invitation to pray and exaggerated demonstration of a ready stance, Sophie, the youngest in the group, looks on as the rest of the children bow their heads and fold their hands and close their eyes. Lynn, a parent volunteer, provides general support by seating herself on the floor behind Sophie. But Dana, one of the oldest children in the class, who is sitting next to Sophie, opens her eyes and offers a more direct intervention:

> Dana: ((*whispering*)) Close your eyes, Sophie.
> ((*Dana presses Sophie's hands together and, raising her own clasped hands, models how to fold them.*))
> Like this.
> Sophie: ((*closes eyes and folds hands tightly*))
> Terry: Dear Jesus, thank you for watching over us and our mommies and daddies during the week, and for bringing us back together this Sunday.

In this exceptionally explicit example of peer socialization, one preschool child cultivates prayerful attitude through multiple channels. First, Dana uses a whisper voice. Second, she issues an unmitigated directive to Sophie to close her eyes. Then Dana tackles the matter of praying hands by (1) actually molding Sophie's hands into the correct position and (2) drawing Sophie's attention to her (Dana's) clasped hands visually and verbally. Dana's apprenticeship techniques are effective in that Sophie then assumes the conventional prayerful demeanor.

Socialization into Prayer: Maintenance

Once children's bodies, voices, and language are organized in a state of prayerful readiness, the praying proceeds. However, children do not always maintain the expected kinesic and linguistic inflections of prayer. In many of these cases, parents and teachers react to children's forays by reining them back into a focus on prayer.

Family Grace

While some family grace conventions require only that children assume the appropriate body position and be silent, others expect children to participate in collective or individual recitations of the grace. In the latter cases, sometimes the younger children often appear inattentive or even begin an alternative activity. We saw the beginning of such a disjuncture in the excerpt earlier when David shifted from the Johnny Appleseed grace into a song about Maxwell's silver hammer. After his diversion is squelched and he sings the appropriate grace, however, David rebels once again. He sings the whole first line of the grace along with his parents:

```
David: OH, OH, OH! [OH:::: the Lord is good to me:::::::
Dad:    [OH the Lord is good to me, and so I
Mom:    [Oh the Lord is good to me, and so I
```

At this point David shifts his comportment and his language:

```
        David: [(((opens eyes, hurls fork to the floor))
               [BANG! BANG! Maxwell's silver fork!
        Dad:    [thank the Lo::rd↑
→       Mom:    ((softly)) Throwing hands aren't praying hands
        David: [TIME FOR MAXWELL! ((laughing))
        Dad:    [for GIVING ME::: the things I need,
```

When David still does not comply, Mom manipulates his hands back into prayerful frame, while joining Dad in grace:

```
        Dad:    the sun and the rain and [the apple see:::d.
→       Mom:                             [(((takes
                David's hands, presses them together in prayer position))
                                         [the apple seed.
        Dad:    [The Lo:::rd is good to me. AMEN!
        Mom:    [The Lo::rd is good to me. Amen.
        David: AMEN! [AMEN, AMEN, AMEN!
        Dad:          [AMEN! [AMEN! AMEN!
        Mom:                 [Amen, Amen.
```

While Mom's corralling is not fully successful, David does manage to display his participation in the closing down of the grace with a boisterous round of "AMEN!"s.

Children's prayer often diverges from the constraints of the genre in ways that are more subtle than David's capricious shifts. For instance, children also display difficulty maintaining the explicit performative purpose of particular subgenres of prayer, as when the message content bifurcates from the ostensible function of the prayer under way. As noted (see also Hendry 1972), there are a number of functional varieties of prayer, for example, petitions, intercessions, praise and thanksgiving, and confessions. These functions are often codified through predicates as in: *Help me/us, I/We pray for . . . , Thank you,* and *Forgive me/us.* Among more expert members, the content of prayer is typically consonant with these functions. Thus, petitions and intercessions solicit support for a desired circumstance (e.g., *Help us to eternal life*); prayers of praise and thanksgiving appreciate the source of a desirable circumstance (e.g., *we thank you for the beautiful creations*); and confessions admit transgressions. In this way, the requirements of the genre filter which experiences are put into words. Conformity to the requirements of the genre appears especially difficult for young children, as becomes evident when their prayers stray from highly formulaic discourse to recount particular, personal situations.

Such inconsistency between ostensible function and content characterizes young Laurie's grace, the opening to which was excerpted earlier. At first, Laurie adheres to conventional expectations concerning grace:

Laurie: Jesus? -
      please - um - help us to love
      and .hh um - Thank you for letting it be a <u>n:ice</u> day,
      and for taking a fun nap?

This portion of the grace displays generic features of prayer: invocation of God ("Jesus?"), petition for assistance ("please - um - help us to love") and thanksgiving ("Thank you for letting it be a <u>n:ice</u> day, and for taking a fun nap?"). However, Laurie's prayer then diverges from the thanksgiving format:

Laurie: .hh - a:nd - for (letting) Mommy go bye
      and I'm glad that I cwied to[day?
      cuz I [like cwying .hh and
Annie: [((*snicker*))
Roger: [((*snicker*))
Laurie: I'm glad (that anything/everything) happened today in Jesus' name
      ((*claps hands*)) <u>A:</u>-MEN!
Roger: [amen ((*clapping lightly*))
Mother: [amen
Jimmy: [A:MEN

While Laurie continues to frame her experience as positive ("I'm glad"), the recounted events themselves ("Mommy go bye," "I cwied today") appear to clash with these sentiments. Indeed, the utterances "I'm glad that I cwied today" and "I like cwying" seem emotional oxymorons, in that crying that follows departure of a loved one usually signals distress. Whereas Laurie's earlier account of pleasant events fits well with the design features of thanksgiving, the evolving problem-centered narrative is dramatically discrepant. A more practiced grace sayer would likely have (1) formulated this experience within the format of a petition for assistance in avoiding or handling future instances of separation, (2) selected an unambiguously pleasing circumstance for which to give thanks, or (3) emphasized positive aspects of the distressing event (e.g., "Thank for helping me to be strong and letting me say good-bye to Mommy," or, "I'm glad that I cried today, because afterward I felt better").[1] Finally, it is likely that the discrepancy between the message content of Laurie's grace and the performative functions that evokes snickering between her older siblings, Annie and Roger, at this point in the prayer. Although far subtler than the socialization strategies delineated thus far, laughter is a potent, widespread resource for marking norm violations (Coser 1959; Goffman 1967).

Sunday School Prayers

Breaking prayer frame is also a routine occurrence among the children in Sunday school, leading their teacher, Terry, to remind them of what they should be doing. In the interaction that follows, the children do not bounce back and forth between activities as did David. Rather, they drift gradually from a focus on the sacred to more profane matters. The students are seated on blue mats when Terry begins reciting a thanksgiving prayer, which elicits a contribution from young Maggie:

> Terry: Dear Jesus, thank you for watching over us and our mommies and
>   daddies during the week, and for bringing us back together this Sunday.
> Maggie: And thank you for watching our dogs.
> Terry: Yes, and thank you for watching our dogs and our cats.

At this point, however, Maggie begins a shift in footing, both kinesically and verbally, which is taken up by her classmate Joe:

> Maggie: ((*opens her eyes*)) Jesus sees everything. He can see you all the time.
> Joe: ((*opens his eyes, unfolds his hands*)) How can he see e::verything? Does he
>   have a microscope? ((*laughs*))

Several children then open their eyes; some unfold their hands, while a few remain in praying position. The children begin to discuss the topic raised by Maggie and challenged by Joe:

> Susan: No, probably a telescope, right Terry?
> → Terry: [((*exhales loudly*))
> Sophie: [Or maybe glasses.
> Joe: ((*turns to Sophie*)) NO::::! You can't see everything just because you
>   have glasses. YOU can't see everything with your glasses, Sophie.

Terry and the parent volunteer, Lynn, then begin to urge them back into prayer:

> → Terry: [((*raises her folded hands and extends them toward the center of the
>   circle, eyes closed*)) Help us to remember that we're praying now.
> Sophie: [((*closes eyes and folds hands*))
> Susan: [((*closes eyes and folds hands*))
> Joe: [((*folds hands*))
> → Terry: [God, we thank you for our Atrium voices,
>   and for our eyes, so that we can see your beautiful creation,
>   and for glasses that help us see if we need them.

Joe: And help them not to fall in the bathtub.
           ((*laughs*))
→ Lynn: ((*positions self behind Joe, wraps her hands around his, pushing them together in prayer position*))
Terry: Amen.
Joe: [AMEN!
Children: [Amen!

In this passage, Terry repeats her exaggerated display of appropriate behavior by exhaling, closing her eyes, and raising her praying hands for perusal. She also adds a verbal reminder/admonition ("Help us to remember that we're praying now"; "thank you for our Atrium voices"), which conveys the message that the slips in comportment and verbal content constitute a departure from the activity of praying. And she attempts to maintain the continuity of the prayer discourse by incorporating a key element of discussion (glasses) into her prayer of thanksgiving ("thank you . . . for glasses that help us see if we need them"). When these strategies fail to corral Joe, Lynn tries a more direct approach: she physically shapes his hands into the desired position.

Bedtime Prayer

The Sunday school prayer of thanksgiving indicates how topics brought up in prayer may touch off other language activities, for example, an argument about God's ability to see everyone on earth. Children's bedtime prayers also lapse into secular discussions. Moreover, prayer and other forms of discourse may interpenetrate, as was the case when Laurie tucked a compressed narrative about her day at kindergarten into a prayer of thanksgiving. In the following example, David, at two years, nine months of age, interlaces prayer and narrative while saying a bedtime prayer with his father:

Dad: Should we say our prayers?
David: Ummm: <u>Okay</u>. ((*folds hands*))
Dad: De::ar God.
       Bless Mo::mmy↑
David: and Daddy↑
Dad: and <u>David</u>.
David: and Gra::nny↑ and <u>Veronica</u> and Kira↑ and Sonya↑
       (.4 pause)
       and <u>O::H</u> don't forget RU↑BY↓
       (.3 pause)
       and <u>Raymond</u>=and Ellie:: ↑ and Sandro and <u>crazy</u> Ma::r↑co↓ and my <u>BIG</u> truck and my little trucks and
       (.2 pause)
→   <u>OH</u> do you? Do you? Do you remember
       when Sandro said, when Sandro said,
       "Hello David?
       You bring my <u>little</u> trucks over <u>there</u>."
       And I DID↑
       Can we play <u>that</u> game? <u>Can</u> we?

```
        Dad:    and God Bless Bop and Nanna↑
        David:  and Uncle Todd↑
    →           and do you know what Uncle Pete's
                other name is?
                "MY FRIEND UNCLE PETE!"
                'Member when Uncle Pete came to my home?
                But I don't think Spike and Nate are coming,
                no. No I don't think so.
        Dad:    God bless Spike and Nate.
    → David:    But I play basketball
                and I say, "Spike and Nate, YOU DON'T PLAY!
                YOU STAY THERE."
                How about we put Spike and Nate in the basement.
        Dad:    Yea::h, I remember that.
                Spike and Nate are big dogs aren't they.
        David:  But I think↑ they're not coming.
        Dad:    When Uncle Pete comes on Saturday?
                Yeah he probably won't bring Spike and Nate.
                Yeah.
        David:  Yeah.
```

As David petitions blessings on numerous persons and objects in his life, he bursts into associated narratives. It is as if each of the blessed entities holds for him a store of memories and emotions that he is compelled to air. His petition to bless "Sandro and crazy Ma::r↑co↓ and my BIG truck and my little trucks," for example, touches off an invitation to ". . . remember . . . when Sandro said, 'Hello David? You bring my little trucks over there.' And I DID↑." These pride-infused remembered events then touch off a desired projection of these events in the future: "Can we play that game? Can we?" Similarly, David's petition to bless "Uncle Pete↑" inspires his recollection that "Uncle Pete's other name is . . . 'MY FRIEND UNCLE PETE'" and the events that transpired "when Uncle Pete came to my home" with his dogs, Spike and Nate. In David's rendering, happy and worrisome past events intermingle with projected events ("But I don't think Spike and Nate are coming," "How about we put Spike and Nate in the basement"), and he seems to use prayer to sort out what the past holds for his future.

In this bedtime interaction, David's dad extensively scaffolds the activity of praying: He launches the activity by inviting David to "say our prayers," provides the opening prayer frame ("De::ar God. Bless Mo::mmy↑"), supplements the list of persons to bless ("and David," "and Uncle Todd↑"), and models intonation and voice quality. Moreover, he attempts to maintain the practice of praying by redirecting David's forays into conversational narrative back to prayer-inflected discourse. When David interjects a bid for permission to play the truck game, his dad responds by continuing to solicit blessings on friends and family using intonation inflected for prayer. In addition, akin to Sunday school teacher Terry's incorporation of a source of divergence into message content of her prayer, when David digresses into recollections about Uncle Pete's visit with the dogs, his dad attempts to rein him in and maintain continuity by invoking God's blessing on the animals ("God bless Spike and Nate"). In these ways, David's father socializes David into conventional practices for transitioning into and maintaining the discourse of praying.

Socialization into Prayer: Ending

The transition out of prayer-inflected discourse into other daily life activities is also an interactional achievement, such that socialization into prayer involves mastering conventionalized practices for marking the ending of a prayer and reentry into other communicative practices. Consistent with their difficulties maintaining prayer postures, gestures, and language practices over the course of the activity, children often shift out of prayer and into other forms of discourse without signaling whether or not the activity of praying has come to a close.

After the preceding excerpt from David and his dad's bedtime prayer, for example, and after contemplating the likelihood that Uncle Pete will bring Spike and Nate to his house, David requests that his dad "tell the story of David's day":

David: Daddy, can you tell a story about what David did today?

David's dad agrees to do so, but before launching into the story, he asks David whether they are finished praying. David's dad's remark both draws David's attention to the fact that he has segued out of prayer into a new discourse activity and conveys the need to mark the close of the prayer before doing so. In response, David recruits a fundamental resource to this end: "Amen."

Dad: Okay, are we done with our prayer?
David: AMEN! AMEN! AMEN!

Indeed, in the interactions analyzed here, *amen* is the most commonly recruited resource for bringing a prayer to completion. Moreover, use of the ritual closing *amen*, which literally means "it shall be so!/so be it!," allows those present to verbally affirm the sentiments expressed in the prayer and thus to reinforce their roles as co-participants, further establishing the collective nature of the activity.

Family Grace

Analysis of prayer interactions suggests that children acquire a sense of the importance of marking the shift from assumption of a prayerful attitude to more mundane daily life activities and that they learn that this transition must be accomplished in specific ways. In particular, the prayer must be closed down in a manner that reflects the spirit of the practice, manifest in maintenance of prayer-inflected body postures, gestures, and tone of voice in addition to lexical content. This is evident in the following excerpt from a dinner grace that involves Father (F), Mother (M), and their daughters, Holly (H), who is six and a half years old, and Shelly (S), who is almost five years old:

F, M, S, H: God is great, goo::d
- a:nd we <u>thank him</u> for our foo:d
creatures <u>A:LL</u>↑- great and SMA:LL↑- -
<u>praise</u> him with thanksg<u>i::</u> ↑-ving

M, S: [A:men ((*Mother unclasps hands and starts reaching for food.*))

Holly: [A:men ben ((*singsong, mock southern accent*))

Father   A:men

Holly: <u>Ame</u>[n ben ((*Holly looks away from Father.*))

Father: [you str:aighten up((*to Holly with his hand beside her*))

In this interaction, Holly voices the requisite lexicon for finishing grace in a playful manner. Her father's reprimand, "You str:aighten up," indicates that this rendition of "Amen" is not an acceptable means of expressing the sentiments behind the word or of ending the activity and points to the necessity of displaying a "straight" (i.e., reverent) demeanor until the closing is complete.

Similarly, as grace is brought to a close at another family dinner, Father's (F) and Mother's (M) responses to four-year-old Kimberly's (K) behavior illuminate the importance of achieving a complete closing before jumping into the next activity, which in this case is dinner:

F, M, K: Come Lord Jesus be our guest,
[and let these gifts to us be blessed.
[(((*Kimberly reaches for a roll, takes a bite.*))

F, M, K: Amen.

Father: Kimberly, <u>no</u> eating before Amens.

Mother: You know that, sweetie.

This interaction demonstrates the requirement that the closing of the prayer and associated shift out of a prayerful attitude be achieved *prior* to, not simultaneous with, entry into a subsequent activity.

Sunday School Prayers

Sunday school teachers also endeavor to facilitate clear demarcation of boundaries between ending prayer and beginning other activities. In the following excerpt, for example, five-year-old Carly offers a prayer of thanksgiving while kneeling at the "prayer table":

Carly: ((*kneels at table, folds hands, closes eyes*))
Dear Heavenly Father, Jesus is <u>beautiful</u>.
Thank you for beautiful Jesus,
and for my beautiful dress,
and for all the flowers.
((*unfolds hands, looks up, remains in kneeling position at prayer table*))

Although Carly does not provide the expected, though not mandatory, "Amen," Terry, who is standing nearby, seems to interpret Carly's unclasped hands and open eyes as a signal that she is finished praying. Terry compliments Carly on her prayer and engages her in conversation, seemingly accomplishing a transition out of prayer:

> Terry: That was a <u>lovely</u> thank-you prayer, Carly.
> We have a <u>lot</u> to be thankful for.
> Carly: Umhm. Yesterday was Travis' birthday,
> and he got a <u>lo::t</u> of presents.
> And I had to keep reminding him to say thank you.
> Terry: It's important that we remind each other to say thank you.
> Carly: Even if you don't like what you got.

At this point Carly, who is still kneeling at the prayer table, addresses Jesus with a prayer of thanksgiving. Yet her comportment violates the vocal, gestural, and content requirements of the genre: she uses a raucous, singsong voice, she does not close her eyes or fold her hands, and she gives thanks for objects she deems "yucky":

> Carly: ((*singsong voice*))
> Thank you Jesus for the yucky truck! ((*laughs*))
> Thank you Jesus for the yucky crackers! ((*laughs*))

Terry responds by endeavoring to prompt Carly to close down the prayer. Like David's dad, she attempts to do so by asking Carly if she is through praying (i.e., suggesting that she is not praying), citing her unclasped hands as evidence that this is the case:

> Terry: Are you through at the prayer table, Carly?
> I don't see your praying hands.

Yet rather than expediently terminating the prayer, for instance, by offering a ritual "Amen," Carly denies that she is finished praying and begins anew, this time with a prayer of thanksgiving that is appropriate to the content domain of the subgenre and displays prayer-inflected body comportment, voice tone, and language:

> Carly: No:::: ((*bows head, folds hands, closes eyes*))
> Dear Jesus, Thank you for the crackers that I <u>do::</u> like.
> I love you Jesus.
> Amen.
> Terry: Amen.

Here Carly's transition out of prayer is complete: she says, "Amen," opens her eyes, unclasps her hands, and rises from her position at the prayer table. Terry's "Amen" further contributes to the successful closing of the prayer and the construction of an opening for collective entry into another communicative activity.

Conclusion

These analyses illuminate the social, kinesic, and linguistic underpinnings of the achievement of a prayerful attitude. Distinct from other genres, prayer offers a template for reach beyond oneself to enter into the presence of the Divine—whether it be nature or a deity. Many experience a profound sense of unification (James 1902/1982:395): "I felt that I prayed as I had never prayed before and knew now what prayer really is: to return from the solitude of individuation into the consciousness of unity with all that is." Prayer thus helps to bring about a sense that one is not alone, that one has accessed a higher power, and that one's voice is being heard. This model of prayer presumes a dialogic relation between the individual who prays and the higher power to whom the prayer is directed. Yet such a model does not account for the social nature of many prayers. As we have seen, people often pray in the company of others. In these situations, the interaction is multi-party rather than strictly dyadic. Further, the activity of praying unites participants with each other and with the Divine, as well as with the presence of entities invoked in the prayer.

Examination of children's socialization into the practice of praying underscores the centrality of the body in accomplishing prayerful attitude. It also demonstrates the difficulty of maintaining a consistently inflected genre over interactional time. Yet rather than viewing these difficulties as imperfections to be overcome, we can perhaps best understand children's forays out of language and conduct inflected for the sacred into mundane modes of communicating as evidence of the routine interpenetration of genres in everyday life. That is, the endeavor to formulate and publicly instantiate understandings of self-in-the-world, which relies on the recruitment of conventional moral frameworks, is *likely* to contain features of multiple genres. Further, while we do not suggest that when people initiate a conversational narrative or formulate a plan they enter directly into dialogue with the Divine, the interweaving of genres manifest here may also point to the human proclivity to orient toward a higher good in attempting to make sense of life events (Taylor 1989).

NOTES

The authors gratefully acknowledge support for this project from the Wenner Gren Foundation for Anthropological Research through a predoctoral grant to L. Capps.

1. As previously noted (Ochs and Capps 2001), such paraphrases are more semantically cogent and contextually appropriate than Laurie's prayer but may undercut emotional authenticity.

REFERENCES

Bakhtin, Mikhail M. 1981. *The Dialogic Imagination: Four Essays.* Ed. M. Holquist. Trans. C. Emerson and M. Holquist. Austin: University of Texas Press.
Bakhtin, Mikhail. 1986. *Speech Genres and Other Late Essays.* Trans. V. W. McGee. Austin: University of Texas Press.
Cavalletti, Sofia. 1992. *The Religious Potential of the Child.* Trans. P. M. Coulter and J. M. Coulter. Chicago: Liturgy Training Publications.

Coser, Rose L. 1959. Some social functions of laughter *Human Relations* 12:171–182.

Duranti, Alessandro. 1991. On the organization of collective activities: Saying grace in a Samoan village. Paper presented at the Annual Meeting of the American Anthropological Association, Chicago, IL, December 1991.

Goffman, Erving. 1967. *Interaction Ritual: Essays on Face-to-face Behavior.* Garden City, NY: Anchor.

Goffman, Erving. 1979. Footing. *Semiotica* 25:1–29.

Hendry, George. 1972. The lifeline of theology. *Princeton Seminary Bulletin* 65:22–30.

James, William. 1902/1982. *The Varieties of Religious Experience.* New York: Penguin.

Ochs, Elinor. 1994. Stories that step into the future. In E. Finegan and D. F. Biber (eds.), *Sociolinguistic Perspectives on Register,* 106–135. Oxford: Oxford University Press.

Ochs, Elinor, and Lisa Capps. 2001. *Living Narrative.* Cambridge, MA: Harvard University Press.

Scheff, Thomas. 1977. Distancing emotion in ritual. *Current Anthropology* 18(3): 483–490.

Schegloff, Emanuel J. 1995. Discourse as an interactional achievement III: The omnirelevance of action. *Research on Language and Social Interaction* 28(3): 185–211.

Taylor, Charles. 1989. *Sources of the Self.* Cambridge, MA: Harvard University Press.

4

Producing Sense with Nonsense Syllables

Turn and Sequence in Conversations with a Man with Severe Aphasia

CHARLES GOODWIN, MARJORIE H. GOODWIN, & DAVID OLSHER

This chapter investigates the collaborative production of meaning and action in the speech of a man in his early eighties named Chil diagnosed with severe nonfluent aphasia.[1] Our data are drawn from over 200 hours of videotaped naturally occurring interaction in Chil's home recorded by Charles Goodwin and Marjorie Harness Goodwin over the past seven years.[2] In 1981 a massive stroke in the left hemisphere of Chil's brain left him with extremely limited language capacities; the right side of his body is paralyzed (thus making gesture possible only with his left arm and hand), and his entire vocabulary consists of three words: *yes, no,* and *and.* He can also produce vocal response cries such as *oh* and *ah.* Chil possesses not only a restricted vocabulary but also a restricted phonology. Most of his lexically empty syllables begin with either a voiced alveolar stop (*d*) or an Aleveopalatal glide (*y*) followed by a limited number of vowels. Despite his severely limited resources, Chil is an effective conversationalist. Indeed, he is a recognized figure in his town and strikes up conversations with strangers as he uses his electric scooter to do the family's shopping, go to restaurants and movies by himself, buy cappuccino at Starbuck's, and so forth. How is this possible?

While lacking a rich vocabulary,[3] Chil can produce syllables such as *deh, duh,* and *yih.* These syllables lack both a semantics and a syntax and could be termed "nonsense syllables." Chil cannot use them as arbitrary, conventionalized signs to perform reference (e.g., he has no terms for cats, dogs, tables, people, or indeed anything). However, Chil can concatenate multiple syllables into larger tone units. Pitch movement, stress, rhythm, and loudness are varied within these units to produce recognizable tunes in, as we will demonstrate in this essay, a meaningful and conversationally relevant fashion. To use prosody without a lexicon Chil relies upon semantic structure in the surrounding talk. Chil is thus able to build appropriate conversational action with talk that lacks a lexicon by using prosodic resources with fluency and skill (see Couper-Kuhlen and Selting 1996 for the importance of taking sequential organization into account in the analysis of prosody). The prosodic resources used by Chil are subtle and complex. In earlier versions of this analysis we attempted to use both pitch tracks and a variety of transcription devices (such as musical notation) to try to capture on the printed page relevant aspects of Chil's prosody. However, none of what we could do provided an adequate visual record. Thus, in the remainder of this essay we will sometimes have to tell the reader about crucial differences in Chil's prosody without demonstrating those differences in the detail that we would like. This is not because we consider the precise description of Chil's prosody unimportant. Precisely the contrary: the analytic problems at issue here are too crucial to pretend to capture with transcription tools that we ourselves recognize as inadequate. We hope in the future to make progress on this issue.

In addition to Chil's ability to vary his prosody in an intricate and locally relevant fashion, he can also precisely slot his talk into the sequential organization provided by the talk of others. Unlike some aphasics, he possesses an excellent sense of timing and uses his restricted repertoire without hesitation, indeed with a fluency of interactional pacing, tracking, and movement that is comparable to that of normal speakers.[4] Through his fluent command of prosody Chil is able to display a wide range of affect and, moreover, to link this affect to the performance of relevant conversational action, such as evaluation and assessment.[5]

Chil is able to supplement the resources in his speech production with a range of different kinds of embodied action (gesture, displays of orientation and intentional focus, etc.). Moreover, he makes extensive use of phenomena in his environment that are already rich with meaning. We will argue that he builds action in concert with others by juxtaposing semiotic resources from a range of different phenomenal fields (e.g., talk, gesture, posture, resources in the environment, etc.). Rather than affecting him alone, his inability to produce speech leads to changes in the ecology of sign systems used by multiple participants within conversation to accomplish meaning and action. Fluent speakers themselves produce speech with lexical content that elaborates and is elaborated by their gestures. However, Chil can produce only gesture and not the lexically rich talk that typically stands in a relationship of mutual elaboration with gesture. One consequence of this is that in conversations with Chil actions that are routinely produced by a single individual in a *single turn* often require a *multiparty sequence*. This interplay between turn and sequence in his interaction is the theme of this chapter.

Building an Utterance by Tying to the Talk of Others

Figure 4.1 is an example of Chil's ability to say something meaningful. Chil and his wife, Helen, are talking with their daughter-in-law Linda in the living room.

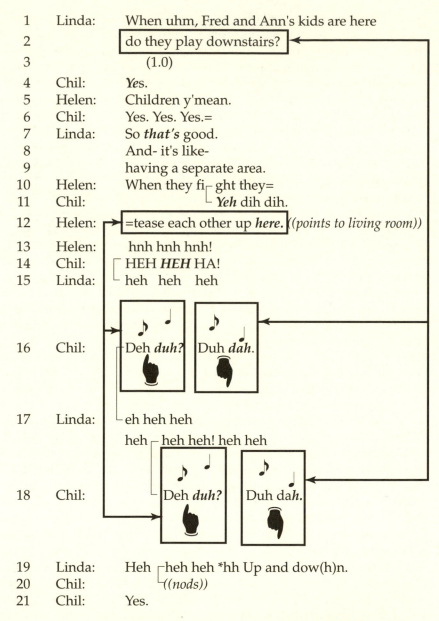

1	Linda:	When uhm, Fred and Ann's kids are here
2		do they play downstairs?
3		(1.0)
4	Chil:	*Yes.*
5	Helen:	Children y'mean.
6	Chil:	Yes. Yes. Yes.=
7	Linda:	So *that's* good.
8		And- it's like-
9		having a separate area.
10	Helen:	When they fight they=
11	Chil:	*Yeh* dih dih.
12	Helen:	=tease each other up *here.* ((points to living room))
13	Helen:	hnh hnh hnh!
14	Chil:	HEH *HEH* HA!
15	Linda:	heh heh heh
16	Chil:	Deh *duh?* Duh *dah.*
17	Linda:	eh heh heh
		heh heh heh! heh heh
18	Chil:	Deh *duh?* Duh da*h.*
19	Linda:	Heh heh heh heh *hh Up and dow(h)n.
20	Chil:	((nods))
21	Chil:	Yes.

Figure 4.1. Combining pitch, gesture, and sequential positioning to say something meaningful.

Linda inquires about their grandchildren, well known for their rough, enthusiastic play, asking if the children play downstairs in the basement (lines 1–2). After Chil answers, "*Yes*" (line 4), Helen comments that they "tease each other up here" (line 12) while pointing to the living room where they are seated. Chil and Linda look at each other and simultaneously produce synchronized three-syllable laughs (lines 14–15). Chil in line 16 then raises his good left arm above his head while holding his hand flat and produces a two-syllable, "Deh *duh?*" with rising pitch.[6] He then drops his hand while producing another two-syllable unit, only this time with falling pitch: "Duh *dah*." As Linda laughs with appreciation, he repeats this sequence of actions in line 18, producing another four lexically empty syllables (hereafter referred to as nonsense syllables). The first two, which carry a pitch rise, are again accompanied by a rising hand, and the final two, which fall in pitch, occur simultaneously with the drop of the gesturing hand. After laughing in response, Linda glosses what Chil has just said as, "Up and dow(h)n," and Chil answers, "Yes."

For Linda the nonsense syllables that Chil produces in lines 16 and 18 constitute an appropriate and relevant move within their conversation and, moreover, communicate a prepositional content that she glosses as "Up and dow(h)n" (line 19).

Chil's ability to produce conversationally relevant meaning and action here is made possible through the creative deployment of a range of different semiotic resources:

- First, the iconic properties of pitch allow him to make visible a contrast between high and low within his talk.
- Second, this is both focused and elaborated by his simultaneous gesture. Indeed, the way in which both pitch movement and unit boundaries in the stream of speech are precisely matched by the boundaries of gesture movements making visible the same high–low contrast is consistent with Dwight Bolinger's (1986, 1989) suggestion that at least some gesture should be included within the domain of prosody.
- Third, the indexical properties of language and most crucially the sequential organization of conversation allow Chil's iconic nonsense syllables to be tied to semantic structure provided by the talk of others. This is accomplished not only by the way in which his prosodic gestural packages make visible iconically a salient semantic contrast in the immediately prior talk but also by additional sequential work on his part. Thus, his laugh in line 14 is visibly tied to what Helen has just said while simultaneously acting as a preface, an interpretive framework, for the prosodic contrast that immediately follows.
- Fourth, by selectively reframing and reinterpreting what has just been said Chil makes an original contribution to the conversation. As Helen in line 12 talks about the children fighting and teasing upstairs she points toward that very place, the room they are sitting in. If reference were all that was at issue in Chil's action he could have easily used a similar pointing gesture. Instead, he links the description in lines 10 and 12 to an earlier one (line 2) by using features of prosody to establish a contrast between two spaces, as well as the possibility of movement between them (e.g., the children are running up- and downstairs, in effect all over the house).

- Fifth, this contrast is further elaborated through repetition. Moreover this repetition seems to carry information about aspect, for example, to display a repetitive state of affairs.[7]
- Sixth, this repetition occurs within a participation framework marked by a relevant affective stance as displayed by Linda's ongoing appreciative laughter at what he is saying.
- Seventh, the sequential organization of conversation provides participants with resources for checking their understanding of what Chil is saying. Chil's talk does not make use of an arbitrary, conventionalized sign system. Determining precisely, or even roughly, what he is saying and assuring that his interlocutors' understandings are compatible with Chil's is a pervasive, systematic problem. In line 19 Linda formulates what he has displayed iconically in explicit language, and in line 21 Chil affirms the correctness of that gloss with a, "Yes." On other occasions refusals by Chil to accept his interlocutors' glosses lead to quite extended sequences (Goodwin 1995, 2000b).

In brief, though Chil is able to use prosody and gesture to perform relevant action, the unit required for the analysis of how this is done is not him alone but rather the larger community of interacting participants within which his actions are embedded (e.g., he borrows meaning from their talk) and the sequential structures that make possible the public accomplishment of relevant meaning and action within conversation.

Summons Request Sequences

In the data just examined Chil built complex action by tying his actions to phenomena in earlier talk. This parasitic organization provides resources that can be used to build complex next actions. However, if Chil wants to initiate new action he is deprived of these sequential resources, and indeed getting others to understand something novel that does not emerge from talk or activity already in progress is a pervasive problem for Chil (see Goodwin 2000b). We will now investigate how he does this.

Performing a Variety of Different Actions Within a Single Turn

The theme of this chapter is turn and sequence. One of the phenomena we want to explore is the way in which actions that can be done in a *single turn* by fluent speakers require a *multiparty sequence* for Chil to accomplish. To establish this contrast we will first look at an action built within a single turn by a fluent speaker, Chil's daughter Pat. Then we will argue that Chil lacks some of the resources deployed by Pat and examine the sequential resources he and his interlocutors use to adapt to this state of affairs.

In Figure 4.2, by saying, "Bring that in Jere," Pat successfully requests that someone else perform a specific action. What resources does she use to accom-

Pat: Bob was up early,

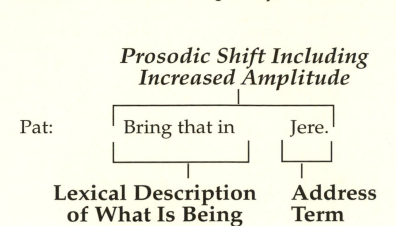

Pat:

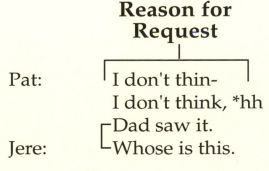

Pat: I don't thin-
I don't think, *hh
Dad saw it.
Jere: Whose is this.

Figure 4.2. Multiple actions within a single turn.

plish this? In these data Pat, her daughter Jessica, and Chil are sitting at the kitchen table on Christmas day. From there Pat can see Jere in the living room. Pat has been talking about her brother Bob (see figure 4.2, above).

Central to what Pat does here is her ability to use the lexical, syntactic, and prosodic resources of language to construe with fine precision a range of phenomena relevant to the action that she is performing. First, by using a name as an address term she can specify one particular addressee from a larger pool of potential recipients. Note also that this particular addressee, Jere, is positioned to perform the action being requested in a way that others present aren't (i.e., he is the one holding the present being requested). Pat's ability to produce a name thus not only identifies an addressee but also helps specify what precisely is being requested. Second, she is able to precisely formulate what she wants done by saying, "Bring that in." Linguistic resources include the lexical verb *Bring* and the imperative form. The use of the demonstrative (*that*) to reference something that she can see that Jere is already attending to displays her ongoing analysis of the actions he is engaged in. This specification could also have been done with a noun such as *the calendar.* Third, she provides a reason for the request. Fourth, she uses increased amplitude (and other prosodic phenomena that are beyond the scope of this essay) to mark that the request to Jere is disjunctive with her earlier talk to Chil. The increased amplitude can also signal a shift in addressee, for example, that instead of continuing to talk to Chil and Jessica, who are at the table with her, Pat is now addressing a more distant recipient.

A Request by Chil

The only one of Pat's resources available to Chil is prosody. We will now look at how he initiates a new action that does not depend upon structure in the immediately prior talk. Chil is having pancakes on the deck of his son Keith's house. Because Chil's paralysis affects muscles on the left side of his throat, Chil can choke if his food is not cut into small pieces. Just after giving Chil a plate with pancakes on it Keith is called away to the phone, and Chil is left alone.

(1)

```
1                    (9.5)
2  Chil:   Dih dih duh: :.
3                    (1.8)
4  Chil:   DUH DUH DUH:.
5                    (2.5)
6  Linda: Yeah Dad?
```

In line 4 Chil produces a loud three-syllable utterance that is responded to several seconds later by Chil's daughter-in-law Linda, with an upwardly intoned, "Yeah Dad?" The sequence appears to be a variant of what Schegloff (1968) has analyzed as a Summons Answer sequence. It functions to bring two participants into a state of mutual accessibility and interaction. Moreover, Linda's "Yeah Dad?" is both a subsequent move to Chil's summons and, with its rising intonation, a new first pair part addressed to Chil. Like the answers analyzed by Schegloff, it displays a readiness to attend to further, as yet unspecified action.[8]

However, Pat's call to Jere, examined earlier, demonstrated how participants, indeed members of this same family, can build utterances with a quite different structure to request action from a co-participant who has temporarily left the room. Rather than summoning Jere, Pat told him immediately what she wanted him to do.

It is important to note that the stream of nonsense syllables that carry the prosody of Chil's utterance cannot target a particular addressee. Chil can't use names as address terms. In this case that may not be consequential. Anyone in the house can cut Chil's pancakes. However, as will be demonstrated later in this chapter, on many occasions a particular addressee is crucial to the constitution of the precise action being formulated.

In brief, what we find here is an instance of a pervasive sequence type used to align participants for subsequent interaction. Despite his drastically impaired ability to produce language, Chil is using basic sequential resources to accomplish interactive tasks. However, this sequence is occurring in an environment where other ways of requesting what Chil wants done would be far more economical and effective. By the end of this multiutterance, multiparty sequence Chil has accomplished far less than Pat did with her single utterance. Linda is now attending to Chil but does not yet know what he wants. An extended sequence has been entered but not brought to a close.

Before we examine how Chil tells the party he has summoned what he wants done, the range of resources he can use to initiate a summons sequence will be further investigated. We will pay particular attention to the problem of addressee selection.

Securing the Orientation of a Co-Participant

Those around Chil recurrently interpret a set of utterances from him as requests for their orientation, that is, as first moves in the particular kind of Summons Answer sequences being investigated here. The following provide some examples. We will not examine in detail what is happening in each example. For the moment we simply want to demonstrate that others do orient to Chil after talk like this and that, moreover, by producing utterances such as, "What?," "Yeah?," and "What do you want Chil?" these parties display that they are prepared for and awaiting further action from Chil:

(2)

> Chil: Dih dih *duh:*.
>   (2.0)
> Pam: What?

(3)

> Chil: Yih dih *duh:*.
>   (0.3)
> Keith: Yeah?

(4)

> Chil: Dih *duh* duh.
>   (0.4)
> Chil: °Duh:
> Helen: What do you want Chil?

In brief, a pervasive sequential pattern in Chil's interaction takes the form of his using a brief string of nonsense syllables (typically three), with a distinctive prosodic shape (the analysis and precise description of which is beyond the scope of this essay) when others are not oriented to him. Parties who hear such an utterance treat it as a summons and shift their orientation to Chil while displaying their expectation of further action on his part.

Addressee Selection

In the data just examined Chil was able to call for an addressee but not to specify a *particular* addressee from a larger pool of potential recipients, as Pat did in Figure 4.2 by using Jere's name as an address term. Without the ability to speak names is Chil completely deprived of the ability to perform one of the core actions instantiated in the turn-at-talk, specifying an addressee and/or next speaker?

Despite his inability to speak names, Chil is able to perform limited types of addressee selection when summoning someone. Many of his methods accomplish this task negatively, that is, by *excluding* potential addressees so that only a very limited set (frequently one) of those present remain as valid candidates. In Figure 4.3 Chil produces a summons. However, instead of responding to the summons by turning to Chil to find out what he wants, his son Keith *relays* the summons to a third party, calling Arnie by name. How is Keith able to find a specific addressee in an utterance that contains only nonsense syllables? Chil can use a variety of iconic resources, including both volume and gaze, to display attributes of participants in terms of how they are positioned in the local surround. In Figure 4.3 Arnie has just left the kitchen to carry out a bag of garbage.

Chil's utterance carries a distinctive summoning contour, marked in part by the way in which the last syllable in each unit is stressed. The precise description of the prosodic features used by Chil to produce a hearable summons is beyond the scope of this essay. The utterance is spoken with markedly loud volume (indicated by uppercase letters in the transcript). Such an action would be inappropriate as a move directed to someone standing right next to the speaker, and indeed Keith hears it as addressed to someone who has just left the room. Other embodied resources are also being deployed to accomplish addressee selection here. Chil is gazing toward the door where Arnie has just exited, and in his relay Keith also gazes toward that door. In brief, though Chil lacks a lexicon he is able to use other embodied resources, including volume contrast, gaze, and postural orientation, to help show those present to whom a summons is being addressed. Note how his use of these resources depends upon an analysis of the current situation (for example, where relevant participants are positioned). Moreover, by using such methods systematically Chil is relying upon his co-participants to embed the actions he produces within a similar analysis.

What is at issue is not simply a difference in volume but an action that displays an analysis of the particulars of the setting in which it is embedded. The talk is specifically designed for a distant addressee. Such use of prosody in no way makes up for Chil's inability to use names to select targets for his action. However, it does demonstrate the importance of not restricting analysis of a conversational move, such as a summons, to morphosyntactic phenomena. Here we find a turn structured as a multimodal performance in which the resources provided by the body

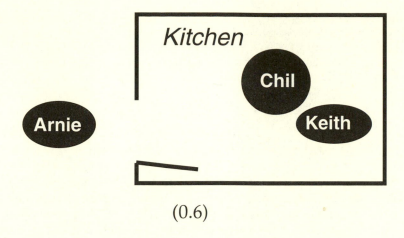

(0.6)

Chil: UH DIH *DUH*. DIH *DUH*.
Keith: Arnie!

Figure 4.3.   Multi-modal designation of a distant addressee.

and the setting where interaction is occurring are used in differentiated ways to
show others what is relevant in the actions of the moment.

Lines 10–12 of the following provide another example. Here three people are
sitting at the table with Chil, while Keith is at a counter behind them making cappuccino with his back to the group at the table. Everyone present unproblematically
locates Keith alone as the addressee of lines 10–12, and moreover, the action is analyzed as a summons. While speaking lines 10–12 Chil gazes toward Keith. No one at
the table responds to Chil's utterance, while Keith turns to see what Chil wants and
produces a prototypical summons response ("Hm?") in line 13:

(5)

>   *Chil is seated at the table with Helen, Jessica, and Julia. Keith is making cappuccino at*
>   *the counter behind them.*
>   1 Julia: How is it.
>   2 Chil: Yeah.=Eh dih *de:* ⌜h.
>   3 Keith: ⌞Yeah.=
>   4 Keith: =But we're gonna⌜get *some*thing else=
>   5 Chil: ⌞Yih
>   6   =that makes it even better.
>   7   (0.3)
>   8 Chil: *Yes*.
>   9   (0.5)
>   10 Chil: DUH DUH *DUH*.
>   11   (0.3)

```
12  Chil:   DUH DUH DUH.
13  Keith:  Hm? ((Keith turns quickly to Chil.))
14                  (0.4)
                    ((Chil waves his fingers
                    from Keith to himself,
                    signaling that he wants
                    something to be brought to him.))
15  Keith:  I will.
16                  What.=You want me ta bring-
17                  Ya want- the chocolate?
```

Two additional observations about these data will be briefly noted. First, line 12 exhibits another property of summonses as analyzed by Schegloff (1968; see also Goodwin 1981 for such recycling *within* the turn itself): recycling a summons that doesn't get an answer and then stopping the recycling when someone at last responds (Keith turns to Chil in the silence immediately after line 12). Second, these data further demonstrate the importance of Chil's prosodic contour in specifying action and addressee. Note that line 2 also contains a three-syllable unit with a strong final accent ("Eh dih *de:h.*"). Moreover, the talk that occurs before both this unit in line 2 and the summons in line 10 is a *Yes*. Just before line 2 Julia has been watching Chil taste a new kind of coffee. Her, "How is it," asks for his evaluation of the coffee. His initial, "*Yeah*," in line 2 is spoken with noticeable appreciation. Unlike line 10, the prosody of line 2 makes visible an enthusiastic assessment, an action that constitutes an appropriate answer to the request in line 1.[9] It immediately follows the "*Yeah*" that answers Julia's, "How is it," and continues the prosodic display of appreciation found there. The *Yes* provides a preface for the three-syllable unit that follows. By way of contrast, line 10 follows Chil's just-prior "*Yes*" in line 8 only after a noticeable silence. Indeed, rather than prefacing what is to follow, that *Yes* is tied to lines 4 and 5 just before it and constitutes a way of closing and bounding that earlier sequence. Moreover, there is a marked voice shift between the "*Yes*" in line 8 and the summons in line 10. This shift includes both an increase in volume and a new intonation contour hearable as a summons, something quite different from the assessment prosody produced in line 2. The talk produced here displays entry into a new action unrelated to what its "*Yes*" was responding to. These data illustrate, first, some of the resources deployed by Chil to select a particular addressee from a larger pool of potential recipients and, second, how he can vary his prosody in order to make visible different kinds of action over syllable strings with a similar structure. Moreover, through increased amplitude he signals that he is not selecting someone at the table as an addressee (as in line 2, for example) but someone more distant, that is, Keith, who is standing behind them.

Determining What Chil Is Requesting

The successful completion of a Summons Answer sequence creates an environment in which the party responding to the summons is orienting to Chil in the expectation that he will produce further action to indicate what he wants done. How is this accomplished? In a situation where the party making the request cannot produce lexical descriptions (as Pat did in Figure 4.2) how do he and his interlocutors publicly and mutually establish what is being requested? To begin to investigate this issue we will return to the example in which Chil is requesting help with his pancakes, picking up where we left off at line 7, that is, at the place where Chil has secured the orientation of a recipient through his Summons Answer sequence:

(6)

```
 1                 (9.5)
 2 Chil:   Dih dih duh: :.
 3                 (1.8)
 4 Chil:   DUH DUH DUH:.
 5                 (2.5)
 6 Linda: Yeah Dad?
 7                 (1.0)
 8 Chil:   ((Chil makes hand motion (cutting) over his plate.))
 9 Linda: No?
10                 (0.5)
11 Linda: Oh. Cut it?
12                 (0.3)
13 Chil:   Hmph.
```

By line 8 Linda can see Chil and is thus positioned to try to determine why she has been summoned. What resources does she use to formulate a candidate proposal (e.g., in lines 9 and 11) as to what Chil might be saying? How does Chil contribute to this process? Work on the organization of interaction *within* the turn provides a point of departure. While much research in CA has been concerned with how sequences of actions and turns follow each other, another line of investigation has focused on the interior of individual turns and actions as phenomena accomplished through the coordinated action of multiple participants. Not only talk but also visible nonvocal action (hearers are largely, though not exclusively, silent) is central to the organization of this process. Thus, Charles Goodwin (1981, 1984) has demonstrated how the construction of both the turn and the utterances and phrases within it is accomplished through an ongoing process of interaction in which the hearer is as active a co-participant as the speaker. Similarly, Marjorie Harness Goodwin (1980) has demonstrated how speakers modify ongoing descriptions to take into account the operations being performed on that talk by her addressee(s) (see also Goodwin and Goodwin 1987). In the data being examined here, at the end of the Summons Answer sequence interlocutors typically find themselves in a position where they are looking at Chil (though there are exceptions). This creates a participation framework characterized by the simultaneous action of structurally different participants. Chil, the "speaker," produces action of some type (this need not involve talk and might be done entirely through gesture) while his addressee analyzes that action. Note that what is involved here is not hearership as a passive process of waiting for the next opportunity to speak but a participation framework characterized by active, differentiated work within a single turn. Thus, Chil waits until his interlocutor is positioned to see what he is doing and expects her to be actively analyzing what he is doing so as to be able to produce an appropriate next action, for example, a proposal about what he wants done. The interior of the turn that occurs once Chil and his interlocutors are positioned to produce a next action to his summons is organized as a process of multiparty interaction in which differentiated participants are actively taking into account what each other is doing.

How does what the interlocutor sees when she responds to Chil's summons provide her with resources for formulating a proposal about what he is requesting, that is, for building their next move in the sequence?

In the sequence being examined here, when Chil at last secures Linda's orientation he places his functioning hand an inch or two above his pancakes, closes the hand as though grasping something, and pushes it rapidly back and forth over the pancakes. Linda correctly interprets this gestural display as miming the act of cutting the pancakes.

What phenomena must Linda take into account in order to appropriately see what Chil is doing here? With a few notable exceptions (for example, Streeck 1996a, 1996b; LeBaron and Streeck 2000; Hutchins and Palen 1997; Ochs, Gonzales, and Jacoby 1996; Haviland 1993), most analysis of gesture has drawn an analytic bubble around the body of the speaker/gesturer and investigated gesture as something done by the body alone. In the sequence being examined here, something in the physical environment, the plate of pancakes, is as crucial to the meaningfulness of Chil's action as his moving hand. The intelligibility of Chil's gesture arises not only from the actions of his hand but also from the conjunction of action displayed through the hand and other kinds of semiotic structure in the surround (see Goodwin 2000a). Pancakes and the tools used to prepare them for eating are lodged within recognizable, culturally organized activities. Chil actively works to make the conjunction between tools for cutting and the activity he wants to pursue visible to his addressees by moving his hand as close as possible to the pancakes. More generally, the way in which Chil lives and moves through an environment that is already richly sedimented with many different kinds of semiotic meaning provides him with some of his most crucial resources for accomplishing intelligible action. To co-participate in this process his interlocutors must attend to not only his talk but also his body and meaningful structure in the surround.

From a slightly different perspective, one might ask how someone whose entire gestural resources are restricted to somewhat limited movements of his face, left arm, and hand is capable of gesturally indicating the extraordinary variety of objects, actions, and events that are relevant to what he might want to communicate. Note that Chil doesn't attempt to depict the shape of a knife (for example, by using a moving finger to outline its shape) but instead performs his gesture by demonstrating how a human body would use the tool being demonstrated. More generally, the human body, as the primordial locus for tool use and the production of action in the world, provides an omnipresent resource for making visible all of the different kinds of phenomena it might articulate in some way. This use of the body as the master template for depicting objects and actions is by no means restricted to someone who can't speak. For example, while telling a story about a "big fight" at an auto race, a speaker makes visible one of the protagonists picking up a "goddamn iron bar" not by depicting the shape of the bar but instead by using a gesture that shows the character holding it. This mode of presentation not only achieves a natural economy by using the body's interaction with objects, rather than the objects themselves, as an organizing focus but also simultaneously integrates the object being depicted into the action being described.

However, people who can speak can disambiguate the inherent ambiguity of an iconic sign system through concurrent talk. Chil can't do this, and in line 9 Linda initially interprets the waving hand over the pancakes as a signal that Chil doesn't want them (e.g., "get rid of them"). The structure of her talk in both lines 9 and 11, in which Linda proposes that Chil wants his pancakes cut, provides an example of a most frequent action type produced by Chil's interlocutors in many different kinds of sequences. The speaking interlocutor does what Chil can't: she uses the full resources of language to provide a guess about what Chil might be trying to say. Note that here, as in most cases, the status of what is being said as a candidate proposal is indicated by producing the guess with a rising contour: "Cut it?" (Though structurally different, the use of rising intonation here seems related to the analysis of Try Markers in Sacks and Schegloff 1979.) Chil can then accept or reject the proposal. On occasion these sequences can become quite extended (see Goodwin 1995 and Goodwin 2000b for more detailed analysis). What we want to note here is that the single-party, within-turn, unproblematic use of lexical and syntactic resources to form a request (e.g., what we saw with Pat's action to Jere in Figure 4.2) here becomes a multiparty sequence that exhibits a particular division of labor. While the fluent speaker produces a description, the only party able to establish the correctness of that move is the addressee, Chil, who lacks the ability to produce language of his own. In terms of the categories proposed by Goffman in "Footing" (1981), Chil is the *principal* and *author*, while his interlocutor is the *animator*. This particular division of talk-relevant identities and labor is made visible through the display of tentativeness produced through the interlocutor's rising intonation.

Once Linda has formulated a proposal about what Chil might be asking her to do, the next move in the sequence is an answer from Chil, accepting or rejecting her proposal. How is this done? Though Chil could say, "Yes," and/or "No" (and in other cases does), here he (1) continues the cutting movement after Linda's incorrect guess in line 9 and thus signals that the task of establishing a relevant gloss of his gesture should be continued, but (2) stops the cutting movement and relaxes his posture after the correct proposal ("Cut it?") in line 11. By terminating the gesture, without initiating a new action, he displays that Linda has appropriately understood the gesture.

It is possible to analyze what happens here as a sequence of actions with some turns, such as Chil's gesture, being accomplished entirely through use of semiotic resources other than lexico-syntax. However, it is crucial to take into account the way in which any such "action" or "turn" is constituted not by Chil's signs alone but instead through the differentiated actions of multiple participants. Linda's informed seeing of what Chil is doing is as necessary as his gesture. More generally, Chil depends upon his interlocutors' functioning as fully embodied social actors who use not only their ears but also their eyes to see relevant events in both

Chil's body and the setting where interaction is occurring. If an addressee such as Linda can't see this, she will lack the resources necessary to build her next move in the sequence: a gloss of what he is requesting.[10]

The very beginning of this sequence provides some demonstration of just how important the visual orientation of the addressee to the gesture is. Chil, in fact, pointed toward the pancakes with a cutting motion before Keith left. However, just as this happened Keith was called away, and he never saw the gesture. Chil was thus unable to eat and initiated the sequence we find here. Keith's failure to see provides further demonstration of how important relevant embodied actions of the interlocutor are to the constitution of action by Chil. The assembly of the particular set of meaning-making practices necessary for the social constitution of a particular action is very much an ongoing, contingent accomplishment, something that can fail by virtue of something as simple as a shift in gaze.

The following example provides an opportunity to explore some of these phenomena further. It is a December day and Chil and Keith are making plans to go out. As the transcript begins, Keith is walking past Chil toward the front door. Immediately after the summons in line 1, Keith interrupts his walk to turn around and look at Chil. As soon as Chil sees Keith orient, he lowers his gaze to the front of his own body and then sweeps his hand over his chest. In line 7 Keith formulates what Chil is requesting with "Uh: jacket."

(7)

> *Keith is walking out the door past Chil.*
> 1 Chil: Yeh deh de:h!.
> 2   (0.3) ((*Keith turns around to Chil.*))
> 3 Keith: Yeah?
> 4   (0.6)
> 5 Chil: ((*hand motion in front of chest*))
> 6   Yeh deh=
> 7 Keith: Uh: jacket.
> 8   (0.3)
> 9 Chil: ((*nods*)) Yeh.
> 10 Keith: Uh: sweater.
> 11   (0.2) ((*shaking head*))
> 12 Chil: ⌈°No
> 13 Keith: ⌊Uh oh uh sws
> 14   Uh *more* than a sweater.
> 15   (0.6)
> 16 Chil: No:.= ((*starts to gesture from neck to head*))
> 17   =Deh deh deh.⌈deh deh dih
> 16 Keith: ⌊Yeah. And a hat,
> 17 Chil: Yes.
> 18 Keith: Right. Right. Right.

These data exhibit the same pattern found in earlier data. A summons secures the orientation of an interlocutor. As soon as that party gazes toward Chil, he produces a gesture. As demonstrated by the candidate proposal that the interlocutor produces as a next action, "Uh: jacket"(line 7), this gesture is treated as providing information about what is being requested. Chil, in fact, performs additional work to show Keith that he should take this gesture into account in building a next move. Thus, as Chil begins the gesture he looks down toward his hand and the region it is moving over. Gaze constitutes a prototypical method for displaying intentional focus (Goodwin in press). By showing what region he is focusing on, Chil can display to Keith what he should take into account in order to produce a course of action tied to Chil's.

Indeed, Chil's body makes visible a complex juxtaposition of quite different kinds of displays here. Like the pancake under the cutting gesture, the chest/shirt under the gesturing hand provides a substantive focus for what the hand might be indicating, and indeed Keith's proposal of a "jacket" is precisely something that would fit (quite literally) the region being gestured toward. The gesturing hand, rather than miming the use of a tool, focuses attention on the place where the object being requested will be used. This combination of gesture and target is itself framed by Chil's own gaze, which spotlights the relevance of what is happening precisely here for the actions of the moment. Chil's body is simultaneously (1) the target of a gesture, (2) the entity performing the gesture, and (3) the visible locus of the focal actor's orientation as displayed through his own gaze. This gesture is thus accomplished through the juxtaposition of multiple visual fields with quite different properties. Moreover, it is designed for someone else. As Keith begins to speak, Chil switches to gaze at Keith and thereby shows that he is positioned to receive a response to what he has just done.

Several other features of the setting may also be relevant to Keith's ability to quickly formulate a candidate proposal as to what Chil might be requesting. First, this talk is embedded within an encompassing activity, leaving the house after breakfast. Second, this conversation occurred in December in the northeastern United States, that is, when it was quite cold outside.

However, in large part because of their iconic generality, such gestural displays are inherently partial and incomplete. A range of quite different things can be attached to the body, and in cases where gestures depict the manipulation of objects the body holds quite diverse tools in similar ways. This is not a problem for parties who can speak, since co-occurring talk can provide other crucial meaning-making resources (e.g., the lexical formulation of what is being gestured about as an "iron bar"). By way of contrast, Chil's inability to provide a lexical construal of what his gesture is about is a real and pervasive problem. He and his interlocutors frequently require extended sequences to determine what in fact he is saying. In the current data Keith in line 10 changes his proposal from a "jacket" to a "sweater" (in fact, Chil's typical outdoor garment was a Scandinavian cardigan, something woven as a thick sweater but tailored like a jacket with buttons). Chil rejects this new proposal in line 12. In line 14 Keith revises this to "*more* than a sweater." Chil's rejection of this is accompanied by another gesture that is structurally analogous to the gesture in line 5. Chil lowers his gaze to his own body, then places his hand near his neck and, while shifting his gaze to Keith, moves the hand up around the side and top of his head, an action that Keith correctly glosses as "a hat" (line 16). Once again, Chil's body performs multiple displays. A gesture being made with the hand targets another region of the body, while Chil's gaze both highlights the gesture and then looks toward its addressee for a response. The lexical formulation of what is being gestured about, an action typically provided simultaneously or almost simultaneously by a gesturer who can speak, here becomes the next move in the sequence, a move that will be performed by Chil's addressee.

Collapsing the Sequence

The data examined so far exhibit a sequence structured so that different tasks are accomplished at different places within the sequence. First, a Summons Answer sequence is used to align a recipient so that he/she is orienting to and gazing at Chil. Only after this has been accomplished does Chil begin to indicate what he is requesting. This action is followed by a candidate proposal by the interlocutor of what Chil might be asking. If Chil rejects the proposal, the sequence is recycled with an alternative (Goodwin 1995). When a proposal is accepted the requested action is performed.

It is, however, possible to collapse moves in this sequence so that some of these tasks are accomplished simultaneously. In situations where an appropriate addressee is already present, Chil can both summon his or her attention and display what he wants simultaneously. The following provides an example: Chil is sitting at the table with his wife and two grandchildren while his daughter-in-law stands behind them. His granddaughter Jessica has just started college. She has been talking about her dorm room and has also brought a package of photographs that are sitting on the table as the sequence to be examined here begins. Detailed analysis of the talk about the dorm room is not relevant to the points to be investigated here. We've used arrows to highlight those sections of the transcript that are relevant to the current analysis. What we want to focus on is how Chil summons Jessica with speech while showing her that he is proposing to look at her pictures by visibly picking them up.

(8)

> Jessica is talking about her room at college. A package of pictures she has brought is sitting on the table.

→   1   Chil: Neh nen em?
→   ((*Chil reaches for Jessica's pictures and gazes toward Jessica.*))
     2   Jessica: *Ours* are pretty simple rooms though.
     3   (0.5)
     4   Jessica: Our roo(h)m's go(h)nna t(h)otall(h) ch(h)ange=
     5   =wh(h)en w(h)e g(h)o ba(h)ck from Chri(h)stma(h)s=
     6   ='cause I got so much stuff.*hhh
     7   Linda: Yea⌈h.
     8   Jessica: ⌊for Christmas.
     9   ta decorate (it) with.
→   10   Chil: Dih dih *duh*?
→   ((*Chil lifts pictures while gazing at them. At the end of his talk Jessica gazes at him.*))
→   11   (0.8)
→   12   Jessica: Want me to *show* them to you?
                  Jessica moves to sit next to Chil.

In both lines 1 and 10 a single turn is built through the juxtaposition of multiple meaning-making practices lodged in different phenomenal fields. While summoning Jessica, Chil simultaneously displays orientation toward the pictures. Chil thus uses talk to summon his addressee, while using the orientation of his body, intentional focus toward specific phenomena in the surround, and gesture to display to that person what he wants, that is, something about the pictures that Chil has just picked up. Though initially Jessica continues her conversation with Linda, just after line 10 she gets up and moves next to Chil, an action that puts her in a position where she can perform the requested action in line 12, that is, showing the pictures to Chil. Though her utterance formulates an offer, her use of "them" to reference the pictures at issue displays that she is unproblematically treating these pictures as the substance of the action Chil is proposing. In her response she thus explicitly takes into account the materials he has displayed to be relevant through the embodied behavior that accompanies his talk. Here the move to request the orientation of an addressee and the display that indicates what that addressee is being requested to do occur simultaneously.

In these data, unlike the events examined earlier, the interlocutor who will be a co-participant in the action that Chil is proposing is already sustaining a co-participation framework with him. Jessica is seated at the table with Chil. This provides one structural basis for Chil's ability to perform his request with a shorter sequence. It is not necessary to first secure the availability of an addressee through a Summons Answer presequence (though something like this might still be necessary in cases where someone seated at the table is engaged in interaction that excludes Chil). Thus, Chil's action here differs in a number of ways from his utterances examined earlier. First, it is spoken, with normal rather than raised volume and is thus appropriate to an addressee who is already sitting with him. Second, it ends with a rising rather than falling contour. In part by virtue of this, his action here is hearable as a request to move to a new activity, rather than an insistent demand for attention. Third, we find here another method for selecting a particular addressee from larger pool of potential recipients. The pictures are tied to events in Jessica's life and not the lives of anyone else at the table. By indicating that they are the focus of his request, he simultaneously selects Jessica as his next interlocutor.

A More Complicated Sequence

We will now examine a slightly more complicated sequence that brings together many of the phenomena noted so far in this chapter, including addressee selection and making visible the object of a request. In Figure 4.4 Chil is taking his pills at breakfast. Most of those present in the house are in the kitchen with him, except for his daughter Pat, who is in another room. The sequence begins with Chil raising a query about one of his pills. At the end of the sequence it becomes clear that he has discovered that he has received only one of a particular kind of pill, instead of his usual two. Pat tells him that his doctor has changed his dosage.

Pervasively, throughout this sequence, Chil's interlocutors use the visible intentional focus of his body to make sense out of his talk. As Chil produces his first

Chil is seated at the breakfast table examining his morning pills.
Helen, Jessica, and Julia are also sitting at the table. Keith and
Linda are working at the kitchen counters. Keith leaves at line 10.
At line 13 Pat walks into the room, but then leaves again immediately.

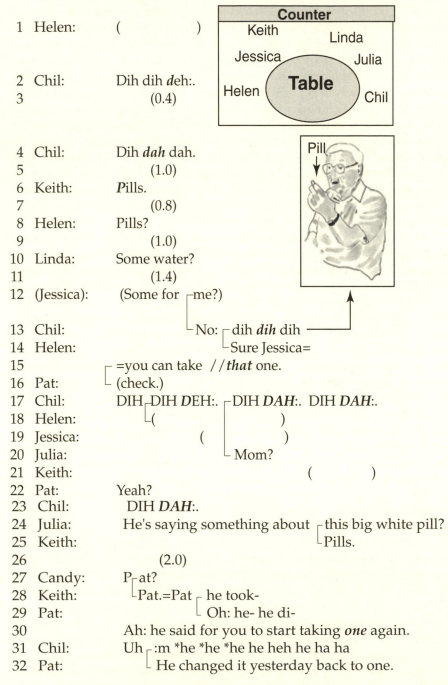

```
 1  Helen:        (               )
 2  Chil:         Dih dih deh:.
 3                      (0.4)

 4  Chil:         Dih dah dah.
 5                      (1.0)
 6  Keith:        Pills.
 7                      (0.8)
 8  Helen:        Pills?
 9                      (1.0)
10  Linda:        Some water?
11                      (1.4)
12  (Jessica):    (Some for ⌐me?)
                           |
13  Chil:            ˪No: ⌐dih dih dih ──────┐
14  Helen:                ˪Sure Jessica=     |
15            ⌐=you can take //that one.     |
16  Pat:      ˪(check.)                      |
17  Chil:         DIH⌐DIH DEH:. ⌐DIH DAH:.  DIH DAH:.
18  Helen:           ˪(              |      )
19  Jessica:             (          |      )
20  Julia:                          ˪Mom?
21  Keith:                                    (        )
22  Pat:          Yeah?
23  Chil:           DIH DAH:.
24  Julia:        He's saying something about ⌐this big white pill?
25  Keith:                                     ˪Pills.
26                      (2.0)
27  Candy:        P⌐at?
28  Keith:         ˪Pat.=Pat ⌐ he took-
29  Pat:                     ˪ Oh: he- he di-
30                Ah: he said for you to start taking one again.
31  Chil:         Uh ⌐:m *he *he *he he heh he ha ha
32  Pat:             ˪ He changed it yesterday back to one.
```

Figure 4.4.   The interactive achievement of a request.

call for attention in line 2, he is looking at his pills and placing them in his fingers. In line 6, Keith correctly formulates Chil's request as having something to do with pills. Note that though Keith can see what Chil is attending to by looking at his embodied behavior, he apparently does not understand in detail Chil's activity. Keith's continuing failure to recognize what Chil might be asking suggests that he sees Chil doing "something" with pills but not performing the specific action of counting them (i.e., Keith and everyone else do not realize that Chil has discovered that he is missing a pill). This penumbra of uncertainty around Chil's seeable action leads to other inaccurate proposals about what he might be requesting. Thus, in line 10 Linda asks if he wants some water (e.g., something that can be used to take pills). Others present are using Chil's visible orientation to the pills as a point of departure for trying to figure out what he is requesting. Once again, the basic unit required for the visible constitution of action is one in which an array of multiple meaning-making practices instantiated in a range of semiotic media with quite different properties (talk, the visible body, gesture, phenomena in the surround, etc.) are being juxtaposed in order to make visible something relevant to the projected course of interactive action.

Note also that the activities that Chil's interlocutors perform in order to act as appropriate hearers (e.g., parties able to attend to what Chil is saying and doing in order to build an appropriate next move) in no way fit an information flow model of communication. Rather than simply decoding a message from Chil, others present actively operate on both what they hear and what they see, while taking into account features of the setting and the seeable activities in progress, in order to try to figure out what might be at issue in Chil's current action. Rather than succeeding or failing to recover his "message," they act as participants engaged in an ongoing, dynamic pursuit of the shape and substance of the action they are attempting to build a response to. As they check their candidate understandings with Chil this pursuit is organized as a thoroughly interactive process.

Within this process, contingencies emerge that can be creatively exploited. Linda's offer of water in line 10 provides one example. Rather than simply declining the water (Chil, in fact, takes his pills in applesauce), Chil uses the sequential frame provided by her request to focus attention on something that is relevant. Instead of simply saying, "No," Chil looks at Linda and then picks up one of his pills while visibly holding it in front of his face. He thus exploits the sequential structure provided by a request to publicly locate the pill as a crucial component of his query. The rejection of "water" provides him with a slot for the production of the correct item. For fluent speakers "No" after an offer (e.g., "Do you want a banana?") is frequently followed by a move that states an alternative to what is being rejected (e.g., "No. I want an orange"). Though Chil can't say "pill," he can try to indicate an alternative to water. His "No:" is immediately followed by a three-syllable utterance that is coordinated with the action of lifting the pill. He thus positions it in the contrast slot made available by Linda's request for specifying the topic of his query. While doing the emphatic summonses that follow in line 17 Chil continues to hold the pill up high, in a focal "front stage" position, while gazing toward it (see the drawing on the transcript). His body becomes publicly visible as an intentional agent, an active person focused on a specific entity, the pill, while summoning aid. He thus organizes his body to produce a public display of intentionality that can be read and used by others as part of the process of building a response to the action he is performing.

In line 17 Chil produces three multisyllable calls in quick succession, followed a moment later by a fourth in line 23. All are spoken very loudly. However, in these data four people are in the kitchen with Chil, three of them sitting at the table with him. And indeed just before this at line 4, another summons, without heightened volume, received an answer from Keith. Further examination of the sequence reveals that the issue Chil is summoning help for can only be dealt with by one person, his daughter Pat, who is not in the room. As becomes clear at the end of the sequence, Chil has found that he's been given one of a particular pill, rather than the two he normally takes in the morning. His daughter Pat, who is a nurse, is the person in the household responsible for dispensing his pills. When the people in the kitchen are unable to formulate a relevant gloss of what he is trying to say, Chil shifts to the one person who is an expert on this issue.

Chil lacks the ability to call Pat by name or, more generally, to use lexical forms to specify a particular addressee from a larger set of participants. However, by using the resources provided by prosody, that is, his ability to systematically vary volume, Chil is able to display that none of those in the room with him count as possible addressees for the action now being performed. The structure of the activity in progress requires specification of a particular addressee, something that Chil can't do lexically. Prosody is thus creatively used to overcome linguistic impairment. It provides a resource for accomplishing the task of specifying the addressee of the current action. This deployment of prosody is in turn embedded within and shaped by a larger course of conversational action, for example, getting a particular recipient, such as Pat, to provide an answer to a relevant query.

All of these hearable and visible practices (e.g., visible orientation toward the pill, volume, prosody, etc.) are taken into account by Julia in line 24 when she glosses Chil's utterance as *saying* something about the pill that Chil is positioning as the focus of attention: "He's saying something about this big white pill?" And indeed, through this artful deployment of multiple semiotic resources, Chil is not just rattling off nonsense syllables but, as Julia states, "saying something about" something, that is, producing a full-fledged utterance that constitutes a recognizable, relevant action within conversation.

Conclusion

This essay has explored how damage to the linguistic resources of a speaker leads to a reorganization of the situated practices used by multiple participants to build meaning and action within interaction. Embodied displays, frequently linked to semiotic structure already sedimented within the material and social arrangements that make up Chil's lifeworld, replace a lexicon and syntactic structure as Chil's primary resources for building turns at talk.

Despite his inability to produce meaningful language, Chil not only understands the talk of others but also makes extensive use of the sequential organization of their talk to produce consequential action of his own. In this process his interlocutors provide the lexical and syntactic structure that he can't. They must shape their contributions in quite specific ways, for example, by using rising intonation to formulate what they are saying for him as a candidate proposal, an action that makes relevant a subsequent response from Chil. What others can do within a single turn instead requires sequences for Chil and his interlocutors. This process has clear structural affinities with events at the opposite end of the life cycle, the talk of caregivers with children just acquiring language (Ochs 1988; Ochs and Schieffelin 1986).

As the first example demonstrated, the meaningfulness of Chil's utterances is not "encoded" in his talk alone. Instead, the production of meaning and action draws upon resources provided by the sequential organization of the unfolding conversation he is contributing to. Chil relies upon the ability of his interlocutors to link what he is displaying through prosody and gesture to specific lexical items provided by their earlier talk. From a slightly different perspective, Chil's aphasia becomes a crucible for the analysis of the body in interaction. His inability to produce syntactic utterances poses for the participants themselves the task of analyzing how a range of phenomena in the stream of speech, the body, and the setting where action is emerging are used to build both turns and sequences.

Traditionally, aphasia has been analyzed as an individual impairment, something lodged within the individual, who loses crucial linguistic competencies such as the ability to produce syntactic units. From such a perspective various paradoxes emerge. For example, it has been noted that people with damage to the right hemisphere who have relatively intact linguistic abilities nonetheless have more problems in social interaction than someone, such as Chil, with severe left hemisphere damage. The data analyzed in this chapter suggest that the relevant unit for the analysis of Chil's capacity to build meaning and action within states of talk is not, however, confined to his skull or to phenomena within the speech he produces. Instead, it must encompass the talk and action of others that provides the enabling context for building meaningful utterances out of what might otherwise be considered nonsense syllables. The practices Chil uses to build meaning and action are not lodged within his body alone but instead within a unit that includes his interlocutors, the sequential environment, and a semiotically structured material setting. It is here, and not through examination of linguistic output alone, that the ability to constitute meaning within states of talk must be assessed. What we see in Chil's family is a process of development, though one situated within the social group rather than the individual and one occurring at the end of the life cycle rather than the beginning.

Interaction with a person with severe aphasia also has a moral dimension. It would be easy to treat someone who can't speak as something less than a full-fledged person, someone whose efforts to communicate can be dismissed or not taken seriously. Indeed, this is the way Chil's doctors sometimes treated him right after his stroke. However, despite Chil's inability to produce language his family does not ignore him but instead treats him as someone who has something to say. They invest considerable effort in working out together just what that might be. All parties to the conversation adapt the way they build turns and sequences to the specifics of Chil's situation. By virtue of this, the social production of meaning and action—the center of human social and cognitive life—remains an ongoing accomplishment despite Chil's inability to produce fluent language. This is made possible by the sequential organization of conversation, including its inherent flexibility, which provides participants with the resources necessary to adapt the organization of both turns and sequences to the details of their particular situation. Through this process not only meaning but also Chil's status as person able to think for himself and build action through conversation is reproduced on a moment-by-moment basis.

NOTES

1. His medical records at discharge in 1981 report "severe expressive and moderate receptive aphasia, moderate dysarthria and verbal apraxia." There has been little improvement in his condition since that time.

2. Chil is the father of one of the authors of this chapter, Charles Goodwin.

3. In this essay Chil's use of *yes* and *no* to construct meaningful action by guiding the talk of others will be noted only in passing. However, both his use of this vocabulary and his ability to say something gesturally by using his hands to display numbers are analyzed in other work (Goodwin 1995, 2000b). Through use of these resource Chil is able to co-construct a wide variety of intricate statements by embedding his limited talk within the talk of others. In essence, he and his interlocutors co-construct meaning and action through use of the sequential resources provided by the organization of conversation.

4. Interestingly, this fluency might arise in part from the very severity of his impairment. Since he has almost no vocabulary, his speech production is free from word searches and repetitive efforts to pronounce words in an acceptable fashion.

5. This study contributes to a growing body of research that is linking the study of speech disorders that arise from brain trauma and other factors to the analysis of conversational interaction. See, for example, Holland (1991), Klippi (1996), Kolk and Heeschen (1992), Laakso (1997), Local and Wooton (1995), Milroy and Perkins (1992), Schegloff (1999), Simmons-Mackie, Damico, and Nelson (1995), and Wilkinson (in press).

6. In this essay we follow the standard transcription system developed by Gail Jefferson for the analysis of conversation (Sacks, Schegloff, and Jefferson 1974: 731-733). We use **bold italics** rather than underlining to mark talk spoken with special emphasis.

7. Roger Andersen (1990) has called for analysis of tense and aspect that is not restricted to a narrow set of syntactic and morphological markers but instead takes into account the wide range of resources that speakers use to signal tense and aspect.

8. By aligning participants specifically for a subsequent sequence, that is, what Chil will then request, the Summons Answer sequence thus also constitutes what Schegloff (1980) has analyzed as a presequence.

9. This assessment quality of this prosody is exhibited in part by the glide over the terminal syllable of this unit. For more detailed analysis of Chil's assessments, including both their prosody and his orientation to a recognizable activity structure, see Goodwin and Goodwin (2000).

10. In appropriate circumstances Chil can design speech for parties who can't see him, and indeed he engages in lengthy phone conversations. Here we are focusing on one particular but pervasive methodology he uses to accomplish social action by getting others to understand what he wants to tell them.

REFERENCES

Andersen, Roger. 1990. Verbal virtuosity and speakers' purposes. In H. Burmeister and P. Rounds (eds.), *Variability in Second Language Acquisition*, vol. 1, 1–24. Eugene: University of Oregon, Department of Linguistics.

Bolinger, Dwight. 1986. *Intonation and Its Parts: Melody in Spoken English*. Stanford: Stanford University Press.

Bolinger, Dwight. 1989. *Intonation and Its Uses*. Stanford: Stanford University Press.

Couper-Kuhlen, Elizabeth, and Margret Selting. 1996. Towards an interactional perspective on prosody and a prosodic perspective on interaction. In Elizabeth Couper-Kuhlen and Margret Selting (eds.), *Prosody in Conversation: Interactional Studies*, 11–56. Cambridge: Cambridge University Press.

Goffman, Erving. 1981. Footing. In Erving Goffman (ed.), *Forms of Talk*, 124–159. Philadelphia: University of Pennsylvania Press.

Goodwin, Charles. 1981. *Conversational Organization: Interactions Between Speakers and Hearers*. New York: Academic Press.

Goodwin, Charles. 1984. Notes on story structure and the Organization of participation. In J. Maxwell Atkinson and John Heritage (eds.), *Structures of Social Action: Studies in Conversation Analysis*, 225–246. Cambridge: Cambridge University Press.

Goodwin, Charles. 1995. Co-constructing meaning in conversations with an aphasic man. *Research on Language and Social Interaction* 28(3): 233–260.

Goodwin, Charles. 2000a. Action and embodiment within situated human interaction. *Journal of Pragmatics* 32:1489–1522.

Goodwin, Charles. 2000b. Gesture, aphasia and interaction, 84–98. In David McNeill (ed.), *Language and Gesture: Window into Thought and Action*. Cambridge: Cambridge University Press.

Goodwin, Charles. In press. Pointing as situated practice. In Sotaro Kita (ed.), *Pointing: Where Language, Culture and Cognition Meet*. Hillsdale, NJ: Erlbaum.

Goodwin, Charles, and Marjorie Harness Goodwin. 1987. Concurrent operations on talk: Notes on the interactive organization of assessments. *IPRA Papers in Pragmatics* 1(1): 1–54.

Goodwin, Marjorie Harness. 1980. Processes of mutual monitoring implicated in the production of description sequences. *Sociological Inquiry* 50:303–317.

Goodwin, Marjorie H., and Charles Goodwin. 2000. Emotion within situated activity. In Nancy Budwig, Ina C. Uzgiris, and James V. Wertsch (eds.), *Communication: An Arena of Development*, 33–54. Greenwich, CT: Ablex.

Haviland, John B. 1993. Pointing, gesture spaces, and mental maps. Paper published online in the Third Language and Culture Symposium. http://www/cs/uchicago.edu/l-c/archives/

Holland, Audrey L. 1991. Pragmatic aspects of intervention in aphasia. *Journal of Neurolinguistics* 6(2): 197–211.

Hutchins, Edwin, and Leysia Palen. 1997. Constructing meaning from space, gesture and talk. In Lauren B. Resnick, Roger Saljo, and Clotilde Pontecorvo (eds.), *Discourse, Tools and Reasoning*, 23–40. Berlin: Springer-Verlag.

Klippi, Anu. 1996. *Conversation as an Achievement in Aphasics*. Helsinki: Studia Fennica Linguistica 6.

Kolk, Herman, and Clause Heeschen. 1992. Agrammatism, paragrammatism and the management of language. *Language and Cognitive Processes* 7(2): 89–129.

Laakso, Minna. 1997. *Self-initiated Repair by Fluent Aphasic Speakers in Conversation*. Helsinki: Finnish Literature Society.

LeBaron, Curtis D., and Jürgen Streeck. 2000. Gestures, knowledge, and the world. In David McNeill (ed.), *Gestures in Action, Language, and Culture*, 118–138. Cambridge: Cambridge University Press.

Local, John, and Anthony Wootton. 1995. Interactional and phonetic aspects of immediate echolalia in autism: A case study. *Clinical Linguistics and Phonetics* 9(2): 155–184.

Milroy, Lesley, and Lisa Perkins. 1992. Repair strategies in aphasic discourse; towards a collaborative model. *Clinical Linguistics and Phonetics* 6(1 and 2): 27–40.

Ochs, Elinor (ed.). 1988. *Culture and Language Development: Language Acquisition and Language Socialization in a Samoan Village*. Cambridge: Cambridge University Press.

Ochs, Elinor, Patrick Gonzales, and Sally Jacoby. 1996. "When I come down I'm in the domain state": Grammar and graphic representation in the interpretive activity of physicists. In Elinor Ochs, Emanuel A. Schegloff, and Sandra A. Thompson (eds.), *Interaction and Grammar*, 328–369. Cambridge: Cambridge University Press.

Ochs, Elinor, and Bambi B. Schieffelin. 1986. *Language Socialization Across Cultures*. New York: Cambridge University Press.

Sacks, Harvey, and Emanuel A. Schegloff. 1979. Two preferences in the organization of reference to persons in conversation and their interaction. In G. Psathas (ed.), *Everyday Language: Studies in Ethnomethodology*, 15–21. New York: Irvington.

Sacks, Harvey, Emanuel A. Schegloff, and Gail Jefferson. 1974. A simplest systematics for the organization of turn-taking in conversation. *Language* 50(4): 696–735.

Schegloff, Emanuel A. 1968. Sequencing in conversational openings. *American Anthropologist* 70:1075–1095.

Schegloff, Emanuel A. 1980. Preliminaries to preliminaries: "Can I ask you a question." *Sociological Inquiry* 50:104–152.

Schegloff, Emanuel A. 1999. Discourse, pragmatics, conversation analysis. *Discourse studies* 1:405–435.

Schegloff, Emanuel A. 1994. With half a mind: Observations on the conduct of interaction in commisurotomies. Paper presented at the Program for the Assessment and Renewal of the Social Sciences, University of Pennsylvania. An earlier version was presented at a Rector's Colloquium, Tel Aviv University, May 1991.

Simmons-Mackie, Nina N., Jack S. Damico, and Holly L. Nelson. 1995. Interactional dynamics in aphasia therapy. Submitted to the Clinical Aphasiology Conference.

Streeck, Jürgen. 1996a. How to do things with things. *Human Studies* 19:365–384.

Streeck, Jürgen. 1996b. Vis-à-vis an embodied mind. Paper presented to the panel Between Cognitive Science and Anthropology: A Re-Emerging Dialogue. Annual Meeting of the American Anthropological Association, San Francisco, CA, November 21, 1996.

Wilkinson, Ray. In press. Aphasia: Conversation Analysis. In M. Perkins and S. Howard (eds.), *Case Studies in Clinical Linguistics*. London: Whuri.

5

Contingent Achievement of Co-Tellership in a Japanese Conversation

An Analysis of Talk, Gaze, and Gesture

MAKOTO HAYASHI, JUNKO MORI, & TOMOYO TAKAGI

The research presented in this chapter is intended as a contribution to an understanding of the mutual bearing of linguistic resources and interactional practices (cf. Ochs, Schegloff, and Thompson 1996). Our interest is in elucidating the embodied nature of language as action in social interaction. To this end, we undertake a detailed analysis of a single episode of talk-in-interaction taken from a videotaped conversation among speakers of Japanese. Our study has three closely related goals: (1) to offer a demonstration of the complex interconnection of linguistic structures and social actions, (2) to underscore the need to include the examination of co-occurring nonvocal behavior in the analysis of language in face-to-face interaction, and (3) to examine the interactive achievement of a contingent participation structure, that is, that of co-tellership, within the activity of telling.

Our first goal is to demonstrate that language is essentially an "instrument of action" by showing how deeply language is embedded in actions in social interaction. Functionally oriented linguists who study grammar in discourse have tended to analyze linguistic structures from textual/structural or cognitive/psychological perspectives (e.g., Chafe 1979, 1980, 1987, 1993; Du Bois 1980, 1985, 1987; Givón 1979, 1983, 1989; Hopper 1979; Hopper and Thompson 1980; Li 1976; van Dijk and Kintsch 1983) and not address their functions in everyday interaction of the members of society.[1] Also, much of discourse-functional grammarians' work has been preoccupied with making generalizations (often with quantitative methods) about linguistic features that are found to form certain discourse patterns and has not paid sufficient attention to the details of how language figures in the situated actions of the participants in particular instances of social interaction. If such generalizations are intended to account for speakers' linguistic behavior in discourse, they should be able to deal with linguistic behavior of participants in single episodes of interaction. In other words, analysis of discourse, we believe, must be answerable to the details of actual, natural occurrences of discourse. It is from this perspective that we undertake a detailed analysis of a single episode of talk-in-interaction.[2] We aim to elucidate how, on the one hand, linguistic features serve as instruments to carry out particular interactional work that the participants engage in and how, on the other hand, moment-to-moment interactional contingencies shape the structuring of linguistic forms deployed in situated actions of the participants.[3]

This study examines a fragment taken from talk-in-interaction in Japanese. Discourse-functional linguists who studied Japanese have accumulated insights into such linguistic features of Japanese as zero-anaphora, utterance-final particles, word-order variability, and so forth, by examining the aggregate of discourse data and providing generalized accounts of such features (e.g., Clancy 1980; Cook 1992; Hasunuma 1992; Hinds 1982; Kamio 1994; Maynard 1993; Ono and Suzuki 1992; Simon 1989; Szatrowski 1994). This study aims to add a contribution to this body of research by taking a different approach to those linguistic phenomena. That is, by closely analyzing the moment-to-moment unfolding of talk-in-interaction in a single episode, we hope to shed light on how such linguistic features of Japanese as the verb-final structure, zero-anaphora, and sentence-final particles become consequential to the conduct of the participants and how such features are mobilized to accomplish actions in interaction among Japanese speakers.

Our second goal is to emphasize the importance of analyzing the participants' body behavior, such as gaze, gesture, and body orientation, as an integral part of their conduct in talk-in-interaction. Much work on conversational discourse has focused on the linguistic aspect of interaction and has tended to neglect the roles of nonlinguistic conduct of the participants. In this chapter, we will explicate the intricate processes of coordination of talk, gaze, and gesture observed in our data and will thereby show how the participants utilize such body conduct as resources to collaboratively frame, sustain, and negotiate participation in talk-in-interaction (this approach is also taken in Kendon 1972, 1977, 1990; C. Goodwin 1979, 1980, 1981, 1984, to appear a, to appear b; M. H. Goodwin 1980; Heath 1984, 1986, 1992; Schegloff 1984; Streeck 1994, 1996; LeBaron and Streeck 1997; Tannen 1990).

Our third goal is to explicate contingently achieved participation structure among four participants involved in a particular kind of "telling sequence." As stated by Schegloff (1995), conversational participants may form a "party" in interaction not necessarily by virtue of extrainteractional ties such as those of couples, families, and economic or political associates but by virtue of interaction-specific contingencies and conduct. We closely examine the manner in which two of the participants come to present themselves as "co-tellers" or one "party" jointly making a claim, while the other two come to display their recipiency. The linguistic and nonlinguistic resources mentioned previously will be examined in the light of the achievement of this moment-by-moment shift in participation structure.

Various studies have explored how the telling-specific identities such as teller, addressed recipient, unaddressed recipient, knowing recipient, and co-teller are mutually constructed by the participants through their talk and body conduct (e.g., C. Goodwin 1981, 1984, 1986; M. H. Goodwin 1990; Jefferson 1978; Lerner 1992; Mandelbaum 1987, 1993; Ochs et. al. 1992; Sacks 1974, 1978, 1992; Schegloff 1992).[4] For instance, Sacks (1974, 1978, 1992: Lecture 2, Spring 1970) documents the systematic manner in which participants negotiate their warrant to tell a story or a personal experience in mundane conversational interaction, where the role as a teller is not preassigned to any specific party. Intending tellers may produce story prefaces wherein they offer to tell or request a chance to tell a story and elicit the co-participants' consent. Further, instead of instantaneously announcing the initiation of a telling, intending tellers need to indicate, at least vaguely, how their forecasted telling is connected to the ongoing talk (Jefferson 1978).

Once a party manages to initiate a telling, the others may withhold the initiation of full turns and remain as recipients until a possible closing of the telling (Sacks 1974, 1978, 1992). However, this does not mean that the recipients must refrain from taking an active role in the development of the telling. The recipients may ask questions, make comments, or, in some cases, overtly contribute to an emerging telling. The ways in which the recipients respond to an ongoing telling, including their withholding of explicit responses, largely influence the subsequent course of the telling. In this sense, all the recipients of a telling could be considered "co-authors" or "co-narrators" of the telling (Duranti 1986; C. Goodwin 1986; M. H. Goodwin 1990; Ochs and Taylor 1992; Ochs et al. 1992; Ochs 1997). However, it is also recognizable that the recipients of different levels of knowledge of, or interest in, the details of a given story exhibit different manners of participation in the ongoing telling (C. Goodwin 1986). Among the recipients, those who have heard the story before or have independent or shared access to the source events of the telling are more likely to actively engage in the ongoing telling. From this perspective, the term "co-teller" generally refers to a participant who joins in the telling initiated by another participant on the basis of the shared knowledge or direct experience of the source event of the telling. Lerner (1992) and Mandelbaum (1987, 1993) investigate how such knowing participants manipulate their contributions and how their contributions affect the course of a telling during its initiation, delivery, and reception.

The case of "co-tellership" documented in this chapter, however, differs from this sort of "assisted explaining" examined by Lerner and Mandelbaum. That is, the "co-tellers" in the current case do not share the knowledge of the described event; only one of them took part in the reported event. Nonetheless, the two participants with differential knowledge align themselves as "co-tellers" or a party jointly making a claim. Specifically, the telling of a personal experience by one is triggered by the proffering of a claim by another. Each of the two participants' contributions mutually occasion and reinforce the other's. This chapter aims to describe the steps through which this particular kind of telling sequence unfolds.

In brief, this study undertakes a close examination of syntactic, prosodic, gestural, and sequential features of the target segment of interaction. Through this analytic undertaking, we will show that the conduct of the participants in this particular episode is accountable in terms of various types of interactional resources that are recurrently employed in talk-in-interaction. In particular, we hope to demonstrate a renewed appreciation of the linguistic features of Japanese, including the verb-final structure, zero-anaphora, and utterance-final particles. The significance of these features is reviewed in relation to social actions that provide context for their use and are accomplished by their use. That is, as we scrutinize each step taken in the development of the sequence for the achievement of "co-tellership", we elaborate on how these resources are deployed according to the contingencies in the moment-by-moment progression of talk-in-interaction.

The Data

The conversation in which the current episode occurred was videotaped at an evening gathering at the house of one of the participants in Chiba (near Tokyo), Japan, in June 1995. The four participants, Emi, Hana, Mari, and Yoko, are all females in their forties and are long-standing friends. They are seated around a rectangular table as shown in Figure 5.1: Emi and Hana are seated at the same longer edge of the table, both facing Yoko. Emi is on the right of Hana. Mari is seated at the shorter edge of the table, facing Hana and Emi on her right and Yoko on her left.

In example (1), we present the full transcript of the target segment, including word-by-word glosses and approximate English translations.[5] Prior to the beginning of the segment, Emi has been telling about wearing a kind of dress that emphasizes the body line; she explains that she has never lost the "dream" of wearing such a dress. However, she admits that, as a middle-aged woman, she ends up avoiding it and choosing more loose-fitting clothes. Yoko joins the description of the ways in which they try to cover up their body line. This reference to various styles of clothes leads into the discussion of the current fashion and, subsequently, the fashion currently popular with the younger generation (lines 1–13). Then, in lines 14 and 16, Mari suggests that the styles worn by the current youth appear to be a recycling of the styles that were popular in the 1970s. In response to this claim by Mari, Yoko delivers her agreement with

Figure 5.1.   Seating arrangement of the participants.

Mari, repeating a part of the previous turn. Subsequently Yoko initiates a personal story that verifies that claim made by Mari (from line 19 on). We will investigate the development of the sequence that starts with Mari's turn referring to the recycling of the popular fashion style (lines 14 and 16). To supply the reader with a sense of how the interaction leads up to the target sequence, the transcript in example (1) starts several turns earlier than the beginning of the segment we examine:

(1)

1 Mari:		[*demo Ima sooyuu no ha*[*yari da kara,* s- (.)
		but now such N popular CP because
		"But because those (clothes) are popular now, s- (.)"
2 Yoko:		[*so-*
		"So-"
3 Mari:	*ii n janai.*=	
	good N TAG	
	". . . it's okay, isn't it?"	
4 Yoko:	=*de*[*mo sono*] *han*[*taini ima no ko hora:,*	
	but that contrary now LK kid you.know	
	"But on the contrary, today's kids are, you know,"	
5 (Emi):	[°*u:::n*°]	
	"°Uh huh°"	
6 Mari:		[*BIGguna kanji no,*
		big like LK
		"Something big,"
7 Mari:	*a!* [*WAkai ko no ne:::::::*	
	oh young kid LK FP	
	"Oh! Young kids' (clothes), ri::ght.""	
8 Yoko:	[*I:ma no ko minna pita::* [*jjanai.*	
	now LK kid all tight TAG	
	"Today's kids are all (wearing) tight (clothes), right?"	
9 Hana:		[*wakai ko no (fuku toka)*
		young kid LK clothes etc.
		"Young kids' clothes,"
10 Mari:		[*chuugakusee kookoosee wa*
		middle. schooler high schooler TP
11	[*minna:-*	
	all	
	"Middle school students, high school students are all,"	
12 Hana:	[*u::n.*	
	"Uh huh"	
13 Yoko:	[*S O O.* [*pita: yo.*]	
	so tight FP	
	"Right, (wearing) tight (clothes)."	
14 Mari:		[*demo are*] *mukashi wa, aya-* (0.2) *a*[*nna no*=
		but that past TP such N
		"But, in the past, (0.2) those kinds (of clothes) . . ."
15 Yoko:		[°*a!*°
		oh
		"°Oh!°"

16 Mari: =*hayatta   desho?*=
              was.popular TAG
              ". . . were popular, weren't they?"
17 Yoko: =*hayatt(a)*.
              was.popular
              "Were popular."
18   (.)
19 Yoko: *wata*[*shi ne::, atta   no ne::,*=
              I   FP   existed FP FP
              "I found (them),"
20 Mari: [*on'naji yo ne::::*.
                   same   FP FP
              "(They) are the same, aren't they?"
21 Emi: =*U:N. a:ru* [*wa yo*.
                      exist FP FP
              "Yeah, sure."
22 Yoko: [*miho* [*ga kiteru   no*.]
                       Miho SB is.wearing FP
                       "Miho is wearing (them)."
23 Hana: [*mukashi no sha*]*shin?*
                           past   LK picture
                       "Old pictures?"
24 Mari: *a!*=
              oh
              "Oh!"
25 Hana: =*E!* [*jibun no* [*mono o?*
              oh self   LK thing O
              "Oh, your stuff?"
26 Mari: [*ho:nto::*.
                   really
              "Rea::lly."
27 Yoko: [*Un. burausu*.
                           blouse
                       "Yeah, blouses."
28   (0.5)
29 Hana: >*hon*<*to:?*=
              really
              "Rea::lly?"
30 Yoko: =*atashi ne* [*nanmaika atta   no yo:*[:, *sute*[*naide::*.=
              I   FP several   existed FP FP   throw.way:NEG
              "I found several (of them), didn't throw (them) away."
31 Mari: [*oiteatta n da*:::::
                       kept   N CP
              "(You)'ve held onto (them)."
32 Hana: [*u:::n
                                    "Uh huh"
33 Emi: [*u::n u-
                                    "Uh huh"
34 Emi: =[*u:::n
              "Uh huh"

35 Mari: =[*era::::i.*
                 impressive
              "Impre::sive."
36 Yoko: *soshitara* [*sore,*
              and.then that
              "And now, those,"
37 Emi: [*kirareru?*
                            can.wear
              "Are (they) okay to wear?"
38   (.)
39 Yoko: *ts- kireru   no.*
                 can.wear FP
              "(They) are!"
40 Mari: °*u:*[:*n.*°
              "°Uh huh°"
41 Emi: [*a! so*[*o::::.*
                 oh so
              "Oh, is that right?"
42 Hana: [*hee:::::::::::::?*
                       wow
              "Wo:::::w"
43 Yoko: [*Ima no katachi to mattaku*
                       now LK shape   as exactly
44   *on'*[*naji.*
              same
              "(They) are exactly the same as the recent styles."
45 Mari: [*on'na*[*ji yo eri   mo.*
                 same   FP collar also
              "Same, the collars, too."
46 Emi: [*A! hon*to::.
                       oh really
              "Oh rea::lly."
47 Yoko: *MAt*[*taku* [*on'naji.*
              exactly   same
              "Exactly the same."
48 Hana: [*honto::.*
                       really
              "Rea::lly."
49 Mari: [°*u::n*°
              "°Uh huh°"
50 Emi: [*un un un*
              "Uh huh, uh huh, uh huh."

Given that conversational participants gradually shift the topical thrust of
their talk, it was difficult to delimit the target segment for this analysis. The claim
concerning the recycled clothing fashion emerges in the step-by-step transition
of topical talk from Emi's telling of her personal experience and sharing of her
frustration to the discussion of the currently popular styles. After the segment
introduced in the transcript, the telling by Mari and Yoko continues for another

several minutes. While we are aware that the analysis of this particular segment might be enriched by situating it in yet "another context" (Schegloff 1992), that is, the larger course of talk within which it occurs, we decided to limit the scope of this study to the description of the three recognizable steps involved in the emergence of the joint telling: (1) Yoko's initiation of her personal experience in conjunction with Mari's proffering of a claim; (2) Yoko's delivery of the telling in response to the different types of recipiency displayed by Emi, Hana, and Mari; and (3) Mari's reengagement in the telling at a possible closing of Yoko's telling.

In the following three sections, we will explicate the intricate coordination of talk, gaze, and gesture through which the participants organize their contributions while shifting their specific identities with respect to the telling.

Entry into the Telling of a Personal Experience

In this section, we describe in detail how the entry into the telling sequence in question is accomplished in the contingencies in the unfolding interaction. We focus on the ways in which Yoko organizes her participation vis-à-vis other participants' conduct so that she emerges from being an unaddressed recipient to becoming the teller of a personal experience within a single turn at talk.

Let us start off by examining example (2), which represents the juncture at which Yoko launches into the telling of her personal experience. Here we are concerned with how Yoko's turn in lines 17–19 is deployed by reference to Mari's turn in lines 14 and 16:

(2)

```
14 Mari:        [demo are] mukashi wa, aya- (0.2) a[nna no=
                but   that past     TP              such  N
            "But, in the past, (0.2) those kinds (of clothes) . . ."
15 Yoko:                                              [°a!°
                                                      oh
                                                      "°Oh!°"

16 Mari:  =hayatta     desho?=
            was.popularTAG
          ". . . were popular, weren't they?"
17 Yoko:  =hayatt(a).
            was.popular
          "Were popular."
18            (.)
19 Yoko:  wata[shi ne::, atta     no ne::,=
            I        FP    existed FP FP
          "I found (them),"
20 Mari:       [onnaji yo ne::::.
                same   FP FP
          "(They) are the same, aren't they?"
```

In lines 14 and 16, Mari produces a turn in which she mentions that the types of clothes that are currently popular among young people were also popular in the past. Mari constructs this turn as a request for confirmation (see *desho?* at the end of line 16), which is designed to solicit confirmation from her recipient(s) (cf. Hasunuma 1992; Szatrowski 1994). Immediately on possible completion of Mari's confirmation request, Yoko starts up and "latches" her turn onto Mari's (as shown by the equal sign in the transcript). Yoko first repeats the verb used in Mari's prior turn (line 17),[6] thereby confirming and agreeing with what Mari has just proposed about the recycled fashion trend. Following a micropause (line 18), Yoko moves on to produce a bit of talk (line 19) that will later turn out to be the initiation of a telling of her personal experience presented in support of Mari's proposal in the preceding turn.

The focus of the discussion in this section is on investigating what "work" is accomplished by Yoko's turn that spans lines 17–19. To explicate that "work," we will analyze the sequence in example (2) by embedding what we can glean from the transcript within the analysis of a broader range of organizations of the participants' conduct. In particular, we will examine the intricate process of coordination between talk, gaze, and other body conduct that takes place at that juncture. The discussion will first focus on what happens before Yoko starts her turn in line 17. It will then move to the analysis of how Yoko's turn is deployed in the contingencies of the moment.

Prior to Yoko's Initiation of Her Turn

Let us first note that at the beginning of her turn in line 14, Mari makes a drastic shift both in her gaze direction and in her body orientation. Prior to that turn, Mari had been maintaining mutual gaze with Yoko for some time (Figure 5.2). Immediately before she reaches the beginning of her turn in line 14, however, Mari quickly moves her gaze away from Yoko and brings it to Emi and Hana, where she receives reciprocal gaze from both these participants. Further, while Mari produces the initial part of line 14, *demo are mukashi wa* ("but, in the past"), her upper body leans forward in the direction of Emi and Hana. Immediately following this shift in gaze and body orientation by Mari, Emi also leans forward to Mari. As a result, then, Emi, Hana, and Mari have formed a "circle" of mutual orientation (Figure 5.3). It is in this configuration of gaze and body orientation among the participants that Mari produces the confirmation request, *anna no hayatta desho?* ("Those kinds [of clothes] were popular, weren't they?") in lines 14 and 16.

Yoko, who had been maintaining mutual gaze with Mari before line 14, is now left out of the circle of mutual orientation formed by the other three participants. It is precisely at this moment that Yoko moves to produce the stretch of talk discussed earlier. Let us consider how she situates her talk in the contingencies of the moment.

Immediately after Emi, Hana, and Mari have established the circle of mutual orientation, Yoko quickly leans forward in the direction of Mari. She prefaces this body movement with *a!* (*oh!*) produced in a soft voice (line 15) in overlap with

Figure 5.2.   Lines 7–11.

Mari's *anna* ("such") in line 14. Then, while leaning her upper body forward, Yoko quickly reaches out her right arm and touches Mari's left arm at the moment Mari utters the word *hayatta* ("were popular") in line 16 (Figure 5.4). It is in this body configuration that Yoko launches into her turn's talk in line 17.

What significance do these body movements have to our understanding of the action that Yoko engages in in her subsequent turn at talk? We propose the following as some of their important aspects: First, by prefacing her body movements with *a!*, a marker of "realization" (which seems to work similarly to *oh* in English [cf. Heritage 1984b]), Yoko provides her co-participants with the context in which her subsequent body movements should be interpreted. That is, with that preface, she publicly displays that some sort of realization has taken place on her part, and with such a public display of realization, she provides a resource for her co-participants to interpret the "meaning" of her subsequent body movements when they occur. Second, by overtly selecting Mari as the target of her body movements, Yoko makes visible to her co-participants that the realization that she has undergone has some primary relevance to Mari. Thus, the *a!*-prefaced body movements as a whole establish the framework of interpretation in which Yoko's subsequent turn's talk is to be understood.

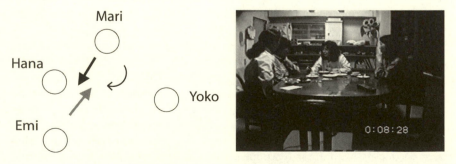

Figure 5.3.   At the beginning of line 14.

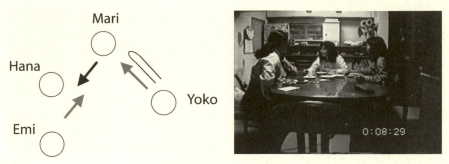

Figure 5.4.   Line 16.

How Yoko's Turn Is Produced

Now let us examine Yoko's turn in lines 17–19 in the light of what we just discussed. As described earlier, she starts her turn immediately on possible completion of Mari's turn in line 16, without leaving time for any beat of silence between the turns. Recall here that Yoko comes to this juncture in the conversation after Mari has produced a confirmation request while facing Emi and Hana and leaning toward them in a circle of mutual orientation. In such a configuration of participation, there is a strong possibility that someone other than Yoko will start to talk after Mari's turn, which may result in Yoko's losing an opportunity to get the mentionable produced. Thus, the contingencies of the moment have created a pressure, motivated by the turn-taking organization, for Yoko to start up as soon as possible to become the first starter after Mari's turn.

What Yoko produces there is a repetition of the verb that Mari has just used in her preceding turn. There is some strategic import to Yoko's initiating her turn in this way. First, among other things that can be achieved through a repetition, repeating an item or items in a preceding turn is one way of showing explicitly that the current turn is responsive to that preceding turn. This observation may seem trivial, but it is quite significant to Yoko in the interactional contingencies in which she finds herself. That is, having been left out of the circle of mutual orientation in which talk is proceeding, Yoko appears to be making a strategic entry into the circle by displaying explicitly in the turn-initial position that her turn has been prompted by and is responsive to what has been going on in the talk in the circle that excludes her.

Second, repeating an item in the preceding turn does more than show responsiveness to that turn. While a range of actions can be achieved by a repetition (cf. Jefferson 1972; Schegloff 1996a; Tannen 1987a, 1987b, 1989), here it is employed to show agreement with and confirmation of what the preceding speaker has said.[7] With respect to the strategic entry from outside of the focal circle of mutual orientation discussed earlier, then, an entry with an immediate repetition of the verb in the prior turn that exhibits explicit agreement appears to be a more effective device than initiating the turn with a more pro forma acknowledgment token such as *un* ("yeah"). This is because such a pro forma acknowledgment token may *claim* responsiveness to the prior turn but may not *evidence* that the current speaker was in fact attending to the details in the ongoing talk in the preceding turn. Thus, Yoko's repetition of the verb *evidences* (i.e., does not just claim) that she was actually attending closely to Mari's preceding turn even though she was left out of the circle as an unaddressed recipient.

Third, it should be noted that, by beginning the turn with a turn-constructional unit (TCU)[8] dedicated to showing agreement to Mari's preceding turn, Yoko in effect closes the sequence opened up by Mari's preceding turn. That is, Mari's confirmation request in lines 14 and 16 constitutes an adjacency pair first pair part (cf. Schegloff and Sacks 1973), which makes certain types of response (in this case, confirmation or disconfirmation) relevant next. And Yoko's confirmatory TCU constitutes an appropriate second pair part, which potentially closes the sequence opened by Mari's first pair part turn.

Fourth, the placement of Yoko's *hayatt(a)* ("were popular") with respect to the gaze shift by her addressed recipient reveals an illuminating fact regarding Yoko's turn construction. As described earlier, toward the end of Mari's turn in line 16 Yoko quickly leans forward and reaches her right arm out to touch Mari's left arm. In response to this "solicit for attention" by Yoko, Mari starts to turn her head quickly to the left on completion of her turn (i.e., at the end of *desho?* in line 16) and brings her gaze to Yoko (Figure 5.5).

Now, close examination of the coordination of talk and gaze shift shows that Yoko's production of *hayatt(a)* is so timed that it is produced while Mari is shifting her gaze, and by the time Mari's gaze reaches her Yoko has virtually completed *hayatt(a)*.[9] In other words, she has "tucked in" a TCU that constitutes agreement with the prior speaker before she obtains mutual gaze with that prior speaker.

These observations lead us to the following considerations of the "work" that Yoko achieves through her talk, gaze, and gesture and their placement vis-à-vis other participants' conduct:

1. By tying her turn to Mari's preceding turn with agreement, Yoko displays turn-initially that Mari's preceding turn has provided grounds for initiating her current turn. That is, by so starting, she publicly locates Mari's preceding turn as the "point of departure" for her turn.

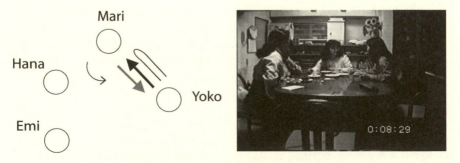

Figure 5.5. At the end of line 16.

2. By closing the sequence opened up by Mari's preceding turn with a turn-initial agreeing TCU and moving on to initiate the telling of a personal experience, Yoko accomplishes shifting the topical focus within a single turn from a general observation of recycled popular fashion styles to her personal experience. Further, by packaging these two actions (i.e., closing a prior sequence and opening up a new one) in a "multi-unit turn" (Schegloff 1982, 1996b), Yoko manages to emerge, within a single turn at talk, from an unaddressed recipient left out of the circle of mutual orientation into the teller of a personal experience.[10]

3. By "tucking in" and completing the turn-initial, sequence-closing TCU before her addressed recipient's gaze arrives at her, Yoko achieves the state of mutual gaze at the precise moment when she moves on to launch the new sequence. In other words, she manages to obtain her addressed recipient's gaze at the precise moment when she begins to display herself as the speaker of a new telling.

To sum up: Prior to the initiation of her turn in line 17, Yoko foreshadows an upcoming action with the *a!*-prefaced body movements, which publicly display that some realization that has prime relevance to Mari has taken place during Mari's turn. With the turn-initial agreeing TCU in line 17 then, Yoko explicitly anchors her contribution to Mari's preceding turn and thereby locates that preceding turn as providing the grounds for initiating her contribution there. Having provided groundwork with that initial TCU, then Yoko launches into the telling of her personal experience at the moment she achieves mutual gaze with her addressed recipient. Yoko organizes this shift in her participation from an unaddressed recipient to a teller within a single turn at talk, and she accomplishes it by packaging a range of actions in a multiunit turn format.

Conclusion

In this section, we investigated the process in which Yoko initiates (what will turn out to be) a telling of her personal experience as a contingent achievement through a fine-tuned coordination of talk, gaze, and other body conduct distributed among the participants. We observed that Yoko's telling is locally occasioned by Mari's preceding turn's talk about the recycled trend of popular fashions and examined how that local occasioning is organized and displayed through the deployment of a multiunit turn.

In the next section, we will turn to the processes in which the recipients of Yoko's telling pursue recipiency in their own differentiated ways. We will examine how Yoko's telling develops through accommodating these differentiated displays of recipiency by her co-participants.

Differentiated Display of Recipiency

In the previous section we described how Yoko's telling is occasioned by Mari's preceding turn, which provides Yoko with warranted grounds for her telling initiation. In this section we will examine how Yoko's telling initiation develops into a telling presented in support of Mari's claim that the old-fashioned style is becoming popular again. It will be shown that this process is achieved through co-construction of the sequence with the recipients of the telling initiation. We first focus on the way in which each of the co-participants displays recipiency toward Yoko's telling initiation. In particular, we will pay special attention to how Mari's way of displaying recipiency differs from that of the other two recipients. Then we will look at how Yoko, the teller, deals with the recipients' differentiated orientation to her telling in order to accomplish her action as agreement with Mari's claim. Thus, this section explores how the participants locally organize their contributions in relation to differential stances toward Yoko's telling.

The "Unexpressed" Referent in the Telling Initiation

Before turning to close examination of co-participants' actions that display recipiency, a few remarks should be made regarding the grammatical structure of Yoko's telling-initiating utterance *watashi ne::, atta no ne::* ("I found") in line 19 in example (1), which is reproduced here as example (3):

(3)

```
19 Yoko: wata[shi ne::, atta    no ne::,=
          I         FP   existed FP FP
          "I found (them),"
```

Translating this utterance as "I found" (as if the object of the verb is missing) is in fact misleading. The verb in the clause *atta* literally means "existed," and the first element, *watashi ne::* ("I") is not interpretable as the subject of the verb.[11] *Watashi ne::* appears to serve only to preface what follows it as something from the speaker's experience or opinion. Thus, the subject, not the object, of the verb *atta* is left unexpressed. That is, "what existed" (hence "what Yoko found" in the approximate translation) is not overtly expressed or is expressed as what has been traditionally called zero-anaphora. This feature of Yoko's turn crucially affects the way the telling sequence is developed. Let us look a little further at what happens in the subsequent turns.

(4)

```
19 Yoko: wata[shi ne::, atta    no ne::,=
          I         FP   existed FP FP
          "I found (them),"
20 Mari:      [on'naji yo ne::::.
               same    FP FP
          "(They) are the same, aren't they?"
21 Emi:  =U:N. a:ru [wa yo.
               exist FP FP
          "Yeah, sure."
```

22 Yoko: [*miho* [*ga kiteru   no.*]
                             Miho SB is.wearing FP
                             "Miho is wearing (them)."

23 Hana: [*mukashi no sha*]*shin?*
                                     past   LK picture
                                  "Old pictures?"

24 Mari: *a!*=
            oh
            "Oh!"

25 Hana: =*E!* [*jibun no* [*mono o?*
                   oh self LK thing O
            "Oh, your stuff?"

26 Mari: [*ho:nto::.*
                   really
            "Rea::lly."

27 Yoko: [*Un. burausu.*
                               blouse
                             "Yeah, blouses."

28   (0.5)

29 Hana: >*hon*<*to:?*=
            really
            "Rea::lly?"

30 Yoko: =*atashi ne* [*nanmaika atta   no yo:*[:, *sute*[*naide::.*=
             I   FP several   existed FP FP   throw.way:NEG
            "I found several (of them), didn't throw (them) away."

31 Mari: [*oiteatta n da:::::*
                      kept   N CP
            "(You)'ve held onto (them)."

32 Hana: [*u:::n*
                                              "Uh huh"

33 Emi: [*u::n u-*
                                                 "Uh huh"

34 Emi: =[*u:::n*
            "Uh huh"

35 Mari: =[*era::::i.*
             impressive
            "Impre::sive."

36 Yoko: *soshitara* [*sore,*
            and.then that
            "And now, those,"

37 Emi: [*kirareru?*
                        can.wear
            "Are (they) okay to wear?"

38   (.)

39 Yoko: *ts- kireru   no.*
            can.wear FP
            "(They) are!"

40 Mari: °*u:*[:*n.*°
            "°Uh huh°"

41 Emi: [*a! so*[*o::::*.
                oh so
           "Oh, is that right?"
42 Hana: [*hee::::::::::::?*
                        wow
                     "Wo:::::w"
43 Yoko: [*Ima no katachi to mattaku*
                        now LK shape   as exactly
44   *on'*[*naji.*
            same
           "(They) are exactly the same as the recent styles."
45 Mari: [*on'na*[*ji yo eri   mo.*
                same   FP collar also
           "Same, the collars, too."

Let us first focus on lines 19 through 22 in example (4). Yoko's utterance in line 22, though following intervening turns by Emi and Mari, is produced as a continuation of her talk in line 19. The pitch at the end of the utterance in line 19 is not fully falling, hence forming a continuing intonation contour. Yoko's body posture is held until the stretch of talk in line 22 is completed. Furthermore, she holds Mari's arm while leaning toward Mari and keeps this body posture across the possible completion point marked with the continuing intonation at the end of line 19. *Miho ga kiteru no* ("Miho is wearing") in line 22 again involves an unexpressed referent: it does not explicitly express the object of the verb *kiru* ("to wear"). However, by virtue of the fact that it is produced as a continuation of the talk in line 19, the unexpressed referent in both utterances can be inferred as one and the same: what is not overtly expressed in these utterances is something that Yoko found and Miho is wearing.

In Japanese conversation, unexpressed referents are massively *not* treated as "absent" or "omitted." In a quantitative analysis of Japanese narrative data, Clancy (1980) confirmed that excluding the cases of introducing new referents, the most common coreferential form was "ellipsis" (73.2%).[12] This suggests that not expressing referents overtly is a regularly occurring practice that co-participants can exploit to co-construct the meaning of the utterance.[13] However, note that in the current case, there is no explicit mention of the referent in the previous turns with which the unexpressed referent in Yoko's turns can be identified. Indeed, in lines 23 and 25, one of the recipients, Hana, responds with "other repair initiation" (Schegloff, Jefferson, and Sacks 1977) by offering a candidate understanding of the unexpressed referent, namely, *mukashi no shashin?* ("old pictures?") and *E! jibun no mono o?* ("Oh, your stuff?"). This "understanding check" by Hana indicates that the identity of the unexpressed referent is in fact problematic to her. In the following, we start our close examination of the participants' actions with this process of reference negotiation initiated by Hana in line 23.

In order to follow the temporal emergence of how each of the co-participants demonstrates her recipiency of Yoko's turn across multiple turn transitions, we will highlight one participant at a time. We should keep in mind, however, that display of recipiency is first and foremost a socially distributed activity that cannot be produced independently of actions of other participants. Accordingly, description of each necessarily involves understanding of the other participants' actions intertwined with that of the participant being described.

Establishing Unexpressed Referent

Hana is the one who "officially" treats Yoko's utterance as involving a "missing" referent. That is, in line 23 Hana offers a candidate for the unexpressed reference, *mukashi no shashin?* ("old pictures?"). This is done before Yoko completes the added segment in line 22, which could have helped Hana guess the unexpressed referent by the occurrence of the verb *kiru* ("to wear") narrowing down the possible candidates to those that can be an object of that verb. However, Hana's first guess is not random. She chooses *shashin* ("pictures") as a candidate unexpressed referent, which is reasonable at this sequential position, that is, after Yoko's agreement to Mari's claim about the old-fashioned style becoming popular again (*hayatta* ["Were popular"]), which could be heard as the beginning of a collaborative reminiscing action. Notice also that the word *mukashi*, meaning "old time," in *mukashi no shashin* first appears in Mari's utterance in line 14. Thus, Hana treats Yoko's utterance with the unexpressed reference as responsive to Mari's preceding utterance in some way or another and shows her understanding that the unexpressed referent should be inferred along these lines. In other words, this instantiates inter-subjective work that seems to underlie participants' capability of co-constructing meaning in talk-in-interaction, even with frequent unexpressed referents.

Furthermore, Hana's next turn in line 25 reveals remarkable sensitivity to the talk produced in overlap with her own talk: she appropriately captures the grammatical structure and the contiguity between Yoko's turns in line 19 and line 22. Hana's utterance *E! jibun no mono o?* ("Oh, your stuff?") in line 25 demonstrates that she now understands that the unexpressed referent is not only somehow related to "old time" but also "can be worn" by Yoko's daughter, Miho. Notice that Hana uses the object marker *o*. By deploying the grammatical practice of object marking, Hana ties her utterance to Yoko's utterance in line 22, thereby instructing the recipients to interpret her utterance as built on what it is responding to, that is, Yoko's utterance. Note also the way Hana chooses words to express the referent yet to be clarified. *Jibun no mono* ("your stuff") at this position of the sequence is particularizable enough to imply not simply "your stuff" but "your old clothing stuff." It is at the same time conveniently indistinctive. That is, it is not clear yet what kind of clothes they are, hence the use of the general term *mono*, referring to any kind of thing. Hana's second try is acknowledged by Yoko, who says *Un. burausu* ("Yeah, blouses") in line 27.[14] By virtue of this fact that it is responsive to Hana's preceding turn, the noun referent (i.e., *blouses*) in Yoko's turn is hearable as offered as further specification of Hana's general reference (*mono*, "the stuff"). Thus, Hana and Yoko engage in collaboratively establishing the unexpressed referent.

The close examination of Hana's participation across multiple turns thus seems to reveal that Hana's action of negotiating the unexpressed referent is specifically adapted to the immediate sequential environment that is constantly reshaped moment-by-moment, as the talk proceeds.

Emi's Shift in Participation

The action of another recipient, Emi, appears to be puzzling when one pays attention to her first response to Yoko's telling-initiation turn. In response to Yoko's *watashi ne, atta no ne* ("I found"), Emi says *un aru wa yo* ("yeah, sure") (literally, "Yeah, X exists," where X is not expressed). Unlike Hana, Emi immediately treats the unexpressed referent as understood and unproblematic and does not invoke the necessity of reference checking. She utters an acknowledgment token *U:N* with prosodic emphasis and then uses the same verb as used in Yoko's utterance with the final particle *yo*, which has been described as indicating that the speaker is knowledgeable of the fact expressed in the clause (Cook 1992; Kamio 1994; Maynard 1993; Suzuki 1990). It is evident then that Emi interpreted Yoko's turn or, more specifically, the unexpressed referent in this turn in line 19 differently from Hana. In other words, unlike Hana, Emi presents herself at least initially as a "knowing" participant vis-à-vis Yoko's telling.

However, Emi quickly shifts herself from a "knowing" to "unknowing" recipient as the reference negotiation between Hana and Yoko proceeds. As she utters the turn in line 21 Emi looks toward Mari and moves her upper body slightly backward as if she were confidently affirming Mari's claim about the recycled fashion trend. While Hana pursues the clarification of the unexpressed referent in Yoko's utterance by asking *E mukashi no shashin?* ("the old pictures?"), Emi moves her upper body back forward, bringing her left elbow to the table and resting her chin on her left hand. As she completes this sequence of body movements, she brings her gaze to Yoko, who is now emerging as a teller through the process of the reference negotiation with Hana. Consequently, upon the completion of the series of movements, Emi orients her body to Yoko, organizing her body posture such that it displays preparedness for recipiency. Figures 5.6a, 5.6b, and 5.6c capture a few points in sequence in this series of Emi's movements.

Figure 5.6a.   Emi leans backward.

Figure 5.6b.   Emi moves forward.

Furthermore, after Yoko's redoing of the telling-initiation in line 30,[15] Emi produces a series of recipiency token *u::n u- u:::n* that displays her alignment as a recipient of Yoko's reinitiated telling. Emi then produces the anticipatory question *kirareru?* ("Are [they] okay to wear?") the moment Yoko completes the connective *soshitara* ("then"), thereby pre-empting what could follow the connective. The occurrence of this connective at this particular position (i.e., after the turn restating that Yoko found her old clothes, namely, after retelling the source event) projects the consequence of the source event as next-to-come. Thus, although Emi's initial response to Yoko, *U:N, aru wa yo* ("Yeah, sure/ [X] exists"), could have had the effect of downgrading the newsworthiness or tellability (Sacks 1992: Lecture 1, Fall 1968, Lecture 3, Spring 1970) of Yoko's emergent telling, her own quick shift

Figure 5.6c.   Emi rests her chin on her left hand.

from presenting herself as a "knowing" participant to an "unknowing" recipient appears to cancel such an effect. Indeed, this turn by Emi is not taken up by any of the other participants.

Mari's Participation as a "Knowing" Participant

Let us now turn to what Mari does in this sequence. After Yoko's additional talk *miho ga kiteru no* ("Miho is wearing") in line 22, Mari starts producing the news receipt token, *a! ho:nto::.* ("Oh! Really"). in lines 24 and 26, facing Yoko. This indicates that Mari takes as news the fact that Yoko has old clothes that are still good enough for her daughter to wear. Recall that Mari has already shown that she knows that the current youth's fashion was popular in the past.[16] Accordingly, she organizes her recipiency in such a way as it displays her treatment of the fact that Yoko kept her old clothes for such a long time (rather than the fact that the old fashion is popular again) as the newsworthy part of Yoko's telling. The timing of Mari's initiation of the news receipt token provides support for this observation. Upon the completion of Yoko's utterance in line 22, it becomes public that Yoko found something that was in fashion in the past and that is worn by her daughter now, and it is at that moment that Mari responds with the news receipt token (lines 24 and 26). That is, Mari starts producing the news receipt token exactly at the point at which this much information is disclosed. The significance of this placement of Mari's news receipt token becomes more evident if we compare it to the placement of Hana's news receipt token. Note that Hana produces *her* news receipt token only after she learns that Yoko's daughter wears her old blouses.[17] In other words, Hana treats the fact that Yoko's daughter wears her mother's old blouses as newsworthy. This difference in the ways of displaying recipiency is further demonstrated later in the sequence. In line 31, in overlap with Yoko's restated claim that she found several of her old blouses, Mari produces a turn that shows her understanding of Yoko's telling, *oiteattan da:::::* ("[you]'ve held onto [them]"), and then an assessment term, *era::::i* ("impressive"). This indicates that Mari recognizes this particular position in the telling sequence as a place for displaying appreciation of the telling (e.g., Sacks 1974; Schegloff 1984; M. H. Goodwin 1990; Goodwin and Goodwin 1987, 1992). This positioning of her display of appreciation demonstrates her treatment of Yoko's telling as "a story of Yoko's keeping old clothes for such a long time without throwing them away."[18] However, Hana and Emi seem to take Yoko's telling as "a story of Yoko's old blouses, which her daughter is wearing now." As we have seen, Emi issues an anticipatory question of whether the blouses are still good enough to wear in line 37. After Yoko's emphatic affirmative answer to Emi's question, Emi and Hana respond with vocalizations that show surprise in lines 41 (*a! soo::::*, "Oh, is that right?") and 42 (*he:::::::::::?*, "Wo:::::w"), respectively, whereas Mari simply produces an acknowledgment token in a low volume in line 40 (°*u::n.*,° "°Uh huh°").

As already implied in the foregoing analysis, these differentiated ways of displaying recipiency can be accounted for by noting how this sequence is initiated. Recall that it was Mari who first indicated noticing the recycled fashion style (lines 14 and 16). Yoko's introduction of her personal experience is occasioned by the occurrence of Mari's utterance that invites agreement and is formulated as providing support for Mari's claim. In other words, the way in which Mari responds to Yoko's telling appears to be shaped by the fact that she was the one who claimed the knowledge of the recent style and that Yoko's telling is prompted by Mari's claim of this knowledge. Thus, this case documents the ways in which co-participants establish and demonstrate their telling-specific identities in the course of co-constructing a telling sequence.

Dealing with Differentiated Recipiency

Let us now look at how Yoko, the teller, deals with the diverse stances toward her telling displayed in the recipients' actions. Yoko's turn in line 30 seems to provide us with a rich locus for discussion of this matter. Note that this turn is produced at the point at which the unexpressed referent has been established and that it has a turn shape similar to the turn with which she has initiated her telling in line 19. These two turns are juxtaposed in examples (5) and (6) with the repeated linguistic items in boldface:

(5)

> 19 Yoko: *wata*[*shi ne::, atta   no ne::,*=
>   I   FP   existed FP FP
>   "I **found** (them)."

(6)

> 30 Yoko: =*atashi ne* [*nanmaika atta   no yo:*[:, *sute*[*naide::.*=
>   I   FP   several   existed FP FP   throw.way:NEG
>   "I **found several** (of them), didn't throw (them) away."

While the addressed recipient of the telling initiation in line 19 was Mari, by the time she starts producing her turn in line 30, Yoko is gazing at Hana as the result of her gaze shift in response to Hana's question *jibun no mono o?* ("your stuff?") in line 25. Thus, the turn at line 30 can be seen as a "redoing" of the telling initiation addressed to a different recipient party (Charles Goodwin 1981; Ford and Fox 1996). The "redoing" nature of this turn is further demonstrated by Yoko's body movement and hand gesture. As she produces *nanmaika atta no yo::* ("I found several [of them]"), she makes short, quick repetitive waving motions with her right hand (see Figures 5.7 and 5.7a). Embedded in this sequential position, these hand movements are not only consistant with the concept of plurality expressed by *nanmaika* ("several"), but are also distinctively marking the reannouncement of the existence or discovery of her old blouses. As she does this hand gesture, she brings her upper body back to upright position. As described in detail earlier, Yoko leaned her upper body toward Mari in launching into the telling initiation. She keeps this leaning position throughout the reference negotiation sequence and then returns to the upright position as she produces the turn in line 30. Thus, by bring-

Figure 5.7.   Yoko's hand gesture in line 30.

ing her upper body into more stable, upright position, or what can be called "home position" (Sacks and Schegloff 1975, Schegloff in press), she puts herself in more neutral posture vis-à-vis each of the other participants, marking "return to the beginning."

Remaining in this neutral position, she extends her turn by adding *sutenaide* ("not throwing away"). Note that *sutenaide* ("not throwing away") is in a way an upgraded version of Mari's appreciative expression *oite atta n da* ("[you]'ve held onto [them]"), whose literal translation would be something like "[they] have been kept." As she produces this added stretch of talk, she moves her gaze to Mari, the original recipient of the telling initiation, resulting in mutual gaze (see Figure 5.8).

Figure 5.7a.   Yoko's hand gesture in line 30.

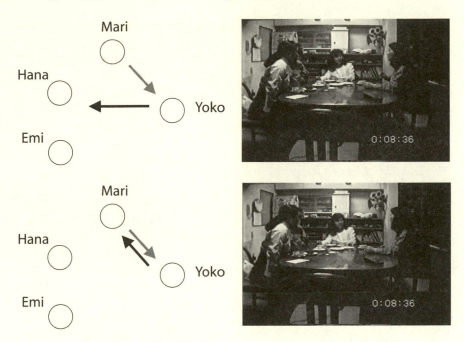

Figure 5.8.   Yoko shifts her gaze from Emi and Hana to Mari.

Extending the turn in the way Yoko does seems to effectively manage complex interactional exigencies in the following respects. Within a single turn, Yoko can:

1. deal with the ever-changing configurations of participation—having produced the first telling initiation addressed to the participant who has provided the turn by which the telling is triggered, she now readdresses it to the other participants who have demonstrated "involved" recipiency
2. recomplete the action of telling initiation by bringing her gaze back to the original recipient while the extended part is being produced, which retroactively makes the reference negotiation sequence reanalyzable as "inserted"
3. acknowledge Mari's appreciation produced in overlap with her own talk by restating and upgrading it.

Thus, a careful analysis of this single turn by Yoko reveals finely tuned coordination of talk, gaze, and body conduct sensitive to immediate interactional contingencies as well as to the sequential organization of telling. Having recompleted the telling initiation and having re-presented the part of the telling that describes the source event, the teller can occasion another opportunity to tell the consequence or outcome of the event. Note that this opportunity is made available not only to the current teller but also to another co-participant who can present herself as a co-teller. As examined in this section, Mari has been demonstrating markedly differential stances to the telling. In other words, the opportunity for Mari to participate as a co-teller at this juncture is methodically staged through the development of the telling.

In this section we have examined how each of the recipients of the telling, through intricate coordination of talk, eye gaze, and body movements, displays her recipiency in such a way that exhibits and constructs her telling-specific identity as well as accommodates emergent moment-by-moment interactional contingencies. The following section explicates the way in which Mari comes to present herself as a co-teller.

From an Unaddressed Recipient to a Co-Teller

In this section, we examine how Mari reengages in the claim she made earlier, that is, the current fashion being a recycling from the 1970s, by joining in a possible closing of Yoko's telling of her personal experience.

By the time Yoko completes her utterance in lines 43–44, *Ima no katachi to mattaku on'naji* ("[They] are exactly the same as the recent style"), the other three participants have demonstrated their acknowledgment of Yoko's emerging telling and directed their gaze to the teller, Yoko. At this point, Yoko faces Emi and Hana and thereby selects these two as addressed recipients. Consequently, Mari, who was originally the addressed recipient of the telling, has become an unaddressed recipient (see Figure 5.9). However, during the subsequent turn in line 45, Mari shifts her participation status from that of an unaddressed recipient of Yoko's telling to a "co-teller" or a member of the party jointly asserting the claim that the current fashion appears to be similar to that of the 1970s. This section provides detailed description of the makeup of Mari's turn in line 45. Through the description, we explicate how Mari accomplishes the shift in her participation status by utilizing syntactic, prosodic, and gestural as well as sequential resources available at that moment.

"Getting the Mentionable Mentioned" Through Anticipatory Completion

Let us first consider the initiation of Mari's turn in line 45 in relation to Yoko's turn in lines 43–44. As shown in example (7), Mari initiates her turn in line 45 a moment before Yoko completes her turn, which delivers the assessment of her old blouses

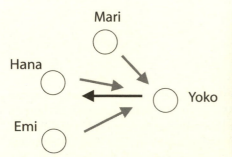

Figure 5.9.   Lines 43–44.

being exactly the same style as the ones currently popular. Mari starts out this turn by closely echoing the assessment term, *on'naji* ("same"), produced by Yoko.

(7)

```
43 Yoko:        [Ima no  katachi to mattaku
                 now LK shape    as exactly
44              on'[naji.
                 same
                "(They) are exactly the same as the recent styles."
45 Mari:    [on'na[ji yo eri     mo.
                 same    FP collar also
                "Same, the collars, too."
```

These two adjacent turns exhibit a practice described as "anticipatory completion" or "collaborative finish" by researchers such as Lerner (1991, 1996), Lerner and Takagi (1999), Hayashi and Mori (1998), Ono and Eri Yoshida (1996), Susan Strauss and Yumiko Kawanishi (1996), and Noriko Akatsuka (1997). Mari initiates the turn in line 45 before Yoko's preceding turn reaches a possible completion point, and Mari's turn supplies the assessment term identical to the one produced by Yoko in overlap. The timing of Mari's delivery of this turn and the fact that Mari and Yoko almost simultaneously produce the identical term indicate that Mari has anticipated the final component of Yoko's turn. What exactly enables Mari to appropriately anticipate the ending of Yoko's turn? What does Mari accomplish by producing the identical assessment term in chorus with Yoko? The close observation of the construction of Yoko's turn in lines 43–44 and of the development of the target sequence provides answers to these questions.

By the time Mari initiates her talk in line 45, Yoko's turn-so-far in lines 43–44 has introduced the adverbial phrase *ima no katachi to* ("as the recent styles"), which is a target of comparison, and the intensifier *mattaku* ("exactly"), which is further emphasized by high pitch accent. Such a development of Yoko's turn appears to help Mari anticipate the upcoming assessment term, *on'naji* ("the same"), or it at least helps her perceive the emerging activity as an assessment. This particular timing of Mari's initiation of the overlapping turn reminds us of Goodwin and Goodwin's (1987, 1992) analysis of the following segment taken from their English conversational data:

(8)

```
Nancy:  Jeff made an asparagus pie
         it was s::so[: goo:d.
Tasha:              [I love it. °Yeah I love that.
```

Goodwin and Goodwin point out that the intensifier *so* produced with enhanced intonation (indicated by the italics and colons in the transcript) exhibits Nancy's involvement in her display of heightened appreciation before the assessment adjective is actually spoken. Further, they suggest the possibility that the recipient uses the intensifier to anticipate what is to be said next and thereby initiates her own concurrent assessment at the end of the intensifier. Goodwin and Goodwin's account appears to coincide with the current case.[19] Mari initiates her turn in line 45 right after the prosodically marked intensifier *mattaku* ("exactly"). A difference is that Tasha in Goodwin and Goodwin's example does not say exactly the same thing as Nancy (i.e., Nancy's *goo:d* as opposed to Tasha's *I love it*), whereas Mari in our case does use the exact same term to join in the assessment activity.

Goodwin and Goodwin explain this variance in the two participants' ways of expressing their assessment by referring to the differential access to the assessed item, that is, asparagus pie. On the one hand, Nancy delivers her assessment in the past tense, indicating her reference to the specific pie made by Jeff. On the other hand, Tasha, by using the present tense, talks about asparagus pie as a generic food category. Thus, choosing the particular structure for her assessing turn, Tasha makes visible her different access to what is being assessed. In the current case as well, the two participants, Yoko and Mari, do not share the experience of the particular event told by Yoko. And yet they do use the identical term to deliver their assessment. We can offer an account for this use of the identical term by Mari and Yoko by reviewing the development of the telling sequence.

Recall that Yoko's telling has been triggered by Mari's initial reference to the recycling of the trend in popular fashion. As has been discussed in the previous sections, it was Mari who initially referred to the fact that the current fashion appears to be similar to what was popular years ago. We should also note that Mari has actually used this assessment term *on'naji* ("the same") once before in line 20, delivered in response to Yoko's partial repetition of Mari's comment but in overlap with Yoko's initiation of the telling.

(9)

```
16 Mari:  =hayatta      desho?=
              was.popular TAG
          ". . . were popular, weren't they?"
17 Yoko:  =hayatt(a).
              was.popular
          "Were popular."
18           (.)
19 Yoko:  wata[shi ne::, atta    no ne::,=
              I        FP   existed FP FP
          "I found (them),"
20 Mari:       [on'naji yo ne::::.              ←
               same   FP FP
          "(They) are the same, aren't they?"
```

(10)

```
43 Yoko:           [Ima no katachi to mattaku
                    now LK shape   as exactly
44         on'[naji.
            same
          "(They) are exactly the same as the recent styles."
```

45 Mari: [*on'na*[*ji yo eri   mo.*   ←
             same   FP collar also
          "Same, the collars, too."

The similarity and the difference in the makeup of these two turns by Mari as well as their placement in relation to Yoko's telling of her personal experience provide important clues for our understanding of this particular case of anticipatory completion and of the accomplishment of "co-tellership."

Note that in both cases the assessment term *on'naji* is followed by the utterance-final particle *yo*. As discussed earlier, the use of *yo* generally indicates that the speaker assumes that she is more knowledgeable toward the information marked by the particle than the recipients. Thus, the use of the particle *yo* in these turns points to Mari's assertion of her knowledge of the recycled styles, which plays an essential role in the establishment of tellership.

However, the particle *ne*, which only occurs in line 20, is considered to index "affective common ground" (Cook 1992) or to be used to seek agreement, confirmation, or reconfirmation (Kamio 1994; Maynard 1993; Suzuki 1990). Therefore, by marking the utterance in line 20 by the combination of *yo* and *ne*, Mari reasserts her claim made in lines 14 and 16 and seeks reconfirmation of Yoko's alignment with Mari.[20] As this turn by Mari overlaps with Yoko's initiation of the telling of her personal experience, the reconfirmation projected by the particles *yo ne* is not realized right away. However, Yoko develops her telling precisely as supporting evidence for the claim initially made by Mari. Further, at a possible closing of the telling, Yoko explicitly refers to the relevancy of her telling to the preceding claim made by Mari (lines 14 and 16), using the assessment term *on'naji* ("the same"). It is at this moment that Mari joins in Yoko's talk and reclaims her original point, using the utterance marked by the evidential stance marker *yo*. Thus, the timing of Mari's initiation of her turn in line 45 and her choice of the word *on'naji* ("the same") seem to be a result of the interactional exigency not to miss an opportunity to reassert her original claim, in other words, to "get the mentionable mentioned" at the precise moment in the temporal progression of the talk-in-interaction. By initiating the turn in line 45 before the completion of Yoko's turn, that is, before the point where the initiation of next turn by any other recipients become relevant, Mari efficiently presents herself as the original claimer of the recycled fashion trend. While merging into the possible closing of Yoko's telling of her personal experience, Mari, in alignment with Yoko, "tells" the other two participants that the current popular styles are exactly the same as those that were popular in the 1970s.

As we discussed earlier, in this example the two participants do not necessarily share the experience of the source event of Yoko's finding her old blouses. It is evident from the preceding talk examined in the previous section that Mari has not seen Yoko's old blouses. This means that there is a difference between what is being assessed by the term *on'naji* in Yoko's turn in lines 43–44 and Mari's turn in line 45. In Yoko's turn, the term specifically refers to the blouses that she has kept. What Mari describes by this same term is not those particular blouses of Yoko's but the recycled style in general. However, unlike Tasha in Goodwin and Goodwin's example (8), Mari does not make the difference explicit in her talk. Rather, by not marking this difference, Mari seems to make a seamless transition from Yoko's telling of her personal experience to her own telling about the current recycled fashion in general.

Extension of Mari's Turn and Concurrent Body Conduct

As we have observed so far, the timing of its initiation and the nature of its initial component demonstrate important features of Mari's turn in line 45. But this turn does not end with just supplying the final component of Yoko's turn. Passing the syntactic completion marked by the adjective and the sentence-final particle *yo*, Mari adds a new piece of talk, *eri mo* ("the collar, too"), which is an NP appended to the preceding adjective. This second component provides more specific information about the style being recycled. These two syntactic components, that is, the adjective *on'naji* marked by the particle *yo* and the following NP, *eri mo*, are uttered in a single continuous intonation contour with no recognizable prosodic break between them. Thus, it appears that these two components are delivered as a single unit of talk. An apparent puzzle for linguists here is Mari's choice of this particular word order. That is, if she utters these two syntactic components as a single unit, why doesn't she choose the canonical, predicate-final word order, as in *eri mo on'naji yo* ("the collars are also the same")?

Previous studies on the word order variability in Japanese (e.g., Hinds 1982; Simon 1989; Ono and Suzuki 1992) have explained the motivations for such a noncanonical word order as follows: "the speaker expresses the predicate and then qualifies it with an element indicating discourse-pragmatic information" (Ono and Suzuki 1992:440) and "important information comes to the speaker's mind first and uttered first, thus frequently resulting in uncanonical, postposed sentences" (Simon 1989:198).[21] While these generalized accounts may provide a basic understanding for this recurrent practice, the detailed observation of the construction of this particular turn, located in this particular sequence, provides a richer understanding of how the linguistic structure gets realized in and serves to accomplish the ongoing interactional activities.

The choice of word order in Mari's turn could be explained partially by the possibility that the turn is produced through the anticipation of the ending of the preceding turn. As discussed earlier, Yoko's unfolding turn that has developed with the adverbial phrase *Ima no katachi to* ("as the recent styles") and the intensifier *mattaku* ("exactly"), produced with high pitch, projects the following element to be some kind of assessment term. This suggests that if Mari used the canonical word order, *eri mo on'naji yo* ("the collars are also the same"), the transition between Yoko's prior turn and this turn would indicate a sense of discontinuity.

(11)

> ?*Ima no katachi to **mattaku** eri mo **onnaji** yo.*
> "The collars are also exactly the same as the recent styles."

Instead, Mari appears to smoothly join in Yoko's telling by making her turn syntactically continuous with the preceding turn by Yoko.

(12)

> | *Ima no katachi to **mattaku*** | *onnaji* | *yo eri mo.* |

That is, in this particular interactional environment, this "marked" word order seems to serve better than what has been considered the "canonical" or "less marked" word order.

The coordination between these two turns by Yoko and Mari is achieved not only through their talk but also through their body conduct. Let us now turn our attention to the delivery of this second element, that is, the postpredicate NP *eri mo* ("the collar, too"), which describes the specific feature of the recycled fashion. If we look at the transcript alone, this specification may appear to be a new contribution to this context brought up by Mari. But the visual record of the interaction reveals a striking fact: this NP, *eri mo* ("the collar, too"), voiced by Mari, appears to correspond to the gesture performed by Yoko during the prior turn. That is, Mari utilizes not only talk but also gesture to demonstrate her alignment with the primary teller at the moment, Yoko. To better understand the construction of Mari's turn in question, let us examine in detail the body movements that accompany the talk in this short segment.

As Yoko utters *katachi to* ("as the styles"), she raises her hands up to her upper chest and stretches her thumb and index finger as shown in Figure 5.10a. Then, as she produces the first syllable of the intensifier *mattaku* ("exactly") with emphasis, she quickly drops down her hands while narrowing the space between the thumb and the index finger. For the rest of the turn, then, she holds her hands at the end point of this gesture as shown in Figure 5.10b and Figure 5.10c.

Figure 5.10a.   Illustration of collar shape gesture.

Figure 5.10b.   Movement of collar shape gesture.

Figure 5.10c.   Gesture indicating the shape of collar.

(13)

|up → |down → | hold → |

43–44 Yoko: *Ima no katachi to ma̱ta̱ku on'naji.*
                  now LK shape as exactly same
                  "(It's) exactly the same as the recent shape."

As discussed earlier, right before the completion of Yoko's turn in lines 43–44 Mari, who has been attending to Yoko's talk, starts her turn with the assessment term *on'naji* ("the same"). Prompted by Mari's initiation of the turn (line 45), Yoko shifts her gaze from the direction of Emi and Hana to Mari (see Figure 5.11).

On achieving mutual gaze with Yoko, Mari delivers her interpretation of Yoko's preceding gesture, *eri mo* ("collar, too"). Mari's immediate as well as appropriate incorporation of Yoko's gesture into her talk is significant for the display of her co-tellership. Mari's ability to assign the relevant "meaning" to Yoko's gesture provides evidence of Mari's knowledge of the recycled style. While producing the

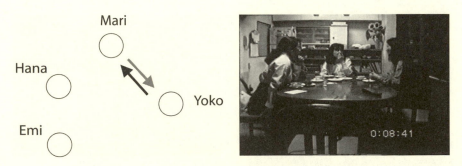

Figure 5.11.   Yoko shifts her gaze from Emi and Hana to Mari.

utterance *eri mo* ("collar, too"), Mari also raises her hands up to her chest and initiates the very same gesture that Yoko has just performed in the prior turn (see Figure 7.10a).

As Mari's turn comes to completion, Yoko shifts her gaze back to Emi and Hana and restates the last portion of her prior utterance, *MAttaku on'naji* ("exactly the same"), placing a stronger emphasis on the first syllable and slightly prolonging the double consonant (line 47 in example [1]). During Yoko's production of the first word, *MAttaku* ("exactly"), Mari, who has her hands at the initial position of the gesture, brings her hands down forming the shape of collars. Simultaneously Mari shifts her gaze from the teller, Yoko, to the recipients, Emi and Hana. During Yoko's next word, *on'naji* ("the same"), Mari holds her hands at the end point of the collar gesture as shown in Figure 5.10(b), producing a minimal vocalization *u::n* and a nod, which appear to reaffirm the jointly asserted claim.

The gaze directions illustrated in Figures 5.9, 5.11, and 5.12 alone indicate how Mari changes her participation from an unaddressed recipient to a co-teller while producing the turn in line 45. But Mari's talk and gesture also support our analysis of the astute manipulation of her shift in participation status. Mari's display of her alignment with Yoko, the other teller, seems to involve at least three steps. First, the appropriate anticipation of the ending of Yoko's talk enables Mari to announce that she has been closely attending to the details of Yoko's talk and to get Yoko's attention to her. Second, by assigning a meaning to Yoko's gesture, Mari can further indicate that she has been attending to not only Yoko's talk but also her gesture. Third, by producing the utterance *eri mo* ("collar, too") under mutual gaze with Yoko, Mari can suggest to Yoko that she has come up with the piece of talk not independently, by herself, but in accordance with Yoko's gesture. In other words, Mari can display her acknowledgment of Yoko's authorship for that piece of talk. Finally, Mari's reproduction of the gesture upon securing Yoko's gaze reassures her alignment with Yoko, which has been developed through the preceding actions. Through these various media, Mari demonstrates her alignment with Yoko. To be more precise, Mari accomplishes her alignment with Yoko not just as a recipient who appreciates Yoko's telling but also as a member of the party jointly asserting the claim. She establishes, or reestablishes, herself as a "co-teller" or "co-

Figure 5.12.   Line 47.

proponent" by masterfully utilizing grammatical and gestural as well as sequential resources.

The co-telling by Mari and Yoko in this segment ends with a remarkable co-ordination of Yoko's talk and Mari's gesture (line 47), as described earlier. During this joint production, Mari shifts her gaze from Yoko to Emi and Hana. As a result, the co-tellers' gazes becomes parallel, and both address the recipients together. This final segment of the target sequence demonstrates how the participants efficiently incorporate their own as well as the others' gestures in building turns and sequences. Gesture and talk are coordinated to provide a mutual framework for interpretation: gesture is understood by virtue of its placement in a particular sequence of talk; at the same time, gesture provides a resource for how the subsequent talk unfolds (cf. Kendon 1972, 1977, 1990; Charles Goodwin 1979, 1980, 1981, 1984, 2000a, forthcoming b; Marjorie Harness Goodwin 1980; Streeck 1994, 1996; LeBaron and Streeck 1997).

Conclusion

In this section, we have examined, from multiple perspectives, how Mari reestablishes her co-tellership through joining in a possible closing of Yoko's telling, which was originally occasioned by Mari's earlier proffering of her noticing of the recycling of the fashion trend. The detailed description of the design of Mari's turn in line 45 has allowed us to discover the intricate process in which the two participants, who have different types of knowledge concerning the recycled fashion, manage to align as co-tellers. This case presents a compelling example of how the participants efficiently and effectively utilize various resources available, including syntax, intonation, gaze, and gesture, as well as sequential development, to organize their participation in a telling sequence.

Concluding Remarks

Our investigation in this chapter focused on the moment-to-moment development of a particular telling sequence documented in a single episode of talk-in-interaction in Japanese. Through that investigation, we attempted to explicate the complex ways in which the participants utilize a range of resources available to them to interactively manage their participation in the activity in progress. In particular, our examination centered on the processes in which two participants emerge as "co-tellers" through their differentiated but coordinated actions within the here-and-now contingencies of the interaction.

Through our discussions of a rich array of phenomena observed in the single case of telling sequence, we hope to have made several points regarding the goals of the study we set up at the beginning of this chapter.

First, we suggested that the "functions" of such grammatical features of Japanese as zero-anaphora and word order variability can be elucidated further if we closely examine their situated workings in actual social interaction. Our analysis demonstrated how such grammatical features are deployed to carry out the par-

ticipants' real-life projects. These grammatical features can have significant interactional consequences in the following ways: (1) they can engender an interactive
activity that multiple participants engage in and thereby shape the structure of
participation in the subsequent course of interaction (cf. the discussion of "zero-
anaphora" and "reference negotiation"); and (2) they can be mobilized to accomplish interactive tasks engendered by the activity in which the participants are engaged (cf. the discussions of the "postpredicate" extensions of turns and final
particles). These observations underscore the importance of conceiving of language
(and its grammatical resources) as an instrument of *action* deployed in the situated occasions in the real-life social interaction of the participants. We thus hope
that this study will serve as encouragement for others to explore social functions
of linguistic features as well as the bearing of linguistic structures on the organization of social interaction.

Second, our analysis of the intricate processes of coordination among talk, gaze,
gesture, and body orientation revealed that the participants in interaction are engaged in a local, situated analysis not only of talk in progress but also of multiple
aspects of their emerging local interactional circumstances, including body movements and spatial orientation. As we demonstrated in the previous sections, talk and
other body conduct provide mutually elaborating framework of interpretation in
which they reflexively elaborate each other's meaning. This observation of the reflexive relationship between talk and other conduct helps us see the process of how
the participants "make definite sense with indefinite resources" (Heritage 1984a) that
are available to them in the immediate interactional matrix. This then blurs the traditional distinction between linguistic and nonlinguistic behaviors. These different
sorts of behaviors mutually inform and reinforce each other, and therefore they may
not always be neatly or usefully segregated. Rather, it may be more profitable to come
to terms with the complex interaction among multiple semiotic activities (e.g., those
with linguistic signs, prosody, gestures, spatial/postural configurations, etc.) to understand how the participants in interaction make sense of each other's conduct.

Third, our analysis of the process of the contingent achievement of "co-
tellership" showed how the activity of telling provides for the relevance of differentiated actions for a range of different types of participants (e.g., knowing participant, unknowing recipient, co-teller, etc.) and how these participants analyze
and make use of the emerging structure of the activity to organize their participation in it. These observations highlight the fact that telling of a personal experience,
story, narrative, and so forth, in talk-in-interaction is essentially a multiparty, collaborative activity. That is, the activity of telling cannot be achieved unilaterally by a
single participant. Rather, each participant engages in a situated analysis of the activity in progress in order to organize his/her participation in it. Co-participants'
analysis of each other's actions is displayed in their own actions. Such displayed observable analysis is in turn used to accomplish further actions. The actions of different types of participants, which are differentiated but coordinated, constitute an
activity of telling. Through our close examination of the moment-to-moment shifts
in the participation structure in the development of the particular telling sequence
in this study, we hope to have added another contribution to an understanding of
telling as an interactive achievement.

Our analysis of the target sequence identified several interactional practices (i.e., repeating an item in a prior turn, talking in a multiunit turn, and anticipatorily completing another's turn) documented in previous work in CA. We observed how these formally described practices are deployed to accomplish situated interactive tasks in the particular contingencies in the distinctive local context. Schegloff once formulated "the big problem" for the analysis of interaction as follows: "How is it that with the use of abstract formal resources interactional participants create idiosyncratic, particularized to some here-and-now, interactions?" (1988a:154). In other words, in the connection to our case how is it that those participants use the recurrently employed practices like repetition, multiunit turn, and anticipatory completion to meet the particular interactional demands they face in the particular moments in the particular interaction in which they find themselves? Our analysis in this chapter, then, provides an example of how the tools of a formal sequential analysis advanced in CA are shown to incorporate sensitivity to particular local contexts.

Finally, we would like to close this chapter by proposing that single-case analyses like the one presented here are important analytic exercises for discovering hitherto undescribed practices and gaining a renewed appreciation of what has been described so far. While our ultimate goal is to advance our understanding of the mutual bearing of linguistic resources and interactional practices in general, we believe that the understanding of such a general phenomenon can only be achieved by building it on careful examination of each situated occasion of language use in the participants' real-life social interaction. We believe so because without grounding the analysis in the details of situated language use, the proposed account of a general phenomenon will remain equivocal as to whether it in fact accounts for what people do in talk-in-interaction. This study, thus, is an attempt to ground our accounts of some grammatical features and interactional practices in a detailed examination of what the participants are demonstrably doing with them on a situated occasion and to gain a new appreciation of the significance of those phenomena we examined. We hope that our study will serve as an encouragement for others to closely examine the details of language use in actual social interaction and as a point of departure for them to contribute collaboratively to a further understanding of the complex linkages between language and social interaction.

Appendix: Abbreviations in the Interlinear Gloss

CP	Copula
FP	Final Particle
LK	Linker
N	Nominalizer
NEG	Negative
O	Object Particle
QT	Quotative Particle
SB	Subject Particle
TAG	Tag Question–Like Expression
TP	Topic Particle

NOTES

The authors have contributed equally to this essay. Different versions of this study were presented at the LSA Linguistic Institute (Albuquerque, New Mexico, July 1995) and at the International Pragmatics Conference (Mexico City, July 1996). We are grateful for the comments and encouragement that we received from the audiences at these meetings. We also thank Carleen Curley, Charles Goodwin, Marjorie H. Goodwin, Reiko Hayashi, and Hiroko Tanaka, who carefully read earlier versions of this chapter and provided us with invaluable comments and suggestions. Our special appreciation goes to the editors of this book, Cecilia E. Ford, Barbara A. Fox, and Sandra A. Thompson. Any remaining short-comings in this chapter are entirely our responsibility.

1. Major exceptions are the work of interactional sociolinguists, such as Schiffrin (1987) and Tannen (1989).

2. Examination of single fragments of interaction to explicate orderly practices of the participants in talk-in-interaction is found in Schegloff (1987, 1988b, 1990, 1992), C. Goodwin (1984, 1987), Jefferson (1980), and Ford and Fox (1996).

3. In this regard, this study is most informed by the work in CA, which has developed rigorous methods for analyzing situated actions of the participants in talk-in-interaction (e.g., Schegloff and Sacks 1973; Sacks, Schegloff, and Jefferson 1974; Goodwin 1981; Atkinson and Heritage 1984; Drew and Heritage 1992). Other related work that analyzes "language as social action" includes that of linguistic anthropologists (e.g., Hymes 1962; Gumperz 1982; Silverstein 1977; Ochs 1988; Hanks 1990; Duranti 1994) and of speech act theorists (e.g., Austin 1962; Searle 1969).

4. For a more extensive review of studies of storytelling in general, see M. H. Goodwin (1990: chap. 9) and Ochs (1997).

5. As anyone who has attempted to translate conversations from one language to another is fully aware, it is impossible to make translations correspond perfectly to the original. This becomes especially problematic when the structures of the two languages are as different as they are between Japanese and English. In this essay, we do our best to supply necessary information in the main text as well as in the notes to allow the reader to grasp approximately how the original Japanese utterances were produced. We also pro-vide interlinear glosses in order to indicate the temporal relationship of each linguistic item being produced (see appendix for the abbreviations used in the interlinear gloss). How-ever, such word-by-word glosses do not completely solve the problem, since it is controver-sial what grammatical classification and/or semantic meaning should be assigned to some of these items. See Moerman (1988, 1996) for a discussion of the methodological issues involved in the presentation and analysis of conversations in languages other than English for an English-speaking audience.

6. Though it is translated as an adjective in English, *hayatta* is a verb in Japanese.

7. Japanese does not have so-called pro-verbs such as the auxiliary *do* in English (e.g., "Did you finish your homework yet?," "Yes, I did."), and repeating the predicate in the preceding turn asking a question or asking for confirmation is recurrently em-ployed to accomplish the same sort of work that the English auxiliary *do* does. Here are some examples:

(i)

    T: *festiba** ima tomattemashita?* ((*name of car))
         Festiva now was.parked
         "Was (your) Festiva parked (outside when I came in) just now?"

H: *tomattemashita yo.*   ←
   was.parked   FP
   "Was parked."

(ii)

H: *Ikkai   no ne*
   1st.floor LK FP
   "The first floor's,"

K: *un un un*
   "Yeah, yeah, yeah"

H: *uriba   tte sonna hirokunai to   omou[shi sa:,]*
   sales.area QT that   large:NEG QT think   FP
   ". . . sales area is not that large, I don't think."

K: [*hirokuna*]*i.*   ←
                                          large:NEG
                                          "Not large."

8. A turn constructional unit (TCU) is a unit with which a speaker sets out to construct a turn. A TCU may consist of a word, a phrase, a clause, or a sentence depending on the context in which it is deployed. What is crucial about a TCU is that it can constitute a possibly complete turn by itself and that on its possible completion transition to a next speaker becomes relevant. See Sacks, Schegloff, and Jefferson (1974) for more detail.

9. We say "virtually" because the final syllable of the word *hayatt(a)* is realized almost as a glottal stop and Mari's gaze arrives at Yoko about the time Yoko produces this glottal stop.

10. Although there is a micropause (line 18) after the deployment of the initial TCU, the whole posture Yoko maintains at that juncture, that is, leaning forward to Mari, reaching her arm out to touch Mari's arm, and gazing at Mari, appears to make it transparent to her co-participant that she is continuing to talk after the completion of the initial unit. This body configuration, however, does not eliminate the possibility that her co-participants may orient to the completion of the initial unit (and the ensuing micropause) as a place where they can properly start talking. In fact, Mari's overlapping talk in line 20 is hearable as a response to the first unit in Yoko's turn, and it suggests that Mari might indeed orient to the completion of the initial unit of Yoko's turn (or the ensuing micropause) as a place for her to start up.

11. The presence of the particle *ne* does not help us judge the grammatical relation between the preceding NP and the verb. However, regarding these two elements as holding a subject–verb relation, which would mean "I existed," is excluded both because of the semantic incongruity in this context and because the verb *aru* cannot be used with an animate subject.

12. Clancy (1980) limits the analysis to third-person human referents and uses the term "coreferential" to mean "referring to characters already introduced into discourse."

13. In fact, because of this "default" nature of "zero," some researchers question the approaches that postulate "zero" in analyzing Japanese conversation (Matsumoto 1981; Okamoto 1985). Ono and Thompson (1997) also propose an alternative view of this issue based on the observation of the predicates that occur frequently in conversation.

14. Though Yoko's turn, *Un . burausu* ("Yeah, blouses"), is produced before Hana's preceding turn in line 25 comes to a completion, it appears to be responsive to Hana's turn rather than Mari's intervening turn in line 26. First, Yoko shifts her gaze toward Hana by the end of her turn in line 27. Further, Hana's utterance can be recognized as approaching its

completion at the point because the combination of the noun *jibun* ("self") and the linker *no* can be understood as a complete NP that means "yours." As Jefferson (1984) suggests, recipients can often recognize what the rest of the turn is going to be like even before it is actually produced and they may start responding at the point when such a recognition is achieved.

15. We will discuss this turn in more detail in the following subsection titled "Dealing with Differentiated Recipiency."

16. Note that in overlap with Yoko's telling-initiation utterance, Mari asserts in line 20 that the recent tight-fitting fashion was popular in the past by producing the high-pitched *onnaji yo ne:::* ("they are the same"). See the following section titled "From an Unaddressed Recipient to a Co-teller" for the analysis of this turn.

17. One might argue that Hana's utterance in line 25, *E! jibun no mono o?* ("Oh, your stuff?"), also displays her surprise and treats the prior turn as news. However, this utterance is designed as an understanding check of the unexpressed referent, whereas the news receipt token *ho:nto::* (line 26); *>hon<to:?* (line 29) ("Really?") is primarily designed to register "understanding" and "appreciation" of the newsworthiness of the telling. Thus, the news receipt token officially marks the recipient's treatment of the prior talk as having come to the crux of the telling.

18. This analysis is further supported by Mari's own utterance that occurs about half a minute later, which states that she threw away her old clothes when she moved and that there were some clothes among them that could have been worn now. The analysis of the premature timing and praising expression in her story appreciation *oiteattanda::: era:::i* ("[you]'ve held onto [them], impressive") is further enriched in the light of this context.

19. The following case extracted from a Japanese conversation also exhibits the same kind of structure. That is, the recipient joins in the assessment activity right after the intensifier is produced in a loud voice. The participants are talking about tokens of appreciations received at different weddings. Kayo just mentioned that she got a very expensive tray at a friend's wedding. Yuki knows this friend and her family quite well. Yuki joins in the assessment activity after the prosodically marked intensifier *MEccha* ("really").

Kayo: *.hh datte   sonnan   asoko   MEccha* [(   )]
            because you.know that.family really
        ".hh because you know that family really ( )"
Yuki: [*kane   kake*]*ru*
                           money spend
       [*mon na::.*]
       N   FP
       "spends money, yeah."

20. Akatsuka (1997) describes the combination of *yo* and *ne* as indicating a stronger agreement.

21. These explanations are provided for cases in which a postpredicate element is produced in a single intonation contour with the preceding predicate. These studies provide separate accounts for cases in which a postpredicate element is produced after a pause.

REFERENCES

Akatsuka, Noriko. 1997. On the co-construction of counterfactual reasoning. *Journal of Pragmatics* 28(6): 781–794.
Atkinson, J. Maxwell, and John Heritage (eds.). 1984. *Structures of Social Action: Studies in Conversation Analysis.* Cambridge: Cambridge University Press.

Austin, John L. 1962. *How to Do Things with Words*. Oxford: Oxford University Press.

Chafe, Wallace L. 1979. The flow of thought and the flow of language. In *Syntax and Semantics*, vol. 12: *Discourse and Syntax*, edited by T. Givón, 159–181. New York: Academic Press.

Chafe, Wallace L. 1980. The deployment of consciousness in the production of a narrative. In W. L. Chafe (ed.), *The Pear Stories: Cognitive, Cultural, and Linguistic Aspects of Narrative Production*, 9–50. Norwood, NJ: Ablex.

Chafe, Wallace L. 1987. Cognitive constraints on information flow. In R. Tomlin (ed.), *Coherence and Grounding in Discourse*, 21–51. Amsterdam: John Benjamins.

Chafe, Wallace L. 1993. *Discourse, Consciousness, and Time: The Flow and Displacement of Conscious Experience in Speaking and Writing*. Chicago: University of Chicago Press.

Clancy, Patricia M. 1980. Referential choice in English and Japanese narrative discourse. In W. L. Chafe (ed.), *The Pear Stories: Cognitive, Cultural, and Linguistic Aspects of Narrative Production*, 127–202. Norwood, NJ: Ablex.

Cook, Haruko M. 1992. Meaning of non-referential indexes: A case study of the Japanese sentence-final particle *ne*. *TEXT* 12(4): 507–539.

Drew, Paul, and John Heritage (eds.). 1992. *Talk at Work: Interaction in Institutional Settings*. Cambridge: Cambridge University Press.

Du Bois, John. 1980. Beyond definiteness: The trace of identity in discourse. In W. L. Chafe (ed.), *The Pear Stories: Cognitive, Cultural, and Linguistic Aspects of Narrative Production*, 202–274. Norwood, NJ: Ablex.

Du Bois, John. 1985. Competing motivations. In J. Haiman (ed.), *Iconicity in Syntax*, 343–365. Amsterdam: John Benjamins.

Du Bois, John. 1987. The discourse basis of ergativity. *Language* 63(4): 805–855.

Duranti, Alessandro. 1986. The audience as co-author. *TEXT* 6(3): 239–247.

Duranti, Alessandro. 1994. *From Grammar to Politics: Anthropology in a Western Samoan Village*. Berkeley and Los Angeles: University of California Press.

Ford, Cecilia E., and Barbara A. Fox. 1996. Interactional motivations for reference formulation: *He* had. *This* guy had, a beautiful, thirty-two O:lds. In B. Fox (ed.), *Studies in Anaphora*, 145–168. Amsterdam: John Benjamins.

Givón, Talmy 1979. *On Understanding Grammar*. New York: Academic Press.

Givón, Talmy (ed.). 1983. *Topic Continuity in Discourse: A Quantitative Cross-Language Study*. Amsterdam: John Benjamins.

Givón, Talmy. 1989. *Mind, Code, and Context: Essays in Pragmatics*. Hillsdale, NJ: Lawrence Erlbaum.

Goodwin, Charles. 1979. The interactive construction of a sentence in natural conversation. In G. Psathas (ed.), *Everyday Language: Studies in Ethnomethodology*, 97–121. New York: Irvington.

Goodwin, Charles. 1980. Restarts, pauses, and the achievement of mutual gaze at turn-beginning. *Sociological Inquiry* 50:272–302.

Goodwin, Charles. 1981. *Conversational Organization: Interactions Between Speakers and Hearers*. New York: Academic Press.

Goodwin, Charles. 1984. Notes on story structure and the organization of participation. In J. Maxwell Atkinson and John Heritage (eds.), *Structures of Social Action: Studies in Conversation Analysis*, 225–246. Cambridge: Cambridge University Press.

Goodwin, Charles. 1986. Audience diversity, participation and interpretation. *TEXT* 6(3): 283–316.

Goodwin, Charles. 1987. Unilateral departure. In Graham Button and John R. Lee (eds.), *Talk and Social Organisation*. Clevedon, England: Multilingual Matters.

Goodwin, Charles. 2000. Gesture, aphasia and interaction. In David McNeill (ed.), *Language and Gesture*, pp. 84–98. Cambridge: Cambridge University Press.

Goodwin, Charles. Forthcoming b. Pointing as situated practice. In Sotaro Kita (ed.), *Pointing: Where Language, Culture and Cognition Meet.* Cambridge: Cambridge University Press.

Goodwin, Charles, and Marjorie Harness Goodwin. 1987. Concurrent operations on talk: Notes on the interactive organization of assessments. *IPrA Papers in Pragmatics* 1(1): 1–54.

Goodwin, Charles, and Marjorie Harness Goodwin. 1992. Assessments and the construction of context. In A. Duranti and C. Goodwin (eds.), *Rethinking Context: Language as an Interactive Phenomenon*, 147–189. Cambridge: Cambridge University Press.

Goodwin, Marjorie Harness. 1980. Processes of mutual monitoring implicated in the production of description sequences. *Sociological Inquiry* 50:303–317.

Goodwin, Marjorie Harness 1990. *He-Said-She-Said.* Bloomington and Indianapolis: Indiana University Press.

Gumperz, John J. 1982. *Discourse Strategies.* Cambridge: Cambridge University Press.

Hanks, William F. 1990. *Referential Practice: Language and Lived Space Among the Maya.* Chicago: University of Chicago Press.

Hasunuma, Akiko. 1992. Nihongo no danwa maakaa "daroo" to "zya nai ka" no kinoo—kyootuu ninshiki kanki no yoohoo o tyuusin ni. (The function of the Japanese discourse markers "daroo" and "janaika" as an evocation of shared knowledge.) In Shigeko Imada, Tazuko Ueno, Michiko Sasaki, Taeko Nakamura and Suzuko Nishihara (eds.), *Koide kinen nihongo kyooiku kenkyuukai ronbunsyuu.* Tokyo: Nihongo Kyooiku Kenkyuukai.

Hayashi, Makoto, and Junko Mori. 1998. Co-construction in Japanese revisited: We do "finish each other's sentences." In S. Iwasaki (ed.), *Japanese Korean Linguistics*, vol. 7, pp. 77–93. Stanford: CSLI.

Heath, Christian. 1984. Talk and recipiency: Sequential organization in speech and body movement. In J. Maxwell Atkinson and John Heritage (eds.), *Structures of Social Action: Studies in Conversation Analysis*, 247–265. Cambridge: Cambridge University Press.

Heath, Christian. 1986. *Body Movement and Speech in Medical Interaction.* Cambridge: Cambridge University Press.

Heath, Christian. 1992. Gesture's discrete task: Multiple relevancies in visual conduct in the contextualization of language. In Peter Auer and Aldo di Luzio (eds.), *The Contextualization of Language*, 101–127. Amsterdam: John Benjamins.

Heritage, John. 1984a. *Garfinkel and Ethnomethodology.* Cambridge: Polity Press.

Heritage, John. 1984b. A change-of-state token and aspects of its sequential placement. In J. Maxwell Atkinson and John Heritage (eds.), *Structures of Social Action: Studies in Conversation Analysis*, 299–345. Cambridge: Cambridge University Press.

Hinds, J. 1982. *Ellipsis in Japanese.* Carbondale and Edmonton, Canada: Linguistic Research.

Hopper, Paul. 1979. Aspects and foregrounding in discourse. In *Syntax and Semantics*, vol. 12: *Discourse and Syntax*, edited by Talmy Givón, 213–241. New York: Academic Press.

Hopper, Paul J., and Sandra A. Thompson. 1980. Transitivity in grammar and discourse. *Language* 56:251–299.

Hymes, Dell H. 1962. The ethnography of speaking. In T. Gladwin and W. C. Sturtevant (eds.), *Anthropology and Human Behavior*, 13–53. Washington, DC: Anthropological Society of Washington.

Jefferson, Gail. 1972. Side sequences. In D. Sudnow (ed.), *Studies in Social Interaction*, pp. 294–338. New York: Free Press.

Jefferson, Gail. 1978. Sequential aspects of storytelling in conversation. In J. Schenkein (ed.), *Studies in the Organization of Conversational Interaction*, 219–248. New York: Academic Press.

Jefferson, Gail. 1980. On "trouble-premonitory" response to inquiry. *Sociological Inquiry* 50:153–185.

Jefferson, Gail. 1984. Notes on some orderliness of overlap onset. In V. D'urso and P. Leorardi (eds.), *Discourse Analysis and Natural Rhetoric*, 11–38. Padua, Italy: Cleup.

Kamio, Akio. 1994. Theory of territory of information. *Journal of Pragmatics* 21:67–100.

Kendon, Adam. 1972. Some relationships between body motion and speech. In A. W. Seigman and B. Pope (eds.), *Studies in Dyadic Communication*, 177–210. Elmsford, NY: Pergamon Press.

Kendon, Adam. 1977. *Studies in the Behavior of Social Interaction*. Lisse: Peter De Ridder Press.

Kendon, Adam. 1990. *Conducting Interaction: Patterns of Behavior in Focused Encounters*. Cambridge: Cambridge University Press.

LeBaron, Curtis D., and Jürgen Streeck. 1997. Built space and the interactional framing of experience during a murder investigation. *Human Studies* 20:1–25.

Lerner, Gene H. 1991. On the syntax of sentences-in-progress. *Language in Society* 20:441–458.

Lerner, Gene H. 1992. Assisted storytelling: Deploying shared knowledge as a practical matter. *Qualitative Sociology* 15(3): 247–271.

Lerner, Gene H. 1996. On the " semi-permeable" character of grammatical units in conversation: Conditional entry into the turn space of another speaker. In Elinor Ochs, Emanuel A. Schegloff, and Sandra A. Thompson (eds.), *Interaction and Grammar*, 238–276. Cambridge: Cambridge University Press.

Lerner, Gene H., and Tomoyo Takagi. 1999. On the place of linguistic resources in the organization of talk-in-interaction: A co-investigation of English and Japanese grammatical practices. *Journal of Pragmatics* 31:49–75.

Li, Charles N. (ed.). 1976. *Subject and Topic*. New York: Academic Press.

Mandlebaum, Jenny. 1987. Couples sharing stories. *Communication Quarterly* 35(2): 144–170.

Mandlebaum, Jenny. 1993. Assigning responsibility in conversational storytelling: The interactional construction of reality. *TEXT* 13(2): 247–266.

Matsumoto, Yoshiko. 1981. Noun phrase ellipsis in Japanese discourse. Ms.

Maynard, Senko K. 1993. *Discourse Modality*. Amsterdam: John Benjamins.

Moerman, Michael. 1988. *Talking Culture: Ethnography and Conversation Analysis*. Philadelphia: University of Pennsylvania Press.

Moerman, Michael. 1996. The field of analyzing foreign language conversations. *Journal of Pragmatics* 26:147–158.

Ochs, Elinor (ed.). 1988. *Culture and Language Development: Language Acquisition and Language Socialization in a Samoan Village*. Cambridge: Cambridge University Press.

Ochs, Elinor. 1997. Narrative. In T. A. van Dijk (ed.), *Discourse as Structure and Process*, pp. 185–207. London: Sage.

Ochs, Elinor, Emanuel A. Schegloff, and Sandra A. Thompson (eds.). 1996. *Interaction and Grammar*. Cambridge: Cambridge University Press.

Ochs, Elinor, and Carolyn Taylor. 1992. Family narrative as political activity. *Discourse and Society* 3(3): 301–340.

Ochs, Elinor, Carolyn Taylor, Dina Rudolph, and Ruth Smith. 1992. Story-telling as a theory-building activity. *Discourse Processes* 15(1): 37–72.

Okamoto, Shigeko. 1985. Ellipsis in Japanese discourse. Ph.D. diss., University of California, Berkeley.

Ono, Tsuyoshi, and Ryoko Suzuki. 1992. Word order variability in Japanese conversation: Motivation and grammaticization. *TEXT* 12(3): 429–445.

Ono, Tsuyoshi, and Sandra Thompson. 1997. Deconstructing "zero anaphora" in Japanese. *Berkeley Linguistics Society* 23. Proceedings of the Twenty-Third Annual Meeting of the Berkeley Linguistics Society, pp. 481–491.

Ono, Tsuyoshi, and Eri Yoshida. 1996. A study of co-construction in Japanese: We don't "finish each other's sentences." In N. Akatsuka, S. Iwasaki, and S. Strauss (eds.), *Japanese Korean Linguistics*, vol. 5. Stanford: CSLI.

Sacks, Harvey. 1974. An analysis of the course of a joke's telling in conversation. In R. Bauman and J. Sherzer (eds.), *Explorations in the Ethnography of Speaking*, pp. 337–353. Cambridge: Cambridge University Press.

Sacks, Harvey. 1978. Some technical considerations of a dirty joke. In J. Schenkein (ed.), *Studies in the Organization of Conversational Interaction*, pp. 249–269. New York: Academic Press.

Sacks, Harvey. 1992. *Lectures on Conversation*. Ed. Gail Jefferson. Oxford: Basil Blackwell Volumes 1 and 2.

Sacks, Harvey, and Emanuel A. Schegloff. 1975. Home position. Paper presented at the American Anthropological Association Meeting in San Francisco, December 6, 1975.

Sacks, Harvey, Emanuel A. Schegloff, and Gail Jefferson. 1974. A simplest systematics for the organization of turn-taking in conversation. *Language* 50(4): 696–735.

Schegloff, Emanuel A. 1982. Discourse as an interactional achievement: Some uses of "uh huh" and other things that come between sentences. In Deborah Tannen (ed.), *Georgetown University Roundtable on Language and Linguistics (GURT)*, 71–93. Washington, DC: Georgetown University Press.

Schegloff, Emanuel A. 1984. On some gestures' relation to talk. In J. Maxwell Atkinson and John Heritage (eds.), *Structures of Social Action: Studies in Conversation Analysis*, 266–296. Cambridge: Cambridge University Press.

Schegloff, Emanuel A. 1987. Analyzing single episodes of interaction: An exercise in conversation analysis. *Social Psychology Quarterly* 50(2): 101–114.

Schegloff, Emanuel A. 1988a. Discourse as an interactional achievement II: An exercise in conversation analysis. In Deborah Tannen (ed.), *Linguistics in Context: Connecting Observation and Understanding*, 135–158. (*Advances in Discourse Processes* 29.) Norwood, NJ: Ablex.

Schegloff, Emanuel A. 1988b. On an actual virtual servo-mechanism for guessing bad news: A single case conjecture. *Social Problems* 35(4): 442–457.

Schegloff, Emanuel A. 1990. On the organization of sequences as a source of "coherence" in talk-in-interaction. In B. Dorval (ed.), *Conversational Organization and Its Development*, 51–77. (*Advances in Discourse Processes* 38.) Norwood, NJ: Ablex.

Schegloff, Emanuel A. 1992. In another context. In A. Duranti and C. Goodwin (eds.), *Rethinking Context: Language as an Interactive Phenomenon*, pp. 191–227. Cambridge: Cambridge University Press.

Schegloff, Emanuel A. 1995. Parties and talking together: Two ways in which numbers are significant for talk-in-interaction. In P. ten Have and G. Psathas (eds.), *Situated Order: Studies in the Social Organization of Talk and Embodded Activities*, 31–42. Washington, DC: University Press of America.

Schegloff, Emanuel A. 1996a. Confirming allusions: Toward an empirical account of action. *American Journal of Sociology* 102(1): 161–216.

Schegloff, Emanuel A. 1996b. Turn organization: one intersection of grammar and interaction. In Elinor Ochs, Emanuel A. Schegloff, and Sandra A. Thompson (eds.), *Interaction and Grammar*, 52–133. Cambridge: Cambridge University Press.

Schegloff, Emanuel A. 1998. Body torque. *Social Research* 65(3): 535–596.

Schegloff, Emanuel A., Gail Jefferson, and Harvey Sacks. 1977. The preference for self-correction in the organization of repair in conversation. *Language* 53(2): 361–382.

Schegloff, Emanuel A., and Harvey Sacks. 1973. Opening up closings. *Semiotica* 7:289–327.

Schiffrin, Deborah. 1987. *Discourse Markers*. Cambridge: Cambridge University Press.

Searle, John R. 1969. *Speech Acts: An Essay in the Philosophy of Language*. Cambridge: Cambridge University Press.

Silverstein, Michael. 1977. Cultural prerequisites to grammatical analysis. In M. Saville-Troike (ed.), *Linguistics and Anthropology: Georgetown University Roundtable on Languages and Linguistics (GURI)*, 139–151. Washington, DC: Georgetown University Press.

Simon, M. E. 1989. An analysis of the postposing construction in Japanese. Ph.D. diss., University of Michigan.

Strauss, Susan, and Yumiko Kawanishi. 1996. Assessment strategies in Japanese, Korean, and American English. In N. Akatsuka, S. Iwasaki, and S. Strauss (eds.), *Japanese Korean Linguistics*, vol. 5, pp. 149–165. Stanford: CSLI.

Streeck, Jürgen. 1994. Gesture as communication II: The audience as co-author. *Research on Language and Social Interaction* 27(3): 239–267.

Streeck, Jürgen. 1996. How to do things with things. *Human Studies* 19:365–384.

Suzuki, Ryoko. 1990. The role of particles in Japanese gossip. *Berkeley Linguistics Society* 12:315–324. Proceedings of the Twelfth Annual Meeting of the Berkeley Linguistics Society.

Szatrowski, Polly. 1994. Discourse functions of the Japanese epistemic modal DESYOO. *Berkeley Linguistics Society* 16:532–546. Proceedings of the Sixteenth Annual Meeting of the Berkeley Linguistics Society.

Tannen, Deborah. 1987a. Repetition in conversation: Toward a poetic of talk. *Language* 63(3): 574–605.

Tannen, Deborah. 1987b. Repetition in conversation as spontaneous formulaicity. *TEXT* 7(3): 215–243.

Tannen, Deborah. 1989. *Talking Voices: Repetition, Dialogue, and Imagery in Conversational Discourse*. Cambridge: Cambridge University Press.

Tannen, Deborah. 1990. Gender differences in conversational coherence: Physical alignment and topical cohesion. In B. Dorval (ed.), *Conversational Organization and Its Development*, 167–206. (*Advances in Discourse Processes* 38.)Norwood, NJ: Ablex.

van Dijk, Teun, and Walter Kintsch. 1983. *Strategies of Discourse Comprehension*. New York: Academic Press.

6

Saying What Wasn't Said

Negative Observation as a Linguistic Resource for the Interactional Achievement of Performance Feedback

SALLY JACOBY & PATRICK GONZALES

Grammar, of course, is the model of closely ordered, routinely observable social activities.   Sacks, 1992

An increasing number of studies of language and social interaction have begun to explore grammar-in-use as an interactionally positioned structuration of language (e.g., Goodwin 1979; Schegloff 1979; Lerner 1991; Ford 1993; Heritage and Sorjonen 1994; Heritage and Roth 1995; Ford and Wagner, 1996; Ochs, Schegloff, and Thompson 1996; He and Tsoneva 1998). In a similar spirit, this chapter investigates the linguistic design, sequential placement, and interactional import of a class of turn format that we call "saying what wasn't said." In and through various linguistic formulations of this turn format, one participant states or alludes to something that another participant failed to say in the just-prior activity. More specifically, based on the particular context from which our data are drawn, saying what wasn't said is a turn type recurrently deployed by a research physics group's senior scientist to point out relevant communicative omissions in a just-rehearsed conference presentation. We argue that this kind of turn is deployed by the senior scientist and oriented to by presenters as a resource for accomplishing the interactionally complex but routine problem-solving activity of face-to-face critique and collaborative improvement of practice conference presentations.

While our analysis is drawn from a highly specific communication culture and activity context, we nevertheless believe that the phenomenon of saying what wasn't said is a more general one, potentially part of any cultural form of members' "indigenous assessment" (Jacoby 1997, 1998; Jacoby and McNamara 1999) of communication competence. Indigenous assessment of communication competence is any formal or informal activity in which at least one person (1) offers feedback to another person on a communication performance (whether written, oral, or multimodal), (2) articulates directly or indirectly what (in their view) is noticeably successful or problematic in that performance and why, and (3) recommends remedies (directly or indirectly) for whatever is deemed to be problematic. In addition, the practice of saying what wasn't said is of Conversation Analytic interest because it appears to be a context-specific type of the more general interactional practice of voicing a complaint through a negative observation (Schegloff 1988; Ford 1993; Jacoby 1998).

It was striking to us that of the forty instances of saying what wasn't said and three additional borderline instances in our data, forty-one (95%) were produced by the principal investigator of the research group.[1] While we realize that studying only one physics group precludes us from drawing any statistical inferences, we nevertheless feel that the highly skewed frequency distribution of this practice among these particular participants deserves comment, especially since other participants also routinely give feedback to presenters and rely on very different sorts of linguistic formulations when they occasionally communicate what they perceive to be problems of omission. We tentatively suggest in our analysis that saying what wasn't said may be especially suited to constructing authority in the potentially negotiable interactional processes of feedback-giving and problem-solving.

Our data come from a larger ethnographic and Conversation Analytic study of the discourse practices of a group of university research physicists—comprising graduate students, post-doctoral fellows, visiting scholars, and a senior investigator—all of whom specialize in various theoretical and experimental aspects of solid state, condensed matter physics, including spin glasses, random magnets, and superconductivity. Our investigations were primarily focused on the group's weekly meetings, when members came together to, among other activities, take care of business, update one another on ongoing research, solve research problems together, and rehearse upcoming conference presentations.[2]

The routine meeting activity most relevant to this discussion is the rehearsing of upcoming presentations in the weeks prior to professional conferences (Ochs and Jacoby 1997; Jacoby 1998; Jacoby and McNamara 1999).[3] Group members working on presentations for conferences typically came to particular weekly meetings prepared to run through their presentations under simulated performance conditions, including talking the rehearsal audience through a set of overhead transparencies projected onto a screen and trying to finish within a strictly observed ten-minute time limit. In the six months of primary data collection, fifteen different rehearsals were held during seven different group meetings, six in preparation for a magnetism conference in October 1990, nine in preparation for the 1991 annual March Meeting of the American Physical Society, perhaps the largest general meeting of research physicists in the world (ca. 4,500 papers). All rehearsals were videotaped, then transcribed using notation conventions long established in the research tradition of CA (e.g., Ochs, Schegloff, and Thompson 1996: 461–465).

Each rehearsal is organized by the participants as having two main phases: (1) an uninterrupted timed runthrough of the presentation, in which the participants co-construct a make-believe conference session; and, immediately following the runthrough, (2) feedback delivered to the presenter by various group members, but especially by the principal investigator (Ron),[4] the only participant who routinely takes copious notes during each runthrough performance (Jacoby 1998).

Post-runthrough feedback is essentially comprised of a series of "comment sequences," defined as:

> a stretch of talk and interaction, with a recognizable opening and closing, during which some particular problem in the just-rehearsed conference presentation is raised or alluded to, the status and remedy of which may be negotiated until verbal or nonverbal agreement is achieved by the participants, before moving on to the next comment or the next activity. (Jacoby 1997)

In other words, the raising of a comment (in whatever form) launches an interactional sequence within which participants pursue agreement as to both the existence and scope of a candidate problem in the conference presentation and the acceptability of a candidate remedy to fix that problem. Once adequate displays of agreement regarding both the problem and the remedy are perceived by the participants, the comment sequence is quickly brought to a close and a next comment sequence (or the shutdown of the entire rehearsal) is begun by the same or a next comment giver.[5]

A preliminary analysis of post-runthrough comment sequences (Jacoby 1998: 361–456) proposes that comment sequences are a context-specific type of "expanded," "extended," or "big package" sequence (cf. Jefferson and Shenkein 1977; Jefferson and Lee 1981; Jefferson 1988; Schegloff 1990; Psathas 1992; Sacks 1992, vol. 2: 354–359; Schegloff forthcoming: 76–92). Starting with the base adjacency pair of complaint–remedy, Jacoby demonstrates that although there is great sequential variation across individual comment sequences in terms of how a sequence is launched, how a problem is raised, how a remedy is proposed, how a sequence is terminated, what can contingently happen if participants display disagreement with the formulation of a problem and/or its remedy, and what is made explicit or left implicit, there nevertheless seem to be recurrently recognizable subsequences of actions and an underlying topical and interactional agenda to which participants are routinely oriented (cf. Schegloff 1986). The proposed underlying organization of any comment sequence is the following:

1. the sequence is launched
2. a complaint is raised
3. a response to the complaint is produced
4. agreement is pursued regarding the complaint
5. a remedy is suggested
6. a response to the remedy is produced
7. agreement is pursued regarding the remedy
8. the sequence is shut down

(cf. Jacoby 1998:376)

Moreover, participants orient to the achievement of mutual displays of agreement (e.g., exchanges of "Okay," head nodding, etc.) regarding both the complaint and its remedy as closing-implicative for any current comment sequence (cf. Beach 1993, 1995). Notably in post-runthrough comment sequences, and in contrast to a classic complaint–remedy adjacency pair sequence, both the raising of a complaint and suggesting its remedy are produced by the same participant: the comment giver.

On one level, post-runthrough feedback appears to be a relentless face-threatening barrage of explicit and implicit criticisms as well as explicit or implicit recommendations for improvement, requiring the presenter to acknowledge his/her lapses of competence and to display a willingness to invest time and effort in redesigning the presentation. On another level, however, post-runthrough feedback is a collaboratively achieved, supportive problem-solving activity through which colleagues and mentors help one another shape co-authored public reports to maximum effect, with the generally tacit (and sometimes overtly articulated) understanding that they are saving one another from potential performance disasters, public humiliation, and damage to their individual and collective professional reputations (Jacoby 1998).

Our examination of the linguistic structure, sequential placement, and interactional import of saying what wasn't said, as a class of comment-giving practices deployed in post-runthrough comment sequences, links two traditionally unrelated discussions in the research literature: linguistic and literary discussions of reported speech, on the one hand, and Conversation Analytic discussions of complaints and negative observations, on the other.

At first glance, turns designed as saying what wasn't said appear to be related to the much discussed linguistic and literary topic of reported speech in general and of indirect reported speech in particular, the latter of which has been identified by, among other things, the presence of a reporting verb in the past tense (e.g., *said, told, suggested*) followed by the use of the complementizer *that* to introduce the report of another's words or thoughts in a subordinate clause (Partee 1973; Munro 1982; Greenbaum and Quirk, 1990).[6] In terms of their linguistic structure, turns designed as saying what wasn't said seem specifically to be variant forms of grammatically or lexically negated reported speech, as in the following examples drawn from our corpus[7]:

(a) RO LAB 10-24-90

    Ron: An- you a:lso did not say that the samples came from uh:: (.) Kling.

(b) RO LAB 2-21-91

    Ron: You never o:nce sai:d (.) why that was important.

(c) RO LAB 10-17-90

    Ron: Secondly you never define alpha.

(d) RO LAB 10-24-90

    Ron: You forgot to define what field cooled was.

(e) RO LAB 10-24-90

Ron: You never <u>stat</u>ed that that was field cooled.

(f) RO LAB 10-25-90

Ron: You didn't say relaxation of <u>wha</u>:t.

(g) RO LAB 3-14-91

Ron: But never <u>o</u>nce did you say that there was a compe<u>ti</u>tion

(h) RO LAB 10-17-90

Ron: (Yeah but) you didn't say that.

(i) RO LAB 3-14-91

Ron: You had- you didn't say that <u>o</u>nce in the talk.

Unlike this brief list of examples, the vast transdisciplinary research literature on written and verbal manifestations of reported speech in various languages and dialects overwhelmingly focuses on non-negated grammatical forms (e.g., Jakobson 1971; Bateson 1972; Partee 1973; Grice 1975, 1978; Goffman 1981; Munro 1982; Sternberg 1982a 1982b, 1991; Davidson 1984; Haiman and Thompson 1984; Quirk et al. 1985; Comrie 1986; Coulmas 1986; Li 1986; Levinson 1987; Tannen 1989; Clark and Gerrig 1990; Mayes 1990; Yule Mathis, and HopKins 1992; Lucy 1993; Halliday 1994; Waugh 1995; Holt 1996). Moreover, the focus in this literature has been on structures employed by speakers to report the fictional or real speech and thoughts of themselves or others that allegedly were (or could have been) uttered or thought in some other event, at some other place and/or other time than the "now" of the current conversation or narrative telling.

In contrast, three main design features distinguish saying what wasn't said utterances in our corpus from bona fide reported speech utterances:[8] (1) all of the utterances we have collected are grammatically negated (e.g., *did not say, didn't define, never stated, haven't talked about*) or otherwise lexically formulated to indicate that something was not said (e.g., *forgot to say, missed an opportunity, lack of references, left out*); (2) overwhelmingly, the utterances are addressed to a co-present participant (the presenter) and therefore are typically formulated with the pronoun *you*;[9] and (3) the utterances refer in various ways to a co-present participant's prior talk (or lack thereof) in the current ongoing activity. The forms of saying what wasn't said that we discuss in detail here thus seem structurally related to reported speech but in fact represent a type of metacommunicative assertion in which one interlocutor tells another co-present interlocutor what that other interlocutor recently failed to say (or otherwise communicate) in the activity in which they are currently engaged.[10]

Saying what wasn't said is perhaps more closely related to Schegloff's (1988) single-case analysis of how an asserted negative observation—"you didn't get an ice cream sandwich"—is interactionally oriented to by interlocutors as a complaint, warranted by the failure to perform an apparently previously promised action. That seemingly nonevaluative utterances, such as statements and descriptions, can be heard as complaints, accusations, or blamings in particular interactional environments is well attested in the Conversation Analytic literature (e.g., Atkinson and Drew 1979; Drew 1978, 1992; Clayman and Whalen 1988/1989; Schegloff 1988, 1988/1989; Beach 1990/1991, 1996). It has also been noted that various forms of complaints make remedies a relevant next topic to take up in unfolding talk (Schegloff and Sacks 1973).

Three main features, however, distinguish the practice of saying what wasn't said from most Conversation Analytic discussions of negative observations and complaints: (1) the hearable complaint is a failure to perform an action of a particular kind, namely, an action of communication; (2) given the future-oriented "dry-run" nature of the rehearsal activity, the linguistic design of the complaint not only implies how the omitted communicational action could have been remedied in the rehearsal performance in the recent past, it also simultaneously implies how the omission ought to be remedied in an actually anticipated, improved version of the discourse performance (whether a next rehearsal or the upcoming conference); and (3) the hearable complaint is not about the failure to perform a previously promised action but a failure to perform a rhetorically expected or rhetorically effective communicative action, whose absence becomes observable only in hindsight as a conference presentation is practiced for indigenous assessment by co-present others.

Thus, the general phenomenon of saying what wasn't said is a context-specific kind of negative observation complaint. Like all negative observations, saying what wasn't said turns are designed and sequentially deployed to be heard as complaints about observably relevant "noticeable absences" (Schegloff 1988; Sacks 1992, vol. 1:190, 293–294; vol. 2:35–36). In the context of a simulated conference presentation, many different kinds of criticisms and complaints are put forward in post-runthrough feedback by various participants, in a wide range of linguistic formats, targeting a wide range of perceived communicative problems (Jacoby 1998; Jacoby and McNamara 1999). Most of these criticisms target problematic aspects of what was communicated or how something was communicated. Saying what wasn't said complaints, in contrast, locate problems in what was never communicated. On the one hand, by asserting an ability to perceive absences of communicative actions in a practice version of a future discourse performance, the senior scientist displays an expertise not claimed by the other comment-giving participants in the physics group. On the other hand, by formulating these perceptions as negative observations, he makes hearable the relevance of particular absent actions to a professionally competent, rhetorically effective, and audience-friendly conference presentation. Paradoxically, then, a particular act of criticism—saying what is lacking in a discourse performance— is simultaneously hearable as a corrective appeal to the moral and rhetorical ethos of scientific practice (cf. Prelli 1989). This communicational complexity aligns with Goffman's (1981) theoretical assertion that participants who offer evaluative feedback following someone's speech performance assume the complex interactional roles of judges of competence, delineators of failure, proposers of remedies, and agents of social control, since they articulate and orient not only to constructs of allegedly normative discursive practice and effective performance but also to the larger social purposes for which the performance is being prepared in the first place (ibid.:197–232).[11]

Analysis of comment sequence organization in the physicists' post-runthrough feedback has shown that hearably critical comments can be and are formulated in a wide variety of linguistic and actional formats, for example, as corrections, assessments, remedy suggestions, directives, questions, descriptions—and with varying degrees of directness and mitigation. Saying what wasn't said turns are interactionally interesting in this regard because while they mitigate the act of criticism by being linguistically designed as descriptive assertions (rather than as explicitly negative assessments), they are also interactionally unmitigated due to their linguistically blunt epistemic certainty. This apparently contradictory encoding of indirectness and directness is achieved in the practice of saying what wasn't said despite specifiable variation in linguistic choices, sequential organization, and resulting interactional consequences for the unfolding of particular comment sequences in post-runthrough feedback. It is to the details of some of this linguistic, sequential, and interactional variety that we now turn.

General Similarities and Differences among Saying What Wasn't Said Turns in Sequential Context

To appreciate the variational details in Ron's design and sequential deployment of saying what wasn't said turns, we first overview a number of general features common to the corpus as a whole plus several features that grossly distinguish among them. Consider, for example, the following four instances (in sequential context) of saying what wasn't said:

(1) RO LAB 10-24-90

	Ron:	S:- you've <u>go:t</u> to do that.
		[(1.2)
		[((*Miguel leans against window wall; nods head.*))
→	Ron:	An- you [a:lso did not say that
		[((*Marsha looks at Ron.*))
		[the samples came from uh:: (.) Kling.
		[((*drops knuckles on table; shakes head*))
		(.)
	Miguel:	Ye:s.
		(1.0)
	Ron:	[Nuhhunhhh!=
		[((*smiles; turns hand and head to right*))
	Gary:	=It should be right [on the [front page.
		[((*Ron looks toward Gary.*))
	Marsha:	[That's-
		[That's a ma:jor. That's first page.
		[((*nodding*))

(2) RO LAB 2-21-91

> Gar?: It's true:. [It's true. It's very true.
> Ron: [heh heh. .hh Okay. .h O:ver and o:ver again you stress the issue of
>   baseline.
>   (0.4)
> → Ron: You never o:nce sai:d (.) why that was important.
>   (2.0)
> Ron: If you don't have a baseline, (0.2) is that important?,
>   (0.8)
> Ron: >I mean< I: didn't even know what you meant by: not having a baseline.

(3) RO LAB 10-17-90

> Ron: But now (.) I have (ju) one more question. You said that uh: (.) how do we
>   see do- (0.2) you say therefore we see domains in the zero <fie:ld cooled (.)
>   case> for T greater than T field coo:led [of (H)
> Miguel: [Yeah that's because the uh
>   (0.4) mts that's because (0.4) here (.) the: uh:m (1.0) the field cooled proce-
>   dure you only see domains. You never [see:
> → Ron: [(Yeah but) you didn't say that.

(4) RO LAB 10-24-90

> Ron: You're missing the point.
>   (0.4)
> Ron: (Y- y-) you're almost you're almost there.
>   (0.4)
> Ron: What's happening when you cool in a field i:s that you set up domains.
>   (0.4)
> Ron: uh: (0.2) and they're pi:nned by the random field.
>   [(0.3)
>   [((Miguel nods.))
> Ron: And therefore the correlation length (.) cannot gro:w. (0.2) beyond that
>   size.=
> Miguel: = [Yes. °I know.°=
>   [((nodding))
> → Ron: = But you didn't [say that.
>   [((bows head to Miguel, smiles))

The highlighted utterances in the above four segments share some common features. First, in each instance, the main comment giver (Ron) indicates that the
presenter failed to articulate particular words or accomplish a specific rhetorical
action in the just-completed rehearsal runthrough. In particular, in Segments (1),
(3), and (4) Ron either specifies precisely (Segment (1)) or anaphorically refers
(Segments (3) and (4)) to words and/or ideas that were not communicated in the
rehearsal runthrough. In Segment (2), Ron points out that the presenter failed to
include a necessary rhetorical move in a part of the scientific argument: explaining
the importance of a key concept ("baseline").[12] Second, as mentioned earlier, each
of the preceding targeted utterances is constructed through a grammatically ne-

gated reported speech frame addressed to the presenter (e.g., "you didn't say . . ."), which focuses attention on those aspects of the oral presentation that the comment giver deems are missing.

Third, on the surface, each highlighted utterance is a simple assertion that some communicative action did not take place, that some words were not spoken or point made. However, within its particular sequential environment the negated polarity of each targeted utterance also implies that what is being pointed out as missing should have been there; that what is missing should not be missing in the future. Thus, though grammatically designed as a simple assertion (as a counterfactual, to be more precise), each utterance is potentially hearable as a criticism of the performance and a recommendation for remedying that criticism. As noted by Schegloff (1988) and Sacks (1992, vol. 1:190, 293–294; vol. 2:35–36), the making of a negative observation announces not only that its speaker has perceived an absence but also, more important, that its absence is a relevant omission. In particular situations, the relevance of an omission may not be readily recoverable or even fully articulated. However, embedded within an activity entirely devoted to the critiquing of a just-rehearsed conference talk—an activity to which all participants to the interaction are jointly oriented—the relevance of a negative observation to both the physicists and the ongoing interaction is provided by and understood to be intricately connected to the activity itself. Thus, while more generally a negative observation is hearable as a complaint regarding a relevantly noticeable failure to perform some anticipated action (Schegloff 1988), it is within the institutional context of a conference talk rehearsal that a negative observation is hearable as a criticism of a presenter's prior discourse performance and as an implied recommendation for remedying that criticism.

Fourth, while negative observations provide one possible way of delivering criticism, this particular way is accomplished without the use of explicit negatively loaded assessment terms. Therefore, though not specifically formulated in the language of negative assessment, negative observations nevertheless imply, in the context of the rehearsal activity, that something is problematic in the presentation because something is missing, not because something that was done was done badly. This suggests that saying what wasn't said may be one way to design a complaint about a presenter's performance such that the criticism appears less directed to what a presenter did incompetently and more oriented (in the complaint turn itself) to improving the performance for the future audience.[13] Still, as mentioned earlier, all the instances of saying what wasn't said are epistemically unmitigated—that is, the negative observation assertions are linguistically packaged with full certainty. There are no qualifying expressions that mitigate either the matrix sentence as a whole (e.g., 'It seems that . . .') or the verb phrase (e.g., 'you may not have said, . . .'). This interactionally schizoid design in saying what wasn't said turns, however, may be just what allows Ron to display his orientation to the complex institutional task in which he is engaged as experienced old hand, mentor, quality controller, and co-author: to deliver honest but constructive feedback in the interest of both whipping presentations into shape and counteracting or mitigating the face-threatening nature and potentially unpleasant interactional repercussions inherent in criticizing another's actions (Goffman 1981).[14]

However, while all of the negative observations in Segments (1) through (4) are similar in that they may be heard as criticisms, complaints, and remedies, further examination reveals that they are nevertheless differentiated in their linguistic design and sequential placement in a comment sequence. Linguistically, the vast majority of negative observations in the talk of the physicists are of the form *you didn't say*, with several instances that add adverbial emphasis to the assertion of omission (e.g., *you never define, never once did you say*). Other saying what wasn't said turns are formulated with communicative verbs other than say, such as *define, use, left out*, or *explain*. In addition, several saying what wasn't said negative observations are linguistically formatted with semantically negative lexical constructions, such as *forgot to say, missed an opportunity*, or *lack of references*, rather than with a grammatically negated verb. Certain lexical forms of negation allow Ron to frame the omission as the result of an assumed oversight on the presenter's part rather than as an unaccounted for absence. Specifically, to declare that the presenter *forgot to say* something or *missed an opportunity* presupposes in the presenter a competent knowledge of what to say. In contrast, simply asserting that the presenter didn't say something does not display a clear stance as to whether the presenter is being given the benefit of the doubt that s/he at least has knowledge of what is declared as having been absent from the runthrough.

Sequentially, some negative observations are deployed to launch comment sequences, especially when Ron is referring to his written notes taken during the rehearsal runthrough (Segments (1) and (2)). By placing a negative observation at or near the beginning of a comment sequence, Ron proffers the next criticism topic of ongoing post-runthrough feedback. Other negative observations, however, are contingently raised well into a comment sequence already in progress (Segments (3) and (4)). These in-progress comment sequences typically had been originally launched with a complaint on Ron's part of being confused or misled by unsatisfactory explanations and interpretations of matters of physics in the presenter's scientific argument.[15] Such comment sequences are not launched by a saying what wasn't said assertion; that is, they start out as complaints about the logic, clarity, or consistency of what was said, with or without bona fide reported speech utterances. At some point in these comment sequences, in pursuit of clearing up confusion and misleading elements, discussion between Ron and the presenter will veer into clarifying their understanding of matters of physics, and when pressed in some way by Ron's questions or explanations about physics in the course of this clarifying discussion, the presenter will claim to know or understand some aspect of the physics. As soon the presenter makes such a claim, however, Ron will swiftly counter with a negative observation that asserts that what the presenter has just claimed to know in the current discussion was nevertheless not said in the presentation. Through such contingently raised negative observations of saying what wasn't said, Ron thus interactionally undercuts a presenter's claim to be a competent physicist with a counter-claim of incompetence as a presenter of physics. By abruptly shifting the focus of discussion away from clarifying matters of physics to assessing matters of performance, Ron redirects the comment sequence back to the original complaint that launched it. The implication of such contingently raised negative observations is that had the presenter said what was only now contingently discovered to be known but not to have been said, the original problem of confusion about what was said would likely not have arisen in the first place.

Another general difference observable among Segments (1) through (4) is that different negative observation turn formats and sequential environments provide corrective suggestions at various levels of explicitness for remedying the alleged omission. By formatting the complaint turn in a full-blown indirect negated reported speech frame, for instance, Ron can point out that a presenter has failed to include particular words or phrases in a presentation and, through the design of the turn, incorporate, in the negative observation itself, a version of the desired words or phrases (e.g., (1): "An- you a:lso did not say that the samples came from uh:: (.) Kling.") On other occasions, Ron may merely assert that the presenter failed to perform a particular rhetorical action (e.g., Segment (2): "You never o:nce sai:d (.) why that was important."), leaving it entirely to the presenter to find the appropriate wording to accomplish that missing action in a revised version of the presentation. When negative observations are contingently raised well into a comment sequence that began with complaints of confusion, Ron routinely points out, through anaphoric reference (mostly *that* but less frequently *this* and *it*),[16] that something wasn't said (e.g., "You didn't say that"). Ron may thus contingently make use of immediately prior talk in the clarifying discussion, whether produced by the presenter (Segment (3)) or himself (Segment (4)), to indicate a just-now discovered omission in the rehearsal runthrough. Sequence types such as Segments (3) and (4) potentially provide the presenter with an anaphoric pathway through the local feedback and clarifying discussion discourse to recover the words or gist that ought to be included in an improved future performance.

Segments (1) through (4) are generally representative of negative observations in the rehearsal feedback of the physicists. In the remainder of this essay, we examine the implications of detailed variations in linguistic and sequential structure for the joint achievement of face-to-face delivery of criticism. In addition, we will explore the ways in which Ron makes use of these formulations of saying what wasn't said as a resource for socializing less experienced group members into particular norms of speaking, arguing, and performing, framed as being relevant for success in a physicist's professional communication culture.

Type 1: Launching a Comment Sequence with *Saying What Wasn't Said*

As the previous discussion has intimated, the placement of a saying what wasn't said negative observation in a rehearsal comment sequence has consequences not only for how the negative observation is grammatically formulated but also for the shaping of the comment sequence itself. As in Segments (1) and (2), in the following segments of interaction a comment sequence is launched with a negative observation placed at or very near the beginning of a new comment sequence. In this position, a negative observation immediately or very quickly focuses attention on some topically new, until now never raised, problem in the presentation, which Ron has now chosen to comment on, once a prior comment sequence has been brought to a close. Launching a comment sequence with a negative observation is therefore a way for Ron to take the earliest opportunity in a new comment sequence both to set the topic for the next bit of feedback and to place the perceived problem on the table for other participants' inspection:

(5) RO LAB 10-24-90

      ((*after a comment sequence focused on the confusion caused by the presenter having divided two related pieces of information on two separate viewgraphs*))

→   Ron: ((*Ron looking at notes*)) um (0.4) Th- there's something that y- (.) that you forgo:t [to say and it('s) <u>terribly</u> important

              [((*looks up at projection screen*)) and that is that the AT line is- is calculated for an <u>I</u>sing spin glass.
              (0.8)

    Ron: You only used the word <u>Hei</u>senberg at the <u>very</u> end of the ta:lk. °(You started) talking [about it.

              [((*Gary looks away from Ron, toward projection.*))
              (0.4)

    Ron: You've <u>got</u> to say that AT line is calculated for an (0.2) <u>I</u>sing spin glass.
              (.)

    Ron: And that the Gabay-Tou<u>lou</u>se is for a Heisenberg (0.2) spin glass.

(6) RO LAB 10-17-90

      ((*after a comment sequence (prefaced with "first of all") for on criticizing the presenter's use of lowercase letters for technical abbreviation that should be represented in uppercase letters*))

→   Ron: <u>S</u>econdly you never define alpha.
              (0.8)

    Miguel: <u>Ye</u>s: I say- >oh< <u>a</u>lpha:,
              [(1.0)
              [((*Miguel nods.*))

    Ron: You define(d) alpha <u>p</u>rime.

    Miguel: [>Well.<
              [((*nodding*))
              (0.3)

    Ron: Alpha('s a) speci- specific exponent for what.

    Miguel: The random exchange (uh:)

    Ron: (°Okay°) sa:y that.
              (0.5)

    Ron: Or ju- just write it down on the viewgraph or something.
              (.)

    Ron: But it has to: you have to define it.

(7) RO LAB 10-24-90

      ((*after a comment sequence focused on the presenter's overall time management and specific apportioning of time to important parts of the talk*))

    Ron: ((*reading from notes; low volume*)) u:m (0.4) The: (0.8) the decrease?, (2.4) °the decrease in temperature with the same° > Oh.< For <u>f</u>ield cooled. .hh You

→   forgot cooled. .hh You forgot to define what field cooled was.
        [(1.0)
        [(((*Gary looking off into distance*))
Gary: Oh:oh:o[kay.
→ Ron: [You- you never <u>stated</u> that that was field cooled.<What you said was
        .hh that you decreased in zero field, you turned on the field and increased you
        defined that as a zero field (0.2) cooled state, and then you said and then you
        (0.2)
Gary: Come back in a [field,
Ron: [Come back in a field, then just- just <u>say</u> it. <u>That</u>'s the field
        cooled.=
Gary: =°Okay.°
Ron: That's the definition of field cooled.

(8) RO LAB 10-25-90

        ((*after a comment sequence focused on the presenter's incomplete discussion of
        a mathematical derivative expression displayed on a viewgraph*))
Ron: Now in your: description of the experimental protoco:l (0.8) you said <u>both</u>
        relaxations are exactly the same. That was when you adjusted T W and T W
        prime?,
Miguel: That's right.
        (.)
→ Ron: You didn't say relaxation of <u>wha</u>:t.
        ((0.8)
        (((*Miguel still sorting through viewgraphs*))
Miguel: >We:ll< I was talking about (.) thermorem [nant
Ron: [No: you weren't. That had- that
        was a lo::ng time before.
        (.)
Ron: Just <u>say</u> it again.

(9) RO LAB 3-14-91

        ((*after a comment sequence focused on clarifications the presenter should in-
        clude regarding experimental results in her own and others' work*))
Ron: And then: uh: also: uh:: I think it's important
?:   (   )
Ron: that you: uh:: (.) you did in: in-introduce the neo<u>dy</u>mium, and make thee
        argument that <u>tha</u>t (0.4) ap<u>par</u>ently tha- (.) gives some evidence of mov-
→   ing: on site. .hh But <u>never</u> <u>once</u> did you say that there was a compe<u>ti</u>tion
        (0.4) between the sin[gle ion (   )
Marsha: [That was e- >you know you know< <u>ho</u>:nestly: <u>hon</u>-
        estly I- I get into that very clearly with the hollandite and I got very
        distr(h)acted b(h)y ou(h)r hh
        [our noi:se=
Ron: [Okay,
Ron: =but=
Marsha: =okay?, .hh But I can <u>do</u>: that okay. Aright.

Segments (1), (2), and (5) through (9) represent a subset of twenty-seven instances of saying what wasn't said in our corpus, which play a role in launching individual comment sequences, once a prior comment sequence or prior activity phase has been brought to closure. Essentially, either any new comment sequence can begin right away with a formulation of the complaint regarding the runthrough performance or the complaint can be slightly delayed after particular types of prefatory actions (cf. Jacoby 1998:379–431). A similar sequential variation was found with regard to the launching of comment sequences with complaints of saying what wasn't said negative observations. Specifically, the negative observations made by Ron in Segments (1), (5), (6), and (7) are deployed in sequence-initial and turn-initial position, meaning that the saying what wasn't said utterance is both the first turn constructional unit (TCU) and the first possibly complete turn in the new comment sequence.[17] In Segments (1) and (6), for instance, the negative observation is the first statement made, following brief phrases ("Secondly," "And . . . also") that introduce the upcoming comment as "another" comment on Ron's list of notes. In Segment (5), the negative observation is begun straightaway ("The- there's something that y- (.) that you forgo:t to say"), but the grammatical and ideational completion of the criticism ("and that is that the AT line is- is calculated for an Ising spin glass.") is slightly delayed until after an intervening clause unit is inserted to stress the importance of the omission ("and it('s) terribly important"). In Segment (7), a first version of the negative observation ("You forgot to define what field cooled was.") is formulated as a failure to perform a rhetorical action (to define) but then is subsequently redone as a failure to communicate particular words ("You- you never stated that that was field cooled.").[18]

In contrast, the negative observations in Segments (2), (8), and (9) are produced after an initial TCU, whether within the first possibly complete turn of the comment sequence, as in Segments (2) and (9), or in a subsequent turn, after the presenter has responded to a preface leading up to a complaint, as in Segment (8). In Segments (2) and (9), the negative observation in each case ((2): "You never o:nce sai:d (.) why that was important."; (9): "But never once did you say that there was a competition (0.4) between the single ion . . .") emerges as a description of what the presenter did not communicate in retrospective contrast to what Ron has just acknowledged was communicated in the rehearsal runthrough ((2): "O:ver and o:ver again you stress the issue of baseline."; (9): "you did in: in- introduce the neodymium, and make thee argument that tha:t (0.4) apparently tha- (.) gives some evidence of moving: on site."). In Segment (2), Ron's articulation of the criticism— here a missing rhetorical action ("you never o:nce sai:d (.) why that was important.")—follows a prior TCU, delivered as a prior turn at talk: "O:ver and o:ver again you stress the issue of baseline." In Segment (8), the negative observation ("You didn't say relaxation of wha:t.") follows the presenter's confirmation ("That's right.") of Ron's try-marked utterance[19] ("Now in your . . . you adjusted TW and TW prime?,"), which itself follows Ron's bona fide reported speech formulation of what the presenter said in the rehearsal runthrough ("Now in your: description of the experimental protoco:l (0.8) you said both relaxations are exactly the same.").

Strikingly, the TCUs that precede the negative observations in Segments (2), (8), and (9) are all instances of Ron revoicing what the presenter said during the rehearsal runthrough, that is, saying what *was* said through bona fide reported speech constructions. These reports of things said in the practice performance range in the degree to which they purport to quote the prior talk: some are constructed as more direct forms of reported speech (Segment (8): "you said <u>bo</u>th relaxations are exactly the same"), while others are constructed as more indirect forms (Segments (2): "O:ver and o:ver again you stress the issue of <u>b</u>aseline"; and (9): "you did introduce the neo<u>d</u>ymium, and make thee argument that . . ."). Prefacing a negative observation with a report of what was said in the rehearsal runthrough serves to link the criticism that follows to the precise location in the presentation that triggered the comment giver's noticing of an absence (when the runthrough was in progress). Thus, much like background statements that news interviewers use to frame subsequent questions (e.g., Heritage 1985; Clayman 1988; Greatbatch 1988; Heritage and Greatbatch 1991; Clayman 1992; Greatbatch 1992), non-negated reported speech statements in the physicists' rehearsal feedback provide a warrant for the comment that follows, making some specific prior talk in the run-through phase of the rehearsal activity relevant for the current action in the feed-back phase. A bona fide reported speech preface at the beginning of a comment sequence thus projects that the feedback comment is yet to come, but it also cre-ates a sequentially relevant place for the articulation of the comment, which will be raised some time after the conclusion of a runthrough, depending on the num-ber of comment givers participating, the number of comments delivered, and the order in which comments are raised. There is evidence that the deployment of bona fide reported speech to project some further talk is a common practice in the talk repertoire of these physicists (Gonzales 1996). Furthermore, such prefatory actions serve to cast and recast an immediately past activity for here-and-now purposes that are ultimately aimed toward some future objective (Bakhtin 1981; Goodwin and Goodwin 1992; Schegloff 1972, 1991b; Ochs and Jacoby 1997).[20]

Segment (7) is an instance in which the bona fide reported speech produced by Ron in contrast with the saying what wasn't said comment follows, rather than prefaces, the negative observation. Specifically, the reported speech component ("<What you said was .hh that . . . and then you") follows quick on the heels of the second version of the negative observation ("you never <u>sta</u>ted that that was field cooled.") which launches this particular comment sequence. If we compare the grammatical structures and sequential placement of non-negated reported speech utterances in comment sequence launchings, then, it appears that reported speech utterances that preface a saying what wasn't said comment are canonical reported speech constructions, while those that follow a saying what wasn't said comment are (or can be) constructed as wh-cleft reported speech utterances.

Regardless of whether a Type 1 saying what wasn't said utterance is sequence and turn initial (in the first turn at talk) or delivered as a subsequent TCU (in the first or in a slightly later turn at talk), the point of a newly launched comment se-quence (i.e., the complaint, the raising of a problem) becomes clear as soon as the negative observation is formulated. In the case of comment sequences that begin straightaway with a negative observation, the entire comment sequence is launched with the complaint. In the case of comment sequences launched with prefaces that sequentially delay the complaint component, the negative observations are linguistically designed and sequentially positioned to say what wasn't said in contrast to what was said in the rehearsal runthrough. Comment givers may achieve this contrast by launching the comment sequence (in the first TCU of the first turn) with a non-negated bona fide reported speech frame before giving voice to saying what wasn't said, that is, by prefacing their pointing out what wasn't said with a report of what was said. It was also mentioned earlier that the contrast between what was and what wasn't said can be sequentially organized in reverse: that is, that the comment sequence is launched with a saying what wasn't said complaint that is then followed by a contrastive bona fide reported speech utterance. That sequentially juxtaposed grammatical oppositions can be effectively deployed in the delivery of criticism certainly seems to support Schegloff's (1996) position that grammatical oppositions can be a relevant resource for constituting social activity (see also Ford 1994).

Type 2: Saying What Wasn't Said as a Contingently Raised Negative Observation

The second major type of saying what wasn't said negative observation in the feedback that followed physicists' rehearsal runthroughs of upcoming conference presentations includes those complaints of omission that are discovered to be relevant in the course of a comment sequence that was originally launched as a complaint about confusion, misleading statements, or insufficient clarity in what was said in the practice presentation. In the corpus for this study, thirteen of the forty clear instances of saying what wasn't said are of this second type, and all are grammatically designed with anaphoric pronouns (e.g., "You didn't say that") linking to prior utterances for retrieval of what wasn't said. In such cases, Ron and the presenter momentarily leave off directly discussing the runthrough performance in favor of collaboratively attempting to sort out the complained-about confusion or vagueness in the physics content of a conference talk, much as they do in nonrehearsal activities, such as informal research progress discussions (cf. Gonzales 1996). These clarification discussions effectively lead to major sequence expansions of the original complaint–remedy comment sequence, which often are jointly produced as a series of questions posed by Ron for the presenter to answer. One recurring sequential variation of contingently raised negative observations is the following:

Ron: [asks a clarification question about matters of physics]
Presenter: [produces an explanation that both clarifies and displays detailed
            knowledge of relevant matters of physics]
Ron: [points out that what presenter has just now said s/he failed to say in
            the rehearsal runthrough]

In other words, despite Ron successfully getting the presenter during post-runthrough feedback to flesh out matters of physics that were explained less successfully during the runthrough, Ron reasserts the complaint with which he launched the current comment sequence by anaphorically pointing to what the presenter just now said as what was not said earlier. What the presenter just said as an act of clarification is thus reframed by Ron as the remedy for solving the communicative problem the current comment sequence has been addressing all along.

If the presenter displays difficulty in answering Ron's questions, Ron may answer his own question himself, occasionally even launching into brief physics mini-lectures in order to demonstrate to the presenter a more adequate clarification of the matters of physics in question. Displaying that they hear these extended explanations by Ron as potentially assuming an incomplete knowledge of physics on the part of the recipient, presenters often defensively respond by claiming to already know what Ron has just elucidated in detail. This interactional environment leads to the second recurring kind of sequence variation of contingently raised, saying what wasn't said negative observations:

> Ron: [clarifies a point of physics in an extended turn]
> Presenter: [claims prior knowledge of the explanation]
> Ron: [points out that what presenter has just now claimed to know s/he failed to say in the rehearsal runthrough]

In other words, despite Ron getting the presenter during post-runthrough feedback to claim adequate knowledge of matters of physics that were inadequately explained during the runthrough, Ron reasserts the complaint with which he launched the current comment sequence by anaphorically pointing to what he just now clarified more adequately as what the presenter didn't say earlier. Ron's own just-said act of clarification is thus reframed by Ron as the remedy for solving the communicative problem the current comment sequence has been addressing all along. Whether it is of the first kind or second kind of sequential variation, however, Ron displays a quick ability to contingently seize upon something just now said in the clarification discussion and point out to the presenter that it wasn't said in the rehearsal runthrough performance but by implication should have been and ought to be said in an improved version of the presentation.

Segments (3) and (4) represent both these interactional environments for saying what wasn't said negative observations. We noted earlier that while contingently raised negative observations are linguistically tied through anaphoric reference (e.g., *that*) to some prior talk in the comment sequence in progress, such referential pro-terms in Ron's complaints of omission can thus be sequentially deployed to refer to different kinds of antecedent talk: something that the presenter or Ron just said (Segments (3) and (4), respectively). We now look more closely at how these two variational forms of contingently raised saying what wasn't said are achieved.

Segments (3) and (10) are both instances of Ron making use of a presenter's just-prior talk in a clarification discussion during feedback to point out contingently that something wasn't said in the presentation runthrough. In Segment (3), for instance, Ron appears to be starting a comment sequence with a bona fide reported speech preface (as in Segment (8)) ("You said that uh: (.) how do we see do- (0.2) you say therefore we see domains in the zero <fie:ld cooled (.) case> for T greater than T field cooled"). But before Ron can contrast his report of what was said with a complaint about what wasn't said, the presenter (Miguel) overlaps the tail end of the reported speech component to produce an account of why he said what Ron reports him to have said ("Yeah that's because the uh (0.4) mts that's because (0.4) here (.) the: uh:m (1.0) the field cooled procedure you only see domains."). Through his hasty response, Miguel displays that he has interpreted Ron's in-progress report of what was said in the presentation as the focal complaint of the newly launched comment sequence. It is important to note that the content of Miguel's explanation of "why" is not an explanation oriented to "matters of rhetoric"—that is, rhetorical organization, technical constraints, graphic design, or audience impact of the presentation (Ochs and Jacoby 1997). Instead, his explanation is oriented to "matters of physics"—that is, the physical processes under investigation as he understands them. In the context of apparently having heard or anticipated in Ron's reporting assertion a challenge to his physical argument, Miguel pre-emptively brings forth his account as supportive evidence for the claim he made during the runthrough.[21]

At this point in Segment (3), just as Miguel begins a second TCU ("You never see:"), apparently in prosecution of furthering his explanation, Ron counters with his own interruptive overlap to anaphorically point out that what Miguel was just saying now was not said in the runthrough ("(Yeah but) you didn't say that."). The particular formulation of Ron's contingently raised negative observation has two parts. The first TCU is a pro-forma agreement token ("(Yeah)"), which displays that Ron is not taking issue with the matters of physics as such, and thus it also serves to block Miguel's pre-emptive interpretive trajectory that Ron's complaint was oriented to an insufficiently supported physical claim. Pressing on with his possibly contrastive second TCU, however ("(but) you didn't say that."), Ron asserts that his complaint is that Miguel failed to say in the runthrough what he just said in the comment sequence

There is no way to know, of course, whether Ron was planning to make this particular negative observation the complaint of focus all along or he considered Miguel's response to the prefatory statement in the comment sequence opening to be correct in terms of whatever comment of focus Ron had originally been aiming for.[22] What is discernible is Ron's sequentially contingent exploitation of a presenter's display of expertise in physics as the discursive anchor, through anaphoric reference, for the raising of a saying what wasn't said negative observation, a complaint of omission, regarding the recently rehearsed conference presentation.

Segment (10) is another, but sequentially variant, example of Ron making use of a presenter's clarification of a point of physics during the feedback phase to contingently raise a negative observation about the practice presentation in the runthrough phase of the rehearsal activity:

(10) RO LAB 10-25-90

> ((*from a comment sequence that began as a complaint about Miguel's under-specification of the term "relaxation" in a statement made during the runthrough*))
> ((*Complying with Ron's request, Miguel displays viewgraph of his experimental protocol.*))

Ron: Okay. What I want you to say i:s (.) that uh: what you <u>said</u> was (.) both re-
              laxations are exactly the same.<Relaxation of <u>wha</u>t.
Miguel: Well that's why I'm I'm
              [(basically:) (.) T R M.
              [((*turns and points to screen*))
              (0.8)
Miguel: But I can sta:te
              [(0.3)
              [((*Miguel nods.*))
Ron: (It) says modified T R M. Where does (it) talk about [relaxation of T R M.
                                                         [((*Miguel cocks head to*
              side.))
              (1.0)
Miguel: >Okay.<
              (.)
Miguel: Uh::m (.) most- uh-
              [actually I didn't <u>wri</u>:te (0.4) everything I
              [((*turns briefly and points to screen*))
              was (.) <u>s:ay</u>ing o[:r-
→ Ron: [>No that's okay. But you didn't <u>say</u> it.< Even orally.
              (.)
Ron: A:n I (u-) what you said was confusing.
Miguel: °Okay.°

Unlike Segment (3), Segment (10) comes much later in the comment sequence of which it is a part, indeed in that part of the extended comment sequence that appears to be the first mention of a candidate remedy to the prior complaint of not giving enough clarifying detail when explaining matters of physics. This is evident in Ron's first turn. Not having gotten an adequate response from Miguel until this point regarding the specification of which kind of relaxation was involved, Ron at first decides to redirect the comment sequence by formulating a specific wording remedy ("Okay. What I want you to say i:s (.) that uh:"). However, Ron soon abandons his remedy trajectory to redo another version of the original complaint, first by producing a bona fide reported speech preface[23] about what Miguel did say in the presentation ("what you <u>said</u> was (.) both relaxations are exactly the same."), then by quickly asking a clarification question about what was said ("Relaxation of <u>what</u>.").

Miguel first begins an answer with what seems to be the start of a justification ("Well that's why I'm I'm (basically)"), but he abandons that tack in favor of offering a direct answer to Ron's question ("T R <u>M</u>."), while pointing to the relevant part of the projection.[24] When Miguel's answer receives no uptake from Ron, Miguel displays that he can perceive a problem in the way he may have communicated the point at issue by beginning to offer his own rewording remedy ("But I can sta:te"). Before Miguel articulates any actual candidate wording, however, Ron finally responds to Miguel's prior turn ("T R <u>M</u>.") and pointing gesture, first by giving voice to a particular phrase visible on the viewgraph ("(It) says modified T R M."), then by pointing out, through a question, the absence of the term they have been discussing all along ("Where does (it) talk about relaxation of T R M.")

and perhaps by implication the discrepancy between what Miguel has said ("[re-laxation of] TRM") and what the viewgraph says ("modified TRM"). Again, Miguel at first responds to what Ron has raised by (apparently) starting an explanation of matters of physics ("Uh::m (.) most- uh"), but he abandons that trajectory in fa-vor of an admission that the transparency may not reflect all the information he conveyed in the ("o:r-"[ally?]) spoken part of his presentation ("a- actually I didn't wri:te (0.4) everything I was (.) s:aying o:r-").

Displaying that he has grasped where Miguel is going with his response before it is fully articulated, Ron intervenes pre-emptively with a recognitional overlap (Jefferson 1983), successfully heading off the completion of what he has already interpreted as Miguel's in-progress claim to have inadvertently failed to specify on the viewgraph what he has just now demonstrated he knows (i.e., that the under-specified relaxation in question is relaxation of TRM). Ron does this first by coun-tering Miguel's framing of the viewgraph as faulty in terms of its representation of relevant matters of physics (">No that's okay."), then by finding fault with Miguel's localization of the problem to the written display alone. It is this latter action that Ron accomplishes through a contrastively prefaced anaphoric and contingently raised saying what wasn't said TCU (But you didn't say it) and a rapidly appended post–possible completion positioned adverbial extension ("< Even orally."). Through this seemingly minor grammatical amendment of his possibly complete saying what wasn't said TCU Ron communicates (as an afterthought) a great deal: (1) that the discursive scope of his complaint of omission is relevant beyond the viewgraph they have been discussing, (2) that he has interpreted Miguel's last syl-lable in the prior turn, and (3) that he is going on record as disagreeing with Miguel's limiting of the problem to the visual rather than oral modes of the presentation.[25]

Another structural difference between Segment (3) and Segment (10) is that the antecedent of the pro-term in the contingently raised negative observation TCU in Segment (10) (i.e., "it") is not recoverable from the presenter's just-prior turn at talk, which was the case for the antecedent of "that" in the saying what wasn't said turn component in Segment (3). Instead, the antecedent to which "it" refers in Segment (10) is located earlier in the sequence: Miguel's answer ("T R M.") to Ron's first clarification question ("Relaxation of what."). That additional exchanges of clarification and disagreement have intervened in Segment (10) between a ques-tion and its answer may explain why Ron follows his complaint of what wasn't said with an explicit negative assessment of what was said ("A:n I (u-) what you said was confusing."). This additional complaint, not in the form of a negative obser-vation, widens the scope of what is being taken to be problematic and appears to be understood by Miguel as "the final word" on this particular comment, since Miguel immediately produces a sequence-closing implicative display of agreement ("°Okay.°").

Segments (4) and (11) are similar to Segments (3) and (10) in that they, too, are instances of contingently raised, saying what wasn't said negative observations. Like Segments (3) and (10), Segments (4) and (11) emerge in the course of an in-progress comment sequence whose topical focus is a particular problem of clarity or confusion regarding matters of physics. Unlike Segments (3) and (10), however, the negative observations in Segments (4) and (11) anaphorically refer to Ron's just-prior talk in the clarification discussion rather than to that of the presenter. In general, this sequential structure unfolds when Ron clarifies a point of physics, then, in response to the presenter's intervening claim to already know what Ron has just clarified, Ron counters the presenter's claim of knowledge with an anaphorically designed saying what wasn't said complaint. Thus, like the first type of contingently raised negative observation (exemplified in Segments (3) and (10)), this second type of saying what wasn't said abruptly moves the discussion away from matters of physics back to matters of communicative performance. It differs from the first type, however, in that Ron makes use of his own recent contribution to the clarification discussion as the discursive anchor for the negative observation, rather than the presenter's contribution. What Ron first offers as clarifying information is thus retrospectively reframed as the remedy for the contingently raised complaint of omission that follows.

To illustrate this, let us now look more closely at the details of turn design and sequential structure in Segments (4) and (11). Segment (4) begins at a point in a larger comment sequence where Ron displays his rejection of the presenter's prior attempts to clarify a matter of physics. First, Ron negatively assesses what Miguel has been saying until now as "missing the point." When no response is forthcoming from Miguel, Ron seems to interpret that silence as a display of some kind of interactional trouble on Miguel's part, for instead of asserting what in his view is the point, Ron downgrades his critical stance by recharacterizing Miguel's contributions to the discussion in a more positive light, as "almost there."[26] Although Miguel again withholds a response at this possible completion point (of Ron's second turn and downgraded complaint), Ron nevertheless proceeds to lay out the matters of physics that (apparently) he was trying to get Miguel to sort out before this segment began.

Specifically, Ron now proceeds to clarify the point of physics under discussion: that is, what happens to the domain structure of a diluted antiferromagnet when it is cooled in a magnetic field.[27] He does this by producing three narratively linked assertions, each designed intonationally and syntactically as a possibly complete sentential TCU. The first of these three turns—"What's happening when you cool in a field i:s that you set up domains."—asserts a cause-and-effect relationship between cooling while a magnetic field is on and the creation of domains. The second of the three assertions—"and they're pi:nned by the random field.—qualitatively describes the frozen dynamics of the domains that result under these physical conditions.[28] The third assertion—"And therefore the correlation length (.) cannot gro:w (0.2) beyond that size."—completes this interpretive argument of what happens to the domains from a quantitative point of view.

As Ron's three-part argument emerges, Miguel is already displaying an emergent stance that Ron's explanation is unnecessary. Following the first assertion, Miguel withholds a response just as he did after Ron's prior two turns.[29] Following the second explanatory assertion, however, Miguel nods in agreement (and/or to display recognition of the information), then latches a two-part verbal response onto Ron's third assertion. Miguel's first spoken response ("=Yes.") upgrades his continuing nonverbal display of alignment with an uneqivocal verbal display of agreement. This minimal response is then itself upgraded in interactional strength (though downgraded in volume) when Miguel produces, immediately after "=Yes.", an equally unequivocal (though acoustically muted) verbal display indicating that what Ron has told him is not news ("°I know.°"). Miguel thus seems to be building a case for his own competence (in terms of expert knowledge of physics) even as Ron's explanation is emerging. This trajectory of Miguel's nonverbal and verbal responses seems designed dynamically to cast Ron's emerging explanation as wrongly assuming that Miguel may not fully understand the matters of physics in question.[30]

Just as quickly as Miguel responds to Ron's third assertion, Ron subsequently retorts with a latched and contingently raised negative observation about Miguel's runthrough performance ("=But you didn't say that."). While this negative observation does not convey disagreement with Miguel's claim of prior knowledge, its turn-initial contrastive conjunction ("But") and saying what wasn't said turn design frame the complaint of omission as important and relevant even if Miguel already knows this information. In building his complaint turn in just this way at just this moment in the talk, Ron displays that it is Miguel's failure to appreciate the relevance of what he knows to the communicative task of performing this particular conference presentation that is the first-order issue, not a possible failure (on Ron's part) to appreciate the adequacy of Miguel's knowledge of physics. Ron's contingently raised negative observation thus asserts the necessity of having spelled out the details of particular physical processes, because it displays Ron's orientation to the original complaint of confusion that led to the clarifying discussion of matters of physics in the first place. By redirecting the focus of discussion away from sorting out theoretical matters of physics and assessing Miguel's competence as a knowledgeable physicist, Ron puts the assessment of Miguel's competence as a performer of a future public scientific report front and center. The hearable implication is that Miguel's argument would have been clearer and thus his performance more competent had he spelled out in his rehearsal runthrough the elucidation of matters of physics that Ron just now spelled out in the rehearsal feedback. While Miguel has just now claimed to know these clarified matters of physics, he seems to be ignoring the fact that it was Ron's negatively critical assessment of Miguel's earlier attempts to explicate the physics that led to Ron taking over the job of clarification in the first place. Like all forms of contingently raised saying what wasn't said complaints then, the complaint turn in Segment (4) also reasserts the larger practical activity in which this local discussion of matters of physics was originally embedded: the institutional tasks of collaborative post-runthrough feedback and improvement of a co-authored (with Ron and others) upcoming conference presentation.

Segment (4) also shows (as Segment (10) displayed) that the referential antecedent of the pro-term in a contingently raised, saying what wasn't said negative observation (in Segment (4), *that*) need not be found in an immediately prior turn, as is the case in Segment (3). Instead, the pro-term *that* in Ron's negative observation in Segment (4) is discursively tied either to the last of Ron's three assertions or to the entire three-part point he made before Miguel displayed agreement and claimed prior knowledge. Thus, to understand the recommendation for improvement of the presentation implied in Ron's negative observation, a presenter (here

Miguel) might potentially have to recover the antecedent to the pronoun over a larger stretch of prior discourse.[31]

Segment (11) is another instance of a contingently raised, saying what wasn't said negative observation whose pro-term anaphorically refers to prior talk produced by Ron in the clarification discussion. Like the negative observation in Segment (4), saying what wasn't said in Segment (11) emerges in the course of a larger comment sequence focused on a problem of clarity and confusion regarding what was said in a rehearsed version of a conference presentation:

(11) RO LAB RO LAB 3-14-91

> ((*from a comment sequence that began as a complaint about the misleading nature of spending too much time on a less relevant matter of physics*))

Ron: Um it seems to me that what you want to conve:y (.) i:s the fact that there's a Coulomb interaction,

Marsha: mmhm=

Ron: =betwee:n the carriers.

Marsha: mmhm,

Ron: which (0.2) minimizes thee energy <by: uh:m uh*::>requi:ring or- (0.2) by fo:rcing

Marsha: mmhm

Ron: the carriers to be equidistant.

Marsha: °mmhm°

(.)

Marsha: Yeah.=

→ Ron: =tha:t's- well you don't sa:y that.

(0.2)

→ Ron: You had- you didn't say that once in the talk.

Much as he did at the start of Segment (4), Ron begins Segment (11) with a turn that frames as inadequate the attempts of the presenter (Marsha) until now to clarify the more relevant aspects of her physical argument. However, while in Segment (4) Ron characterized Miguel's attempts as "missing the point" and "almost there," here Ron's negative assessment of what Marsha has said is observably more indirect and mitigated. Specifically, Ron prefaces his corrective explanation of matters of physics with both a cautiously phrased admission of personal interpretive perspective ("it seems to me") and a footing shift (Goffman 1981) through which he claims to have analyzed and understood what Marsha has been trying to say ("that what you want to conve:y (.) i:s the fact that . . .") despite her unsuccessful attempts to say it.[32]

Another difference between Segment (4) and Segment (11) is the manner in which the presenter in each case displays recipiency of Ron's in-progress extended clarification sequence. In Segment (4), Miguel at first withheld, then nonverbally aligned with Ron's emerging explanation, before finally responding with a verbal display of both agreement and prior knowledge. In Segment (11), as Ron produces his extended clarification of the physical system dynamics uncovered by Marsha's experiments (i.e., that Marsha's findings exhibit a Coulomb interaction[33]), Marsha punctuates Ron's emerging explanation with a series of verbally responsive yet interactionally noncommittal continuers (i.e., *mmhm*).[34] Only when no response from Ron is forthcoming following her fourth *mmhm* does Marsha redo her response as a more overt lexical display of alignment, specifically of understanding, of agreement with, and of knowing all along what Ron has just clarified. Marsha's revision of her fourth response also shows she now recognizes Ron's multi-unit sentential turn to be possibly complete.[35]

For his part, it seems that Ron may have analyzed the pause after Marsha's fourth mmhm and her revised response as indicative of a problem in comprehension or of pre-disagreement, for he latches what appears to be the beginning of still another extension of his point (=<u>tha</u>:t's-). However, Ron immediately abandons this new trajectory to respond to what Marsha's verbal response has intimated, and he does this by producing the first of two contingently raised, saying what wasn't said negative observations. This first negative observation ("well you don't sa:y that."), though delayed by one syllable, does seem oriented to countering the claim of understanding and prior knowledge conveyed by Marsha's verbal display of agreement. As he did in Segment (4) with the conjunction but, Ron prefaces this negative observation (in Segment (11)) with a contrastive, qualifying conjunction ("well") before reasserting the importance of what he just said for Marsha's performance competence ("you don't sa:y that."), even if she does understand, agree, and already know what he has just clarified. The formulation of this complaint as a complaint of omission in the presentation seems also to have the effect of silencing Marsha, who, though a turn space is left for her, does not respond. Apparently orienting to this silence as a possible display of pre-disagreement, Ron self-selects to say something that looks like the start of a comment about what Marsha did say ("you had-"). However, as he did in his prior turn, Ron abandons the beginning of this turn trajectory in favor of a new tack—a second version of the negative observation ("you didn't say that <u>o</u>nce in the talk.").[36]

Finally, as we saw in Segments (10) and (4), the antecedent of the pro-terms in each of the two versions of the negative observation in Segment (11) (that) is not the last thing Marsha said in her prior turn (i.e., to Yeah), but the entire extended clarification turn at talk that Ron produced step-by-step to unpack the details of what he is proposing is a clearer, more explicit interpretation of Marsha's results than any argument Marsha has thus far offered. Saying what wasn't said in this sequential environment thus also possibly calls into question Marsha's claim to already know what Ron took the trouble to explain in detail.

An interesting sequential variant of the kind of contingently raised negative observation represented by Segments (4) and (11) is Segment (12), the only instance of this variant in our corpus. Like Segments (4) and (11), Ron refers pronominally to his own clarifying explanation of matters of physics as that which wasn't said by the presenter, but he does not do so in response to a presenter's claim of prior knowledge of what has just now been clarified:

(12) RO LAB 02-28-91

    ((*from a comment sequence that began as a complaint about confusion regarding the relationship between a series of viewgraph displays and the issues of "waiting time" and "decay" in Daniel's experiment*))

((*Ron is inspecting one of the viewgraph projections.*))

Ron: Now I- I- what I want you to say is I'm gonna <u>moti</u>-eh I want you to <u>moti</u>vate
        people.
        (.)

Ron: You can say that the <u>pre</u>vious viewgraph gave you a vie:w of the magnetization
        decay, (.) an' now I wanna look at <u>ano</u>ther factor that really specifie:s (.) the

→   multi- you did not say thi:s. (0.3) the multi-valley nature of the spin glass state.

In Segment (12), Ron is at a point in the larger comment sequence where he is
proposing a particular concrete performance remedy for sorting out some of the
underspecification that appears to be at the heart of the presenter's confusing
discussion of his experimental results. Ron's tack is to voice for the presenter a
version of the actual wording of the proposed remedy, going back and forth between footings in which he constructs himself as Ron recommending to the presenter in the here-and-now what to say and as the presenter (Daniel) performing the suggested wording in a next version of the presentation. As can be seen
in Segment (12), while speaking in the voice of the presenter Ron cuts off the
"presenter's" utterance in progress to parenthetically note in his own voice that
Daniel failed to say in the runthrough what Ron is now saying. Having produced
this negative observation, Ron then resumes his interrupted utterance and the
footing stance of the presenter. Rather than responding to a presenter's claim to
know what is being specified in greater detail, Ron seems through this sequential placement of a negative observation to be discovering and emphasizing, while
impersonating the presenter as a clearer, more effective communicator, that what
he is saying now was not said by the presenter in the runthrough rehearsal. The
parenthetical placement of saying what wasn't said in the midst of an extended
and impersonated clarification also appears to motivate the selection of pronoun
this over *that*, since the antecedent of the pronominal reference in this case would
be not only Ron's prior talk but also the continuation of his talk that followed
the negative observation.

Contingently raised saying what wasn't said negative observations, as represented by Segments (3), (4), (10), (11), and (12), all share the identifying sequential features of emerging in the course of an already in-progress comment sequence
originally launched with a complaint of confusion or lack of clarity regarding what
a presenter said in his/her runthrough of a conference presentation about matters
of physics. In addition, saying what wasn't said in Segments (3), (4), (10), and (11)
is deployed as Ron's countering response to a presenter's claim of prior understanding and knowledge regarding the matters of physics in question. Saying what wasn't
said in Segment (12) is deployed by Ron as a self-interruption and footing switch,
to underscore that what is being said now as an impersonated version of a remedy
for clearing up confusion is something that wasn't said in the rehearsal performance.
Contingently raised negative observations thus refocus talk away from what had
become a clarfying discussion of matters of physics and back to the business of post-
runthrough feedback: jointly assessing the practice version of an upcoming conference presentation and jointly proposing modifications in the interest of improving the presentation for reception by the actual audience the presenter will face in
the future. Thus, in pointing out that what was just said (or is now being said) in

the clarifying discussion was not said in the rehearsal runthrough (whether what was just said was said by the presenter or Ron himself), Ron retrospectively problematizes prior talk (cf. Gonzales 1996) and reframes the current clarifying discussion about matters of physics as being relevant to the larger activity in which the participants are engaged: the critiquing and remedying of practice conference presentations.

Discussion

Discursive Scope of Saying What Wasn't Said

Whether a negative observation launches a comment sequence or is contingently raised in the course of a comment sequence, we have argued that both main major types of saying what wasn't said are intricately built and variously dependent upon some prior talk. Emerging in the feedback phase of a larger conference presentation rehearsal activity, this general kind of negative observation is a linguistic resource deployed by Ron, the principal research investigator, to communicate what he considers to have been relevant omissions in the presentation runthrough. However, saying what wasn't said negative observations that launch comment sequences directly link the complaint of omission in the feedback phase to prior talk in the runthrough phase of the rehearsal activity, whereas contingently raised saying what wasn't said negative observations directly link the complaint of omission in the feedback phase to prior talk (and sometimes, as in the case of Segment (12), also to talk about to emerge) in the current feedback phase. Contingently raised negative observations in this context-specific activity are thus indirectly linked to prior talk in the runthrough phase through pro-term anaphoric reference in their linguistic design. Figure 6.1 schematically illustrates this sequential and referential difference. The discursive scope of a negative observation deployed to launch a comment sequence thus encompasses the saying what wasn't said turn and the rehearsal runthrough, while the discursive scope of a contingently raised negative observation encompasses the saying what wasn't said turn, the prior talk in the feedback that comprises the antecedent to the pronominal referent in the saying what wasn't turn, and the rehearsal runthrough.

We have also pointed out that a candidate remedy for the complaint of omission hearable in a negative observation—the topical relevance of which is created by the action of complaining—is either embedded in the negative observation turn itself or recoverable through pronominal reference to prior (or later) talk. However, we also note that the implied directives hearable or recoverable through the linguistic design of a negative observation are in fact often explicitly articulated in some form or other soon after a negative observation turn is produced. Examples from our data include:

from Segment (1):

    Gary: =It should be right on the front page.

**Sequence-Initial
Negative Observation**

**Contingently-Raised
Negative Observation**

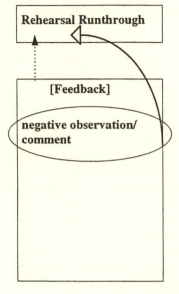
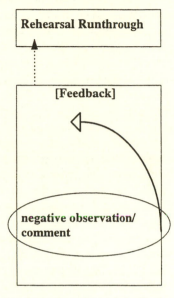

Figure 6.1.   Discursive scope of negative observations in rehearsal runthrough feedback.

from Segment (5):

> Ron: You've <u>got</u> to say that AT line is calculated for an (0.2) <u>I</u>sing spin glass.

from Segment (6):

> Ron: (°Okay°, sa:y that. (0.5) Or- ju- just write it down on the viewgraph or some-
> thing. . . . you have to define it.

from Segment (7):

> Ron: Just <u>say</u> it.

from Segment (8):

> Ron: Just <u>say</u> it again.

Nevertheless, we note that in Segment (9), after providing an account of why she failed to include a particular discussion that Ron had pointed out was missing in the runthrough, Marsha displays agreement with a recommendation for improvement (*I can <u>do</u>: that okay. Aright*) that Ron in fact never uttered . This instance provides important evidence that negative observations are hearable both as complaints of omission and as remedies for the alleged omission, whether or not an explicit directive follows a negative observation.[37]

Negative Observations, Saying What Wasn't Said,
and Relevant Next Actions

Our analysis suggests that the delivery of a negative observation appears to make particular types of next actions relevant. First, saying what wasn't said, as one way that Ron can both criticize and suggest a remedy for improving a conference presentation, invites agreement or alignment by its recipient (Schegloff 1988; Pomerantz 1984a). For instance, in Segment (7) Gary displays a change in his understanding of and alignment with Ron's observation ("Oh:oh:okay.") that he failed to define the term "field cooled."[38] Gary's response further displays that he understands why the definition of the term should be included in a future version of his presentation and thus that he agrees with the remedy proposed by Ron's negative observation. Of course, recipients of negative observations can alternatively respond by displaying disagreement with the complaint itself, as in Segment (6) where Miguel at first counters ("Yes: I say-") Ron's claim that he failed to "define alpha."

Second, as a kind of report, negative observations can sequentially implicate a recipient either to interactionally register his/her informativeness or to claim prior knowledge (Heritage 1984; Schegloff 1988), especially in the case of contingently raised negative observations. For instance, as was discussed earlier in Segment (4) (but which is also true of Segments (3), (10), and (11)), Miguel essentially denies the newsworthiness of Ron's explanation of matters of physics by claiming to "know" it already, thus undermining a potential warrant for Ron's complaint. However, Ron counters with a complaint of omission that in turn undermines Miguel's claim of prior knowledge, in that the negative observation of saying what wasn't said focuses the discussion on the relevant absence of a display of the claimed prior knowledge in the just-rehearsed presentation. Segment (11) indicates that even if a presenter displays alignment with the comment giver's clarifying explanation, a contingently raised negative observation can undermine the interactional adequacy of that display of alignment by transforming a sorted-out confusion into a complaint of omission in the conference presentation performance.

Third, negative observations potentially project more to come, whether from the speaker or the recipient of a complaint of omission. Specifically, saying what wasn't said can project that a presenter may offer an account for why some words were not included or that Ron may further explain why the complaint is warranted (Button and Casey 1984; Ford 1993, 1994; Ford, Fox, and Thompson 1996). For instance, in Segment (9) Marsha accounts for why she failed to "get into" the issue of competition between single ions during her rehearsal runthrough by alluding to the time taken up dealing with noisy window blinds, a side activity that disrupted her runthrough ("I got very distr(h)acted b(h)y ou(h)r hh our noi:se").[39]

A presenter's account for failure to include something in the presentation retrospectively orients to a problem in the runthrough performance. In contrast, when a participant accounts for why a complaint of omission is warranted, he/she is orienting prospectively to a potential problem (if the problem is not remedied) for the performance and/or audience of the presentation at the upcoming conference. For instance, in Segment (1) Gary and Marsha both provide didactic warrants for Ron's negative observation that Miguel failed to adequately cite the source of the samples of condensed matter used in his experiments. Proclaiming that this particular omission is "major" and a "front/first page" expectation, Gary and Marsha emphatically frame the omission of a certain kind of citation as a serious breach of the expectations and standards of professional courtesy and rhetorical conduct allegedly held by the larger scientific community—giving credit where credit is due. A participant's warrant for a negative observation thus implicitly raises the specter of potential future performance disaster (Jacoby 1998). In Segment (1), the possible disaster is concretized as offended future audience members (Jacoby 1998).

Saying What Wasn't Said and Issues of Competence

When Ron produces a negative observation in post-runthrough feedback, he is claiming to have sufficient competence and experience to perceive omissions, to know what should be included in a physics conference presentation, and to anticipate how a future audience might react. At the same time, publicly pointing out what is missing in a rehearsal runthrough questions the competence of the presenter (cf. Jacoby and Gonzales 1991; Heritage and Sefi 1992). Our analysis suggests that negative observations can potentially cast doubts on a presenter's competence as a performer of conference presentations and as a possessor of expert knowledge in physics.

Several of the segments we have analyzed reveal that speakers and recipients of negative observations are oriented to the critique of competence implied in a complaint of omission. For instance, in Segment (9) Ron complains that Marsha failed to mention the competition between ions in her experimental results. In response, Marsha deflects the possible implication that she does not know this fact of physics by asserting that she had planned to include it in her talk ("ho:nestly: honestly I- I get into that very clearly with the hollandite") but was thwarted by a technical interruption during her runthrough. In addition, in Segments (3), (4), (10), and (11), when presenters display or claim competence in expert knowledge in a clarification discussion of matters of physics, Ron can subsequently attack the presenter's performance competence by contingently observing that the knowledge of physics a presenter has just now displayed or claimed in the rehearsal feedback to be familiar with was not articulated in the rehearsal runthrough.

Saying What Wasn't Said, Institutional Identity, and Generalizability

In the feedback that follows the fifteen separate physics conference rehearsals held by the same research group over a six-month period, saying what wasn't said negative observations are clearly an optional turn design format for delivering criticism in general and for pointing out noticeable omissions in particular. However, just as clearly they are primarily deployed by Ron, the senior professor and principal investigator in charge of this group of graduate students, post-doctoral fellows, and visiting scholars, none of whom equal or surpass their mentor's international renown or professional seniority. Nevertheless, this does not mean that only Ron offers feedback comments or that only Ron notices omissions in practice runthroughs.

Although quantitatively less often, other members of the group do initiate nega-tively critical comments of all types, including comments that suggest that some-thing is missing from the presentation and should be included in an improved version. Overwhelmingly it is primarily Ron, however, who opts linguistically to design many of his complaints of omission as negative observations.[40]

One reason for this skewing of the distribution of negative observations in our feedback data may be the interactional contribution such utterances make in con-structing the institutional identity of someone in Ron's position as "boss," inter-national expert, academic mentor, professional trainer, co-author, quality control-ler, and old hand at conference performances. Negative observations are, after all, linguistically designed as epistemically certain, bald assertions of failure on the part of a presenter to say something in the runthrough that by implication ought to have been said and ought to be said in a future version of the presentation. Such linguistically unmitigated assertions may thus be oriented to by the physicists as being too interactionally risky for other than the participant who is most senior, most confident, most experienced, and most responsible for expert mentoring and quality control oversight of research publication output. The privilege of design-ing complaint comments that construct the comment giver as possessing the ex-pert competence to unproblematically perceive what is absent from a discourse performance may be one of the ways that a research group leader can reinvoke and maintain his/her senior status and authority throughout an extended activity such as post-runthrough feedback.

Does this mean, then, that negative observations are a unique and quirky aspect of one person's discourse practices? We think not. In the first place, Ron's saying what wasn't said negative observations are linguistically and sequentially akin to Schegloff's (1988) delineation of negative observation complaints in everyday con-versation. Moreover, as complaints of what wasn't said in a prior self-contained discourse (i.e., the rehearsal runthrough), it seems plausible that negative obser-vations such as Ron's might be produced in similar situations, when some desig-nated competent assessor provides face-to-face feedback to a writer, presenter, teacher, or performer who has just submitted for inspection a draft version or dry run of a discourse performance (whether written, oral, or multi-modal). It remains an empirical question, however, as to whether negative observations might indeed occur in other such task-oriented settings (within or outside of science) as well as to whether negative observations of a failure to perform a communicative action can also be found in everyday conversation.

Conclusions

Negative observations are one of the linguistic and interactional resources through which the community of research scientists we have investigated comes to articu-late, experience, and understand aspects of their working culture. While there are many other ways of delivering criticism and suggesting improvements in the feed-back that follows a rehearsal runthrough for an upcoming conference, negative observations are a linguistic resource deployed by the senior professor to simultaneously criticize and offer a hearable remedy for noticeable omissions in a group member's conference presentation. Negative observations are therefore a locally occasioned practice through which weaknesses in scientific argument can be communicated and less experienced presenters can be socialized into particular ways of speaking and presenting. Through negative observations then, presenters (and, we assume, overhearing participants) are made aware of alleged discourse norms and expectations of their professional culture. Negative observation in general, and saying what wasn't said in particular, is also a practice whereby scientific colleagues and co-authors transform backstage monitoring and criticism of a rehearsal performance into constructive and collaborative problem-solving for the actual performance in the future. Thus, what is on one level just another type of criticism in a seemingly relentless series of criticisms is, on another level, part of a larger collaboratively achieved problem-solving and socializing activity through which colleagues display both that they are saving one another from potentially humiliating public performance disasters and that they are helping to shape co-authored reports to maximum effect. Delivering criticism through negative observations is therefore an important vehicle by which professional and discursive competencies are indigenously assessed, interactionally co-constructed, and ideologically framed as important and normative for communicative success in a particular communication culture. At the same time, saying what wasn't said underscores a presenter's failure to actualize professional and communicative norms and expectations (whether real or perceived), thereby enabling a senior comment giver to call into question a presenter's competence to effectively communicate a publicly performed scientific report, regardless of whether a presenter has (or claims to have) the relevant underlying knowledge necessary for a competent communicative performance.

As important to discussions of art as are the notions of positive and negative space, so, too, should consideration of what participants say and do not say, of what interlocutors report has been said and has not been said, be an integral part of the ongoing study of "language use." If we may make a negative observation of our own, to our knowledge, the research literature on reported speech and the Conversation Analytic literature on complaints and negative observation have not specifically addressed the phenomenon of saying what wasn't said, though these two lines of research seem intrinsically related and relevant to such a communication practice. We have tried to show that saying what wasn't said is a linguistically and sequentially rich conversational practice worthy of analytic attention, since it may be a more pervasively routine practice in everyday and institutional conversation than is currently recognized.

Analysis of the practice of saying what wasn't said also provides insight into the more general topic of how participants interactionally deal with the issue of relevance when asserting or displaying understanding that something is absent or that some event did not occur. As Sacks (1992) formulated the problem in one of his 1966 lectures,

> There's a tremendously tricky problem about talking about things that haven't happened, and that is, if you're going to say some X hasn't happened, then there's an indefinite list of things that could be said not to have happened at that point. And if

that's so, then your case is non-discriminable from the rest of those, and the observation is trivialized. 'Sure he didn't do X, but he didn't do A, B, C, etc., either.' And how do you go about locating, as a significantly sayable thing, that he didn't do, distinctively, X?

. . . There are some occasions under which absences are noticed. If we can characterize the bases for them, we can come up with a usable notion of 'absence.' And such a notion could perhaps be generalized beyond the specific occasion that we happened to construct it in relation to. (Sacks 1992, vol. 1:293–294)

From the outset we have argued that saying what wasn't said is a context-specific form of the more general conversational practice known as negative observation (Schegloff 1988). Our close examination of particular occasions in which the practice of saying what wasn't said is interactionally deployed has been an exercise in respecifying members' methods for locating the relevance rules that render this kind of noticing of absence as "significant" rather than "trivial" in the routine culturally situated activity of rehearsing upcoming physics conference presentations. We also hope to have contributed more generally to the respecification of members' methods for locating the relevance rules that render any kind of negative observation "significant" rather than "trivial" in any sort of culturally situated activity.

This study has demonstrated how a particular grammatical structure—the assertion of what was not said—is a linguistic resource for performing a particular action: a negatively criticial complaint about a relevantly absent communicative act. It has also demonstrated how actions are jointly accomplished through particular deployments of grammatical structure, turn design, and sequential organization. We trust that we have made it clear that any analysis of the co-constructed interactional functions and meanings of grammatical choices is highly dependent upon an analysis of the interactional functions, meanings, and sequential structurings of the routine cultural activity in which a grammatical structure is situated. For, as Schegloff (1996) astutely pointed out and as this study has shown, grammar not only shapes interaction but also is itself shaped by the fundamental features of talk-in-interaction as a sequential phenomenon and a social activity. This means that, in addition to being situated in and fitted to a particular cultural activity and a particular configuration of participant roles, linguistic structures in naturally occurring communication also provide detailed evidence of participants' tacit orientation to the position of a turn constructional unit within a conversational turn, to the position of a turn within a sequence of turns and actions, and to the position of a sequence within a larger context-specific activity.

NOTES

This study was supported by grants from the Spencer Foundation to Elinor Ochs, Principal Investigator: "Socialization of Scientific Discourse" (Grant No. M900824, 1990–1993) and "Collaborative Construction of Scientific Knowledge in a University Physics Laboratory" (Grant No. L940204, 1994–1997). Additional funding was provided by a University of New Hampshire Junior Faculty Development Grant and by the Graduate Division and the Faculty Senate of the University of California, Los Angeles. Earlier versions of this chapter were presented at the 1996 International Pragmatics Conference in Mexico City, the 1998 Workshop on New Developments in Variationist Linguistics in Oulu, Finland, and the 1999 Linguistics Colloquium at the University of New Hampshire. We are grateful to Steven Clayman, Cecilia Ford, Barbara Fox, Agnes Weiyun He, Joan Russell, Emanuel Schegloff, and John Shotter for comments and suggestions along the way.

1. Of the three borderline cases, one is produced by Ron ("The next one isn't labeled"), the other two by other group members ("I haven't said it," "But here you are not showing anything"). The subset of forty unambiguous instances of saying what wasn't said turns are all produced by Ron. We consider these three instances to be borderline cases of saying what wasn't said, although they all appear to be clear instances of negative observations.

2. For detailed analyses of many of the routine activities and discourse practices that occurred during the weekly meetings of this team of physicists, see Jacoby and Gonzales (1991), Ochs, Jacoby, and Gonzales (1994), Ochs, Gonzales, and Jacoby (1996), Gonzales (1996), Ochs and Jacoby (1997), Jacoby (1998), and Jacoby and McNamara (1999).

3. See Jacoby (1998) for a detailed analysis of how the physicists interactionally co-construct the various Phases of a conference presentation rehearsal runthrough, including launching the runthrough, maintaining a mock event, bringing the runthrough to a close, launching post-runthrough feedback, and working through comment sequences.

4. Pseudonyms are used to to protect the privacy of the participants.

5. Comment sequences exhibit enormous variation in length, turn format deployed for their launching, placement of the complaint and/or candidate remedy, degree of explicitness, number of participants, and interactional trouble, such as contingently emerging resistance, disagreement, and withholding of agreement. See Jacoby (1998) for a detailed analysis of comment sequences in the physicists' rehearsal feedback.

6. Reported speech has traditionally been divided into two categories, direct and indirect, though there is increasing evidence that such a sharp line cannot easily be drawn between these two categories (e.g., Clark and Gerrig 1990).

7. We deliberately display these examples as isolated utterances at the outset so as to make some preliminary observations about their linguistic structuration before we devote the larger part of our discussion to an analysis of the relationship among linguistic variation, sequential placement, and interactional import of these types of turns within the culturally specific face-to-face activity in which they occur.

8. It should be noted that bona fide reported speech utterances are found throughout the weekly meeting discourse of the physicists in our study, especially in nonrehearsal activities, when participants report on conversations they had with nonpresent others or when they discuss the published findings of other nonpresent physicists. Our current analysis found a version of bona fide reported speech addressed (by Ron) to a co-present presenter (e.g., "[in the runthrough] you said that . . ."), but this kind of reported speech utterance is routinely deployed to set up a contrastive preface to an immediately subsequent complaint of what wasn't said. See, later in this chapter, a detailed analysis of this kind of slightly delayed sequential placement of saying what wasn't said in a comment sequence. See also later discussion of Segment (7), in which the bona fide reported speech utterance ("What you said was . . .") follows a saying that wasn't said utterance. Gonzales (1996) has identified still another interactional practice related to bona fide reported speech in which one interlocutor displays an understanding of a co-present interlocutor's prior talk in an ongoing problem-solving activity (informal discussion of research findings). In this practice, using present progressive verb tenses (e.g., "So what you're saying is . . ."), one physicist (usually Ron, the principal investigator) will offer an interpretation of the gist or upshot of what another co-present physicist has just said.

9. There is a strikingly exceptional instance in our data in which Ron poses a clarification question to a presenter regarding the physics content of a presentation and the presenter answers, "I haven't said it." Although this sequence provides evidence that members are oriented to the potential link between confusion and omission, we ignore this uniquely interesting excerpt in our current discussion.

10. Though it is not the focus of her discussion, B. L. Dubois (1989) notes in passing a type of "pseudoquotation" in English usage in which a speaker uses a "negative quote formula," as in *and so you didn't say, "Hey, it was you who brought me here"* (ibid.: 348) and *"Hey, she didn't really say it"* (ibid.: 343). Deborah Tannen (1989) also briefly mentions the possibility that reported speech can represent what wasn't said, as in, *You can't say, "Well, Daddy, I didn't HEAR you"* (ibid.: 111). Speakers would use this and other types of "constructed dialogue," Tannen vaguely argues, as "a discourse strategy for framing information in a way that communicates effectively and creates involvement" (ibid.: 110).

11. L. Wittgenstein's (1958) awareness of the communicational complexity of negation as a situated communicative action seems to be relevant to our claim that saying what wasn't said is a complaint also hearable as an implied recommendation to include what wasn't said in an improved version of the presentation:

> The sign of negation is our occasion for doing something—possibly something very complicated. It is as if the negation-sign occasioned our doing something. But what? That is not said. It is as if it only needed to be hinted at; as if we already knew. As if no explanation were needed, for we are in any case already acquainted with the matter. (ibid.: 147, #549)

See also Ford (1993, 1994) and Ford, Fox, and Thompson (1996) for related discussions of how negative assertions, disagreements, and contrasts can project more actions to come, especially *because*-accounts.

12. Of forty instances of saying what wasn't said in our corpus, seven are produced with the missing statement or wording provided in the negative observation utterance itself (as in Segment (1)); twenty are produced as negative observations that a rhetorical action is missing, without incorporation of the missing statement or wording (as in Segment (2)). The remaining thirteen instances are anaphorically constructed saying what wasn't said utterances.

13. See Maynard (1984), Ochs (1993), and Peräkylä (1993, 1995) for discussions of how interlocutors interactionally accomplish an orientation to the future in the here-and-now of what they are currently doing.

14. The delivery of criticism would thus seem to be related to other discursive actions with the potential for unpleasant interactional consequences, such as complaints (Schegloff 1988), accusations (Drew 1978, 1992), blamings (Pomerantz 1978; Watson 1978), advice-giving (Heritage and Sefi 1992), and some forms of evaluations or assessments (Pomerantz 1984a; Goodwin and Goodwin 1987, 1992; Goodwin 1986).

15. See Ochs and Jacoby (1997) for a discussion of how the physicists orient to potentially problematic issues in rehearsed physics presentations as either matters of physics or matters of rhetoric.

16. We have not found any notable interactional contrasts with regard to the alternation of *that* or *it* in the pronominal, contingently raised type of saying what wasn't said turns. We tentatively conclude, however, that alternation with the pronoun *this* may be motivated when Ron leaves off an explanation or demonstration of recommended wording to parenthetically assert that a presenter "did not say this," before bringing the explanation or rewording suggestion to a close. See analysis of final Segment (12) later in this chapter.

17. On the notion of TCU and its role in talk-in-interaction, see Sacks, Schegloff, and Jefferson (1974), Ford, Fox, and Thompson (1996), Ford and Thompson (1996), Ford and Wagner (1996), Schegloff (1996), and Selting (1996). The negative observation in Segment (7) is considered here as the first TCU in the sequence, although technically there is some bit of talk that precedes it. The bit of talk produced before the actual negative observation is Ron reading aloud from his written notes in what appears to be an attempt to recall his reason for having made a notation. We thus consider Ron's utterance in Segment (7): "You forgot to define what field cooled was," as the first utterance in the comment sequence that is designed for and addressed to an intended recipient (i.e., the presenter).

18. In Segment (7), it appears that Ron may have interpreted Gary's long silence that followed the first version of the negative observation as a sign of resistance to the original formulation of the criticism and/or as a problem in comprehending the criticism. While the second version of of the negative observation does begin after Gary has begun to display comprehension (oh: oh:), its onset also seems to have been inadvertently delayed, thus overlapping the end of Gary's turn.

19. See Sacks and Schegloff (1979) for a discussion of try-marked utterances for interactionally sorting out references to persons. The distinctively rising intonational shape of try-marked utterances routinely elicits a display from a recipient that the reference is understood.

20. In this regard, Segment (8) is interesting in that the presenter has apparently interpreted Ron's clarification preface as the comment of focus. However, the negative observation emerges after the presenter's confirmation of Ron's candidate understanding of something he acknowledges as having been communicated. The saying what wasn't said utterance that follows can thus retrospectively reframe the presenter's analysis of the comment sequence until this point as off the mark without explicitly saying that the presenter has jumped the gun in orienting to an aspect of the presentation as problematic that is not (for Ron) at issue. In other words, the negative observation in Segment (8) allows for participants to re-analyze the initial exchange at the beginning of the comment sequence as a prefatory set-up for the actual comment of focus.

21. Cf. Clayman and Whalen (1988/1989) and Schegloff (1988/1989) for analyses of a news interviewee's pre-emptive responses to a journalist's reported speech prefaces, before the journalist has produced the target interview question.

22. Unfortunately, copies of the notes Ron took during rehearsal runthroughs and which he continuously consulted during rehearsal feedback were not collected for this study.

23. The reported speech preface to the complaint (a practice Ron uses in Segments (3) and (8) as well) is analyzable as the first pair part of a pre-sequence to the complaint–remedy base adjacency pair (cf. Schegloff 1990, forthcoming). That is, the action of asserting what was said can potentially be responded to by a recipient (e.g., agreeing/confirming or disagreeing/correcting what the speaker alleges the recipient has said), whether the recipient responds or not before a next target action sequence trajectory is pursued. In Segment (10), Ron rushes through to his question ("=Relaxation of <u>what</u>."), which by the way accomplishes a complaint of omission without relying on the linguistic format of a negative observation or, specifically, saying what wasn't said.

24. "T R M" is an abbreviation for "thermoremanent magnetism," pockets of magnetic atomic order retained by a substance that has been heated and subsequently cooled (Halliday, Resnick, and Walker, 1993:931).

25. Ron's adverbial extension of the TCU that contains the negative observation is also a form of self-correction at a possible turn completion point (Schegloff, Jefferson, and Sacks 1977) and thus a post–possible completion, or recompletion, of his TCU (Schegloff 1996).

26. See Pomerantz's (1984b) discussion of different ways speakers respond to a lack of response (or delay in responding) on the part of recipients. Pomerantz (ibid.: 159–161) specifically demonstrates that when a recipient fails to respond to a speaker's assertion, particularly when that assertion is a complaint, speakers may subsequently assert an amended, even opposite, position. Pomerantz suggests that the recipient's silence leads the speaker to see "an implication or consequence that he or she had not considered" (ibid.: 161) when making the original assertion. Thus, in Segment (4), Ron's second turn is evidence that he may have interpreted the "trouble" behind Miguel's silence as a display of pre-disagreement with his first turn, the design of which he now realizes can be heard as a dismissive attack on Miguel's competence as a physicist.

27. A "domain" is a dynamically growing or already frozen pocket of correlated atomic order (and therefore a local magnetic region) in a piece of condensed matter whose atoms are otherwise randomly and nonmagnetically arranged (Halliday, Resnick, and Walker 1993:930).

28. The interpretive implication in Ron's second assertion is that the presence of a random magnetic field when cooling takes place eventually "pins" (i.e., freezes) the dynamic process of domain creation.

29. It is not entirely clear why Miguel does not respond at this point. First, Miguel may hear in Ron's first explanatory turn a bid to speak at length and thus may be refraining from responding to allow Ron an extended turn space for a story composed of more than one TCU. Second, it may be that this assertion is so obvious in terms of its physics content that Miguel hears it as clearly not the clarifying point that Ron is aiming to make and thus prefatory to some other less obvious point yet to come. Third, Miguel's silence may be a carryover response stance first taken up when Ron dismissed his prior explanations as "missing the point." What is a bit clearer, however, is that Ron appears to have expected some kind of minimal response after his first and second assertions. Not only does Ron in fact leave a space for a possible response after each of them, his second assertion is preceded by interactional evidence of a turn exchange glitch (*uh:* and another brief pause).

30. See Jacoby and Gonzales (1991) and Heritage and Sefi (1992) for discussions of how—through questioning, informing, evaluating, and advice-giving sequences—participants can co-construct and resist the implied identities of "expert" and "novice," in the sense of "knowing more" and "knowing less."

31. See Sacks's (1992) discussion of "tying rules" (inter alia, vol. 1, 150–156), the syntactic and discursive analyses recipients may have to engage in to make sense of particular pronomial expressions in conversation.

32. It is unclear whether through the words "what you want to conve:y" Ron is claiming to have grasped Marsha's intention despite the alleged problem of clarity in her argument or he is making a recommendation as to what Marsha ought to convey. It is of course also possible that Ron's turn is linguistically designed with just these words so as to allow Marsha to hear both communicative possibilities.

33. According to D. Halliday, R. Resnick, and J. Walker (1993:639–640), the formula for calculating the force of interactions between electrically charged particles (which involves among other things the distance between particles) was discovered by eighteenth-century scientist Charles Augustus Coulomb and has never been overturned, thus attaining the status of a "law" of physics. Coulomb's law has been found to account for the electrostatic forces between an atom's positively charged nucleus and each of its negatively charged electrons as well as for the forces that bind atoms together to form molecules and that bind atoms and molecules together to form liquids and solids. This is the level of condensed (solid-state) matter that Marsha is investigating. By spelling out the importance

of Coulomb's law to explain Marsha's results, Ron appears to be indirectly attacking Marsha's competence as a physicist in that he is making explicit a fundamental physical process that she (apparently) had not sufficiently made clear in her own prior version of the argument.

34. See Schegloff (1982) for an analysis of recipients' verbal and nonverbal minimal responses to extended turns, which he terms "continuers." In general, continuers allow a recipient to display recipiency and, at the same time, a willingness to allow the current speaker to produce an extended turn and keep talking beyond the first point of possible turn completion. Such minimal responses also, to varying extents, mute a recipient's display of interactional alignment with the content of a speaker's emerging multi-unit turn, *mmhm* being perhaps the most useful for withholding an overt display of alignment while forefronting recipiency.

35. Cf. Schegloff's (1991a) analysis of a radio talk-show host's upgrading of his *mmhm* response turn to a verbal response turn that showed appreciation for the caller's point. Schegloff argues that this kind of turn design revision displays the host's interactional re-analysis of the caller's prior turn unit as being the last unit in a multi-unit turn rather than just another unit in a still as yet incomplete multi-unit turn.

36. Ron may have analyzed Marsha's failure to respond as a sign of trouble in processing the first version of the negative observation. Possible evidence for this interpretation is that in the second version Ron substitutes the past tense for the present tense and adds a locational reference ("in the talk"). It appears that Marsha's silence may have caused Ron to reconsider his formulation of the negative observation and redo it so that it more clearly evokes what Marsha failed to say in the rehearsal runthrough. This suggests that Ron may have heard the first version of the negative observation as ambiguously analyzable as referring what Marsha failed to say in the current clarifying discussion.

37. Space does not permit us to analyze in detail the interactional emergence of explicit directives and recommendations for improving the conference presentation produced so close on the heels of a negative observation. We do not think that the subsequent production of a directive undermines our claim that a comment giver's candidate remedy for the complaint of omission is hearable in or discursively recoverable from the negative observation turn itself. We do think, based on but a preliminary analysis of this sequential phenomenon, that post-positioned directives are an option for making maximally explicit the remedy inferrable from a negative observation. This apparently redundant spelling out of informational meaning appears to be interactionally motivated when Ron detects that a presenter is displaying resistance to the remedy indirectly proposed by the negative observation or is attempting to negotiate an alternative remedy. See Schegloff (1995) and He (1995) for interactional analyses of other kinds of turns at talk that at first glance appear to be informationally redundant but on closer inspection are seen to be sequentially motivated.

38. See Heritage (1984) for an analysis of *oh* as a speaker's interactional display of a change in his/her cognitive state of understanding.

39. Marsha's rehearsal runthrough on this date was interrupted by a sudden strong wind that noisily and rather violently rattled the venetian blinds that covered the open windows of the rehearsal room. This disturbance continued on for some time, breaking Marsha's performance concentration, until Miguel rose from the audience and raised the blinds beyond the open windows. Subsequently, Marsha resumed her runthrough but ran overtime and had to be cut off before reaching the summary of her experimental conclusions.

40. Some examples of alternative linguistic formats used by participants other than Ron to design complaints of omission include impersonal descriptions (e.g., Gary: "It

doesn't look like there's any data there.") and opting to leave the complaint unspoken in favor of articulating a recommendation to add something (e.g., Jeremy: "As long as you have everything else in the recipe you've made out, you might as well just write turn on a field, because that is a crucial step in this procedure.").

REFERENCES

Atkinson, J. Maxwell, and Paul Drew. 1979. *Order in Court: The Organisation of Verbal Interaction in Judicial Settings.* London: Macmillan.

Bakhtin, Mikhail M. 1981. *The dialogic imagination: Four Essays.* Ed. M. Holquist. Trans. C. Emerson and M. Holquist. Austin: University of Texas Press.

Bateson, Gregory. 1972. A theory of play and fantasy. *In Steps to an Ecology of Mind,* 177–193. New York: Ballantine.

Beach, Wayne A. 1990/1991. Avoiding ownership for alleged wrongdoings. *Research on Language and Social Interaction,* 24:1–36.

Beach, Wayne A. 1993. Transitional regularities for 'casual' "Okay" usages. *Journal of Pragmatics* 19:325–352.

Beach, Wayne A. 1995. Preserving and constraining options: "Okays" and 'official' priorities in medical interviews. In G. H. Morris and R. J. Chenail (eds.), *The Talk of the Clinic: Explorations in the Analysis of Medical and Therapeutic Discourse,* 259–289. Hillsdale, NJ: Lawrence Erlbaum.

Beach, Wayne A. (1996). *Conversations About Illness: Family Preoccupations with Bulimia.* Mahwah, NJ: Lawrence Erlbaum.

Button, Graham, and N. Casey. 1984. Generating topic: The use of topic initial elicitors. In J. M. Atkinson and John Heritage (eds.), *Structures of Social Action: Studies in Conversation Analysis,* 167–190. Cambridge: Cambridge University Press.

Clark, Herbert H., and R. J. Gerrig. 1990. Quotations as demonstrations. *Language* 66:764–805.

Clayman, Steven. 1988. Displaying neutrality in television news interviews. *Social Problems* 35(4):474–492.

Clayman, Steven. 1992. Footing in the achievement of neutrality: The case of news-interview discourse. In Paul Drew and John Heritage (eds.), *Talk at Work: Interaction in Institutional Settings,* 163–198. Cambridge: Cambridge University Press.

Clayman, Steven, and J. Whalen. 1988/1989. When the medium becomes the message: The case of the Rather–Bush encounter. *Research on Language and Social Interaction* 22:241–272.

Comrie, Bernard. 1986. Tense in indirect speech. *Folia Linguistica* 20:265–296.

Coulmas, Florian. (ed.). 1986. *Direct and Indirect Speech.* Berlin: Mouton.

Davidson, Donald. 1984. Quotation. In D. Davidson (ed.), *Inquiries into Truth and Interpretation,* 79–92. Oxford: Clarendon Press.

Drew, Paul. 1978. Accusations: The occasioned use of members' knowledge of 'religious geography' in describing events. *Sociology* 12:1–22.

Drew, Paul. 1992. Contested evidence in courtroom cross-examination: The case of a trial for rape. In Paul Drew and John Heritage (eds.), *Talk at Work: Interaction in Institutional Settings,* 359–417. Cambridge: Cambridge University Press.

Dubois, Betty Lou. 1989. Pseudoquotation in current English communication: "Hey, she didn't really say it." *Language in Society* 18:343–359.

Ford, Cecilia E. 1993. *Grammar in Interaction: Adverbial Clauses in American English Conversations.* Cambridge: Cambridge University Press.

Ford, Cecilia E. 1994. Dialogic aspects of talk and writing: *Because* on the interactive-edited continuum. *TEXT* 14(4): 531–554.

Ford, Cecilia E., Barbara A. Fox, and Sandra A. Thompson. 1996. Practices in the construction of turns: The "TCU" revisited. *Pragmatics* 6(3): 427–454.

Ford, Cecilia E., and Sandra A. Thompson. 1996. Interactional units in conversation: Syntactic, intonational, and pragmatic resources for the management of turns. In Elinor Ochs, Emanuel A. Schegloff, and Sandra A. Thompson (eds.), *Interaction and Grammar*, 134–184. Cambridge: Cambridge University Press.

Ford, Cecilia E. and Johannes Wagner (eds.). 1996. Interaction-based studies of language. Special issue of *Pragmatics* 6(3): 277–456.

Goffman, Erving (ed.). 1981. *Forms of Talk*. Oxford: Basil Blackwell.

Gonzales, Patrick. 1996. The talk and social organization of problem-solving activities among physicists. Ph.D. diss., University of California, Los Angeles.

Goodwin, Charles. 1979. The interactive construction of a sentence in natural conversation. In G. Psathas (ed.), *Everyday Language: Studies in Ethnomethodology*, 97–121. New York: Irvington.

Goodwin, Charles. 1986. Between and within: Alternative and sequential treatments of continuers and assessments. *Human Studies* 9:205–218.

Goodwin, Charles, and Marjorie Harness Goodwin. 1987. Concurrent operations on talk: Notes on the interactive organization of assessments. *IPRA Papers in Pragmatics* 1(1):54.

Goodwin, Charles, and Marjorie Harness Goodwin. (1992). Assessments and the construction of context. In Alessandro Duranti and C. Goodwin (eds.), *Rethinking Context: Language as an Interactive Phenomenon*, 147–189. Cambridge: Cambridge University Press.

Greatbatch, D. 1988. A turn-taking system for British news interviews. *Language in Society* 17:401–430.

Greatbatch, D. 1992. On the management of disagreement between news interviewees. In Paul Drew and John Heritage (eds.), *Talk at Work: Interaction in Institutional Settings*, 268–301. Cambridge: Cambridge University Press.

Greenbaum, Sidney, and Randolph Quirk. 1990. *A Student's Grammar of the English Language*. Essex: Longman.

Grice, H. Paul. 1975. Logic and conversation. In *Syntax and Semantics*, vol. 3: *Speech Acts*, edited by Peter Cole and Jerry Morgan, 41–58. New York: Academic Press.

Grice, H. Paul. 1978. Further notes on logic and conversation. In *Syntax and Semantics*, vol. 9: *Pragmatics*, edited by P. Cole, 113–128. New York: Academic Press.

Haiman, John, and Sandra Thompson, (1984). Subordination in universal grammar. *The Proceedings of the Tenth Annual Meeting of the Berkeley Linguistics Society* 10:510–523.

Halliday, David, Robert Resnick, and Jearl Walker, 1993. *Fundamentals of Physics*, 4th ed. New York: John Wiley.

Halliday, M. A. K. 1994. *An Introduction to Functional Grammar*. 2nd ed. London: Routledge.

He, Agnes Weiyun. 1995. Co-constructing institutional identities: The case of student counselees. *Research on Language and Social Interaction* 28(3): 213–231.

He, Agnes Weiyun, and Snezha Tsoneva. 1998. The symbiosis of choices and control: Toward a discourse-based account of CAN. *Journal of Pragmatics* 29:615–637.

Heritage, John. 1984. A change-of-state token and aspects of its sequential placement. In J. Maxwell Atkinson and John Heritage (eds.), *Structures of Social Action: Studies in Conversation Analysis*, 299–345. Cambridge: Cambridge University Press.

Heritage, J. 1985. Analyzing news interviews: Aspects of the production of talk for an "overhearing" audience. In T. van Dijk (ed.), *Handbook of Discourse Analysis*, vol. 3: *Discourse and Dialogue*, 95–119. London: Academic Press.

Heritage, J., and D. Greatbatch. 1991. On the institutional character of institutional talk: The case of news interviews. In D. Boden and D. Zimmerman (eds.), *Talk and Social Structure*, 93–137. Cambridge: Polity Press.

Heritage, John C., and Andrew L. Roth. 1995. Grammar and institution: Questions and
    questioning in broadcast news interviews. *Research on Language and Social Interac-
    tion* 28(1): 1–60.
Heritage, John and Sue Sefi. 1992. Dilemmas of advice: Aspects of the delivery and recep-
    tion of advice in interactions between Health Visitors and first-time mothers. In Paul
    Drew and John Heritage (eds.), *Talk at Work: Interaction in Institutional Settings*,
    359–417. Cambridge: Cambridge University Press.
Heritage, John, and Marja-Leena Sorjonen. (1994). Constituting and maintaining activi-
    ties across sequences: *And*-prefacing as a feature of question design. *Language in So-
    ciety* 23:1–29.
Holt, Elizabeth. 1996. Reporting on talk: The use of direct reported speech in conversa-
    tion. *Research on Language and Social Interaction* 29:219–245.
Jacoby, Sally. 1997. Rethinking English for science and technology (EST): What can "in-
    digenous assessment" tell us about the communication culture of science? Invited
    paper, Parasession on Pragmatics and English for Specific Purposes in Academic and
    Workplace Contexts, 11th Annual International Conference on Pragmatics and Lan-
    guage Learning, University of Illinois, Urbana-Champaign, April.
Jacoby, Sally. 1998. Science as performance: Socializing scientific discourse through phys-
    ics conference talk rehearsals. Ph.D. diss., University of California, Los Angeles.
Jacoby, Sally, and P. Gonzales. 1991. The constitution of expert-novice in scientific dis-
    course. *Issues in Applied Linguistics*, 2:149–181.
Jacoby, Sally, and Tim McNamara. 1999. Locating competence. *English for Specific Pur-
    poses [ESP] Journal* 18(3): 213–241.
Jakobson, Roman. 1971. Shifters, verbal categories, and the Russian verb. In *Selected Writ-
    ings, Word and Language*, vol. 2:130–147. The Hague: Mouton.
Jefferson, Gail. 1983. Notes on some orderliness of overlap onset. In Gail Jefferson (a) Notes
    on some orderlinesses of overlap onset and (b) On a failed hypothesis: "Conjunc-
    tionals" as overlap-vulnerable; with an appended glossary of transcript symbols. Two
    Explorations of the organization of Overlapping Talk in Conversation: *Tilburg Papers
    in language and literature* 28:1–33.
Jefferson, Gail. 1988. On the sequential organization of troubles-talk in ordinary conver-
    sation. *Social Problems* 35:418–441.
Jefferson, Gail, and J. R. E. Lee. 1981. The rejection of advice: Managing the problematic
    convergence of a 'troubles' telling' and a 'service encounter.' *Journal of Pragmatics*
    5:399–422.
Jefferson, G. and J. Schenkein. 1977. Some sequential negotiations in conversation: Unexpanded
    and expanded versions of projected action sequences. *Sociology* 11:87–103.
Lerner, Gene H. 1991. On the syntax of sentences-in-progress. *Language in Society* 20:441–458.
Levinson, Stephen C. 1987. Putting linguistics on a proper footing: Explorations in Goff-
    man's concepts of participation. In P. Drew and A. Wooton (eds.), *Goffman: An In-
    terdisciplinary Appreciation*, 161–227. Oxford: Polity Press.
Li, Charles N. 1986. Direct and indirect speech: A functional study. In F. Coulmas (ed.),
    Direct and Indirect Speech, 29–45. Berlin: Mouton.
Lucy, John A. (ed.). 1993. *Reflexive Language: Reported Speech and Metapragmatics*. New
    York: Cambridge University Press.
Mayes, Patricia. 1990. Quotation in spoken English. *Studies in Language* 14:325–363.
Maynard, Douglas. 1984. *Inside Plea Bargaining: The Language of Negotiation*. New York:
    Plenum Press.
Munro, Pamela. 1982. On the transitivity of 'say' verbs. In Paul Hopper and Sandra A.
    Thompson (eds.), *Studies in Transitions*, vol. 15: 301–318. New York: Academic Press.

Ochs, Elinor. 1993. Stories that step into the future. In Edward Finegan and Douglas F. Biber (eds.), *Perspectives on Register: Situating Register Variation within Sociolinguistics*, 106–135. Oxford: Oxford University Press.

Ochs, Elinor, Patrick Gonzales, and Sally Jacoby. 1996. "When I come down I'm in the domain state": Grammar and graphic representation in the interpretive activity of physicists. In Elinor Ochs, Emanuel A. Schegloff, and Sandra A. Thompson (eds.), *Interaction and Grammar*, 328–369. Cambridge: Cambridge University Press.

Ochs, Elinor, and Sally Jacoby. 1997. Down to the wire: The cultural clock of physicists and the discourse of consensus. *Language in Society* 26(4): 479–505.

Ochs, Elinor, Sally Jacoby, and Patrick Gonzales. 1994. Interpretive journeys: How physicists talk and travel through graphic space. *Configurations* 2(1): 151–171.

Ochs, E., Emanuel A. Schegloff, and Sandra A. Thompson. (eds.) 1996. *Interaction and Grammar*. Cambridge: Cambridge University Press.

Partee, Barbara H. (1973). The syntax and semantics of quotations. In P. Kiparsky and S. Anderson (eds.), *A Festschrift for Morris Halle*, 410–418. New York: Holt.

Peräkylä, Anssi. 1993. Invoking a hostile world: Discussing the patients' future in AIDS counselling. *TEXT* 13:291–316.

Peräkylä, Anssi. 1995. *AIDS Counselling: Institutional Iinteraction and Clinical Practice*. Cambridge: Cambridge University Press.

Pomerantz, Anita. 1978. Attributions of responsibility: Blamings. *Sociology* 12:115–121.

Pomerantz, Anita. 1984a. Agreeing and disagreeing with assessments: Some features of preferred/dispreferred turn shapes. In J. Maxwell Atkinson and John Heritage (eds.), *Structures of Social Action: Studies in Conversation Analysis*, 57–101. Cambridge: Cambridge University Press.

Pomerantz, Anita M. 1984b. Pursuing a response. In J. Maxwell Atkinson and John Heritage (eds.), *Structures of Social Action: Studies in Conversation Analysis* 152–163. Cambridge: Cambridge University Press.

Prelli, Lawrence J. 1989. The rhetorical construction of scientific ethos. In H. W. Simons (ed.), *Rhetoric in the Human Sciences*, 48–68. London/Newbury Park, CA: Sage.

Psathas, G. 1992. The study of extended sequences: The case of the garden lesson. In G. Watson and R. M. Seiler (eds.), *Text in Context: Contributions to Ethnomethodology*, 99–122. Newbury Park, CA: Sage.

Quirk, R., S. Greenbaum, Geoffrey Leech, and Jan Svartvik. 1985. *A Comprehensive Grammar of the English Language*. London: Longman.

Sacks, Harvey. 1992. *Lectures on Conversation*, vols. 1 and 2. Ed. Gail Jefferson. Cambridge, MA: Basil Blackwell.

Sacks, Harvey, and Emanuel A. Schegloff. 1979. Two preferences in the organization of reference to persons in conversation and their interaction. In G. Psathas (ed.), *Everyday Language: Studies in Ethnomethodology*, 15–21. New York: Irvington.

Sacks, Harvey, Emanuel A. Schegloff, and Gail Jefferson. 1974. A simplest systematics for the organization of turn-taking in conversation. *Language* 50(4): 696–735.

Schegloff, Emanuel A. 1972. Notes on a conversational practice: Formulating place. In D. Sudnow (ed.), *Studies in Social Interaction*, 75–119. New York: Free Press.

Schegloff, Emanuel A. 1979. The relevance of repair to a syntax-for-conversation. In *Syntax and Semantics*, vol. 12: *Discourse and Syntax*, edited by Talmy Givón, 261–286. New York: Academic Press.

Schegloff, Emanuel A. 1982. Discourse as an interactional achievement: Some uses of "uh huh" and other things that come between sentences. In Deborah Tannen (ed.), *Georgetown University Roundtable on Languages and Linguistics (GURT)*, 71–93. Washington, DC: Georgetown University Press.

Schegloff, Emanuel A. 1986. The routine as achievement. *Human Studies* 9:111–151.

Schegloff, Emanuel A. 1988. Goffman and the analysis of conversation. In Paul Drew and Anthony Wootton (eds.), *Erving Goffman: Exploring the Interaction Order*, 89–135. Cambridge, UK: Polity Press.

Schegloff, Emanuel A. 1988/1989. From interview to confrontation: Observations on the Bush–Rather encounter. *Research on Language and Social Interaction* 22:215–240.

Schegloff, Emanuel A. 1990. On the organization of sequences as a source of "coherence" in talk-in-interaction. In Bruce Dorval (ed.), *Conversational Organization and Its Development*, 51–77. (*Advances in Discourse Processes* 38.) Norwood, NJ: Ablex.

Schegloff, Emanuel A. 1991a. Conversation analysis and socially shared cognition. In L. Resnick, J. Levine, and S. Teasley (eds.), *Perspectives on Socially Shared Cognition*, 150–171. Washington, DC: American Psychological Association.

Schegloff, Emanuel A. 1991b. Reflections on talk and social structure. In Dierdre Boden and Don H. Zimmerman (eds.), *Talk and Social Structure: Studies in Ethnomethodology and Conversation Analysis*, 44–70. Cambridge: Polity Press.

Schegloff, Emanuel A. 1995. Discourse as an interactional achievement III: The omnirelevance of action. *Research on Language and Social Interaction* 28(3): 185–211.

Schegloff, Emanuel A. 1996. Turn organization: One intersection of grammar and interaction. In Elinor Ochs, Emanuel A. Schegloff, and Sandra A. Thompson (eds.), *Interaction and Grammar*, 52–133. Cambridge: Cambridge University Press.

Schegloff, Emanuel A. Forthcoming. Sequence organization. *Talking in Interaction: An Introduction to Conversation Analysis.*

Schegloff, Emanuel A., Gail Jefferson, and Harvey Sacks. (1977). The preference for self-correction in the organization of repair in conversation. *Language* 5(2): 361–382.

Schegloff, Emanuel A., and Harvey Sacks. 1973. Opening up closings. *Semiotica*, 8(4): 289–327.

Selting, Margret. 1996. On the interplay of syntax and prosody in the constitution of turn-constructional units and turns in conversation. *Pragmatics* 6(3): 371–388

Sternberg, M. 1982a. Point of view and the indirections of direct speech. *Language and Style* 15:67–117.

Sternberg, M. 1982b. Proteus in quotation-land: Mimesis and the forms of reported discourse. *Poetics Today* 3:107–156.

Sternberg, M. 1991. How indirect discourse means syntax, semantics, poetics, and pragmatics. In R. Sell (ed.), *Literary Pragmatics*, 69–93. New York: Routledge.

Tannen, Deborah. 1989. *Talking Voices: Repetition, Dialogue, and Imagery in Conversational Discourse.* Cambridge: Cambridge University Press.

Watson, D. R. 1978. Categorization, authorization, and blame-negotiation in conversation. *Sociology* 12:105–113.

Waugh, Linda R. 1995. Reported speech in journalistic discourse: The relation of function and text. *TEXT* 15:129–173.

Wittgenstein, Ludwig. 1958. *Philosophical Investigations*. 3rd ed. Trans. G. E. M. Anscombe. New York: Macmillan.

Yule, G., T. Mathis, and M. F. HopKins. 1992. On reporting what was said. *English Language Teaching (ELT) Journal* 46:245–238.

7

Recipient Activities

The Particle No as a Go-Ahead Response in Finnish Conversations

MARJA-LEENA SORJONEN

Across languages, we find particles that are capable of forming an utterance and turn at talk by themselves, deployed by recipients for responding to co-participants' prior talk. During the last fifteen years or so, a line of interdisciplinary work has evolved that focuses on meaning and use of response forms in different languages and cultures (see, for example, Jefferson 1981, 1984, 1993, 1996; Schegloff 1982; Heritage 1984b; Goodwin 1986; Tao and Thompson 1991; Drummond and Hopper 1993a, b; Hakulinen 1993; Gardner 1995; Clancy et al. 1996; Local 1996; Müller 1996; Sorjonen 1996, 1997; Guthrie 1997; Kangasharju 1998:140–184).

These studies, done within Conversation Analysis (CA) or informed by it, have started to tackle the highly indexical meanings displayed by different response forms. They are informed by an understanding of talk as action and the reflexive character of utterances. Thus, it is not merely with respect to structural features of prior talk such as its grammatical structure and prosodic cues that response forms are produced and understood but also, and more important, with respect to the type of action that that prior talk accomplishes through its construction and placement within the ongoing sequence of actions and activity. Hence the action that the response form is responding to is treated as part of its semantics. Furthermore, like all actions, actions accomplished by response forms are reflexive in that they either maintain or alter the line and sense of the activity that they occur as part of (Heritage 1984a:140).

These studies have pointed out, for example, differences between classes of response forms, such as one between responses that receive their prior utterance as
informative (e.g., *oh*; *I see*) and those that, in one way or another, merely register it
(e.g., *yeah*), and differences between response forms within a class. Response forms
appear to be one of the most language- and culture-specific interactional devices with
respect to the kinds of epistemic, affective, and interactional meanings they display.
With this chapter, I would like to contribute to our understanding of the kinds of
meaning and action recipients display with single-word responses by examining the
use of the particle *no* in Finnish conversations when used as a turn of its own.

The meaning of the particle *no* is described by the etymological dictionary of
Finnish as comparable with German particles *nun* and *na*. The dictionary suggests
that *no* is partially an original Finnish word, also found in other Baltic-Finnish and
Sámi languages, and which has also been influenced by foreign languages, most
notably by Germanic languages (*Suomen sanojen alkuperä* 1995).[1]

No is deployed both as a preface to longer utterances and as a turn at talk of its
own. Lauri Carlson (1984:78–80) points out that *no* often comes close to the English particle *well*; however, in some cases its closest counterpart can be *oh*, *why*, or
now. Within his dialogue game approach and using conversations from fiction, he
posits a general rule for *no*: "begin a move by *no* only to terminate a subplay in
progress." He states that the notion of play in progress is meant to capture a range
of situations, including ones where *no* is used to "initiate an action through terminating a period of relative inaction," and his examples include the following case
where *no* forms a turn of its own: *Kuulehan! - No?* 'Listen! - Well?'. Carlson does
not specify how his general rule applies to this example, but if *no* is here understood to terminate the preliminary activity started by *Kuulehan* 'Listen', asking the
speaker to initiate the main action, my findings fit his general rule. Liisa Raevaara
(1989), based on an exploration of conversational data, focuses mainly on *no* as a
preface. She concurs with Carlson and states that *no* displays a marked topical or
activity transition, often a shift either back to the main line of talk or within a larger
activity from one issue to another, within a longer unit of talk such as storytelling.
It is also found as a preface to turns such as dispreferred responses to a first pair
part of an adjacency pair (Schegloff and Sacks, 1973) that, in one way or another,
run against a line of talk made relevant and preferred by the co-participant in the
prior turn. Raevaara (1989:151) also mentions *no* as a turn of its own, providing
an example where she formulates the function of *no* as one of displaying willingness to move to a topic suggested by the prior speaker (*Nyt mä tiedän. - No?* 'Now
I know. - *No?*), a function exhibited by the current data base.

However, the detailed use of *no* as a turn of its own—the character of the sequential contexts in which it is found and the characteristics of the prior utterances
it responds to—is previously unresearched (apart from Carlson and Raevaara, for
other mentions of this usage, see *NS* 1992, s.v. *no*; Routarinne 1997). What I would
like to suggest in this chapter is that as a turn of its own *no* typically provides a
response to a co-participant's prior utterance that acts as a preliminary (*pre*) to
something else yet to come. A core group of preliminaries responded to by *no* are
ones that are constructed through conventionalized utterance types for doing a
preliminary action (e.g., *hei*, 'hey'; *arvaa mitä*, 'guess what'; *tää on tämmönen*

hätäapusoitto, 'this is this kind of help-in-trouble call', when starting the activity of telling the reason for one's telephone call). These utterances initiate a pre-sequence; that is, they act as a first pair part that projects some main action to come, and they make a response relevant next by the co-participant (see, for example, Sacks 1992a:685–692[1967]; Schegloff 1990:60–62). The particle *no* offers a second pair part to the preliminary: it provides a "go-ahead" response (Schegloff 1990:61); that is, it invites the co-participant to get on with the production of the main action. Together with its prior utterance, *no* forms an adjacency pair and a separate miniactivity through which the participants deal with the issue whether there are grounds for the speaker to initiate the main action he/she has projected by the preliminary, and it tells the speaker to initiate that action.

Furthermore, *no* can also be found in some other contexts, such as following an answer to a question or within storytellings. In these cases, the prior utterance *no* responds to reports on an event or state of affairs that runs against some ordinary or agreed-upon course of action without, however, providing a reason or account for that departure. The particle *no* treats the prior utterance as one in need of an elaboration and invites the co-participant to go ahead and specify what has happened. Associated with this kind of treatment is an understanding of the prior utterance as one that reported something special having happened, for which an explanation is needed.

The use of the particle *no* as a turn of its own is basically restricted to the kinds of usages to be discussed in this chapter. Thus, it differs from some other particles that have a wider range of usages as turns of their own. Most notably, these include the particles *nii(n)*, *joo*, and *mm*, which not only respond to preliminaries but also, for example, function as answers to polar questions and responses to directives and displays of stance by the previous speaker (see Sorjonen 1996, 1997, in press; Kangasharju 1998:140–184). In this chapter, I will briefly compare *no* with one of these particles, *nii(n)*: the latter is a particle that comes closest to *no* in its sequential distribution, and it is sometimes found in the same sequential environments as *no* (I will comment on the use of other particles when instances of them occur in data segments being discussed).

As a response to preliminaries, the use of *nii(n)*, roughly equivalent to English *yeah* and *yes* in some of its central usages, differs from the use of *no* in that it seldom provides a response to conventionalized pre-sequence first pair parts: the structure and character of the prior utterance it responds to is variable. Furthermore, contrary to utterances responded to by *no* that initiate a separate miniactivity and an adjacency pair for seeking grounds for initiating some main action, utterances responded to with *nii(n)* have already started the main activity, even though its core, its point, is yet to come. Within the activity, *nii(n)* typically occurs at places of maximum incompleteness, at junctures after which the production of some core action is imminent. However, in rare cases *nii(n)* is found as a response to a conventionalized pre-sequence first pair part, that is, in a sequential environment for the particle *no*, but in these cases it displays trouble with understanding the co-participant's prior utterance.

The data base of this study consists of thirty-two instances of *no* as a turn of its own. Thirteen of them come from a corpus of eighty-six telephone calls between adults.[2] Nine instances come from three telephone calls between two teenage girls (marked as "Girls"). One instance comes from a videotaped doctor–patient consultation, and two are from my written notes (marked as "FN"); that is, there is no audio-recording available. The rest, seven cases altogether, come from videotaped interactions between a father and his five-year-old son (marked as "Child").[3] The data base of the particle *nii(n)* contains all the instances of the particle as a continuer in the aforementioned corpus of eighty-six telephone calls, totaling eighty-some instances. It should be noticed, however, that these cases form only a portion of the instances of *nii(n)* as a turn of its own in the corpus: there are a great number of occurrences of *nii(n)* as a turn of its own when given as a confirming response to noninterrogative polar questions and as a response to displays of stance by the previous speaker. These cases fall outside the current study (see Sorjonen 1996, 1997, in press). In most of the cases in the current data, both the particle *no* and the particle *nii(n)* are produced with a nonfalling terminal contour.

In the following, I will first discuss the kinds of presequence first pair parts to which *no* offers a response. I will then explore cases where *no* is used as a response to prior utterances that report an out-the-ordinary state of affairs or event. And finally, I will briefly compare the use of *no* with the use of the particle *nii(n)*.

No *as a Response to Pre-Sequence First Pair Parts*

Response to Summonses and Attention-Getting Devices

The clearest cases of *no* as a response to a pre-sequence first pair part are what Schegloff (1990:60) has termed "generic pres," that is, summonses and other "attention-getting" devices (Schegloff 1972 [1968]). Generic pres provide no specification of the type of main action initiated by the speaker with the pre. They are especially found in co-present interactions where, for example, they are used for securing the attention of a nongazing recipient. Example (1) comes from an interaction between a five-year-old Lasse (L) and his father, Vesa (V), who are playing with small electric cars. At the beginning of the segment Lasse announces yet another derailment of his car. In line 6, he addresses his father with the noun *Isi*, 'Daddy'[4]:

(1)

```
    [Child/Aeroplane]
    1 L:    T(h)aas .nff t(h)aas .nff taas mu-l:ta
            again        again       again I-ABL
            A(h)gain .nff a(h)gain .nff again mi:ne
    2       suis[tu.hh           ]
            got off.hh          ]
                [                ]
    3 V:        [Pan-na-an se t]änne,
                [put-PAS-4 it here+TO
                [Let's put it here,
```

```
 4 L:    Aina    mu-lta suis°tuu°.
         always I-ABL get off
         Always mine gets °off°.
 5 V:    [((coughs))]
         [          ]
 6 L: →  [Isi,      ]
         [Daddy,    ]
 7 V: ⇒  Noh,
 8 L:    >Mä e-n    o< koskaa (1.0) mitää (0.2)
         I    NEG-1 be ever        any(PAR)
         >I have not< ever (1.0) any (0.2) aeroplane
 9       lentokone-tta koon-nu          yksin e-n-kä
         aeroplane-PAR assemble-PPC alone NEG-1–and
         assembled alone nor
10       l- laivaa.
         a s- ship.
11 V:    ((Coughs and sneezes.))
12 L: →  Niin saa-n-k-s      mä tänää?
         PRT may-1–Q-CLI I today
         May I today?
13 V:    No  ei-kö-hän    se järjest-y.
         PRT NEG-Q-CLI it arrange-REF
         Well I think it can be arranged.
```

At the time of Lasse's utterance in line 6, he and Vesa are back-to-back, both working with their cars. Through the address term, Lasse seeks the attention of his father for making some yet-to-be-produced action. In line 7, Vesa responds with the particle *no*. With this response, he displays that he is attending to Lasse and invites him to go ahead with his action. In lines 8–10, Lasse continues his talk with an utterance through which he reports actions he has never done alone, delivering thereby a possible complaint (see Schegloff 1988b:121; Pomerantz 1978). This utterance provides background for a yet-to-be-made main action, and it can be heard to imply a request for permission to do the kinds of actions reported. The utterance is done as a prosodic unit of its own, produced with a falling terminal contour. Since the speaker does not continue, the recipient could use the opportunity and provide a response, for example, to pre-empt the request. However, at that point Vesa only coughes and sneezes, and in line 12 Lasse moves on, now producing a request. This request is heard as the main action launched by Lasse with his summons in line 6.

In this case, the particle *no* presents a preferred response, a go-ahead, to a summons with which the speaker secures the attention of a nongazing recipient who was engaged in an activity of his own. Following the *no* response, the speaker proceeds to a further preliminary and subsequently produces the main action.

Response to Pre-Announcements and Other Pre-Tellings

Another set of prior utterances that act as pre-sequence first parts and regularly get a *no* response from the recipient are ones that project some sort of announcement or telling to come. In example (2), *no* is given as a response to a pre-announcement (cf. Terasaki 1976). Earlier in the talk, Marja had suggested to Eeva that they have a Campari later in the evening. Eeva had agreed, suggesting that they would have the drink at her place. The plan then is that Marja, who is calling from work, will fetch the Campari from home and come to Eeva's. In line 1, Eeva encourages Marja, who in the meantime has revealed that she had another plan for the evening, which she now abandons, to visit her:

(2)

```
[Eeva/Dog: 9–10]
1  E:    .hh @Tuu          tänne      [vaa:,h@ ]
             come(IMP) here+TO [just      ]
         .hh @Just come    here:,h@            ]
                                       [        ]
2  M:                                  [(Joohh) ]h [(   )   ]
                                       [(Yeahh) ]h [(   )   ]
                                               [        ]
3  E: →                                [Mut ↑ar]vaa
                                       [but  guess(IMP)
                                       [But  ↑guess

4        mitä,=
         what,=
5  M: ⇒ =No:[:?           ]
             [           ]
6  E: →      [Nyt-hän mä:] keks-i-n.=
             [now-CLI I   ] invent-PST-1
             [Now I:      ] realize.=
7  M: ⇒ =[No:?]
             [  ]
8  E: →  =[.hh ] Mu-lla-han on tuolla jääkaapi-ssa
         [     ] I-ADE-CLI is  there refrigerator-INE
      →  =[.hh ] I've got y'know there in the fridge
9     →  iso pullo samppiooni-a.
         big bottle brand, a domestic version of Campari
         a big bottle of Champion.
```

In line 3, in overlap with Marja's display of acceptance of the plan, Eeva initiates a new sequence with an utterance that exhibits a canonical way of building up a generic pre-announcement in Finnish: the utterance contains the verb *arvata*, 'guess,' in the second-person singular imperative form *arvaa*, followed by the question word *mitä*, 'what'. The utterance projects a telling of a piece of news to come but does not reveal any details of its subject matter. In line 5, Marja latches into Eeva's turn the particle *no*, which is delivered with a stretch and a rising terminal contour.

Through the particle *no* here, the recipient gives a go-ahead to the speaker; that is, *no* offers a second pair part that encourages the speaker to get on with the production of the core action and the base first pair part (Schegloff 1995) projected by the pre-announcement. However, in overlap with *no*, the speaker (line 6) produces an elaboration of the pre-announcement that formulates the announcement to come as something just realized. The utterance acts as a pre-announcement of its own. This preliminary also gets a *no*-formulated go-ahead response from the recipient. Following this *no*, the speaker (line 8–9) produces an utterance that delivers the announcement and simultaneously acts as an offer (an offer to drink Eeva's Champion, a domestic version of Campari, instead of having Marja go home and fetch her Campari).

No is also found as a response to utterances that project a telling of a joke to come, as in example (3). The example is part of a larger segment of talk in which Kake is telling a series of jokes about ways in which the inhabitants of the city of Tampere speak; his recipient, Veke, has just before mentioned that he will soon take a business trip to Tampere. In line 1, Veke is laughing at the previous joke:

(3)

```
       [Tiina/Fatty: 17]
        1 V:     Aa hah [hah hah haa .ha              [.ih .ih .ih
                        [                             [
        2 K: →          [eh heh heh .hhh £Niih, ja [tie-t   sä   mikä
                                            PRT   and know-2 you what
                        [eh heh heh .hhh £Yes, and do you know how
        3   →  on [kuljettaja£        tamperee-ksi,
               is [driver Tampere dialect-TRA
               is [((bus))driver£ in Tampere dialect,
                  [
        4 V:      [.ih hhhh
        5         (0.2)
        6 V: ⇒  #N:::noh#?
        7 K: →  Myy:rä.=.hh On-k-s    su-lla     myy-rä lippu-j-a
               mole        be-Q-CLI you-ADE sell-INF ticket-PL-PAR
               Myy:rä. (('mole')) =.hh Do you have tickets to myy-rä (('sell'))
        8       ((fake laughter:)) @ah[h ahh (.) hahh@
                                        [
        9 V:                           [.hh hh
       10 V:   °ih hih hih [.hhh #eee.#                      ]
                           [                                 ]
       11 K:              [Hausko-j-a     vits(h)e-j(h)-ä] £vai£,=
                          [funny-PL-PAR joke-PL-PAR ] PRT
                          [Funny jo(h)ke(h)s            ] £huh£,=
       12 V:   =#£Sä oo-t ol-lu    Tamperee-lla.£#
                  you be-2 be-PPC city name-ADE
               =#You've been in Tampere.£#
```

Kake's utterance in lines 2–3 is formed as a polar question, and on the surface it inquires about Veke's knowledge of how "bus driver" is said in the Tampere dialect. However, instead of inviting an affirmation or a rejection as its response, this utterance is heard as a "pre" that projects a joke to come and checks that the recipient does not already know the joke. It acts as a first pair part, and it prefers as its response a go-ahead by the recipient. After a short silence, the recipient (line 6) responds with *no*, which is stretched and carries a rising terminal contour. *No* treats the prior talk as a preliminary and invites the speaker to proceed to the main action. In line 7, the speaker delivers the joke.[5]

In example (4), from my written notes, A produces an utterance that projects a telling to come, checking simultaneously that what will be told is news to the recipients:

(4)

> [FN August 1996]
> 1 A: → *Hei mä kuul-i-n   yhe-n   hyvä-n   jutu-n.*
>   PRT I   hear-PST-1 one-ACC good-ACC story-ACC
>   Hey I heard a good story.
> 2 B: ⇒ *No:.*
> 3 A: *Ehkä   te   oo-tte kuul-lu   se-n.*
>   maybe you(PL) be-PL2 hear-PPC it-ACC
>   Maybe you have heard it.
> 4 B: ⇒ *No.*
> 5 A: *Se on semmonen nais-juttu.* [*JUTTU*]
>   it is such   woman-story
>   It's like a women's story. [STORY]

A's utterance in line 1 is another recurrent way of building up a pre-announcement in Finnish. It contains the first-person singular subject pronoun and the verb form *kuulin*, 'heard', followed by an object NP that refers to and characterizes what will be told. The characterization contains a general noun ("prospective indexical," Goodwin 1996), *jutun*, 'story', and the modifier *hyvän*, 'good', which further specifies the nature of what will be told. In line 2, B responds with the particle *no*, with which she treats A's prior turn as a "pre" and invites her to get on with the telling. However, instead of starting the telling, A now addresses the possibility that her recipients may already have heard the story. In line 4, B again responds with *no*, providing a further go-ahead to A. And in line 5, A first offers a more specific characterization of her story and then moves to the telling of what turns out to be a joke (data not shown).

In all three examples, *no* is given as a response to a turn that acts as a pre-announcement or other kind of pre-telling. In all of them, the prior turn is constructed through a conventional format of doing a pre-announcement or pre-telling in Finnish: the status of the turn as a "pre" is made explicit by the speaker. With *no*, recipients offer a preferred response to the prior turn: they treat the prior utterance as one that has not been produced in its own right, and they invite the co-participant to go ahead.

Response to Preliminaries to Preliminaries

A further set of prior turns that get the particle *no* as response are ones that act as preliminaries to preliminaries (pre-pres; Schegloff 1980). Pre-pres are turns and utterances with which a speaker projects an action by mentioning or naming it. However, instead of doing next the action named, the speaker moves to offer further preliminaries to the main action yet to come; hence the name pre-pre. In example (5), the pre-pre in line 3 projects a request for help to come. Raisa has called Tuire. After the greetings and after having been assured that Tuire has time (data not shown), Raisa (line 1) produces an utterance that contains an attention-getting device and prepares the recipient for something special to come:

(5)

```
[Tuire/Help: 1–2]
 1 R:    Kuule.
         Listen.
 2       (.)
 3 R: →  .mt Apu-a      su-lta.
             help-PAR you-ABL
         .tch Help from you.
 4 T: ⟹  >No,<
 5 R:    .mth Kuule tota: tuoll-on t- tuolla hhh höhhöhhöh
         .tch Listen uh: there's t- there hhh uhuhuhuh
 6       .hhh bisnes     studiierillä     on joskus
              business(S) studies(S)-ADE is sometimes
         .hhh at the Business Studies⁶ they have sometimes
 7       ens  vuon-na  sellanen (.) wöörkshoppi.
         next year-ESS such         workshop(E)
         next year like (.) a workshop.
 8 T:    [Nih,]
         [Yes,]
         [    ]
 9 R:    [Ja ] (.) ei-hän  siellä tietyst   mitää    semmos-t
         [and ]    NEG-CLI there of course any(PAR) such-PAR
         [And ] (.) there isn't of course y'know anything
10       mi-stä (.)  mikä o-is     mun ihan om-i-a
         what-ELA what be-CON my  just own-PL-PAR
         about what (.) that'd be just my own
11       asio-i-ta      mutta .hhh mu-n pitäs    nyt (.) yleensä
         thing-PL-PAR but         I-GEN should now     in general
         stuff but .hhh I should now (.) generally
12       siis  niinku °u° teh-dä   kaikke-a.h
         PRT like        do-INF everything-PAR
         I mean like °e° do all kinds of things.h
13 T:    N[ii. ]
          Yes.
          [    ]
14 R:    [.mth] Niin, nin  mu-m pitäs    sinnek-ki
         [    ] PRT PRT I-GEN should there+TO-also
         [.tch] Yes, so I should
15       jotaki      murjo-a.   Ja  ne  puhuu
         something mangel-INF and they talk-3
         get something there too. And they'll discuss
```

```
16        [inflaatiosta. .m[th
          [inflation-ELA
          [inflation.    .t [ch
          [                  [
17 T:     [.hhh             [Jao.
          [.hhh             [Yeah.
18 R: →   Ja  mä kysy-si-n    su-lta    että o-is-    o-is-ko
          and I    ask-CON-1 you-ABL that be-CON be-CON-Q
          And I'd like to ask you that wou- would
19    →   tämmönen otsikko (.) su-m      miele-stä  semmonen
          this kind   title     you-GEN mind-ELA such
          this kind of title (.) to you mind be one
20    →   (.) joka tuota o-is     ruotti-a.
              that PRT be-CON Swedish-PAR
          (.) that uh would be Swedish.
21        (0.3)
22 T:     Joo.
          Yes.
23 R:     ((begins to read the title))
```

In line 3, Raisa produces a verbless utterance with which she announces that she needs help from the recipient without, however, specifying the kind of help needed. This utterance projects a request for help to come. In line 4, Tuire responds with the particle *no*.[7] With *no*, she offers a go-ahead response. This response is followed by talk through which Raisa offers the recipient background information needed for the production of the request; the request itself is delivered in lines 18–20.

In example (6), *no* (line 8) is given as a response to an utterance with which the speaker, the caller, characterizes the kind of action to come through describing the type of phone call she is initiating:

(6)

```
[Tiina/SOS-call: 1]
  1 T:    @No mi-tä      kuuluu@,=
          PRT what-PAR is heard
          @Well how are you@,
  2 J:    =.hhh Ihan hyvä-ä.   <Kiitos muuten>   @viimeise-stä@,
              just  good-PAR thanks by the way last-ELA
          =.hhh Just fine. <By the way thanks> @again@,
  3 T:    >@Ei-pä kestä    toivottava-sti ol-i    ↓mukava-a@.
          NEG-CLI endure hopeful-ADV be-PST nice-PAR
          >@You're welcome hopefully you had a ↓good time@.
  4 J:    @O:l-i@,
          be-PST
          @We di:d?@
  5       (0.2)
  6 T: →  .mh @↑A↓haa@. .mhhh Tota< (.) @tää on tämmönen:::
              PRT            PRT      this  is  this kind
          .mh @↑I ↓see@. .mhh Well< (.) @this is this kind
```

```
 7    →   (.) h̲ätä-apu-soit̲t̲o̲,
               trouble-help-call
               of::: (.) help-in-tr̲o̲uble call?
 8  J: ⇒   N̲o̲,=
 9  T:     =ʼmnen sos: .mhhh Oo-tte-k-s        te
               such   SOS       be-PL2–Q-CLI you(PL)
               =a kind of a SOS:. .mhhh Will you ((PL)) be here
10         v̲iiko-n-lopu-n          täällä̲,
               week-GEN-end-GEN here
               during the w̲eekend,
11  J:     .hh Mä mee-n Nastola-a.
               I   go-1  city name-ILL
               .hh Iʼll be going to Nastola.
12  T:     Te       mee-tte N̲astola-a.
               you(PL) go-PL2 city name-ILL
               Youʼll ((PL)) be going to N̲astola.
13  J:     E-   e-n    mä E̲ila-st      °tiedä°. Mä mee-n.
               NEG NEG-1 I    1nameF-ELA know I    go-1
               N- I donʼt know about E̲ila. I̲ʼll be going.
14  T:     Ahaa. Entä-s          p̲erjantai-na.
               PRT   what about-CLI Friday-ESS
               I see. What about on Fr̲iday.
15         (1.1)
16  J:     ööö M̲i-tä     pitä-s     teh-dä.
               what-PAR must-CON do-INF
               er: Wh̲at should be done.
17  T:     .hhhhh Jo(o) h̲omma     on sellanen että mei-lle
                        job(NOM) is such     that we-ALL
               .hhhhh Yeah the j̲ob is that weʼll have
18         tulee l̲ava             p̲erjantai-aamu-na.
               comes platform(NOM) Friday-morning-ESS
               a pl̲atform coming on Friday morning.
19  J:     Mik̲ä?
               what(NOM)
               What?
20  T:     L̲ava,
               A pl̲atform.
21         (.)
22  J:     [°N̲ii°?,
           [°Yes°?,
           [
23  T:     [Semmonen s̲iirto-lava.=
           [such       moving-platform
           [Like a tr̲ansfer platform.
24  J:     =°N̲ii, [(just°)
           =°Yes, [(right°)
                  [
25  T: →          [Ja   tota: .hhhh sit   ne   ka:ma-t
                  [and PRT       then they stuff-PL
                  [And we:ll, .hhh then the stu:ff should
```

26 → *pitä-s   ne* (.) *seinä-n   jämä-t*
       must-CON they wall-GEN remaining-PL(ACC)
       the (.) remains of the walls
27 → *pitä-s   siirtä-ä   sinne   lava-an.*
       must-CON move-INF there+TO platform-ILL
       should be moved to the platform.

In lines 6–7, at a place for telling the reason for the call, Tiina produces an utterance that describes the kind of call she is making. The utterance is done through the format [X is Y], a predicate nominal clause, which describes the ongoing encounter as a certain type of encounter from the point of view of its speaker, the caller. Through the compound noun *hätäapusoitto*, 'help-in-trouble-call', the utterance projects a request for help to come and portrays the need for help as pressing. However, no details of the request are provided by the speaker. In line 8, the recipient responds with *no*, which carries a level terminal contour.

Through *no*, the recipient treats the co-participant's prior talk as a preliminary and invites her to go ahead. In so doing he also displays that he does not know the specifics of what the pre is leading up to. In line 9, the speaker first responds by an elaboration of her description of the call, adding to the pressing need for help. She then moves to an action other than the projected request for help: she inquires about the recipient's and his wife's circumstances in a way that formulates the request as contingent on the response to this question. When she gets a blocking response from Jari, that is, a response that indicates that he already has a commitment for the weekend, Tiina (line 14) proceeds to ask about the availability of the recipient earlier. At this point, following a trouble-indicative silence (Pomerantz 1984a, b), the recipient (line 16) inquires about the kind of task the caller has in mind, and subsequently, in lines 25–27, the caller provides an indication of the kind of help needed.

In examples (5) and (6) the particle *no* was offered as a response to a pre-pre, that is, to an utterance that described the type of main action to come. In that fashion, *no* made room for the delivery of some background information and assured that there were grounds for doing the main action. Similar to other types of pres discussed earlier, in these cases *no* provides a response that forwards the activity launched by the speaker by inviting the speaker to get on with the production of the larger unit of talk under way.

In sum, the particle *no* is used as a go-ahead response to a prior turn that initiates a pre-sequence. In the cases we have seen, the prior turn has a format that is conventionalized as a way of doing a preliminary in Finnish. The types of prior turn responded to with *no* include certain kinds of preliminaries, such as summonses (e.g., *hei*, 'hey', *Isi*, 'Daddy'), pre-tellings (e.g., declarative clauses that announce that its speaker has heard a good story), generic pre-announcement utterances (imperatives, e.g., *arvaa mitä*, 'guess what') and pre-pres (namings of an action e.g. *apua sulta*, 'help from you'). These utterances, in one way or another, indicate that a pre-sequence has been initiated in order to check that there are grounds for starting some yet-to-come main action, instead of doing the main action straight off. However, we also find *no* as a response to utterances other than conventionalized pre-sequence first pair parts. In these cases, *no* nevertheless treats its prior turn as something that acted in a pre-like fashion. We now turn to these cases.

No *as a Response in Other Environments*

Cases to be explored in this section that get a *no* response from the recipient differ in two ways from instances discussed so far: (1) the prior utterance is not constructed through a conventionalized utterance type for doing a preliminary, (2) the prior utterance does not necessarily initiate a sequence. The prior utterance can even be produced in a fashion that does not seem to provide the recipient an opportunity for a response, for example, as part of a larger telling. However, these instances bear similarities to sequences that involve conventionalized pres. Thus, also in them the prior utterance is hearably incomplete as a telling and/or an expandable utterance. It reports or implies a departure from some normal, ordinary course of action or state of affairs, and its incompleteness lies in the fact that no explanation or account for the departure has yet been provided by the speaker.

In line 10 in example (7), we find *no* as a response to an announcement of a change in a joint plan. The segment comes from a phone call between Tiinu (T) and Mia (M), two teenage girls who are classmates. Just before line 1 they have brought talk about a school exam to a possible completion. Silence ensues, and in line 1 Tiinu breaks it with a loud belch, received by Mia with teasing:

(7)

```
     [Girls/How's school: 19]
      1 T:    mhh .mt ((röyhtäisee äänekkäästi:)) br::::p
              mhh .mt ((a loud belch:)) br::::p
      2        phhh [°eh heh eh              [.hhh
                    [                        [
      3 M:          [(((tekonauru:)) haha,   [Terveisiä
                    [(((fake laughter:)) haha, [Greetings
      4        @si↑ka-la:-s [ta@,      ]
                  pig-NOU-ELA          ]
               @from a ↑pi:g house@,
                            [         ]
      5 T:                  [↑£Mm:,] Joo?,
                            [↑£Mm:,] Yeah?,
      6 M:    @täällä ↑Tii:n [u,
               here   1nameF
               @here's ↑Tii:n[u,
                              [
      7 T: →                  [@.hh@ Ei    hei   vi:tsi,
                              [      NEG PRT PRT
                              [@.hh@ Oh no da:mn,
      8 M: →  Noh.
      9 T: →  .mt E-m    mä voi tul-la    tei-lle    yö-ks?,
                  NEG-1 I  can come-INF you(PL)-ALL night-TRA
               .tch I can't come and stay overnight at your place?,
```

10 M: ⇒ N*o*h.

11 T: .hh ↑No siis ku s*i*t   meiä-n   pitää men-nä sinne
          PRT PRT as then we-GEN must go-INF there+TO
          .hh ↑Well I mean since th*e*n we have to go there

12   tsöötsi-in   se-j   jäl:kee tai sinne (.)   kappeli-i.
          church(E)-ILL it-GEN after   or there+TO chapel-ILL
          to the ch*u*rch after that or to the (.) chapel.

13   (0.5)

14 M: [Mua ei-   ]
          [I don'-   ]
          [   ]

15 T: [T*a*nssi-tunni-j]   jäl .hh ja< m ↑no sinne   mh (0.5)
          [dance-lesson-GEN after   and   PRT there+TO
          [After the d*a*nce lesson .hh and< m ↑well to the mh
          (0.5)

16 M: [↑Ai ni,   ]
          [↑Oh yeah,]
          [   ]

17 T: [mh   ] M*m*. .mhhhh Ni k*i*va kum mä mh .hh >s*i*t
          [mh   ] M*m*. .mhhhh N*i*ce   when I   mh .hh >then

18   mu-l ei   oo mitää   semmos-i-i   vaa:tte-i-ta
          I-ADE NEG be any(PAR) such-PL-PAR cloth-PL-PAR
          I have no such clothes nor

19   ei-kä   mitää   mu-n pitä-s   raijaa niinku
          NEG-and anything(PAR) I-GEN must-CON drag   like
          anything I should drag like all

20   koko omai:suus tänne—
          all   prope:rty here+TO
          the prope:rty here—

Following Mia's second teasing utterance, Tiinu (line 7) produces an excla-
mation that displays that something has just occurred to her. This utterance comes
close to a generic pre: it alerts the recipient to some forthcoming main action and
shifts the talk away from the tease (see Drew 1987 on receipts of teases). In line 8,
Mia offers a go-ahead to Tiinu with the particle *no*. Tiinu (line 9) continues her
talk with an announcement: she cancels what she has agreed upon with the recipient earlier. Through the modal *voi*, 'can', the cancellation is formulated as a lack of
possibility of fulfilling an agreement.[8] As an announcement and cancellation Tiinu's
talk is heard as incomplete at this point: although the modal *voi*, 'can' provides
inability as a reason for the cancellation (cf. Heritage 1988), no specific reason has
been produced yet. However by not continuing, Tiinu makes Mia's response relevant. And in line 10, Mia responds with the particle *no*. With *no*, she treats Tiinu's
announcement as in need of an elaboration. Following *no*, Tiinu moves to specify
the cancellation, marking her utterance as an explanation with the complex connector *siis ku* (see Ford 1994 on English *because* in contexts of remarkable claims).

No can also occur in a third position: it can, for example, receive an answer to
a question, as in line 4 in example (8). After the greetings, Reijo, the caller, has asked
Tuire whether he woke her up (data not shown), thereby treating his call as un-

usual in terms of its timing. Tuire's turn in line 1 elaborates her negative answer to the question:

(8)

```
[Tuire/Furniture: 1–2]
  1 T:    Lehte-ä      lue-n.
          paper-PAR read-1
          I'm reading the paper.
  2 R:    £↑Jaa ja[a. Jaa jaa. [No<       ]
          £↑I se [e. I see.    [Well<      ]
               [            [            ]
  3 T:              [.hh    [No   mi-] mi-stä      soitt-ele-t.
                    [       [PRT    ] what-ELA call-FRE-2
                    [.hh    [Well wh-] where're you calling from.
  4 R: →  Mi↑nä soitt-ele-n tä-llä      kerta-a      Länsi-Pasilasta.
          I       call-FRE-1 this-ADE time-PAR suburb name
          I'm calling this time from Länsi-Pasila.
  5 T: ⇒  No:,hh
  6 R:    Mei-ll' on tul-lu      semmonen äkki-lähtö Helsinki-in
          we-ADE is come-PPC such        hasty leave name-ILL
          We've had like a hasty leave to Helsinki
  7       kun tuota (.) tai se n e::i   nyt  ihan äkkilähtö
          as   PRT     or it  NEG now quite hasty leave
          as uh (.) or it n no::t a hasty leave quite but
  8       mut kuitenki       ni .hhhh (h)ei me tien-nee-t
          but nevertheless PRT       NEG me know-PPC-PL
          nevertheless .hhhh we did not know
  9       joutu-va-mme           tule-ma-am       me: (.) tuo-da-an
          have to-INF-POS1PL come-INF-ILL we      bring-PAS-4
          we'd have to come we: (.) are bringing ((here))
 10       semmos-t suku-kalleut-ta        tuoli-a
          such-PAR family-treasure-PAR chair-PAR
          like a family treasure a chair
 11       joka on hajon-nu—
          that is break-PPC
          that got broken—
```

In line 3, Tuire inquires after the location Reijo is calling from. The mere posing of this inquiry suggests that there may be something out-of-the-ordinary in Reijo's call. In his answer, Reijo (line 4) tells the place he is calling from, a suburb of Helsinki. This utterance contains the time expression *tällä kertaa*, 'this time', which presents the place of calling as different from some other place. The answer consists of this utterance only. For the recipient the answer poses a question about what to make of it here and now. In line 5, the recipient responds with the particle *no*, which is delivered with a level terminal contour.

With *no*, the recipient treats the prior answer as in need of elaboration. A relevant action by the speaker would be giving a reason for being in the place he is. From ethnographic information we know that Reijo lives quite far away from

Helsinki, where Tuire lives, but is calling from a suburb of Helsinki. What this makes relevant is a telling of a reason for him being in Helsinki and also a reason for his call, as he has presented no reason for it yet. His response that starts in line 6 eventuates into a specification of the reason for him (and his family) being in Helsinki, and subsequently (data not shown) he also tells the reason for his call, a suggestion to get together with Tuire and her family.

In example (9) *no* occurs within storytelling in line 9. It is produced in overlap with an utterance in which the speaker, as part of a report of her day, tells about having cried extensively. In line 1, following Eeva's response to her how-are-you question, Marja, the caller, starts a report of her day:

(9)

```
[Eeva/Dog: 1–2]
  1 M:   [he Nii::n .ihhh £Voi: sentä mie täälä
         [   PRT          PRT PRT I    here
         [he Yea::h. .ihhh £O:h go:d I'm here
  2      tö-i-ssä      oo   #ja m [mm#
         work-PL-INE be(1) and  [
         at work uu #and m       [mm#
                                 [
  3 E:                           [↑↑Tö-i-s:sä.
                                 [   work-PL-INE
                                 [↑↑At wo:rk.
  4 M:   >Joo: k'le tänään tulee   tommone< super-pitkä päivä
         PRT hear today  comes that kind   super-long day
         >Yea:h listen it's gonna be a< super long day
  5      ku ensi mä ol-i-n    siel seminaari-s ja sit tul-i-n<
         as first I  be-PST-1 there seminar-INE and then come-PST-1
         as I first attended the seminar and then I came<
  6 →    tul-i-n<    tän:ne   ja ((rykäisee:)) khym .mt ↑mä
         come-PST-1 here+TO and clears throat              I
         I came he:re and ((clears throat)) grhm .tch ↑I
  7 →    oo-n i:tke-ny ku Niagara-n
         be-1 cry-PPC like Niagara-GEN
         have crie:d like the Niagara
  8 →    pu[tous tänää kuule   ] ku .hhhh Riitta tänää
         fall    today hear(IMP)] since 1nameF today
         Fa[lls today y'know   ] since .hhhh Riitta had
           [                    ]
  9 E: ⇒ [No::h,               ]
 10 M:   vika päivä-ä tö-i-s:sä      ja molemma-t ties
         last day-PAR work-PL-INE and both-PL    know-PST
         her last day at wo:rk today and we both
 11      että tä-stä-hä ei   tuu  mitää       tä-stä
         that this-ELA NEG come anything(PAR) this-ELA
         knew that this wouldn't work this
 12      mei#j-ä  hyvästely-stä   ja# .hhh .mt se ol-i
         we-GEN leave taking-ELA and            it be-PST
         #our saying goodbye business and# .hhh .tch she
```

```
13        täälä tö-i-:ssä        ja  me sovi-tt-i-in        et  se
          here  work-PL-INE  and we  agree-PAS-PST-4  that it
          was here at wo:rk and we agreed that she'd slip

14 E:     livahtaa ove-sta      ulos ett-e-n        #mä nää si-tä#.
          slips     door-ELA   out  that-NEG-1 I     see it-PAR
          she'd slip out through the door so that #I won't see her#.

15 M:     Joo::,=
          Yea::,=

16 E:     =.mt Ja  sit   mä sano-i-n    Riita-lle   et   no< kyl
               and then I   say-PST-1 name-ALL that PRT  surely
          =.tch And then I said to Riitta that well<

17        mei-jän  on pakko      silti hala-ta   ku se ol-i
          we-GEN  is obligation still hug-INF as  it be-PST
          we surely still have to hug each other when she

18        menossa siinä  ove-n-rao-ssa            kuule      ni   s-
          going    there door-GEN-hole-INE  hear(IMP) PRT i-
          was there at the door y'know and i- it was y'know

19        se-hän ol-i     ku o-is       pom:mi heittä-ny    kuule
          it-CLI be-PST as  be-CON bomb   throw-PPC hear(IMP)
          as a bom:b had been thrown y'know we both started

20        molemma-t rupe-s    itkee iha  hysteerise-nä  ja
          both-PL    start-PST cry  just hysterical-ESS and
          to cry just hysterically and .hhh

21        .hhh se vaa kuule        paken(h)ee o(h)ve(h)-sta
               it just hear(IMP) escapes      door-ELA
          she just y'know escape(h)s thro(h)ugh the d(h)oor

22        u(h)los (ku   mie) .hhh .mt £(viel) sitte puol
          out     when I                 still  then half
          (when I) .hhh .tch£then it was boiling in my head

23        tunti-i    kuule     keitt-i   pää-ssä£ ↑itk-i-n niin
          hour-PAR hear(IMP) boil-PST head-INE cry-PST so
          (still) for half an hour ↑I cried so

24        ett-ei      oo mitää ↓raja-a  ja   sitte—
          that-NEG be any   limit-PAR and then
          that there is no ↓limit and then—
```

In line 6, the teller intiates a new unit of talk (marked with pitch in rise, indicated by an upward arrow). The utterance eventuates into a beginning of trouble telling: it describes a strong emotion (↑*mä oon i:tkeny ku Niagaran putous tänää kuule*, 'I have cri:ed like the Niagara Falls today y'know', lines 6–8). Here *no* overlaps the description of the manner of crying done with a metaphorical expression at a point at which the expression is recognizable. At this point the telling is incomplete: Marja has provided no reason for her crying yet. The *no* treats the utterance it responds to and what is mentioned in it as a preliminary to some core telling and encourages the teller to go on. Through the delivery features of the particle, the vowel lengthening and utterance-final outbreath (indicated by *h*), she furthermore, I suggest, displays empathy toward the teller. Through *no*, the recipient commits herself as a troubles recipient (see Jefferson 1988). Simultaneously the teller (line 8), independently and without any break in intonation, proceeds to specify the reason for her crying, marking her utterance as an explanation with the connector *ku*, 'since'.

In all three examples in this section, the particle *no* is used as a response to an utterance that offers an informing. This informing can occupy different kinds of sequential environment: it can be an announcement, an answer to a question, or part of a storytelling. What is common to them, however, is that at the point at which the recipient responds with *no* the telling is hearably incomplete. The speaker has described an action or a state of affairs that in some way departs from an ordinary course of action, such as extensive crying, calling from an unexpected location, and failing to fulfill an agreement. The incompleteness of the telling lies in the fact that no reason for the departure or for an out-of-the-ordinary course of action or state of affairs has been provided yet. This reason or account forms an essential part of the telling, and it is to this kind of incompleteness that the recipient orients with the particle *no*.

There is a link between the usages of *no* discussed in this section and its use as a response to conventionalized preliminaries discussed earlier: in both cases it responds to a prior utterance that has implicated something remarkable, something that forms a departure from some normal course of action or state of affairs. The most conventionalized sequential context for a *no* response is after a conventional preliminary such as an attention-getter (for example, *isi*, 'daddy') or a generic pre-announcement (*arvaa mitä*, 'guess what'). In those cases the remarkable character of the prior talk lies in the fact that the speaker has initiated a pre-sequence, instead of proceeding more directly to the main action. The cases we have seen in this section show that recipients also use *no* as a response to turns that explicitly or by reference to shared knowledge (example [8]) report a remarkable state of affairs or an event.

The Particle Nii(n) *as a Response to Incomplete Prior Talk*

There is another particle, the particle *nii(n)*, that—especially when delivered with a nonfalling terminal contour—is used as a response to prior talk that is hearably incomplete. *Nii(n)* is an original Finno-Ugric word that etymologically belongs to the paradigm for the demonstrative pronoun *se* 'it; that' as its instructive (instrumental) case form 'thus, so' in the plural. However, the status of *nii(n)* as a case-marked, inflected element faded early on, and it is now understood to be an uninflected particle. In sentence-internal usages it comes close to the English particle *so* (e.g. , 'She did it so'; 'I'm so glad').[9] *Nii* has moved out of the demonstrative paradigm and also out of clause structure so that it can also occur as an utterance and turn of its own. As a turn of its own, it is used, for example, as a confirming response to noninterrogative polar questions (declaratives, nonclausal questions) and as a claim of agreement with a display of stance by the speaker of the previous turn (see Sorjonen 1997, in press).

The usage that is of interest to us here is the use of *nii* as a "continuer" (see, e.g., Sacks 1992b:410; Schegloff 1982), that is, as a claim of an understanding that the co-participant is building a larger unit of talk that is yet to be completed and as an invitation to the co-participant to continue the production of that larger unit of talk. Thus, similarly to *no*, the particle *nii* also occurs as a response to an utterance that acts as a preliminary, that is, as an utterance that has not been produced in its own right.

However, the types of prior utterances responded to by *nii* differ from ones that get a *no* response. One clear difference is that in the current data base *nii*, with three exceptions (see example [12]), does not occur as a response to conventionalized preliminaries. In other words, there are no pre-sequences that would have *nii* as a second pair part. By contrast, *nii* is found as a response to utterances that through their semantico-pragmatic design and their sequential positioning project some core action yet to come. Here the prior utterance has already started the larger main activity even though its core action and point is yet to be delivered. Within the activity, the utterance to which *nii(n)* responds forms a place of maximum incompleteness. That is, the speaker has reached a place in her talk after which the delivery of a point of the activity is imminent. Before proceeding to the point she momentarily stops her talk, thereby yielding a place for a possible response by the recipient.

In line 5 in example (10), *nii* is offered as a response to an utterance with which the speaker has started to tell the reason for her call. The utterance is being constructed as a multiclause construction ("compound TCU," Lerner 1987, 1991, 1996), in which the first part describes the activity under way and the second part tells the subject matter of the talk. Lines 1–3 belong to a larger segment of talk in which Tuire and Sisko talk about how easy it is to break into the shed of Sisko's summer cottage:

(10)

[Tuire/Birthday: 4–5]
```
  1 S: → [Juu, ja ikkuna-n      särkee. ]
         [PRT and window-ACC breaks ]
         [Yea, and break the window. ]
  2 T:  [Nii,              ]
         [                  ]
  3 S: → [Siinä-hän on °ikku] na-ki°. .hhh ↑No kuule     se
         [it+IN-CLI is  window-CLI      PRT hear(IMP) it
         [There's the window as well see. .hhh .hhh ↑Well
  4   →  asia j- jonka      takia    mä soita-n #oikeesti#,=
         thing which(GEN) because I    call-1   really
         listen the reason I'm calling #in fact#,=
  5 T: ⇒ =NII[:.
            [
  6 S:     [.hhh on Maija-n       synty#mä-päi[vä#.]
            [    is 1nameF-GEN birth-day
            [.hhh is Maija's birth#day#.
                                           [ ]
  7 T:                                     [ JO]O,=
  8 S:  =.hh Että (.) me on nyt >kaikennäkös-tä ohjelma-a
         PRT    we is now all sorts-PAR   program-PAR
         =.hh So (.) we have now scraped together
```

```
 9  S:    haa↑li-ttu,
           scrape together-PPPC
           all sorts of acti↑vities,
10  T:    Mm:.
11  S: →  Laulu-a   ja   tanssi-a    ja   #a#  ↓muu-ta.
           song-PAR and dance-PAR and ?      else-PAR
           Singing and dancing and #e# ↓like that.
12  T: →  NII.=
13  S:    =.hh Nin tota .mhhh #ö m# ↑käv-is-kö     su-lle   että
                PRT PRT              suit-CON-Q you-ALL that
           =.hh So um .mhhh #er um# ↑would it suit you that
14        sää pitä-isi-t    puhee-n.
           you give-CON-2 speech-ACC
           you would give a speech.
15  T:    <.hhhh> No ↑minä-hän voi-n si-tä    mie:tti-ä.hhh
                      PRT I-CLI    can-1 it-PAR think-INF
           <.hhhh> Well ↑I can surely thi:nk about it.hhh
```

In line 3, Sisko begins an utterance that projects the reason for her call to come.
The core of the utterance is initiated (lines 3–4) with a pronominally modified
general noun *asia*, 'reason', to which the speaker, through a restrictive relative
clause, connects the information that she is on her way to tell the reason for the
call. The yet-to-come reason is separated from the preceding talk and formulated
as important through the adverb *oikeesti*, 'in fact'.[10] This adverb forms a possible
grammatical completion of the relative clause (and the NP)[11] and makes a copula
verb syntactically relevant, followed by a complement that would provide an initial characterization of the reason for her call. The utterance so far is constructed
prosodically as a unit of its own through a pitch peak in *soitan*, 'calling' (cf. Schegloff
1988a, 1996) and a momentary break at the end of the adverb (marked by a comma
that indicates level terminal contour indexing continuation). At this point, the recipient latches *nii* onto the utterance (line 5).

Here the particle *nii* is uttered at a point at which the speaker has not yet provided the recipient with any indication about the subject matter of the action she has
projected. *Nii* aligns with the prior state of talk by displaying an understanding that
the prior utterance forms part of a yet-to-be-completed verbal action and invites the
co-participant to go on. The speaker orients to *nii* as a continuer by formulating the
turn at line 6 as a grammatical continuation of her prior utterance.

The segment contains another *nii* response in line 12.[12] In this case, *nii* responds to an utterance after which the delivery of the core action would be relevant. Sisko's utterance in line 11 offers, through three co-ordinated NPs that
form a list (cf. Jefferson 1990), a specification of what she and some other people
have done for the program of a mutual friend's birthday party. The list specifies,
by virtue of its sequential position, the case marking (cf. the partitive case endings,
marked in the gloss lines with *PAR*, lines 8 and 11), the lexical content of the words,
and the fact that there is nothing else in the utterance, the program for the party.
It is offered as a possibly complete utterance through falling intonation contour
and its three-partedness.[13] Having been constructed as a specification of the prior

utterance in lines 8–9 and as a grammatically dependent component of it, the list possibly completes the report on the program. In so doing it forms an internal juncture within the activity and makes relevant a shift from the report to the point of giving it. In line 12, the recipient responds with *nii*. Through it, she orients to the incomplete character of the prior talk and the ongoing activity and invites a continuation of it. This *nii* is followed by a turn that delivers a request (lines 13–14).

In example (10), the *nii* responses occurred at crucial structural junctures within the activity of telling the reason for a telephone call. Within storytelling, *nii* is also found at places of maximum incompleteness. Here its prior utterance forms a juncture within the main story line. An utterance that introduces the main character of the forthcoming telling forms one central prior context for the *nii* response. In example (11), *nii* is given as the first response to the narrative proper at a point at which the main character has been introduced by the teller. Arto's question at line 1 is a response to Tiina's announcement of a place where she and her husband, Veke, spent their Midsummer:

(11)

```
[Tiina/Moving: 2–3]
  1 A:   Ol-i-k-s        kiva-a.=
         be-PST-Q-CLI nice-PAR
         Did you have a good time.=
  2 T:   =.mt ↑Ol-i    mei-l    ol-i     sillai     aika
              be-PST we-ADE be-PST in that way quite
         =.mth ↑Yes we had it quite
  3      mukava-a et (0.2) sillon aato-n-aatto-na
         nice-PAR that    then  eve-GEN-eve-ESS
         nice in that (0.2)a day before the Midsummer eve
  4      torstai-ilta-na?       .hhh ni    m' ol-t-i-i      tuol
         Thursday-evening-ESS      PRT we be-PAS-PST-4 there
         on Thursday evening? .hhh we were creeping
  5      mönki-mä-ssä Veke-n              vanhe-mp-i-en
         creep-INF-INE nicknameM-GEN old-COM-PL-GEN
         through Veke's parents'
  6      kellari-a   ja   katto-ma-ssa   on-k-s   nii-l    siel
         cellar-PAR and look-INF-INE be-Q-CLI they-ADE there
         cellar and checking if they have
  7      kivo-j-a       huone-kalu-j-a       ja  sit  ↑me
         nice-PL-PAR room-thing-PL-PAR and then  we
         nice furniture there and then ↑we
  8      men-t-i-i      vaa ylös    pese-e ↑kä:de-t        ja
         go-PAS-PST-4 just up+TO wash-ILL hand-PL(ACC) and
         went up just to wash our ↑ha:nds and
  9      sit  so-i      puhelin ja .hhh jah tota (.) siel
         then ring-PST phone  and   and PRT   there
         then the phone rang and .hhh and well (.) there
 10      ol-i    semmonen (.) tyttö joka me ol-la-an
         be-PST such          girl that we be-PAS-4
         was this (.) girl whom we had
```

```
11        tava-ttu      sillo neljä vuo-tta    sitte Rooma-ssa.
          meet-PPPCP then four year-PAR ago Rome-INE
          met four years ago in Rome.
12  A: ⇒ Nii?,
13  T:   .mh Ja   tota uusseelanti-lainen tyttö.  .hh ni   se
               and PRT New Zealand-ADJ girl        PRT it
          .mh And um a New Zealand girl.  .hh she
14        (0.2) ol-i     tulo-ssa    Suome-en    pyörä-ile-mä-än,
               be-PST come-INE Finland-ILL bike-FRE-INF-ILL
          (0.2) was coming to Finland to bike,
```

In line 2, Tiina first responds with a slightly downgraded confirmation and then proceeds to specify the events assessed in that way with a report of her and her husband's activities a couple of days before the Midsummer. Within the frame of telling about Midsummer, this talk is heard as a lead-up. It sets up a particular time; it introduces the characters, their location, and the activity they are engaged in with its goal. It then reports subsequent events and, in line 9, the event of the phone ringing. From this Tiina, in lines 9–11, proceeds to describe the caller: a friend and somebody not known to Arto. This description makes relevant some further reporting of the call. Through a falling terminal contour, this utterance is prosodically marked as a juncture within the telling.

At that point, Arto (line 12) responds with *nii*, which carries a slightly raising terminal contour. Through it, he treats Tiina's talk as still incomplete and invites her to continue. And following the *nii* response, Tiina, after a further characterization of the character, moves (data not shown) to give an initial description of the reason for the friend's call that subsequently leads to a description of their Midsummer with the New Zealander as a surprise guest.

Similarly to example (10), also in this example *nii* was offered as response to a narrative at a point of core structural juncture of the activity, at a point in the teller's talk that projected a first core event in the narrative to come next. Notice that before the *nii* response there are hitches in the teller's talk that the recipient could have used as places for a response. A strong candidate for a recipient response is in line 4 at a point at which the temporal anchoring of the events to be told is done with a rising terminal contour, followed by an inbreath; the speaker also takes an inbreath after the mentioning of the phone ringing (line 9). However, these places are not made use of by the recipient. Through his *nii* response, the recipient picks up the place at which the teller has introduced a character who is heard as possibly playing a major role in the forthcoming telling.

In rare cases (in three cases of eighty-some instances in the data base), *nii* is found as a response to an utterance that has been constructed through a conventionalized utterance type for doing a preliminary, that is, in a sequential environment for the particle *no*. Example (12) offers an instance. In it, *nii* is given as a response to an utterance with which the caller initiates a pre-sequence by describing the type of call she is making.[14] In lines 1–3, Raija and Tiina are closing down discussion about the place where they will meet the following day:

(12)

```
[Tiina/Chapel: 6–7]
    1  R:    Hyvä. [Kolme-n    ] [maissa ] Kappeli-ssa.
             good   [three-GEN] [around] cafe name-INE
             Good. [Around three        ] in Kappeli.
                       [          ]
    2  T:            [Joo.      ] [.hhh  ]
                     [Yes.      ] [.hhh  ]
    3  T: →  Joo:. .mh >Oikeen hyvä. .hh Mut ↑itse asi’-s
             PRT       very  good    but  self thing-INE
             Ye:s. .mh >Very good. .hh But ↑as a matter of fact
    4      →  tää  on kutsu-soitto,<
             this is  invitation-call
             this is  an invitation call,<
    5         (0.4)
    6  T:    Siis [meiä-n   tupaan]tuliaiset on kahe-s-kymmene-s=
             PRT [we-GEN housewarming is  two-ORD-ten-ORD
             That is to say our housewarming ((party)) will be
                       [                ]
    7  R: ⇒      [Nii:?           ]
    8  T:    =yheksä-s #päivä#,=
             nine-ORD day
             on the twentyninth,=
    9  R:    =.hh Aha,
             =.hh I see,
   10  T:    mt Lau:antai-na kahe-n    vii#ko-n    päästä,#
                Saturday-ESS two-GEN week-GEN after
             .tch On Sa:turday after two weeks,
   11  R:    Mm:: tadadadaa Pulliainen taitaa ol-la
             PRT            surname  might be-INF
             Mm:: tadadadaa I think Pulliainen is gonna be
   12        etelä-ssä   °sillo°,
             south-INE then
             in the south¹⁵ °then°,
```

At the beginning of the call, as a response to Tiina's "how-are-you," Raija told her that she is coming to the city the following day. This announcement was followed by making arrangements for getting together, and it is the arrangement-making sequence that is being brought to closure by Raija at line 1. In line 3 Tiina, the caller and the initiator of the contact, first confirms (*Joo:.*) and then assesses (>*Oikeen hyvä*, 'very good') the arrangements just completed. However, instead of proceeding into the closings of the call she moves to introduce a new, contrastive line of talk (cf., *mut*, 'but'). This utterance makes an announcement that displays that the caller had an independent agenda (cf. *itse asi's*, 'as a matter of fact'), a reason for her call not yet having been dealt with. The core of the utterance is done with the format [X is Y] through which the ongoing encounter is described as a certain type of encounter from the point of view of its speaker, the caller. The modifying noun in the NP makes a reference to a specific action, that of inviting. However, the utterance does not deliver any specifics of that activity—invitation to what—and that is where its incompleteness lies. This formulation of the action is produced prosodically as an utterance of its own, providing the recipient an opportunity for responding. In line 7 (in overlap), the recipient responds with a *nii* that is stretched and carries a rising terminal contour. Slightly before the *nii* response, however, the co-participant (line 6) has started an utterance through which she delivers an announcement that can be understood as the action projected by the pre, an invitation.

This example bears a resemblance to example (6), in which an utterance that described the type of call being made was responded to with *no* by the recipient; a relevant segment of example (6) is reproduced here:

(6)

     [Tiina/SOS-call: 1]
      1 T: @*No mi-tä*   *kuuluu*@,=
              PRT what-PAR is heard
              @Well how are you@,
      2 J: =.hhh *Ihan hyvä-ä.* <*Kiitos muuten*> @*viimeise-stä*@,
              just good-PAR thanks by the way last-ELA
              =.hhh Just fine. <By the way thanks> @again@,
      3 T: >@*Ei-pä kestä* *toivottava-sti ol-i* ↓*mukava-a*@.
              NEG-CLI endure hopeful-ADV be-PST nice-PAR
              >@You're welcome hopefully you had a ↓good time@.
      4 J: @*O:l-i@,*
              be-PST
              @We di:d?@
      5   (0.2)
      6 T: → .mh @↑A↓*haa*@. .mhhh *Tota*< (.) @*tää on tämmönen:::*
                  PRT   PRT   this is this kind
              .mh @↑I ↓see@. .mhh Well< (.) @this is this kind
      7   →   (.) *hätä-apu-soitto*,
                trouble-help-call
              of::: (.) help-in-trouble call?
      8 J: ⇒ *No,*=
      9 T: ='mnen *sos:* .mhhh *Oo-tte-k-s* *te*
              such SOS   be-PL2–Q-CLI you(PL)
              =a kind of a SOS:. .mhhh Will you ((PL)) be here
      10   *viiko-n-lopu-n*   *täällä*,
              week-GEN-end-GEN here
              during the weekend,

Now, what is the recipient doing by using *nii* instead of *no* in example (12)? Two issues must be noticed. First, the temporal relation of the particle *nii* to its prior talk in example (12) differs from that of the particle *no* in example (6). In example (12), *nii* is delivered after a trouble-indicating silence (line 5) and after the main speaker (Tiina) has broken the silence. The particle *no*, by contrast, is typically, as in example (6), produced without any delay. Furthermore, in example (12) the utterance through which the main speaker (line 6) breaks the silence contains an initially positioned particle *siis*, that projects a reformulation or an explanation to come. That is, *nii* is given as a response in a sequential environment in which both the *nii* speaker (by staying silent in line 5) and the co-participant (by initiating a turn that projects a reformulation of her prior turn to come in line 6) have displayed an orientation to the *nii* speaker having some kind of trouble in understanding the pre. Second, in example (12) the pre that initiates the delivery of the reason for the call is in a particular place in terms of the overall structure of the call: the delivery of the reason for the call is substantially delayed considering the amount of time the participants have already talked (the pre comes on the sixth page of the transcript). Furthermore, before the pre, the co-participant, the recipient of the call, has produced (line 1) talk that may be indicative of an understanding that the encounter has arrived at its closure; that is, she may have interpreted the call as one without any particular reason. The choice of the tense in the preliminary in lines 3–4 may add to the possible disorientation by the recipient: considering how long the participants have already been speaking, it may have been more apt for the speaker to select the past tense instead of the present tense.

What seems to be at issue here is that in addition to acting as a continuer, the *nii* response in example (12) functions as a trouble-indicative device: it displays that its speaker does not quite know what the co-participant is talking about. However, instead of initiating a repair sequence through a conventional repair initiator such as a partial repetition of the co-participant's prior talk, she selects a response that claims that the point of the co-participant's talk has not yet come and invites a continuation. A further central aspect of the trouble-indicative character of *nii* is its intonation, the fact that it is delivered as stretched and with a rising terminal contour.

Example (12) provides further evidence for the suggestion that *no* is a basic way of responding to an utterance with which the co-participant has initiated a pre-sequence with a conventionalized utterance for doing a preliminary. *No* offers the preferred second pair part and a response of the type of "go-ahead" in these cases. When the particle *nii* is used in this kind of environment, it forwards the sequence launched by the co-participant with the pre by inviting the co-participant to continue. It may, however, simultaneously display that the recipient has trouble understanding the kind of action the co-participant did through the pre. However, it should be kept in mind that the sequential environments of *nii* in example (12) and *no* in example (6) are not quite identical in that *nii* is provided in a context where the activity of telling one's reason for the call initiated with the pre is delayed.

Discussion

In this chapter I have discussed the use of the Finnish particle *no* as a turn of its own in conversations. There appear to be two intertwining axes associated with the uses of *no*. One of them has to do with the character of the prior utterance and the current state of talk in terms of its possible completion. Thus, *no* finds its home as a response to an utterance that, in various degrees, exhibits that it has not been produced in its own right but as a preliminary to something else. The clearest cases of these kinds of prior utterances are ones that are conventionalized in the speech community as ways of building up a pre-sequence first pair part of a certain kind such as a summons, a pre-announcement or a pre-telling, and a pre-pre. The particle *no* aligns with its prior talk: it provides a preferred second pair part, a go-ahead, to the first pair part.

The second axis has to do with the character of the prior utterance with respect to some preferred or "normal" course of action or state of affairs. In this respect, *no* often appears to be associated with prior turns that exhibit a departure from some normal or agreed-upon course of action or state of affairs, and here the use of *no* as a turn of its own relates to some of its usages as a preface to longer utterances. Thus, the prior turn may introduce a complication in a joint activity or plan or report some out-of-the-ordinary course of action or state of affairs in its speaker's life. As a response to conventionalized preliminaries the use of *no* can be seen as a conventionalization of an understanding of these preliminaries as departures from some more straightforward way of doing the main action. While providing a go-ahead response to the co-participant, *no* acknowledges and may even in some cases make visible the "deviant" character of what the co-participant has said and/or done and displays willingness to go on with the activity initiated by the other.

We have also discussed briefly the use of the particle *nii* as a response to an utterance that acts as a preliminary. What we have seen is that *nii* and *no* prefer different kinds of sequential environments. While *no* comes as a response to turns that, through utterances conventionalized as preliminaries, initiate a separate small activity through which grounds for moving on to the main action and activity are secured, *nii* is found as a response to utterances that have already initiated the main activity, albeit not the main action. Furthermore, in contrast with *no*, which can be responsive to prior utterances that form a departure from some "normal" or agreed-upon course of action or state of affairs, *nii* is found at points of maximum incompleteness, at structural junctures within a "normal" course of action. And when *nii* enters a sequential environment where *no* regularly occurs, it is heard as an alternative to *no*, for example, as a display of trouble with prior talk.

It should be kept in mind that the current data base of *no* is relatively small; more work is clearly needed in this respect. However, I hope to have demonstrated some of the interactional operations speakers of Finnish display with the use of single-word utterances. Particles such as *no* and *nii* are essentially interactional devices: their meaning and use are tied to the actions produced by the prior speaker, to the kinds of turns (their action features and their semantico-grammatical construction) they respond to, and to the kinds of sequences as part of which they occur. They display two different kinds of stances to the current state and characteristics of the evolving larger activity in framing the prior turn and sequence as something that is incomplete and still on its way to some core action and in so doing participate in the construction of particular coherent activities. There is a need for systematic studies of response forms in their particular sequential, epistemic, affective, and grammatical contexts in different languages as a topic of their own: how would the field of conversational actions discussed here be divided, for example, among the English responses *well*, *yes*, and *why* and among responses in other languages and cultures?

Appendix: Key to the Glossing Symbols

The morphemes are separated from each other with a hyphen (-). Elements that are not separatable but that are contained in a lexeme and carry important semantic information are indicated by adding a plus sign (+) and a capitalized glossing (e.g., *kotoa* home + FROM). The following forms have not been indicated in the glossing (except when there are special reasons for indicating the form): (1) nominative case, (2) singular, (3) third-person singular, (4) active voice, (5) present tense, and (6) second-person singular imperative. Different infinitives and participial forms have not been specified.

Abbreviations used in glossing are:

1	First-person ending	3	Third-person ending
2	Second-person ending	4	Passive-person ending

Case endings (modified from Andrew Chesterman, 1991; *On Definiteness: A Study with Special Reference to English and Finnish* [Cambridge: Cambridge University Press], 90–91) are shown in the following table:

Case	Abbreviation	Approximate Meaning
ablative	ABL	'from'
accusative	ACC	object
adessive	ADE	'at, on'
allative	ALL	'to'
elative	ELA	'out of'
essive	ESS	'as'
genitive	GEN	possession
illative	ILL	'into'
inessive	INE	'in'
nominative	NOM	subject
partitive	PAR	partitiveness
translative	TRA	'to', 'becoming'

Other abbreviations include:

CLI	clitic	POS	possessive suffix
CON	conditional	PPC	past participle
FRE	frequentative	PPPC	passive past participle
IMP	imperative	PRT	particle
INF	infinitive	PST	past tense
NEG	negation	Q	interrogative
NOU	noun	REF	reflexive
ORD	ordinal number	SG	singular
PAS	passive	1nameF	First name, female
PL	plural		

NOTES

I am grateful to Lauri Carlson, Cecilia Ford, Barbara Fox, Auli Hakulinen, and Liisa Raevaara for valuable comments on earlier drafts of this chapter.

1. As a result of an influence of the majority language, Finnish, the Finland Swedish particle *nå* bears similarity to *no*, as compared to the use of *nå* in Sweden Swedish (Lehti-Eklund 1992).

2. The majority of these calls belong to the corpus of conversational Finnish at the Department of Finnish, University of Helsinki. In the examples, the heading of an example indicates a subcorpus within the data base, followed by a name of the call the example belongs to and the page(s) of the segment in the transcript (e.g., [Eeva/Dog: 9–10]).

3. I wish to thank Sara Routarinne for giving me access to her data base of telephone calls between teenage girls and Outi Tekoniemi for providing me examples from father–son interactions.

4. At each numbered line, three lines of text have been provided. The top line in italics offers the Finnish original, the second line is a morpheme-by-morpheme gloss of the Finnish, and the third line presents a more idiomatic translation. For a key to the glossing conventions and for the transcription symbols, see the appendix to this chapter. Notice the following transcription symbols that are in addition to the symbols in the glossary: Talk surrounded by #-signs is said with a creaky voice, the £-sign indicates a smile voice, and the @-sign marks an animated voice.

5. The joke is based on a reanalysis of the infinitival verb form *myyrä*, 'to sell', in the question *Onks sulla myyrä lippuja?* ('Do you have tickets to sell?') in Tampere dialect. In standard written Finnish and in some spoken varieties of Finnish the infinitival form is *myydä*. The Tampere dialect form *myyrä*, 'to sell', is reanalyzed as the noun *myyrä*, 'a mole', used in standard written Finnish and a wide range of spoken varieties of Finnish.

6. *Business Studies* is produced in Swedish by the speaker (marked with [S] in the gloss line); similarly the noun translated as *workshop* in line 7 is in the original produced as the English word (marked with [E] in the gloss line), pronounced in a Finnish fashion. Similarly in example (7), (E) in the gloss line of line 12 indicates that T is using the English word for "church."

7. It should be noticed that in the segment there was already earlier a possible place for a *no* response in line 2 after Raisa's generic pre in line 1. On the basis of the fact that Raisa does not continue her turn after the generic pre but allows a micropause to develop it could be argued that she oriented to the relevance of a response by the recipient. The recipient, however, witholds a response at that point.

8. With this utterance Tiinu cancels an event that among teenage girls is an important part of friendship: staying overnight. Notice that this possible taking of distance is done subsequent to a sequence within which the coparticipant has displayed disapproval toward the speaker's conduct.

9. The sound structure of the response token *niin* varies. The written-language form of the particle contains the final *n*. However, in most of the cases in which the particle is produced as an utterance of its own, there is no final consonant. Therefore, from now on, I will refer to the particle as *nii*.

10. Before the segment at hand, the participants have been talking at length about Sisko's summer cottage, which Tuire has visited in order to return some of Sisko's things. The adverb *oikeesti*, 'in fact', in addition to formulating the issue to come as the most important may also concern the fact that the issue of the summer cottage could have been heard as the reason for the call.

11. The first grammatically possible completion point of the relative clause is, of course, after the finite verb *soitan*, 'call'.

12. In line 7 the specification of the topic of the reason for the call is received as understood with the particle *joo* by the recipient, and in line 10 the first part of the report gets a *mm* response through which the recipient minimally acknowledges the prior report (cf. Sorjonen 1997:398–400).

13. The list in example (10) contains as its third element what Jefferson (1990:66) calls a "generalized list completer." It thus displays an orientation to "'programmatic relevance' of three-partedness for the construction of lists" found in English conversations: the speaker engages in a search for a third item (Jefferson 1990:66–67).

14. In the remaining two cases, *nii* is given as a response to utterances constructed through a format often used as summonses (*hei*, 'hey'; *halloo*, 'hallo'). However, there are features in these cases that display that the prior turn is not the usual kind of a summons: *Hei*, 'hey', evidenced by the fact that its speaker continues his turn after *hei* in overlap with the *nii* response, acts as a turn-initial marker. The particle *halloo*, 'hallo', functions more like an announcement, a telling of 'I'm back' by a speaker who has momentarily left the phone to take care of something in her physical environment.

15. The expression *etelässä*, 'in the south', refers to a warm southern tourist center, a prototypical representative of which is Torremolinos in Spain.

REFERENCES

Carlson, Lauri. 1984. *"Well" in Dialogue Games*. Amsterdam: John Benjamins.
Clancy, Patricia, Sandra A. Thompson, Ryoko Suzuki, and Hongyin Tao. 1996. The conversational use of reactive tokens in English, Japanese and Mandarin. *Journal of Pragmatics* 26:355–387.
Drew, Paul. 1987. Po-faced receipts of teases. *Linguistics* 25:219–253.
Drummond, Kent, and Robert Hopper. 1993a. Back channels revisited: Acknowledgement tokens and speakership incipiency. *Research on Language and Social Interaction* 26(2): 157–177.
Drummond, Kent, and Robert Hopper. 1993b. Some uses of *yeah. Research on Language and Social Interaction* 26(2): 203–212.
Ford, Cecilia E. 1994. Dialogic aspects of talk and writing: *Because* on the interactive-edited continuum. *TEXT* 14(4): 531–554.
Gardner, Roderick. 1995. On some uses of the conversational token "mm." Ph.D diss., University of Melbourne.
Goodwin, Charles. 1986. Between and within: Alternative and sequential treatments of continuers and assessments. *Human Studies* 9:205–218.
Goodwin, Charles. 1996. Transparent vision. In Elinor Ochs, Emanuel A. Schegloff, and Sandra A. Thompson (eds.), *Interaction and Grammar*, 370–404. Cambridge: Cambridge University Press.
Guthrie, Anna M. 1997. On the systematic deployment of *okay* and *mmhmm* in academic advising sessions. *Pragmatics* 7:397–415.
Hakulinen, Auli. 1993. Inandning som kulturellt interaktionsfenomen. [Inbreath as a cultural interactional phenomenon.] In Ann-Marie Ivars, Hanna Lehti-Eklund, Pirkko Lilius, Anne-Marie Londen, and Helena Solstrand-Pipping (eds.), *Språk och social context* [Language and social context], Series B, vol. 15:49–67. Meddelanden för institutionen för nordiska språk och nordisk litteratur vid Helsingfors universitet.
Heritage, John. 1984a. *Garfinkel and Ethnomethodology*. Cambridge: Polity Press.
Heritage, John. 1984b. A change-of-state token and aspects of its sequential placement. In J. Maxwell Atkinson and John Heritage (eds.), *Structures of Social Action: Studies in Conversation Analysis*, 299–345. Cambridge: Cambridge University Press.
Heritage, John. 1988. Explanations as accounts: A conversation analytic perspective. In Charles Antaki (ed.), *Analysing Everyday Explanation: A Casebook of Methods*, 127–144. London: Sage.

Jefferson, Gail. 1981. Caveat speaker: A preliminary exploration of shift implicative recipiency in the articulation of topic. Final report to the British SSRC.

Jefferson, Gail. 1984. Notes on a systematic deployment of the acknowledgement tokens "yeah" and "mm hm". *Papers in Linguistics* 17:197–216.

Jefferson, Gail. 1988. On the sequential organization of troubles-talk in ordinary conversation. *Social Problems* 35:418–441.

Jefferson, Gail. 1990. List-construction as a task and resource. In George Psathas (ed.), *Interaction Competence*, 63–92. Washington, DC: International Institute for Ethnomethodology and Conversation Analysis and University Press of America.

Jefferson, Gail. 1993. Caveat speaker: Preliminary notes on recipient topic-shift implicature. *Research on Language and Social Interaction* 26:1–30.

Jefferson, Gail. 1996. Is 'No' an acknowledgement token? Comparing British and American uses of (+)/(–) tokens. Paper presented at the 11th World Congress of Applied Linguistics, Jyväskylä, Finland.

Kangasharju, Helena. 1998. Alignment in disagreement: Building up alliances in multiperson interaction. Ph.D. diss., University of Helsinki.

Lehti-Eklund, Hanna. 1992. Användningen av partikeln "nå" i helsingforssvenska samtal. [The use of the particle "nå" in Helsinki Swedish conversations] *Svenskans beskrivining* 19:174–184.

Lerner, Gene H. 1987. Collaborative turn sequences: Sentence construction and social action. Ph.D. diss., University of California, Irvine.

Lerner, Gene H. 1991. On the syntax of sentences-in-progress. *Language in Society* 20:441–458.

Lerner, Gene H. 1996. On the "semi-permeable" character of grammatical units in conversation: Conditional entry into the turn space of another speaker. In Elinor Ochs, Emanuel A. Schegloff, and Sandra A. Thompson (eds.), *Interaction and Grammar*, 238–276. Cambridge: Cambridge University Press.

Local, John. 1996. Conversational phonetics: Some aspects of news receipts in everyday talk. In Elizabeth Couper-Kuhlen and Margret Selting (eds.), *Prosody in Conversation: Interactional Studies*, 177–230. Cambridge: Cambridge University Press.

Müller, Frank Ernst. 1996. Affiliating and disaffiliating with continuers: Prosodic aspects of recipiency. In Elizabeth Couper-Kuhlen and Margret Selting (eds.), *Prosody in Conversation: Interactional Studies*, 131–176. Cambridge: Cambridge University Press.

NS = *Nykysuomen sanakirja*. 1992 [1951–1961]. (Dictionary of modern Finnish.) 13th ed. Porvoo: WSOY.

Ochs, Elinor, Emanuel A. Schegloff, and Sandra A. Thompson (eds.). 1996. *Interaction and Grammar*. Cambridge: Cambridge University Press.

Pomerantz, Anita. 1978. Attributions of responsibility: Blamings. *Sociology* 12:115–121.

Pomerantz, Anita. 1984a. Agreeing and disagreeing with assessments: Some features of preferred/dispreferred turn shapes. In J. Maxwell Atkinson and John Heritage (eds.), *Structures of Social Action: Studies in Conversation Analysis*, 57–101. Cambridge: Cambridge University Press.

Pomerantz, Anita. 1984b. Pursuing a response. In J. Maxwell Atkinson and John Heritage (ed.), *Structures of Social Action: Studies in Conversation Analysis*, 152–163. Cambridge: Cambridge University Press.

Raevaara, Liisa. 1989. "No"—vuoronalkuinen partikkeli. ["No"—a turn-initial particle.] Suomalaisen keskustelun keinoja I. Edited by Auli Hakulinen. *Kieli* 4:147–161. University of Helsinki, Department of Finnish Language.

Routarinne, Sara. 1997. Kertomuksen rakentaminen. [Constructing a story.] In Liisa Taino (ed.), *Keskustelunanalyysin perusteita* [Basics of Conversation Analysis], 138–155. Tampere: Vastapaino.

Sacks, Harvey. 1992a. *Lectures on Conversation*, vol. 1. Ed. Gail Jefferson. Cambridge, MA.: Basil Blackwell.

Sacks, Harvey. 1992b. *Lectures on Conversation*, vol. 2. Ed. Gail Jefferson. Cambridge, MA: Basil Blackwell.

Schegloff, Emanuel A. 1972 [1968]. Sequencing in conversational openings. In John J. Gumperz and Dell Hymes (eds.), *Directions in Sociolinguistics*, 346–380. New York: Holt Rinehart and Winston.

Schegloff, Emanuel A. 1980. Preliminaries to preliminaries: "Can I ask you a question." In Language and social interaction, edited by Don Zimmerman and Candace West. *Sociological Inquiry* 50:104–152.

Schegloff, Emanuel A. 1982. Discourse as an interactional achievement: Some uses of 'uh huh' and other things that come between sentences. In Deborah Tannen (ed.), *Georgetown University Roundtable on Languages and Linguistics (GURT)*, 71–93. Washington, DC: Georgetown University Press.

Schegloff, Emanuel A. 1988a. Discourse as an interactional achievement II: An exercise in conversation analysis. In Deborah Tannen (ed.), *Linguistics in Context: Connecting Observation and Understanding*, 135–158. (*Advances in Discourse Processes* 29.) Norwood, NJ: Ablex.

Schegloff, Emanuel A. 1988b. Goffman and the analysis of conversation. In Paul Drew and Anthony Wootton (eds.), *Erving Goffman: An Interdisciplinary Appreciation*, 89–135. Cambridge: Polity Press.

Schegloff, Emanuel A. 1990. On the organization of sequences as a source of "coherence" in talk-in-interaction. In B. Dorval (ed.), *Conversational Organization and Its development*, 51–77. (*Advances in Discourse Processes* 38). Norwood, NJ: Ablex.

Schegloff, Emanuel A. 1995. Sequence organization. Ms., University of California, Los Angeles.

Schegloff, Emanuel A. 1996. Turn organization: One intersection of grammar and interaction. In Elinor Ochs, Emanuel A. Schegloff, and Sandra A. Thompson (eds.), *Interaction and Grammar*, 52–133. Cambridge: Cambridge University Press.

Schegloff, Emanuel A., and Harvey Sacks. 1973. Opening up closings. *Semiotica* 7:289–327.

Sorjonen, Marja-Leena. 1996. On repeats and responses in Finnish conversations. In Elinor Ochs, Emanuel A. Schegloff, and Sandra A. Thompson (eds.), *Interaction and Grammar*, 272–327. Cambridge: Cambridge University Press.

Sorjonen, Marja-Leena. 1997. Recipient activities: Particles "nii(n)" and "joo" as responses in Finnish conversations. Ph.D. diss., University of California, Los Angeles.

Sorjonen, Marja-Leena. In press. *Responding in Conversation. A Study of Response Particles in Finnish*. Amsterdam: John Benjamins.

Suomen sanojen alkuperä. 1995. (The origin of Finnish words: Etymological dictionary.) Vol. 2. Helsinki: Research Institute for Languages of Finland and Finnish Literature Society.

Tao, Hongyin, and Sandra A. Thompson. 1991. English backchannel in Mandarin conversations: A case study of superstratum pragmatic 'interference'. *Journal of Pragmatics* 16:209–223.

Terasaki, Alene. 1976. Pre-announcement sequences in conversation. *Social Science Working Papers*, no. 99. School of Social Science, University of California, Irvine.

8

Oh-Prefaced Responses to Assessments

A Method of Modifying Agreement/Disagreement

JOHN HERITAGE

I want to begin with a text from the "Parade" section of the *LA Times* of Sunday, January 25, 1998. On the cover is a picture of a woman in full firefighting attire, backlit by flames and hosing water at a target that is out of the shot. Superimposed on the picture is a text that reads: "A firefighter, a jockey, a welder, a tobacco farmer, a boxer—these women's stories are as different as their professions, but they all have one sentiment in common: 'Oh, yes I can!'" A significant element of the "sentiment" referred to here is one of rebuttal. This woman, the reader is led to infer, decided to be a firefighter and was told that it is not a job for a woman. The picture with its caption conveys that she has driven back this attack and overcome the opposition of naysayers. A substantial contribution to that understanding, I want to suggest, is made by the *oh*-preface to this quotation. "Oh, yes I can!" conveys something different, in this case more oppositional, than just "Yes I can!": it is this kind of difference that I am trying to reach in this essay.

It has long been recognized that turn beginnings are a significant and strategic aspect of turn design (Sacks, Schegloff, and Jefferson 1974; Schegloff 1987b, 1996; Lerner 1996). As Schegloff (1987b) observes, turn beginnings often project the planned shape and trajectory of the remainder of the TCU to follow, thus providing hearers with resources for anticipating both what kind of action is under construction and what it will take to be complete. Turn beginnings are thus important resources both for the anticipation and organization of sequences of actions and for the management of the turn-taking through which those sequences are implemented.

Turn beginnings are also strategic sites because they are a prime location for the placement of sequential markers that convey some relation between what the current speaker is about to say and what the previous speaker has just said. Turn components like *well, uh, but, so, oh,* and others are all used in this way. For example, turn beginning is the standard position for *well, uh,* and other markers used to index a relationship of dispreference or disaffiliation between the position taken by a previous speaker and the position the current speaker is about to adopt (Pomerantz 1984a; Davidson 1984; Schiffrin 1987). Similarly prefacing a question with *and* is a resource for conveying that the question to follow is part of a continuing activity initiated previously (Heritage and Sorjonen 1994).

The particle *oh* is also used at turn beginnings to convey a stance toward what the previous speaker has said. When persons preface a second or responsive action with *oh,* they are commonly understood to have acted in a fashion that problematizes the action to which they are responding. *Oh*-prefaced responses to questions, for instance, often embody a challenge to their relevance or appropriateness (Heritage 1998). In example (1), taken from a radio talk show, Sir Harold Acton, a celebrated English aesthete, was interviewed by British broadcaster Russell Harty. The interview has turned to a discussion about the manners of the Chinese and some work that Acton was doing in Beijing—teaching modern poetry at Beijing University. Sir Harold Acton's reply to the question "Did you learn to speak Chinese" is *oh*-prefaced:

(1)

```
        [Chat Show: Russell Harty–Sir Harold Acton]
     1  Act:    . . . hhhh and some of thuh- (0.3) some of my students
     2           translated Eliot into Chine::se. I think thuh very
     3           first.
     4           (0.2)
     5  Har:    Did you learn to speak (.) Chine[:se.
     6  Act: →                                 [.hh Oh yes.
     7           (0.7)
     8  Act:    .hhhh You ca::n't live in thuh country without speaking
     9           thuh lang[uage it's impossible .hhhhh=
    10  Har: →            [Not no: cour:se
```

Here, given that Acton taught modern poetry and that his students were the first to translate T. S. Eliot's work, the interviewer's question is clearly vulnerable to the charge that it is questioning the obvious. Acton's responsive *oh yes* manages to convey just that, treating it as evident that he would have learned the language. Subsequently both parties topicalize the self-evident nature of the point. Acton goes on to explain briefly why it was essential to learn the language to live in China (lines 8–9). And this explanation, in turn, is acknowledged by the interviewer (with *Not no: course* [line 10]) in a way that treats the answer to his question as, after all, having been quite self-evident (Heritage 1998).

As I have argued elsewhere, this process of challenging the relevance or appropriateness of a question by *oh*-prefacing the response exploits the "change-of-state" meaning of *oh* (Heritage 1984) to indicate that the question has occasioned a *marked shift of attention*. In the case of questions, conveying a marked shift of this kind can imply that a question was inapposite and, hence, that the respondent is experiencing difficulties with the question's relevance, appropriateness, or presuppositions. In this way, a respondent can challenge or resist the relevance of a question and the course of action that the question may be implementing.

An important feature of this practice is that, through it, respondents can convey that *their own point of view* is the basic framework from which the issue is to be considered and do so inexplicitly yet insistently (Heritage 1998:291–296). In treating their own point of view as the perspective from which some matter should be considered, *oh*-prefacing respondents index (and reaffirm) a claim of epistemic authority over their questioners. This is a theme that will resurface in this analysis of *oh*-prefaced agreement and disagreement.

Oh-*Prefaced Agreements: Epistemic Independence*

In analyzing *oh*-prefaced agreements, we can begin by distinguishing two kinds of agreements. First, there are agreements in contexts where persons have had a joint experience of some kind. Here each person knows that the other has rights, grounded in experience, to assess the object in question (Pomerantz 1984a):

(2)

 [JS II:41)
 1 J: T's- tsuh beautiful day out isn't it?
 2 L: → Yeh it's jus' gorgeous . . .

(3)

 [VIYMC 1:2] ((J and R are in a rowboat on a lake))
 1 J: It's really a clear lake, isn't it?
 2 R: → It's wonderful.

(4)

 [SBL 2:2:3:46]
 1 B: Well, it was fun Cla[ire,
 2 A: →   [Yeah, I enjoyed every minute of it.

In these contexts, agreeing second assessments of the experience are ordinarily produced as simple upgraded agreements or as upgraded agreements prefaced with *yes* (Pomerantz 1984a). These second assessments convey that the second speaker's agreement is grounded in a newly articulated common experience, which is reconfirmed in a common judgment in the "here and now."

Something rather different appears to be going on in the case of *oh*-prefaced second assessments. In example (5), for instance, Gay is giving Jeremy a German telephone number. After she has given eleven digits of the number, thus exceeding the norm (during the 1980s) for a (British) intracountry call, Jeremy comments (line 13) on the length of the number, prefacing his comment with *Gosh*, an expression that indicates that, for him, this is something new, notable, or surprising. Here Gay could have responded with a simple agreement, which, as in examples (2) through (4), would have conveyed that her agreement was grounded in the "here and now" common experience of an interminable telephone number. Instead, her *oh*-prefaced response—*Oh* it doe:s—treats his remark as reviving an earlier observation of the same type that she had made independently of this occasion, and she thereby conveys that, in contrast to Jeremy, she finds it unsurprising.[1] By this means she also manages to indicate that she is an "old hand" at phoning abroad:

(5)

    [Heritage 0I:7:3]
     1 Gay: So the ↑number is (0.2) oh: one oh::.
     2 Jer: Oh one oh:,
     3   (1.0)
     4 Jer: Yeup,
     5 Gay: ↑Four ni:ne,
     6   (0.5)
     7 Jer: Ri:ght?
     8 Gay: Sev'n three, u-six o:ne?hh
     9   (0.6)
   10 Jer: Sev'n three: six o:ne?
   11   (0.3)
   12 Gay: Ei:ght ni:ne,
   13 Jer: → °Gosh° it goe:s (.) goes on'n on
   14 Gay: → Oh it doe:s Germany doe:s.

It may also be noticed that Gay adds a turn component that appears designed to further suggest her expertise about foreign telephone calls. Her postpositioned "adjusting" component (*Germany doe:s*) recalibrates the referent of her response from this particular telephone number to German telephone numbers in general and also works to convey a degree of prior knowledge on the topic. Moreover, with its hint of a further contrast with telephone numbers in other foreign countries, it implies a still broader expertise in the matter of placing telephone calls abroad. Shortly afterward, Gay underscores her expertise, informing Jeremy that the "ringing" sound on a German phone sounds like a "busy" signal on a British phone (data not shown).

    In example (5) the *oh*-prefaced second assessment conveys that the observation being agreed to had already been independently arrived at by the agreeing party on an earlier occasion, and this in turn was used to suggest the agreeing speaker's greater expertise on the topic at hand. In example (6) *oh*-prefacing is again used to convey that the opinion being agreed with was formed earlier and on the basis of independent experience of the referent event. However, in contrast to example (5), there is no indication of particular expertise on the matter under discussion. Here

two Orange County women are talking approximately one week after the assassination of Robert Kennedy in Los Angeles in 1968. The matter on which they agree
is not something of which the speakers have a directly shared experience but rather
something that, by virtue of the public media, they have experienced separately
but in common:

(6)

> [NB II:2:R:2]
> 1 Emm: ↑THE:Y gosh uh <u>this</u> is really been a wee:k <u>ha</u>:sn'it?=
> 2 Nan: → =O<u>h</u>:: it r<u>i</u>lly ha:s. ((sadly))
> 3 Emm: I[t's r i h]
> 4 Nan: [Gee it r<u>i</u>]:ll<u>y</u>, it rilly h<u>a</u>:[s.
> 5 Emm: [<u>A</u>h won't ev'n turn the tee v<u>ee</u> o:n,h

In this example, Emma's assessment of "the week" evidently invokes the assassination event and its aftermath in Southern California.[2] Nancy's *oh*-prefaced response,
like Gay's in example (5), indicates that she has separate and independent access to
the assassination and its aftermath, which Emma alluded to, and moreover that she
has separately and independently arrived at the same conclusion as Emma.

Given that Nancy could have responded with the kind of simple or *yes*-prefaced
agreement that is otherwise commonplace, what is at stake in this marked indexing of epistemic independence? In assessing objects or states of affairs, there are
differences between going first and going second. Specifically:

1. A first assessment can index or embody a first speaker's claim to what might
   be termed "epistemic authority" about an issue relative to a second or to
   "know better" about it or to have some priority in rights to evaluate it. While
   this may mean little and be readily acquiesced to in the matter of the weather
   or the quality of lake water (e.g., examples [2] and [3] respectively), it may
   be resisted in the matter of a grandchild (e.g., examples [18] and [19]), or
   the attractions of one's birthplace (e.g., example [7]).[3]
2. Moreover, a first assessment establishes a context in which a second can be
   found to agree or disagree. In such a context, respondents may be vulnerable
   to the inference that their response is fabricated on the instant to achieve
   agreement or disagreement and is thus a dependent or even a coerced action
   within a field of constraint that is established by the first.
3. These issues can be compounded by the context of the assessment. The priority relationship between a first and second assessment may be less significant in contexts where the parties are joint experiencers of a state of
   affairs (e.g., the weather and lake water cited earlier). However, where a state
   of affairs is separately experienced or known by the parties, going first can
   have a greater impact in implicitly establishing superior access, expertise,
   authority, and rights to assess the matter in question, if only because the
   relative access and expertise of the parties to the state of affairs may remain
   to be negotiated.

Where, out of these and related considerations, a second speaker wishes to convey that he/she has *previously and independently* formed the same view or opinion as the first speaker, *oh*-prefacing is a resource with which to achieve this objective. *Oh*-prefaced second assessments, in short, embody a declaration of epistemic independence. Returning to example (6), the *oh*-prefacing of Nancy's agreement markedly indexes her independent access (via media coverage) to the week's sad events. And it also carries the implied claim that her agreement is based on a judgment that, rather than being constructed in immediate response to Emma's assessment, was formed earlier and in independence from it.

In summary: this chapter argues that *oh*-prefacing both agreements and disagreements to assessments, thus conveying a "change of state of orientation" in response to them, is a systematic way of indicating that a speaker has independent access to and already holds a position on the matter at issue. The baseline claim conveyed in an *oh*-prefaced (dis)agreement is one of *epistemic independence*: in this way, the second speaker conveys that the opinion that follows the *oh*-preface is independent of the "here and now" of current experience and the prior speaker's evaluation. *Oh*-prefacing may achieve this outcome through a "change of state semantics" that conveys that the first assessment has occasioned a review, recollection, and renewal of the speaker's previous experience and judgment and that it is this that forms the basis for the second assessment. As in responses to questions, *oh*-prefacing conveys that the speaker's *own experience* is the basis for the evaluation that follows. This baseline claim of epistemic independence is often associated with and a resource for conveying superior knowledge of and/or rights to assess the matter under discussion.

To demonstrate this phenomenon of epistemic independence, we begin with cases where the agreeing respondent has separate but equivalent access to the phenomenon being assessed and equivalent rights to know or evaluate it. Subsequently, we will move to cases where the second speaker has a priori epistemic authority in relation to the assessed state of affairs, that is, primary or privileged access to it and/or primary or privileged rights to evaluate it.

The data for this essay are drawn from a large number of American and British telephone calls. There are no discernible differences in the deployment of this practice between British and American English.

Equivalent but Independent Access

In this first set of cases, *oh*-prefacing is used to invoke the independent basis of an agreement when "going second" on a matter of common knowledge. For instance, in example (7) Robbie and Lesley, two British teachers connected through a class that Lesley once taught and that Robbie now has charge of, have found, unexpectedly, that they have common origins and family connections in the county of Kent. At this point, the conversation turns to the attractions of their home county, which, it transpires, both visit fairly regularly:

(7)

[Holt 5/88:1:5:21]

```
 1 Rob:    Well that's ri:ght I mean: uh .hhh you know this is the
 2            thing we: miss the trees eh- yu- exactly the same as
 3            you[:
 4 Les:         [eYes:.=
 5 Rob:    =An'[you don't realize until you go u:p just how many=
 6 Les:        [Yes
 7 Rob:    =trees there are [(↑sti [ ll if if ] the:)y [
 8 Les:                     [.hhh [n N o :.]      [Specially in the
 9            Wea:l:d it['s lovely. .hh[hhhhhh=
10 Rob: →            [↑Oh- yes    [Yes
11 Les:    =The Wea:ld I lo:ve:: sti:ll.=
12 Rob: → =Oh:: lovely. You ↑(never) use' to go to a pub called
13            the Wheatsheaf, up at Ide Hill did you?
```

At line 1, Robbie agrees with an earlier observation of Lesley's by remarking on the number of trees there "still" are in Kent, to which Lesley appends, *Specially in the Wea:l:d* (a notably beautiful part of Kent). This remark attracts an *oh*-prefaced agreement from Robbie (line 10). Here Lesley's remark, with its increase in specificity over Robbie's earlier comment about the trees, "ups the ante" on a point that Robbie had already made. Robbie's *oh*-prefaced response, while evidently agreeing, limits this process, formulating her agreement about the Weald as grounded in independent experience and judgment. Robbie responds in a similar way to Lesley's (line 11) subsequent, more general, assessment of the Weald. Here Lesley's left-dislocated turn is designed to be heard as a new "first action," partially disengaged from the prior sequence and reestablishing her previous assessment of the Weald as an action to be addressed. Robbie's *oh*-prefaced response embodies the independence of her own judgment in the matter but again limits Lesley's effort to extend the topic with a brief and dismissive response.[4] In this example, which involves two persons with independent experience of their native county and equal rights to assess it, the agreeing second speaker *oh*-prefaces her agreements to convey their grounding in independent experience. In this way, she invokes an equality of experience with the one who took the lead in the matter.

A similar process seems to be at work in example (8). Here two women are discussing a neighborhood dog:

(8)

[MC:1]

```
 1 A:    They keep 'im awful nice somehow
 2 B: → Oh yeah I think she must wash 'im every [week
 3 A:                                           [God-she
 4        must (h) wash 'im every day the way he looks [to me
 5 B:                                                  [I know it
```

Here neither woman owns the dog, but each of them has equal rights as an "independent observer" in the neighborhood to assess it. Here B's *oh*-prefaced agreement is offered as based in independent experience and judgment: an independence of perspective that she goes on to support with her epistemically upgraded agreement about how frequently the dog must be washed (line 5).

Finally, in a conversation that almost exactly parallels example (6), Emma discusses the Kennedy tragedy and its aftermath with another co-participant.[5] Although she claims (in both calls) not to have followed the television coverage of the events, it transpires a little later that she did watch the ceremony in which Kennedy's body was loaded onto a plane for transportation to the East Coast and that she has a connection with that particular location—she took a chartered flight to Honolulu from the same airfield. In example (9), she makes an effort to introduce this information:

(9)

```
    [NB II:1:R:2]
    1  Emm:    ↑Th<u>a</u>t's where ↑w<u>e</u> took off. The ex<u>a</u>:ct sp<u>o</u>:t. on that
    2            ch<u>a</u>rtered f<u>li</u>:ght.
    3            (0.4)
    4  Lot:    ↓Oh:.=
    5  Emm:    =°where the° pl<u>a</u>:ne came in. <u>I</u> jst watched th<u>a</u>:t but
    6            (0.3)
    7  Emm:    [hhh
    8  Lot:  → [Uh <u>I</u> wouldn'ev'n turn it <u>o</u>:n I [mean I]: js .t.hhh
    9  Emm:                                      [<u>Uh</u>-uh ]
   10  Lot:  → Iss t<u>oo</u> depr<u>e</u>s[sing.]
   11  Emm: →               [Oh:::]:: ↓it is <u>t</u>err:uhble↓=What's n<u>e</u>:w.
   12  Lot:    Gee <u>noth</u>ing Em<u>ma</u> . . . (continues)
```

However, as it turns out, Lottie did not watch the event and justifies this with the observation that it is *too depressing* (line 10). Faced with the failure of her effort to move the conversation toward her own small connection with the assassination events, Emma is reduced to an *oh*-prefaced agreement that renews her earlier stated position on the assassination. Here the *oh*-preface-carried claim of her independence in that viewpoint may help to mask the sense that she is "merely agreeing" with her co-participant in the aftermath of a failed topic launch.[6] In any case, the *oh*-prefaced agreement is here used preparatory to an abrupt topic shift, implemented at line 11 with *What's ne:w.* (See also example [7], line 12, and note 4).

Of course, not every second assessment that is based on separate and independent experience is *oh*-prefaced. In example (10), two neighbors—Emma and Margy—are discussing an associate of Margy's husband who is also known, albeit peripherally, to Emma and her husband. After some talk about the associate's business dealings, the following sequence occurs:

(10)

```
    [NB VII:7]
    1  Mar:    B'd isn'it fun<u>ny</u> <u>Emma</u> how that's all c'nnected
    2            t'g<u>e</u>ther? [.hh
```

```
3  Emm:              ['S that terr:ifih=
4  Emm:  →  =YEAH BECUZ yihknow he's a goodlooking fel'n eez got a
5         →  beautiful wi:fe.=
6  Mar:   →  =Ye:s::. Go:rgeous girl-.hh-.hhh e-We:ll see he'n Larry'v
7            been friends fer a long ti:me.=
```

Here, even though Margy evidently has independent experience of the associate and his wife, her agreement is not *oh*-prefaced. Indeed, example (10) and similar cases are particularly significant because although her assessment is in second position, Margy has a *closer* relationship with the individual referred to and his wife and thus arguably *stronger* rights to assess them. As is shown later, *oh*-prefaced responses to assessments cluster in contexts where the second speaker has epistemic authority in relation to the matter being assessed relative to the first speaker. Thus, cases like example (10), where a second speaker has the "prior and independent access" necessary to assess the referent but does not index it, underscore that *oh*-prefacing in the case of agreements is a practice that markedly and optionally conveys an epistemic position.[7]

In sum, *oh*-prefacing in the context of agreements is a method persons use to index the independence of their access and/or judgment in relation to the state of affairs under evaluation. Sometimes, as in example (8), the *oh* prefaces turn components that add further independent contributions to the matter at hand; in others (examples [7] and [9]), they do not. Thus, the basic claim here is that *oh*-prefacing, in and of itself, indexes epistemic independence: an independence that may or may not be elaborated by other elements of the turn that follows. This indexing is inexplicit, marked, and optional.

"Epistemic Authority" in Access to and/or Rights to Assess the Referent

Oh-prefaced agreements are common in environments where the second, *oh*-prefacing speaker has primary access to the state of affairs being assessed and/or primary rights to assess it. In this context, *oh*-prefacing continues to index "independent access" to the referent, but it may often be additionally understood to index the epistemic authority of the second speaker.

In example (11), for instance, two dog breeders—Norman and Ilene—have been talking about the readiness of one of Norman's younger dogs to have a first litter. At line 9, Ilene ventures a comment about one of Norman's other dogs (Trixie), who apparently began breeding at a young age:

(11)

```
[Heritage 1:11:4]
1  Ile:    No well she's still a bit young though isn't [she<ah me]an:=
2  Nor:                                                 [S h e : :   ]
3  Ile:    =uh[:
4  Nor:                                       [She wz a year: la:st wee:k.
```

```
 5  Ile:       Ah yes. Oh well any time no:w [then.]
 6  Nor:                                    [Uh:::]:[m
 7  Ile:                                          [Ye:s.=
 8  Nor:    =But she[:'s ()]
 9  Ile:  →         [Cuz Trixie started] so early [didn't sh[e,
10  Nor:  →                                  [°O h : :  [ye:s.°=
11  Ile:    =°Ye:h°=
```

Here Norman's *oh*-prefaced agreement (line 10), in conveying the independence of his assessment from Ilene's, also alludes to his epistemic priority with respect to the information in question. At the same moment, Ilene's tag question (line 9) downgrades the epistemic strength of what would otherwise be a flat assertion.

In example (11), the epistemic priority of the second, *oh*-prefacing speaker is available from the topic and context of the interaction and inexplicitly indexed in the talk. In the following cases, the priority between first and second assesser is directly established in the sequence prior to the *oh*-prefaced second assessment. In example (12) Jon and Lyn are talking to Eve, Jon's mother. After Jon's announcement about going to the movie *Midnight Cowboy*, Lyn asks Eve if she has seen it. She replies that she has not and goes on to account for this by reference to a friend, Rae, who reportedly said that the film "depressed her terribly" (lines 5/7):

(12)

```
[JS II:61]
 1  Jon:    We saw Midnight Cowboy yesterday -or [suh- Friday.
 2  Eve:                                         [Oh?
 3  Lyn:    Didju s- you saw that, [it's really good.
 4  Eve:                           [No I haven't seen it
 5       →  Rae [sed it 'n' she said she f- depressed her
 6  ():         [(   )
 7  Eve:  →  ter [ribly
 8  Jon:  →      [Oh it's [terribly depressing.
 9  Lyn:  →              [Oh it's depressing.
```

Here both Jon and Lyn agree with Eve's friend's opinion, but both their agreeing assessments are *oh*-prefaced, thus indexing the independence of their access to the movie and in this context that, relative to Eve, they have epistemic priority: direct, rather than indirect, access to the movie.

A similar gradation of access to a referent is apparent in example (13), which comes from a dinner party at which Shane and Vivian are hosts to Michael and Nancy. The conversation turns to a neighbor who is quite well known to the hosts but not to the guests. Shane makes a number of disparaging remarks about the man, characterizing him as an "asshole" and attracting a protest from Vivian, who is rather less critical, that the guests have not yet met him. When it transpires that the guests have in fact met him briefly in the past, Shane revises his assessment (at line 1): "Nuh 'eez a nice guy 'eez j's sorta dumb." Whereupon the following sequence ensues:

(13)

```
        [Chicken Dinner:10]
         1  Sha:    Nuh 'eez a nice guy 'eez [j's s[orta dumb.]
         2  Mic:                            [(   [    )     ]
         3  Nan:                                   [I've talk'to]'m on the
         4           pho[ne.
         5  Mi?:        [(Yeah)
         6           (0.4)
         7  Sha:    (        [        ).
         8  Viv:              [Oh when you were over he wz ho:me?
         9  Mic:    Hm-hm?
        10           (1.0)
        11  Viv:    So wuddiyou thi:nk.
        12           (2.2)
        13  Sh?:    pwehh °hh
        14  Mic:    I'on'know I couldn' (1.4) I din'rilly git tih
        15           talk to'm that much uh- I can't say.
        16           (1.2)
        17  Viv:    hHuh. (Yuh lucky.)
        18           (0.9)
        19  Mic:    °I can't say.°
        20           (3.2)
        21  Mic: →  He seem'like a nice guy-
        22  Sha:    (Naw) he is.
        23           (0.6)
        24  Sha:    He's [a nice [guy
        25  Vi?:         [(.t)   [
        26  Viv: →              [Oh he's a nice gu:y.
```

Invited by Vivian's *So wuddiyou thi:nk* (line 11), Michael's eventual assessment at line 21 is epistemically downgraded with *He seem*, and this is itself preceded by statements (lines 14–15, 19) in which Michael accounts for his unwillingness to assess the neighbor by reference to his lack of knowledge of him. Though hedged, this assessment hearably disagrees with Shane's position and agrees with Vivian's.[8] The assessment attracts responses from both of them. Shane agrees with Michael (lines 22/24), further backing away from his earlier critical position. Vivian's agreement is *oh*-prefaced. Here although both parties clearly have epistemic priority, Vivian, who has taken a consistently more pro-neighbor position, *oh*-prefaces her agreement, while Shane (the previously antineighbor participant) may be inhibited from an *oh*-prefacing ("knowing better") stance by the inconsistency of the position he is taking relative to his earlier pronouncements.

And in example (14) there is also a gradation of access, this time in relation to the qualities of Burmese cats:

(14)

```
        [TCIIA:1]
         1  Abe:    Well I had this- (1.2) beautiful Siamese fer years yihknow.
         2           (en) [I'm (j's a li'l)- unha:ppy when 'e wuh- when 'e::
```

```
 3   Ben:        [M-
 4   Abe:    had t'be put awa:y tihday,.hh acquired a Bu:rmese.=
 5            =D'yihknow what that breed [is?
 6   Ben:                               [Oh yes indee:d uh we had a
 7            neighbor thet had a couple a' Burmese.
 8            (.)
 9   Ben:    They're ni:ce.
10   Abe: → Oh:: it's a great cat. It's the- only cat I ever saw thet
11            chased do:gs.
12            (0.2)
13   Ben:    [ehh hhu [hh huhh  ]
14   Abe:    [(Hadda)[go out'n r]escue a dog thet wz eight times bigger'n
15            he wz th's  [morning.
16   Ben:                [e- .hhhhhh Hurra::y fer the Burme:se.
17   Abe:    e-huh-huh-[heh-[heh-he:h,]
18   Ben:              [F:::  [ight'n' fo]o:ls.
19            (0.2)
20   Abe:    Pard'n,
21            (0.3)
22   Ben:    .hhh They're fight'n' fools those Burmese,
23   Abe: → Oh I know 'e is.
```

This sequence begins with Abe's report of his acquisition of a Burmese cat and his query as to whether his co-interactant (Ben) knows "what that breed is." As it turns out, Ben does know about Burmese cats, but indirectly through a neighbor, and ventures an assessment, *They're nice* (line 9). Abe responds with a strongly upgraded assessment, which also includes an *oh*-preface that indexed independent judgment and, in this context, invokes his epistemic authority as a Burmese cat owner. Subsequently Abe elaborates his assessment with an account of the fighting abilities of Burmese and offers an event that occurred that very morning and involved his own cat as evidence for this (lines 14–15).[9]

A second sequence that culminates in a second *oh*-prefaced second assessment is launched with Ben's *Hurra::y fer the Burme:se* and his assessment of them as "fight'n' fools." This latter, postpositioned, assessment is produced in overlap with Abe's laughter, and Abe solicits its repetition at line 20. Thus, Ben finds himself producing a sequentially detached assessment of Burmese cats as a new "first action" at line 22.[10] In response, Abe launches a second *oh*-prefaced agreement, involving a shift in reference from Burmese cats in general to his own cat. Here both the *oh*-preface and the emphasis on the word *know* upgrade the strength of his assertion and convey his claim of epistemic authority in the matter.

In examples (11) through (14), the speaker who had rights to know better than the other asserted those rights with *oh*-prefaced second assessments against the implied priority claims of first assessments. However, more problematic issues may be at stake than sheer epistemic priority. In example (15), extensively discussed in Schegloff (1997), Marsha and Tony are the separated parents of the teenage Joey, who was scheduled to drive home to his father in Northern California on the day of this call. Tony, the father, has called to find out when Joey left, only to be informed that Joey is flying home on standby because the soft top of his sports car was stolen and driving north without the top on his car would be too cold. At this point, Tony renews an earlier inquiry about the fate of the car:

(15)

```
    [MTRAC 60:1–2 Stolen]
 1  Tony:      W't's 'e g'nna do go down en pick it up later? er
 2             somethin like (        ) [well that's aw]:ful
 3  Marsha:                    [H i s   friend ]
 4  Marsha:    Yeh h[is   friend  Stee- ]
 5  Tony:           [That really makes] me ma:d,
 6                    (0.2)
 7  Marsha: →  .hhh Oh it's disgusti[ng ez a matter a'f]a:ct.
 8  Tony:                    [P o o r   J o e y ,]
 9  Marsha:    I- I, I told my ki:ds. who do this: down et the Drug
10             Coalition ah want th'to:p back.h .hhhhhhhhh ((1.0 breath))
11             SEND OUT the WO:RD.hhh hnh
12                    (0.2)
13  Tony:      Yeah.
14  Marsha:    °hhh Bu:t u-hu:ghh his friend Steve en Brian er driving
15             up. Right after:: (0.2) school is out.En then hi'll
16             drive do:wn here with the:m.
17  Tony:      Oh I see.
```

Tony's inquiry (lines 1–2), as Schegloff notes, takes the form of a question + candidate response, and Marsha makes two attempts to respond with a description of a plan for Joey to return later with his friends to pick the car up (lines 3 and 4), finally succeeding in its articulation much later at lines 14–16. Marsha's attempt to describe the plan is derailed by Tony's assessments of his son's misfortune at lines 2 and 5. Tony positions the first of these assessments as an immediate follow-on from the completion of his inquiry at line 2 and in overlap with Marsha's first attempt to respond to it. Marsha abandons her response and restarts it with a minimal agreement (*Yeh*) at line 4, before proceeding with a recognizable reinitiation of her previous response to his question. Immediately after her agreement, Tony pursues the issue with an upgrade: *That really makes me ma:d* (line 5). It is to this pursuit that Marsha responds with an *oh*-prefaced agreeing second assessment, embodying an upgrade (from Tony's *mad* to her *disgusting*).

A number of observations can be made about this assessment and its context. First, although she is the one with firsthand access to the event, this is the first explicit evaluation of Joey's misfortune that Marsha has offered.[11] Moreover, second, she produces this assessment having responded with the most "pallid" (Schegloff 1997) of agreements (*Yeh*) to her husband's first assessment at line 2. Thus, third, as Schegloff notes, her assessment at line 7 is vulnerable to the "suspicion that it has been coerced by Tony's interruptive upgrade of his prior assessment in reaction to Marsha's tepid agreement; that Marsha is just going along, saying what is necessary" (ibid.). In this context, Marsha does three things to defeat this suspicion. She completes her first unit of talk with *as a matter of fact*, which, as Schegloff again notes, is a resource for claiming that what is said "is so, and is said, independent of local interactional grounds for saying it" (ibid.). Second, she follows this with an account that describes her expression of that reaction on an earlier occasion to the kids at the "Drug Coalition." The third practice she deploys is the prefacing of her responsive assessment with *oh*, through which she conveys that, "of course," she had "previously and independently" arrived at this upgraded evaluation of this unfortunate state of affairs.

Here, then, Marsha, the one with the firsthand experience of the robbery and its impact on her son, was not the first of evaluate the event. But caught in a persistent and upgraded flurry of assessments by her ex-husband, she was obliged to work hard to provide for the fact that her eventual responsive assessment was not simply a coerced response, from someone who might otherwise be characterized as insufficiently concerned about her son's predicament. *Oh*-prefacing her agreement to convey its epistemic independence from her ex-husband's position was the first of the resources she deployed to that end.

Epistemic Authority and the "Agree + Disagree" Format

In a significant number of cases where *oh*-prefaced agreeing turns involve the second speaker's epistemic priority in the matter being assessed, these turns also involve some qualification or disagreement. In example(16), for instance, Robbie has recently taken over an elementary school class that Lesley was previously teaching. Here, in a conversation in which Robbie seeks and gets reassurance about various aspects of teaching the class from Lesley, her generalized assessment of the children also encounters an *oh*-prefaced agreement. Once again, the *oh*-prefacing conveys that Lesley's opinion was arrived at prior to and independently from Robbie's and, in this context, reinforces the epistemic priority on the matter that Robbie recurrently attributes to Lesley across the course of a lengthy conversation:

(16)

> [Holt 5/88:1:5:4]
> 1 Rob: Oh I'm such a ↑so: gla:d t'have a chat with you cz I ↑↑do want
> 2   t'↓know'n I'm en↑jo:ying it 'n' the children'r ↓love[ly.
> 3 Les: [.tch
> 4 Les: → ↑O̲h̲ ↓yes.=They ↑a̲re lovely:: i[h i̲f a little ex↓citable.
> 5 Rob: [(   )
> 6 Rob: Th[a:t's w̲'t I thought. I'ave ↑thi̲r↓ty in that ro̲o- I=
> 7 Les: [Hm̲↓:.
> 8 Rob: =do̲:. Sympa↓thize with you.↓

However, in addition, Lesley modifies her agreement that the children are "lovely" with the qualification "i̲f a little ex↓citable." Robbie then takes up this shift in the subsequent talk (lines 6/8). In this sequence, we can see an additional motivation for *oh*-prefacing a second assessment. The *oh*-preface indexes an "independent" and "decided" perspective that, in turn, invokes Lesley's epistemic authority in the matter of the children. That epistemic authority is then mobilized as part of a turn that ends in Lesley's qualification of Robbie's enthusiam for the class and Robbie's acquiescence in that qualification.

In example (12), this mobilization of *oh*-prefacing as part of an [agree + disagree] response format (Pomerantz 1984a) is still more overt: both *oh*-preface producers go on to modify their positions in relation to Eve's friend's reported position:

(12)

```
[JS:II:61]
 1  Jon:       We saw Midnight Cowboy yesterday -or [suh- Friday.
 2  Eve:                                            [Oh?
 3  Lyn:       Didju s- you saw that, [it's really good.
 4  Eve:                              [No I haven't seen it
 5             Rae [sed it 'n' she said she f- depressed her
 6  ():             [(    )
 7  Eve:       ter[ribly
 8  Jon:  →       [Oh it's [terribly depressing.
 9  Lyn:  →               [Oh it's depressing.
10  Eve:       Ve[ry
11  Lyn:  →       [But it's a fantastic [film.
12  Jon:  →                             [It's a beautiful movie.
```

In example (13), Vivian's positive assessment of the neighbour is subsequently qualified, albeit at a slight distance, with an addition (lines 30–31) in which Vivian repositions herself closer to Shane's earlier stated position that the neighbor is "sorta dumb" (line 1):

(13)

```
[Chicken Dinner: 10 (extension)]
 1  Sha:       Nuh 'eez a nice guy 'eez [j's s[orta dumb. ]
 2  Mic:                                [(   [    )      ]
 3  Nan:                                     [I've talk'to]'m on the
 4             pho[ne.
 5  Mi?:          [(Yeah)
 6             (0.4)
 7  Sha:       (       [        ).
 8  Viv:               [Oh when you were over he wz ho:me?
 9  Mic:       Hm-hm?
10             (1.0)
11  Viv:       So wuddiyou thi:nk.
12             (2.2)
13  Sh?:       pwehh °hh
14  Mic:       I'on'know I couldn' (1.4) I din'rilly git tih talk to'm
15             that much uh- I can't say.
16             (1.2)
17  Viv:       hHuh. (Yuh lucky.)
```

```
18           (0.9)
19  Mic:     °I can't say.°
20           (3.2)
21  Mic: →   He seem'like a nice guy-
22  Sha:     (Naw) he is.
23           (0.6)
24  Sha:     He's[a nice [guy
25  Vi?:          [(.t)   [
26  Viv: →                [Oh he's a nice gu:y.
27           (0.3)
28  Sha:     I rib um a lot.
29           (2.7)
30  Viv: →   But- when- That's the: prob'm when yih try tih carry
31      →    on a conversation with im
```

And in example (14), having agreed that his cat is a "fight'n' fool," Abe shifts to a strong claim about the affectionate nature of his cat:

(14)

```
[TCIIA1:detail]
1  Ben:     .hhh They're fight'n' fools those Burmese,
2  Abe: →   Oh I know 'e is. But yet 'eez the most affectionate thing I
3           ever saw.
```

In these cases of *oh*-prefaced [agreement + disagreement], it is noticeable that the *oh*-prefaced agreement incorporates the same descriptive terminology that was employed in the first assessment, albeit qualified by the *oh*-prefaced indication of epistemic independence or authority. These *oh*-prefaced repetitions are then recurrently followed by disagreement components. In these cases, the *oh*-prefaced repetitions are the clear harbinger of subsequent disagreement components and are designed to index an epistemically authoritative position ancillary to the project of (re)positioning the speaker as in modified agreement or actual disagreement with the first speaker.[12]

Disagreement within Agreement: Further Refinements

Since *oh* can convey the epistemic independence of a second speaker's assessment from a first, *oh*-prefacing can be part of a process of competitive agreement in which each party, while agreeing with the other, invokes the priority of his/her own experience as the standpoint from which his/her evaluation is made. In such cases, the affiliation that is normally associated with agreement is marred by a form of ego-centered epistemic struggling between the participants. Example (17) is a simple case of this phenomenon. This sequence occurs close to the opening of the phone call, and Lottie is just back from a trip to the Palm Springs area:

(17)

> [NB IV:10:R:1]
> 1 Emm: .h ↑How wz yer tri:p.
> 2 Lot: Oh:: Go:d wonderful Emm[a,
> 3 Emm: [Oh idn'it beautiful do:wn the:re,
> 4 Lot: → Oh:: Jeeziz ih wz go:rgeous::.
> 5 Emm: Wh't a ni:ce ↑wut time'djih git i:n. Jst a li'l whal ago?

Here Emma's (line 3) response, itself indexing "independent access" to the "Palm Springs experience" and a degree of separation from the experiential basis of Lottie's report, is met with a response whose *oh*-preface is part of turn that insists (with the past tense) on Lottie's own immediate experience as the basis for the assessment.[13] Here, as Goodwin and Goodwin (1987) have noted in their work on assessments, the contrast between the tenses used by the two speakers marks two distinct stances toward the item being assessed: Lottie, the speaker with the news, uses the past tense to index a specific experience on which her assessment is based, Emma uses the present tense to index a more generalized stance toward the location.[14]

Examples (18) and (19) are more complex and embattled cases. The context of this conversation is as follows: Vera's married son and grandchildren have been visiting for a day or so. When they arrived at Vera's house, after a long-distance car drive, a note on her door directed them to her neighbor Jenny's, where they had a cup of tea and waited for Vera to return. Now the family has gone home, and Vera and Jenny are discussing the visit. In example (18), Vera responds to Jenny's assessment of the children as "go:rgiss" with a specifically behavioral assessment: the children were "ez good ez go:ld"—a shift in tack that she warrants by adding that she had heard "such bad repo:rts.about them." Jenny's response to this assessment is *oh*-prefaced and (1) agrees with Vera's assessment, (2) disagrees with the "bad reports," and (3) indexes her independent access to the referent—the children's good behavior in her home—as the basis for her position:

(18)

> [Rahman 14:2]
> 1 Jen: An' they look so well.the chilreh theh go:rg[iss   aren't they]
> 2 Ver: [D'you know theh-]
> 3 Ver: → He wz- they w'rr ez good ez go:ld,
> 4   (.)
> 5 Jen: Yes:[:
> 6 Ver: →   [Yihknow ah'v hehrd such bad repo:rts.about them.
> 7 Jen: → Oh:: they w'sm[ashi:ng.]
> 7 Ver: →   [Ah: : : :n]d eh- they w'good here they
> 9   pla:yed yihkno:w,

Now Jenny evidently designs this turn both to agree with Vera and to maximize her disagreement with the "bad reports" that Vera had mentioned (see the section on disagreements and the discussion of example [26]). But the *oh*-preface nonetheless conveys Jenny's independent access to the behavior of the children (who visited her house), and this is confirmed by the *w* in *they w'smashi:ng*, which unambiguously bases the assessment on her personal experience of the children's visit.[15] Here, then, the *oh*-preface contributes to Jenny's claimed right to independently assess children whose conduct Vera, as the grandmother, would ordinarily have exclusive rights to evaluate. Significantly, at line 8 Vera abandons an *and*-projected continuation of her talk at line 6, in favor of mobilizing what we can term a counteragreement that explicitly asserts (with *here*) her own home as the epistemic basis for her claims. This strongly suggests that in the face of Jenny's *oh*-prefaced assessment, the task of asserting her epistemic rights in the matter of assessing the grandchildren's conduct has assumed a real priority for Vera. Here the *oh*-preface-carried claim of epistemic independence has become a source of friction in a sequence otherwise designed to achieve maximal agreement and affiliation.

A similar order of activity seems to be going on in example (19), which is taken from the same conversation and occurred just after example (18). Vera's assessment of the older grandchild, James, culminates in her assertion that he "was mischeevious but he was good" (line 7). This is met with an upgraded agreement from Jenny (line 8), which is *oh*-prefaced[16]:

(19)

```
      [Rahman 14:2]
    1 Jen:    [Yeh James's a little divil ihhh ↑heh heh
    2 Ver:    [That-
    3 Jen:    [.huh .hh[h He:-
    4 Ver:            [James is a little bugger [isn'e.
    5 Jen:                                      [Yeh- Yeah=
    6 Jen:    =[(         ) evrythi]ng.
    7 Ver: →  =[Mindju 'eez good] Jenny, 'e wz mischeevious but w-'e wz good.
    8 Jen: →  Oo 'e wz beautiful here [wuuz↑n't'ee.=
    9 Ver:                           [↓Yes.
   10 Jen:    ='E[wz very well be[he:ved.
   11 Ver: →     [↓Yes.          ['E wz well behaved he:uh [too:.
   12 Jen:                                                 [Ye:s they're
   13           luvly little boy:s.
   14 Ver:    Ye::s,
```

This is a very complicated sequence. At its beginning both speakers have picked out James as the naughtier of the two grandchildren, using quite extreme terms (lines 1 and 4) that encompass the character of the child as well as his behavior.[17] Subsequently Vera, the grandmother, revises her position, describing James as "good" and then explicitly referencing his behavior with the qualified claim that "'e wz mischeevious but w-'e wz good." It is now Jenny's turn to revise her earlier observation that James is "a little divil" and position herself as in agreement with Vera's new position. Jenny also does so by reference to his behavior, specifically the behavior that she has witnessed at her home. Here, although her turn is done as an upgraded agreement (designed to back away from her earlier position and to agree with Vera), the *oh*-preface is part of a turn that, especially with the additional use of the word *here*, markedly invokes Jenny's independent knowledge of the behavior of the children as the basis for her revised position. However, this narrows the scope of her agreement to the behavior that she has actually witnessed.[18] The scope of this agreement is not sufficient for Vera, who reasserts her earlier assessment with a further agreement (*'E wz well behaved hẹ:uh toọ:*) that reasserts her own experience of the children as a further and final basis for the conclusion they are converging upon. Jenny then seizes this opportunity to exit the sequence with a generalization about both children (lines 12–13). Thus, in both examples (18) and (19), while the parties are working to achieve full agreement about the behavior of the children, they are also discomforted over how that agreement is to be managed and which account will have epistemic priority as the basis for the conclusions they are jointly reaching.

Summary: Oh-*Prefaced Agreements*

In sum, *oh*-prefacing in the context of agreements is a practice that embodies the second speaker's claim to have a perspective and opinion that is epistemically independent of the first.[19] As suggested earlier, *oh*-prefacing may achieve this outcome through a "change of state semantics" that conveys that the first assessment has occasioned a review, recollection, and renewal of the speaker's previous experience and judgment and that it is this preexisting experience that is the basis for the second assessment. Through this independence of perspective that is central to the work of *oh*-prefacing in agreement environments, the practice can serve as a resource with which a respondent can talk in a fashion that novelists describe as "decided." It projects the second speaker's mind as "made up" on the topic. And it permits an expression of opinion to be understood as voiced in response to the other's point of view but not altered by it.

   Oh-prefaced agreements are more frequent in cases where (1) the second speaker has epistemic authority in the matter of access to and/or rights to assess the state of affairs in question, and (2) the second speaker is in some disagreement with the first and deploys an [agree + disagree] response to register this. These two circumstances may be primary motivations for the claim to epistemic independence that *oh*-prefaced responses to assertions embody, and they may add associative coloring to the understanding of what an *oh*-preface has indexed. Thus, *oh*-prefacing is associated with, indexes and reflexively embodies claims to epistemic independence that may be understood and glossed by a recipient in terms of authority and disagreement. Further, while the claim of epistemic independence embodied by *oh*-prefaced agreements may be treated as giving enhanced support to the claims of the first speaker, it may also be understood as embodying an element of epistemic competition between the parties. Under certain conditions, speakers may find themselves dealing with both possibilities simultaneously and struggling uncomfortably through a process of "counter-agreement." Thus, across these cases, even the most harmonious, there is an element of epistemic tension between the parties.

Oh-*Prefaced Disagreements*

Given that *oh*-prefacing is clearly associated with various kinds of tensions and trends toward divergence and misalignment in sequences that are primarily occupied with agreement, it will come as no surprise that it is also found in disagreement sequences. We begin with two basic claims about *oh*-prefaced disagreements.

First, persons do not ordinarily *oh*-preface a first disagreeing turn. Rather, *oh*-prefacing is used by disagreed-with parties in responding to a disagreement that is already launched. Although it is obviously possible that *oh*-prefaced "initial disagreement" turns can occur empirically, there are none in the substantial data set I have examined for this essay. It is reasonable to conclude, then, that *oh*-prefacing is rarely a "weapon of first resort."[20]

Second, since *oh*-prefaced disagreements are ordinarily *responses* to disagreement, *oh*-prefacing can be understood as a means of escalating disputes. In this context, its role in indexing a position as "established" and as founded in epistemic independence/priority (whether rhetorically or not) is a significant one.

Oh-*Prefaced Disagreements: "Holding a Position" in Flat Out Opposition*

Although oh-prefacing is relatively uncommon in disagreement contexts, its significance there is unambiguously one of escalation and intensification of disagreement. Example (20) is perhaps prototypical of this. Here two undergraduates, Shirley and Geri, get into a dispute about how many weeks of the Geri's school term are left. Geri's assessment of "*six* er seven more weeks" initially meets with agreement from Shirley (line 4), but the latter then revises her opinion so as to disagree (lines 6–8), calculating that the quarter has only five more weeks to run:

(20)

```
[Frankel TC1:7]
 1  Ger:   A:nd uh:m (0.2) schoo:l is, alri:ght 't's coming alo:ng it['s
 2  Shi:                                                          [Yeah=
 3  Ger:   =it's only seh- seven more six er seven more weeks.
 4  Shi:   Yea:h, rilly,
 5  Ger:   A:::n[d
 6  Shi:        [There's less then tha:t, this's the beginning of
 7          the seventh week a'the quarter. .hhhh Yer off- You have five
 8          weeks left.
 9  Ger:   Uh-uh,
10  Shi:   [Mm-hm,
11  Ger:   [We av more then [fi : : [ve,
12  Shi: → 　　　　　　　　　[.hhh[Oh no Geri five weeks.
13                    (0.7)
14  (S):   .t.hhh
15  Ger:   Wul maybe we 'av six. But we don't have[fi : [ve.
16  Shi:                                          [.hh[Whendju get out.=
17  Shi:   =Christmas week er the week before Christmas.
```

Geri resists at line 9 with _Uh-uh_ and subsequently with a contradictory claim of _more than fi::ve_. It is this disagreement in which Geri holds her original position, which Shirley then attacks with an _oh_-prefaced rejection and a reassertion of "five weeks." At this point Shirley has already underpinned her claim at lines 6–8 with a display of calculation that builds an explicit justification for her position. Faced with continued, but unargued for, disagreement (at lines 9/11), Shirley reasserts the product of her earlier "calculation" with an _oh_-prefaced repetition. Here the _oh_-prefacing of the turn indexes (1) its epistemic independence and (2) the "established" nature of the position she is expressing and thus points to the inappositeness of Geri's questioning something that has already been explicitly stated, thereby indirectly asserting a (claimed) epistemic authority on the matter.[21] By this means the response is made more overtly _reassertive_. Here the practice of _oh_-prefacing is a significant feature of a turn, designed to "hold a position" that has already been taken up and which is now reasserted in intensified fashion.[22] Notably, it induces Geri into a partial backdown from her earlier position (line 15).

_Oh_-prefacing achieves this intensification of a stated position by entering a claim of position-holding epistemic independence while simultaneously providing for the unexpectedness or inappositeness of the (oppositional) assertion to which it responds. Turn-initial position is a strategic site for this provision in that it represents a first possible opportunity at which it can be made. As an initial response component, _oh_ amplifies the impact of the subsequently stated disagreement.

In example (21), as in example (20), _oh_-prefacing is used to further escalate an already thoroughly developed disagreement between a grandmother and her granddaughter whom she suspects of being bulimic.[23]

(21)

```
        [SDCL:G/S:25–40]
   1 G:    I don'(t) know (.) I think you're just (0.2) °(well you're)°
   2       just wearin' yourself out with all your activity >I think if you
   3       slo:w down a li(tt)le bit and rest a little bit more<
   4       (0.4)
   5 S:    GRA:[M M A] YOU'RE SO WEIRD!
   6 G:        [Maybe]
   7 S:    >I don't even know why you say that I- <.hh I am f : i : : ve thr : ee : :
   8       and I still weigh a hundred an' te[n- fif teen po : unds?
   9                                          [((noise))
  10       (0.6)
  11 G: →  O:h ↓you don't weigh a °hundred an'° fifteen ↑pounds .hh all your
  12       clothes are fallin' off of ya everybody tells you ya look thi : : n?
```

Here the grandmother's rebuttal of her granddaughter's disagreement is _oh_-prefaced. The epistemic claim embodied in the _oh_-preface is a fascinating maneuver: surely the granddaughter—especially if she is bulimic—will have an exact knowledge of her own weight. Yet the _oh_-preface can imply that the grandmother knows that the granddaughter is overestimating her weight for argumentative purposes, and indeed at line 12 the grandmother offers two kinds of evidence to support her side of the case.

Even in less intensely contested disagreements, *oh*-prefacing is ordinarily restricted to "second rounds" of disagreement. In example (22), Rich has disclosed that he's working from three to eleven during the weekends—something that Hyla regards as "terrible hours" (line 5):

(22)

```
[Hyla–Rich: 2]
 1 RIC:    Well I go in en outta work from about three to eleven
 2         thirt[y.
 3 HYL:        [tch Oh: yer ki::dding.
 4         (0.3)
 5 HYL:    That's terr[ible hours.]
 6 RIC:               [Jes- jes fe]r (.) jest today en yesterday.
 7 HYL:    O:h.
 8         (.)
 9 HYL:    Those're aw:ful hour:s.
10 RIC:  → Oh but the pay is grea:::t.
```

In this sequence, Rich deflects Hyla's first assessment (at line 5) with the incremental claim that he's only working these hours for two days (line 6). However, on Hyla's subsequent renewal of the negative assessment (at line 9), he again disagrees, citing the pay—something to which he has epistemically privileged access. That disagreement is *oh*-prefaced and, once again, *oh*-prefacing is used to "hold a position" as a weapon of second resort.

In these cases *oh*-prefacing is used when the speaker is rebutting a disagreement and, in my data at least, this is the prototypical context for *oh*-prefaced disagreements. It is thus no accident that it is just this sense that is conveyed in the text with which I began this essay. The women (firefighters and others) described in the text are, we imagine, retorting to naysayers, people who deny their occupational aspirations. It is the *oh*-preface that specifically conveys this, and it does so because *oh*-prefaced disagreements overwhelmingly manifest themselves as disagreements to disagreements.

Oh-*Prefaced Disagreements: "Holding a Position" in Scaled Disagreement*

We have seen that *oh*-prefaced disagreements are predominantly deployed to respond to actions that are themselves disagreeing: in all such cases they "hold a position" that the speaker has already taken up in a prior turn. However, they also occur in environments of downgraded or "weak" agreement (Pomerantz 1984a). Pomerantz (ibid.:68) notes that downgraded agreements frequently engender disagreement sequences in which the participants reassert previous positions. Not surprisingly, some of these reassertions are *oh*-prefaced, as in example (23). Here a strongly positive assessment is met with an agreement token (*yes*) and a downgraded assessment. The producer of the original strongly positive assessment then reasserts her position with a second strongly positive one that is also *oh*-prefaced:

(23)

> [GJ:1 (From Pomerantz 1984a:68)]
> 1 A: She's a fox.
> 2 B: Yeah, she's a pretty girl.
> 3 A: → Oh, she's gorgeous!

Here the *oh*-preface upgrades the disagreement that is expressed in the mismatch between descriptors by underscoring the reassertive "position holding" quality of A's response. A similar process is apparent in example (24):

(24)

> [NB VII:1–2]
> 1 Emm: =Oh <u>ho</u>ney that was a <u>lo</u>vely lunch<u>eo</u>n I shoulda <u>ca</u>:lled you
> 2   s:soo[: ner but <u>I :</u>]l : [<u>lo</u>:ved it.Ih wz <u>just</u> deli:ghtfu[: l.]=
> 3 Mar: [((f)) <u>Oh : : :</u>]   [°(   )   [Well]=
> 4 Mar: =<u>I</u> wz gla[d y o u] (came).]
> 5 Emm: ['nd yer f:] <u>friends</u>] 'r so da:rli<u>:</u>ng,=
> 6 Mar: = <u>Oh</u> : : : [: it wz:]
> 7 Emm: [e-that <u>P</u>]<u>a</u>:t <u>i</u>sn'she a do : [<u>:</u> ll?]
> 8 Mar: [iY e]h <u>i</u>sn't she pretty,
> 9   (.)
> 10 Emm: → <u>Oh:</u> she's a beautiful girl.=
> 11 Mar: =Yeh <u>I</u> think she's a pretty gir[l.
> 12 Emm: [En that <u>Reinam'n</u> : :

Here, too, Emma's (line 10) reasserted position is *oh*-prefaced, indexing that she is holding a position vis-à-vis an unlooked-for, or less than apposite or agreeable, response. This case is notable for the fact that Margy sustains her disagreement into a fourth turn (line 11) with a yes-prefaced turn that preserves the exact assessment value that she offered in her first downgrade at line 8. However, with the yes-preface in place, Margy's utterance, which also "holds a position," manages this in a less argumentative way and is done as a less reassertive disagreement. This example permits us to see that there is a clear distinction between *oh*-prefaced and yes-prefaced position adjustments. While Emma's *oh*-prefaced upgrade comes off as an explicit disagreement, Margy's subsequent yes-prefaced downgrade is managed, like her first (line 8), as a muted disagreement or "pseudo-agreement."

In sum, in the context of direct disagreement, *oh*-prefacing is rarely deployed in a first disagreeing action. Rather, it is normally reserved for disagreements with assertions that are themselves disagreements. In such contexts, the epistemic independence embodied in *oh*-prefacing is hearable first as explicitly holding an earlier stated position and second as implying the inappositeness or untowardness of the counterposition. For this reason, *oh*-prefaced reassertions of upgraded or downgraded assessments relative to another's position underscore the element of disagreement that those actions embody without *oh*-prefacing.

Conclusion

In this chapter, I have argued that *oh*-prefacing is used to convey the epistemic independence of a second judgment or evaluation from a first and primarily in cases where the parties have not had joint access to the referent being assessed. It is used by an agreeing party to markedly indicate access to and/or evaluation of a state of affairs that is independently grounded from that of the first speaker. More commonly than not, it is used in contexts where the second speaker has epistemic priority with regard to the matter under discussion. Thus, it may be motivated as a means of disputing any epistemic priority that is asserted by the sheer "firstness" of a first assessment and to disengage a second speaker's expression of opinion from the taint of being produced merely "in agreement with" or "in conformity with" the first speaker's opinion. A substantial subset of *oh*-prefaced agreements embodies some element of epistemic competition between the parties, often compromising the element of affiliation that is normally embodied in the process of agreement. A further subset involves movement toward position adjustment or disagreement by the second speaker.

Oh-prefaced disagreements embody upgraded disagreement relative to the same turn in the same context without the *oh*-preface and tend to be restricted to subsequent disagreements or disagreements with disagreements.

It might be concluded that *oh*-prefaced responses to assessments are somewhat undesirable actions to encounter. While generally true, this is not always the case. In example (25) Emma is telling her sister about an accusation that Emma's husband has made, as reported to Emma by her married daughter:

(25)

```
[NB IV:10:R:4]
 1 Emm:    . . . she s'z well:< (0.3) DA:D se:z you won't LIVE
 2         IN THE A↓PA:RTMENT in thetcher unHA::PPY UP THERE'n
 3         you want him tuh c'mmute BA:CK 'n forth evry day
 4         ↑which is a Go:d da:mn LIE:,
 5         (.)
 6 Emm:    .hh[hhh<
 7 Lot:  →    [Oh↓:::::::y:eah[c u z]you'd never sai:d tha*:[t.
 8 Emm:                      [e-H e]                       [A:nd uh, . . .
```

Here Emma's sister's *oh*-prefaced response at line 7 simultaneously manages escalated disagreement with Emma's husband's assertion as reported by Emma and epistemically independent agreement with—and thus independent corroboration of—Emma's assessment of that assertion as a "Go:d da:mn LIE:." Her action is the more remarkable as a gesture of raw affiliation with her sister by the fact that her "epistemic independence," though strongly asserted and powerfully voiced, is at best dubious in the context of a "he said, she said" dispute between husband and wife. While *oh*-prefaced responses are often "bad news," they are not invariantly so.

NOTES

1. There is a nice paradox here. *Oh*, which is commonly thought of as the "surprise particle," is here used to convey the reverse.

2. Because Kennedy was assassinated in Los Angeles, its aftermath and many of the funeral arrangements received heavy coverage on local television stations.

3. It is possible that the use of turn components such as tag questions in first position assessments embodies a mitigation of any implied claim to epistemic authority that the turn's position embodies, even in the co-present cases, such as examples (2) and (3).

4. This response is hearably brief and dismissive of an assessment that could have engendered an extended sequence on this topic. Robbie then immediately initiates a new topic, a pub. There is a convergence here with the use of *oh*-prefaced responses to questions to curtail the development of topics projected by the questions (Heritage 1998:313–320).

5. For a more extensive account of these two sequences, see Heritage (1990/1).

6. There is a convergence here with Schegloff's (1996:63) comment that deploying such terms as "actually" or "as a matter of fact" is a practice that can be used to indicate that what follows has a contemporary relevance to the speaker that is distinct from that created by the prior speaker's talk. See also the discussion of example (15).

7. Of course speakers have other ways of indicating the independence and priority of their perspectives. For example, as she elaborates her agreement in lines 6–7 of example (10), Margy underscores the closeness of her relationship to the referenced person, relative to Emma.

8. Michael's reluctance may receive additional motivation from the apparent difference in the stance taken to the neighbor by his host and hostess.

9. It is possible that Abe is referring to his own cat at lines 10–11, thus shifting the reference from Ben's "Burmese cats in general" to his own animal as part of his *oh*-prefaced, epistemically authoritative response. However, his initial *oh*-prefaced response employs a reference form, *it's a*, which is likely designed as a generic reference, by comparison with Abe's later use of *he* at lines 15 and 23 to refer specifically to his own cat.

10. I thank Geoff Raymond, who drew this feature of the sequence to my attention.

11. It probably speaks to the state of the relationship between these two interactants that Marsha did not call Tony to inform him of the altered travel plans and that the call, having been—up to this point at least—focused on the "mechanics" of Joey's return to his father, now turns to the "mechanics" of the return of the car itself. In a variety of other ways Marsha, who is ordinarily an emotionally colorful interactant, attempts to maintain a factual, controlled, and "cool" tone.

12. This observation lends some further support to Anita Pomerantz's argument that nonupgraded agreements convey incipient disagreement.

13. The format of Emma's inquiry—"isn't it. . ."—makes it as close to an assertion in its own right as can be made within interrogative syntax. Questioning in the news media that embodies this format is recurrently so treated. For example:

```
IR:    W'l Mister President in your zea:l (.) for funds during
    →  the last campaign .hh didn't you put the vice president (.)
       an' Maggie and all the others in your (0.4) administration
       topside .hh in a very vulnerable position, hh
       (0.5)
IE:  → I disagree with that.hh u- How are we vulnerable because . . .
```

Here Helen Thomas's (UPI) interrogative syntax is not sufficient for her utterance to be treated by President Clinton as simply a neutral question. Rather, she is treated as having taken a position with which the president, as he puts it, "disagrees." Questions framed in the negative with such beginnings as *Isn't it, Don't you,* and so forth, are characteristically responded to as assertions (Heritage forthcoming).

14. There is a strong parallel here with Goodwin and Goodwin's (1987) treatment of the "asparagus pie" example, to which this discussion is indebted.

15. If Jenny had used *are* instead of *were,* the outcome would have likely been less problematic. It might be added that Jenny's choice of adjective—*smashing*—is a shade overapt as a description of the good behavior of a naughty child!

16. Here the particle preface at line 8, transcribed as *Oo,* is treated as a token of *oh.* Though the shift in its pronunciation may involve some (currently unknown) departure in use and meaning from *oh,* it is part of the "*oh* family" in a way that *ah* (Aston 1987), *eh,* and *uh* manifestly are not.

17. Although Jenny appears to "go first" in offering this assessment, in fact it is interactionally engendered (data not shown). Moreover, Vera's responsive upgraded and agreeing turn at line 4 is ended with a tag question, muting its second position status and offering itself as a claimedly first position object.

18. In this example, it is noticeable that the *oh*-prefaced second assessment is converted into a first action by the addition of the tag question. The tag question here is a further resource that Jenny uses to try to work her way out from a reactive "second position" revision of opinion and to reduce the extent to which her revised assessment of the child will be seen as interactionally motivated.

19. Significantly, an *oh*-prefaced agreement may be abandoned when its producer recognizes that the object to which it responds was not a first hand assessment. Thus in the following case, Lesley is describing a visit to her mother in Kent, which among other things involved helping with the garden (lines 1–2) and taking a trip to Maidstone (line 3). As is clear from the subsequent talk, Lesley is quite distressed by recent changes in the town. The issue is raised by Kevin with a remark—"Yes I hear it's changed a lot"—which could seem, to Lesley at least, to imply exactly the concerns she is about to express. Kevin's turn also embodies (with the evidential phrase *I hear* [Chafe 1986; Pomerantz 1984b] just the kind of reduced epistemic access that is, as we have seen, recurrently associated with *oh*-prefaced second position agreements by epistemic authorities. And indeed this is what Lesley vigorously launches into with *Oh: it (.) was (.) abs-,* where, in light of her later remarks, the cut-off *abs-* was presumably going to be *absolutely.*

```
[Holt U/88–2–2:1–2]
 1 Les:    eYes: u-and uhm, hmhh.t.hhh we helped her with'er garden
 2         an' hhh.hhh weeded 'n::d hh generally messed about,h
 3         But w'↑went tuh ↑Maidsto:ne[.hhhhhhhhhh] [
 4 Kev:                        [—(1.0)—]        [Yes I hear it's
 5         chan[ged a [lot.
 6 Les: →      [↑u-  [Oh: it (.) was (.) abs- e-We came back ↑so
 7         depressed. .hhhh It- (0.2) eh that-that Stoneborough,hhh
 8         uh:m: (0.4) .k.hhhh e-shopp↓ing arcade↓ (.) is: a ↑pi:t.
 9         hh It: (.) is ↑gha:st↓ly. 'N' everything looked taw:↓dry
10         in it.↓ .hhhhh And the ↑↑people looked ↑so ↑shabby.hh
```

However, the turn with which Lesley was about to agree was, on its face at least, relatively "neutral." It describes a report of "change." It does not embody the kind of strongly felt evaluation with which Lesley was evidently preparing to agree. It is likely that Lesley abandons this turn start in recognition of the lack of fit between Kevin's remark and what she had intended as an "agreement." It is noticeable that her revised turn, now of course shorn of the *oh*-preface, reports a notably "subjective" experience—*We came back ↑so depressed*—now positioned as a "first" action reporting "news," rather than a "second" and agreeing action.

20. An exception to this generalization might arise in the context of highly polarized "hot button" public issues, for example the widely circulated Starr Report and the possible impeachment of President Clinton. For such subjects, one might expect to hear: "Oh I completely disagree . . ." as a first position disagreement, though to date (September 1998) I have not heard such a maneuver. Pseudoexceptions might include disagreements over topics that, for example, family members recurrently disagree on. In these latter cases, the *oh*-preface might, through its very use as a weapon of first resort, reinvoke earlier disagreements on the same issue.

21. Shirley also deploys another offensive procedure in this turn: naming her addressee (Clayman 1998).

22. There is a parallel here with phenomena described in Heritage (1998), in which *oh*-prefacing is used to "hold a position" in a context of questioning that embodies components of disagreement. The following, well-known sequence concerns Mike's claim (line 1) that "a guy at work" has two Cords. A Cord is a rare automobile that was briefly manufactured in the United States in the 1930s and is now copied as a "classic car." For these reasons the claim is distinctly newsworthy, especially for the car enthusiasts among the conversation's participants. Mike's claim at line 1 gives rise to a sequence of queries from Curt, of which we are interested in the first two. Curt's initial query is, *Not original*. While this may be deployed merely as a means to register the out-of-the-ordinary nature of Mike's claim, it may alternatively be taken to indicate doubt as to whether the "two Cords" are of original manufacture and therefore "the real thing" or alternatively just modern replicas. At any event, the design of Curt's question strongly favors a, "No," response which, in the unlikely event that it were done, would represent a reversal of Mike's stated position:

```
[Auto Discussion: 13:04–13:15]
    Mik:      Lemme ask a guy at work. He's gotta bunch a' old
              clu[nkers.
    Gar:          [Y'know Marlon Liddle?
              (0.2)
    Mik:      Well I can't say they're ol' clunkers eez gotta Co:rd?
              (0.1)
    Mik:      Two Co:rds,
              (1.0)
    Mik:      [And
    Cur: 1→   [Not original,
              (0.7)
    Mik: 2→   Oh yes. Very origi(h)nal. [lateral "disagreeing" head shake]
    Cur: 3→   Oh:: reall[y?
    Mik: 4→             [Yah. Ve(h)ry origi(h)nal. [vertical "agreeing" head shake]
    Cur:      °Awhhh are you shittin' m[e?
    Mik:                               [No I'm not.
```

Mike's response to Curt's question is composed of two TCUs that (re)assert his claim as to the originality of the cars. The first unit, *Oh yes*, is accompanied by a strong lateral and, in this context, "disagreeing" head shake. It clearly reasserts his earlier claims of lines 5 and 7. The second unit, <u>Very</u> origi(h)nal, which is accompanied by a continuation of the lateral head shake, strongly upgrades that assertion. Curt's second query—oh:: really—is, by contrast with Not original, not in any way oppositional. It is a "newsmark" of a type that, far from inviting a revision of Mike's position, routinely invites reconfirmation of a position and, further, projects its producer's acceptance of that reconfirmation (Heritage 1984; Jefferson 1981). Mike's response to this second query is identical to the first except for two features. The first is that his head movement is revised from a lateral head shake, indicative of disagreement, to a vertical head shake, produced across the entire turn and indicative of agreement. The second feature is that the reassertive oh-preface is removed. This sequence embodies fine-grained evidence that oh-prefacing in response to questions can be specifically designed to disagree with, or rebut the position taken by a questioner and to do so by indexing the "established" nature of the position being defended and pointing to the inappositeness of questioning something that has already been explicitly stated (Heritage 1998) as an ancillary part of holding and upgrading the position that has already been taken. It remains to be added that both of Curt's questions are designed to underscore the "newsworthiness" of Mike's announcement and that the sequence is generally benign. Nonetheless, within that understanding, Curt's two questions are treated in quite distinct ways that are fitted to the preferences they embody. See Goodwin (1980) and Schegloff (1987a) for further discussions of this well-known sequence. I thank Charles and Candy Goodwin for very helpful discussion of this example.

   23. See Beach (1996) for an extended analysis of this conversation.

REFERENCES

Aston, Guy 1987. Ah: A corpus-based exercise in conversational analyisis. In John Morley and Alan Partington (eds.), *Spoken Discourse*, 123–137. Camerino, Italy: Universita di Camerino.

Beach, Wayne A. 1996. *Conversations About Illness: Family Preoccupations with Bulimia*. Mahwah: NJ: Lawrence Erlbaum.

Chafe, W. 1986. Evidentiality in English conversation and academic writing. In W. Chafe and J. Nichols (eds.), *Evidentiality: The Linguistic Coding of Epistemology*, 261–272. Norwood, NJ: Ablex.

Clayman, Steven. 1998. Some uses of address terms in news interviews. *Mimeo*, University of California, Los Angeles.

Davidson, Judy. 1984. Subsequent versions of invitations, offers, requests, and proposals dealing with potential or actual rejection. In J. Maxwell Atkinson and John Heritage (eds.), *Structures of Social Action: Studies in Conversation Analysis*, 102–128. Cambridge: Cambridge University Press.

Goodwin, Charles, and Marjorie Harness Goodwin. 1987. Concurrent operations on talk: Notes on the interactive organization of assessments. *IPRA Papers in Pragmatics* 1(1): 1–54.

Goodwin, Marjorie Harness. 1980. Processes of mutual monitoring implicated in the production of description sequences. *Sociological Inquiry* 50:303–317.

Heritage, John. 1984. A change-of-state token and aspects of its sequential placement. In J. Maxwell Atkinson and John Heritage (eds.), *Structures of Social Action: Studies in Conversation Analysis*, 299–345. Cambridge, Cambridge University Press.

Heritage, John. 1990/1. Intention, meaning and strategy: Observations on constraints on interaction analysis. *Research on Language and Social Interaction* 24:311–332.

Heritage, John. 1998. *Oh*-prefaced responses to inquiry. *Language in Society* 27(3): 291–334.

Heritage, John. (Forthcoming). The limits of questioning: Negative interrogatives and hostile question content. In Philip Glenn, Curt LeBaron, and Jennifer Mandelbaum (eds.), *Studies in Language and Social Interaction.* Mahwah, NJ: Lawrence Erlbaum Associates.

Heritage, John, and Marja-Leena Sorjonen, 1994. Constituting and maintaining activities across sequences: *And*-prefacing as a feature of question design. *Language in Society* 23(1): 1–29.

Jefferson, Gail. 1981. *The Abominable 'Ne?': A Working Paper Exploring the Phenomenon of Post-Response Pursuit of Response.* Occasional Paper no. 6, Department of Sociology, University of Manchester, England.

Lerner, Gene H. 1996. On the "semi-permeable" character of grammatical units in conversation: Conditional entry into the turn space of another speaker. In Elinor Ochs, Emanuel A. Schegloff, and Sandra A. Thompson (eds.), *Interaction and Grammar,* 238–276. Cambridge, Cambridge University Press.

Pomerantz, Anita. 1984a. Agreeing and disagreeing with assessments: Some features of preferred/dispreferred turn shapes. In J. Maxwell Atkinson and John Heritage (eds.), *Structures of Social Action: Studies in Conversation Analysis,* 57–101. Cambridge, Cambridge University Press.

Pomerantz, Anita M. 1984b. Giving a source or basis: The practice in conversation of telling 'what I know'. *Journal of Pragmatics* 8(4): 607–625.

Sacks, Harvey, Emanuel A. Schegloff, and Gail Jefferson. 1974. A simplest systematics for the organization of turn-taking in conversation. *Language* 50(4): 696–735.

Schegloff, Emanuel A. 1987a. Analyzing single episodes of interaction: An exercise in conversation analysis. *Social Psychology Quarterly* 50(2): 101–114.

Schegloff, Emanuel A. 1987b. Recycled turn beginnings: A precise repair mechanism in conversation's turn-taking organisation. In Graham Button and John R. E. Lee (eds.), *Talk and Social Organisation,* 70–85. Clevedon, England: Multilingual Matters.

Schegloff, Emanuel A. 1996. Turn organization: One intersection of grammar and interaction. In Elinor Ochs, Emanuel A. Schegloff, and Sandra A. Thompson (eds.), *Interaction and Grammar,* 52–133. Cambridge, Cambridge University Press.

Schegloff, Emanuel A. 1997. Whose text? Whose context? *Discourse and Society* 8(2): 165–187.

Schiffrin, Deborah 1987. *Discourse Markers.* Cambridge: Cambridge University Press.

9

Turn-Sharing

The Choral Co-Production of Talk-in-Interaction

GENE H. LERNER

Simultaneous speech in conversation, when it occurs, can be treated as a turn-taking problem in need of repair (Sacks, Schegloff, and Jefferson 1974). Speakers may cut short what they are saying or employ devices to compete for exclusive speakership when faced with an overlapping utterance by another participant (Jefferson 1983; Jefferson and Schegloff 1975; Lerner 1989; Schegloff 1987, 2000). However, some forms of participation in conversation are not serially organized—that is, they are not designed for one participant speaking at a time. On occasion, participants may treat more-than-one-at-a-time speaking as properly simultaneous. That is, some simultaneously voiced actions are not treated by participants as a violation or as being in need of repair (Coates 1996; Erickson 1992; Goodwin and Goodwin 1987; see James and Clarke 1993 for a review of research on "supportive and cooperative interruptions").[1] Furthermore, there seem to be systematically describable sequential environments for such simultaneously voiced actions. For example, the beginnings and endings of social gatherings may be marked by collective greeting and leave-taking utterances. Also, consider the appreciative responses that can follow the opening of a gift. These can form a cacophony of verbal and vocal assessments.

Thus far I have only proposed that there are times when simultaneous speech and not just a one-at-a-time contribution seems in order. I have not yet said anything about the form of these simultaneous utterances. In the examples of properly simultaneous speech cited earlier, each speaker's contribution may consist of a somewhat different utterance or a differently timed utterance. This can result in properly overlapping speech but does not reveal a specific orientation to the simultaneity of the speech. Yet at times participants may speak in a fashion that reveals that they are not aiming to produce a separate turn at talk or even a distinct utterance among other simultaneous contributions but are instead aiming to simultaneously co-produce part or all of a turn-constructional unit (henceforth TCU) more or less in unison with another participant, by recognizably attempting to do such things as match the words, voicing, and tempo of the other speaker. This type of turn-sharing can be seen in excerpt (1) at line 12 and again at line 15. Here three young children (speakers A, B, and C) are addressing their remarks to an adult (D):

(1)

```
    [Osborn]
     1    A:  my teacher made me make it
     2        (.)
     3        taught us how to make (gate)
     4        (0.8)
     5    B:  there
     6        (.)
     7    C:  my teacher was
     8    B:  you know what my teacher was gone
     9        fer a week, she went
    10        (.)
    11        [she's in the hospita:l
    12 → C:  [(she's in the) hospita:l
    13    D:  mmm mm.
    14    B:  she has an [operation
    15 → C:              [(opera)tion
    16    C:  she gets this pretty (bathrobe)
    17        (.)
    18    B:  nightgown
```

The difficulty in distinguishing the voices (as indicated by the parenthesized words in the transcript at lines 12 and 15) attests to how very closely matched these utterances are. Though choral co-production of a TCU or TCU component refers to "voicing the same words in the same way at the same time" as another speaker—or at least demonstrating that one is aiming at that result[2]—it is important to note that this does not necessarily mean achieving the same action as the other speaker through that utterance. This chapter describes the ways some choral performances are arranged and then examines how some are used in conversation and other forms of talk-in-interaction. Finally, consideration is given to the phenomenon of gestural matching.

Co-Production—Not Co-Optation

In an earlier series of investigations I described the sequential features of turn construction that furnish participants with the resources to co-opt the completion of the

TCU-in-progress of a current speaker (Lerner 1991, 1996b), and I showed how such anticipatory completions can be employed interactionally (Lerner 1996a; Lerner and Takagi 1999). In the course of that earlier work, I occasionally came across instances of collaboratively produced TCUs that could not be characterized as co-opting the completion of the ongoing turn. That is, they did not seem to be designed to say first what the erstwhile current speaker was about to say, thus pre-empting the current speaker. Rather, these instances appeared to be designed to co-produce a turn's completion. And many of them seemed designed to match the voicing of the current speaker quite closely—that is, they resulted in a fully choral rendition of the turn's completion.

There is a fine distinction between the anticipatory completion of a TCU described in those earlier investigations—in which a speaker aims at taking over or co-opting the voicing of the final part of a compound TCU—and the choral co-productions described in this chapter. However, as one can see in the following comparison, these practices can be oriented to (i.e., composed and treated) as distinct forms of participation.

Anticipatory completions ordinarily begin at a place that allows new speakers to finish the TCU by themselves (and current speakers can collaborate with this by not resuming or continuing their utterance), as in excerpt (2):

(2)

    [Mother's Day]
    R: Well honey,
        (0.5) ((R chews and swallows.))
        in dis world, really truly.
        (.)
    C: you can't be sure.

And even when the new speakers begin a bit late, as in excerpts (3) and (4), they do not attempt to match their utterance to the emerging final component of the current speaker:

(3)

    [US]
    Rich: If they come en' pick it up
            it'll co[st yah
    Mike: [they charge yuh

(4)

    [Theodore]
    A: if you start watering,
        it [will get gree-
    B: [it will come back

In excerpt (3) Mike produces a recognizably alternative final component for the compound TCU whose final component Rich has already begun voicing, and in excerpt (4) speaker A cuts off her utterance to allow B to complete the TCU by herself.

By contrast, in excerpt (5) Shane shifts his use of *I* and *you* in the course of a co-produced idiomatic expression to match Michael's usage:

(5)

> [Chicken Dinner]
>   MIC: [I kne:w you were co:ming so I ba:ked a ca:ke.
> → SHA: [You knew I you coming, so I baked a cake

And in excerpt (6) speaker B also shows herself to be beginning late but designs her contribution to match the now-available beginning of A's TCU. Moreover, she shows that she is aiming at choral co-production through a precise midcourse adjustment of her utterance:

(6)

> [GL:FN:closing]
>   A: Good luck. Nice to [↑ s e e::˙   y o u : :]
> → B: [>Nice to< ↑ see:: you::]

Speaker B begins with the same words, but rather than matching the tempo of the already-produced part of A's utterance, she instead employs a very fast tempo until she catches up with A's utterance and then shifts to a much slower tempo and elevated pitch that match A's voicing, so that they come to complete their utterances in unison.

My aim here has been to highlight the design differences between co-produced and co-opted turn components. However, it is important to keep in mind that one cannot always tell whether a second speaker's contribution is designed to co-opt or to co-produce a turn component, since that speaker's contribution is not always produced with one or the other of these design features. In addition, the co-production or co-optation that results is an interactionally achieved outcome, since the current speakers may or may not halt their utterance—and if they do continue, the result can be more or less choral.[3] In other words, though some instances are clearly designed as either co-production or co-optation, many are not designed and not treated in a distinctive manner. Thus, these two means of conditional entry into the turn space of another speaker might be seen as only partially distinctive alternatives.

Arranging Choral Performances in Conversation

Chorally co-produced turn elements can be set in motion in at least two ways. For the most part in the conversations I have examined, recipients of an emerging turn's talk join in without specific elicitation on the part of the speaker; yet it is also possible for a current speaker to elicit recipient co-participation that takes the form of turn-sharing. I will first describe some of the ways that recipients can use the ongoing talk and context to initiate co-production in an opportunistic fashion, and then I will examine how current speakers can make co-production a relevant practice for their recipients.

Opportunistic Co-Production

The sources of TCU projection are always situated in what might be called the thick particulars of each individual instance of turn construction as it emerges within its circumstances, sequence and turn. Thus, turns at talk are somewhat projectable as they emerge. This projectability furnishes possible next speakers with the resources to locate an upcoming place to begin speaking (Sacks, Schegloff, and Jefferson 1974; Ford, Fox, and Thompson 1996; Ford and Thompson 1996). Moreover, on some occasions the form or even the specific words that will be used to construct a TCU or TCU element can be strongly projected. These foreseeable features of a turn's emergent construction can be used by recipients to accomplish choral co-production of the turn's completion. It should be noted that overwhelmingly it is the final part of a TCU—its terminal item—that is co-produced. Here co-production is not specifically elicited, but an opportunity for co-production is furnished by the enhanced projectability of the TCU.

Ordinarily, what it will take, roughly, to possibly complete a TCU can be projected from the TCU in progress, so that its imminent arrival at possible completion can be warrantably anticipated by recipient action. However, this does not necessarily imply that the particular words employed can ordinarily be projected precisely but only that the form of an action and reflexively the action realized through that turn-constructional form can be projected and its possible completion can be recognized. Yet the position of a TCU (in a sequence of actions) and the composition of that TCU (i.e., its emerging syntactic and prosodic realization) can sometimes enhance the projectability of what it will take to complete a turn, so that the particular items and not just the form of completion can be foreseen.

In excerpt (7), prior actions by the speaker and her co-participants (as well as relevant particularities of content and context) make clear not only the specific word that will complete a TCU but also exactly how it will be pronounced. Here a richly structured TCU is established through a quoted sequence of exchanges that projects a corrected pronunciation as the terminal item (and punch line) of a story:

(7)

```
[SARI]
 1    C:  Now okay having young girls name their children
 2          is one thing, but when you have middle aged
 3          people trying to make their name fancy,
 4    B:  Mm mm
 5    C:  My friend's mother got married right.
 6          I said huh- w'll what's what's
 7          yer stepdad's name. <she said L'roy.
 8 →        <I said no baby, it's [LEROY.]
 9 → A:                          [Leroy ]
10 → B:                          [Leroy ]
11          ((All three participants laugh together.))
```

(It is noteworthy that *no baby* at line 8 carries a horizontal-right-hand-shaking "no way" gesture and that the speaker's right hand goes up in front of her face on *it's.*

Her index finger is then thrust downward at *LEROY*.) In this instance, we can see a number of interactional elements that can be used to establish a place for and enhance the possibility of choral co-production. First, a dichotomy is established between fancy names and plain names; then an example of a fancified name (*L'roy*) is given. This is then rejected using a two-part [No + Correction] format. Further, the speaker sets off the contrasting plain name (which is concomitantly the punch line of her story) with a preparatory gesture at pre–possible completion. (Here the gesture is seeably a feature of the quoted exchange where the gestural accompaniments of [No + Correction] might be glossed as [stop-gesture + make-a-point-gesture]. The hand raise at *it's* is in preparation for the "make-a-point-gesture.") Thus, many elements of the story project the specific terminal item of the TCU and its placement. Moreover, pre–possible completion, as the onset of the transition space, itself opens up the possibility of talk by others, since possible completion is imminent. The fact that both of the speaker's co-participants initiate a choral co-production simultaneously (and simultaneously with the onset of the current speaker's terminal item) argues strongly for the availability of a place that has been prepared for a specific terminal item and thus furnishes the resources for co-production.

In excerpt (7) I showed how concurrently available resources of action and TCU structure can strongly project a place and specific lexical and phonological forms for co-participant entry into the turn.[4] In excerpt (8) (which was briefly considered in note 2) the availability to co-participants of a specially stressed realization of the first syllable of an emerging single word (at line 18) provides enough of a clue to (and opportunity for) TCU completion for a co-participant to initiate a choral co-production[5]:

(8)

```
[SARI]
 1    B:  One of those Kay Sweets brought him a cake.=
 2    C:  =O:h.=
 3    B:  =Oh, let's not talk about it though ahuh huh
 4        (1.2)
 5    A:  Why: [no:t ((smile voice))
 6    C:       [(You don't) one of those sisters.
 7    A:  Oh you mean (.) one of the sweethearts=
 8    B:  =the (        ) Kappa [Sweethearts]
 9    C:                        [Y e a:h s: ]=(mo:re)
10    B:  brought him a cake.
11        (0.7)
12        yep.
13        (0.3)
14        [It was a ni-]=
15    A:  [(      )]    ((A looks to C.))
16    B:  =It was a nice cake, [you kno:w
17    C:                       [You, you just have to
18 →      e:x::p[erience them
19    B:        [perience that
20        ((B and C laugh.))
```

Speaker B actually begins with a preparatory lip close slightly earlier than indicated by the bracket at line 19. B is gazing directly at C as line 18 is produced; thus, she can see the speaker's mouth behavior and her preparation (a kind of "windup") for an emphatic head dip and recoil that punctuates the second syllable of *experience*. In particular, B can see the momentary halt in the speaker's head dip prior to the plosive burst at the beginning of the second syllable. B produces the recoil component of a head dip, though abbreviates the dip itself, which C already has under way before the plosive burst. In other words, B attempts to catch up to the emphatic head dip and recoil by shortening the dip.

By comparison, Tannen (1989) has described a phenomenon that she calls shadowing. She suggests that a recipient hears what someone is saying, syllable by syllable, and then quickly reproduces or copies it in an automatic fashion. Choral co-production is a somewhat different phenomenon. In excerpt (8), as in other co-produced utterances, a recipient hears (and sees) what another participant is saying (in this case, a word's initial syllable) and uses that—along with what came before in the turn and the rest of the context and structure of the talk—to project what is possibly being said and then co-produces that projected TCU component. This case shows that projection may not be precise. In fact, the simultaneity and imprecision support the view that these are not merely instances of shadowing. It should also be clear that choral co-production is not composed as a repetition of a prior or even emerging utterance (cf. Johnstone 1994), though repetition or projected repetition by a speaker furnishes an important resource for contributing a matching TCU component.

The use of the repetition of the structure and content of prior talk as a resource for enhancing the projectability of a TCU can be seen clearly in excerpt (9). Here the specific word that will possibly complete a TCU (and its voicing) is established in the preceding talk. Excerpt (9) follows on from excerpt (7), in which the pronunciation of *Leroy* was at issue. This is another example—that is, it is on the order of a second (reciprocal) story about another person who uses a fancy name:

(9)

    [SARI]
    B: She goes () Joaye Lee.
          I'm like GI:RL you know your
          name is [Joy
    C: [Joy ((lip prep at *is*))

In this case, the fancy and plain pronunciations have been issued several times in the course of rejecting the use of the fancy version prior to the excerpt shown—including several earlier renditions of *you know your name is Joy*. So, when B again addresses the absent target of their evaluations with another correction, the terminal item (*Joy*) is fully foreshown. Since the exact form of the TCU *you know your name is Joy* has been used by the speaker several times, this rendition is hearable and treatable as a repetition—and therefore as known-in-common.

This subsection has shown that the structure of TCUs in their course and context can provide enhanced opportunities for a speaker's co-participants to join in

the production of a turn's talk. Beyond speaking in a way that provides such opportunities for co-production, a current speaker can act in a fashion that seems explicitly designed to draw another participant into co-participation. The following subsection examines several ways that speakers can elicit co-participation and
thereby make co-production specially relevant.

Eliciting Co-Participation

One way to make choral co-production specially relevant is to initiate a shared
reminiscence. In excerpt (10), considered briefly in excerpt (5), Michael draws
Shane into a co-produced rendition of a well-known line from a movie (*I knew
you were coming, so I baked a cake*). At line 14, Michael initiates a common preliminary sequence to accomplish this; he produces a reminiscence recognition
solicit (Lerner 1992):

(10)

```
       [Chicken Dinner]
        1    VIV:   =We got anothuh boddle, jist in case.
        2           (0.9)
        3    NAN:   You knew I wz comin:g.=
        4    VIV:   =Yeh ehh [hih huh heh hn]
        5    NAN:            [The lush is here,
        6    VIV:   So I baked=[a cake.]
        7    SHA:             [hhhuh hu]h[huh huh ]
        8    NAN:                     [Yhhheah ah]h huh hu
        9    MIC:   So I baked a cak[e.yeh.
       10    VIV:                   [nhheh heh he[h huh
       11    MIC:                                [Wuzzat Three Stooges?
       12    VI?:   (°°Yeh.°°) ((Vivian nods.))
       13    VIV:   hheh heh (.) heh
       14  → MIC:   Remember that?=
       15    SHA:   =Yeah
       16    MIC:   [I kne:w you were co:ming so I ba:ked a ca:ke.
       17    SHA:   [You knew I you coming, so I baked a cake
       18    VIV:   [I knew you were coming so I () ca(h)ke heheheh
       19    NAN:   [You watch the Rascals today,
       20    SHA:   En thez about eighteen cakes
       21    MIC:   an Shemp's (sitting there) like [this
       22    SHA:                                   [Yeah, yEAH,
       23           YE(h)AH(h)
       24    NAN:   Didju watch The Rascals tihday? ah luh I love
       25           (tuh watch them ther so fu:nny)
```

At the beginning of this sequence, Vivian, at line 6, retroactively turns Nancy's prior
possibly complete turn into now having been the first component of a two-part
idiomatic expression. Michael recognizes the expression as a line from a "Three
Stooges" movie. He first repeats the second component of the expression and then
requests a confirmation of its source from Vivian. At this point, the source of the

movie line has been proffered and confirmed, but the full expression has not been fully reenacted. Next, Michael addresses Shane, asking if he remembers the line from the movie. Shane turns to directly face Michael, and as he responds at line 15 he can see Michael preparing to deliver the line—including incipient preparation of a gesturally realized cake presentation.

A reminiscence recognition solicit initiates a preliminary sequence that can project a follow-up action. However, the character of mutual reminiscence (with its shared entitlement) blurs the entitlement to perform that next action. The performer need not be the originator of the sequence. For example, if a story is projected by the reminiscence recognition solicit, this presequence does not establish who will begin the telling (Lerner 1992). In the current case, the delivery of the full movie line becomes relevant for both Michael and Shane, after Shane's confirmation. Vivian, who initiated this course of action at line 4, also treats this as a place to deliver the movie line, further demonstrating its shared relevance at this point. Both Shane and Vivian can see that Michael is in the prebeginnings of this reenactment, but nonetheless both join in. In addition, Michael uses the cake presentation gesture to conduct the beats of the joint reenactment, thus showing that he, too, sees this as a locus for shared participation. This is a place—an action environment—in which one-at-a-time speaking is suspended by the participants, by participant conduct, in order to accomplish a specified action. This is not the same thing as saying that turn-taking is irrelevant, since what they are co-constructing is a speaking turn.[6]

In excerpt (10), one speaker (Michael) initiated a sequence of actions (the reminiscence recognition solicit sequence) that established a sequential environment for co-production. This is one method for creating a shared opportunity to participate. Though co-participation is made specially relevant here (and in this sense co-participation has been elicited), I am not suggesting that such participation is conditionally relevant (Schegloff and Sacks 1973) in the sense that it will be a noticeable absence if it does not occur. Here an opportunity can be passed over rather than declined, since other forms of participation by speaker and recipient are also relevant. For example, Michael's co-participants could demonstrate appreciation of his sole rendition of the reenacted line during its production or after its completion (Goodwin and Goodwin 1987).

Before examining another form of elicitation, I will need to briefly pursue the matter of a speaker's entitlement to voice the words that make up his/her turn. In excerpt (10) Michael initiated a sequence of actions that relaxed his entitlement to be the sole animator of a projected turn's talk. Other ways that such entitlement can be relaxed (though there does not seem to be any special elicitation involved) also seem to enhance the conditional entry of other participants into the turn. One form of talk (seen in some of the earlier excerpts) that can relax a speaker's entitlement to a turn—that is, that seems consequential for that entitlement—occurs when speakers are voicing a TCU or TCU component that is not attributable to them as author/owner (in the current turn). Two forms this can take are the voicing of an idiomatic expression and the voicing of an utterance that is attributable to someone other than the speaker (including a categorical other).

This type of relationship to the talk is established in excerpt (11) and seems to provide, along with other features of the talk and its action context, an enhanced opportunity for entry. Again, I am introducing this analysis here not because it exemplifies a form of co-production elicitation but because it establishes a sequential environment for a form of elicitation that I will then describe. It is necessary to show how entitlement is relaxed in this instance before describing how one of the speakers subsequently elicits co-participation, since these actions are accomplished separately in this case. In excerpt (11), A voices the criticism that someone like herself might receive as a way of holding up that sort of thinking to ridicule:

(11)

```
        [SARI]
        A: You have too many white friends. You don't know
            how to be with (.) your p[eople.
        B:                            [people
```

Here speaker A not only voices the turn as the words of others but also specifically marks off its terminal item as idiomatic by momentarily halting the progressivity of the talk and by attaching gestural quotation marks. She constructs a two-handed double-quote gesture at *your*. B produces two quick nods latched to the end of *your* and then enters the turn at its possibly final word and co-produces that final word.

I am now ready to use this instance of opportunistic co-production to introduce a form of co-production elicitation that speaker A employs subsequently. In excerpt (12), which expands excerpt (11), speaker A uses the occurrence of co-production itself to elicit subsequent co-production. As I have mentioned, projected repetition of a TCU or TCU component can provide co-participants with the resources of enhanced projectability. Here speaker A specifically composes and packages subsequent TCUs to project repetition of the (co-produced) terminal item at line 2. Thus, at line 4, she again produces the quotation gesture and post-preposition pause found in line 2. This projected terminal item repetition structures her subsequent TCUs as subsequent items in a list—though not a list with a common syntactic frame but a linked series of accusations held together by projection and repetition of the terminally placed membership category that the target of the accusations has ostensibly become estranged from within the enactment:

(12)

```
        [SARI]
        1    A: You have too many white friends. You don't know
        2        how to be with (.) your p[eople.
        3    B:                            [people
        4 →  A: Why are you not proud of (0.2) [you:r [peo:ple.
        5    C:                                 [you:r [peo:ple
        6    B:                                         [°people°
        7    A: What makes you think that?
        8        You're not seeing enough of your [people.
        9    B:                                    [people.
```

By turning the initial co-produced TCU into now having been the first item in a list of accusations, A can be seen to be setting up a next place for co-production within her turn. This amounts to a method for eliciting continued co-participation. "Elicitation" here, as in the case of the reminiscence recognition solicit, does not constitute a strong form of initiation; it does not make the form of uptake (e.g., co-production) conditionally relevant as an adjacency pair first pair part is understood to do for the type of action it implicates.[7] Nevertheless, I believe it can be seen to be actively encouraging continued co-production. Indeed, speaker C seems to be treating it as just this by gesturally conducting the chorally produced TCU terminal item. Once the list format is established in and as the second list part at line 4 and its terminal item is co-produced by all present, then the next accusation (which takes the form of a follow-up question + answer format) seems recognizable as the third list part even without the explicit marking of a quotation gesture or post-preposition pause. And this terminal item is also co-produced by a recipient.

Launching a search for a word in the course of a turn can be another method for eliciting conditional entry. In excerpt (13), C elicits help from B in a search for a list of names. At line 1 speaker C addresses participant A (who is from the West Coast) to describe a shirt (available at southern universities) to her, then turns to B (a fellow southerner) for help in listing all the names that appear on the shirt. C elicits help by turning to an already knowledgeable participant, while producing what I would call a dispreferred or recognizably inadequate reference form (*all the "M"::s on it*) with a sound stretch on the voicing of the "M." This can count as an embedded clue in a search for the names glossed by "M":

(13)

```
      [SARI]
      1    C:   Oh, we have the (multi) shirts (        )
      2         all the "M"::s [on it. ((C looks to B at all.))
      3    B:                  [Oh yeah.
      4    B:   Ma[:lcolm:, ] Ma[:rtin:, ] ah::
      5 →  C:      [Malcolm:,]   [Martin:, ]
      6    B:   what is that. (It's) Marcus (.)
      7         [Malcolm:, Ma- ]
      8    C:   [(always) ends with] me[::. ] you know ((gaze → A))
      9    B:                           [me:.] yes      ((gaze → C))
```

Note that in this case the original speaker is not the primary recipient of the elicited help. B uses the opportunity to offer assistance in the search to aid in the explanation being addressed to C's original recipient (A). Here is a case where the speaker of record (C) is not the one who selects the words spoken in what to this point has been her turn. Nonetheless, she voices the words in chorus with B as a way to retain speakership and then at line 8 continues the description in her own words. (B drops out at that point and then co-produces the TCU's terminal item at line 9.)

To summarize, I have now shown how recipients can make use of the particularities of turn structure, content, and context to produce simultaneous, matching TCU elements in chorus with the current speaker. I have also shown that current speakers have methods for gaining the co-participation of recipients by eliciting conditional entry into their turn space (e.g., through reminiscence recognition solicitation and word-search initiation) and that this entry can take the form of co-production. In the next section I look more directly at how choral co-production is used in conversation

Using Choral Co-Production

How is co-production employed in conversation? That is, what courses of action are co-productions a part of and what parts do they play in those courses of action? First, the co-production of a component of a TCU can furnish participants with a method for accomplishing action in a conjoined fashion with another participant (see Lerner 1993 for other forms of conjoined participation). Thus, choral co-production can be employed to co-produce an element of an explanation for a third participant, as in excerpt (14) at line 4. (See excerpt [8] for a fuller extract.)

(14)

```
        [SARI]
        1    B:  =It was a nice cake, [you kno:w
        2    C:                       [You, you just have to
        3          e:x::p[erience them
        4 → B:          [perience that
        5          ((B and C laugh.))
        6    A:  You mean Kappa Sweethearts,
        7          they have them in Sacramento
        8    C:  Not like these!
        9          :
       10    C:  You have to experience °them.°
       11    B:  WOO:::::? I mean you're talking
       12          living and dying for the frat.
```

Or choral co-production can be employed to issue a joint complaint to a third participant—which in excerpt (15) may also enact a conjoined request[8]:

(15)

```
        [NC Home]    ((The family is eating dinner))
        1    Jerl:  Mom, why didn't you make
        2           some (·) Che:rr:y  [Che:rr:y  [Cherry P(h)ie::]
        3 → Jasn:                      [Che:rr:y C[herry P i e ],
        4           oowh[y:
        5    Jerl:       [>hah-hah-hah-<
```

These are both forms of action that are ordinarily realized through individual participation but can accommodate conjoined participation. Here conjoined participation is accomplished through the sharing of a speaking turn—addressed to a third participant—that voices the action.

However, joining with another speaker to implement an action addressed to a third participant is only one way that choral co-production can be employed. The action realized through any turn at talk is contingent upon both that turn's composition and its placement in an emerging course of action. This holds for the utterances that comprise a chorally co-produced turn as well. The placement of an utterance in an emerging course of action and the opportunities to participate that are relevant at that moment—especially the opportunities to participate that can be made relevant through the "directionalities of address" associated with each contribution—can prepare differing contexts for action.[9]

Co-producing part of a turn's talk along with another speaker need not implement the same type of action as the other speaker's contribution. For example, choral co-production can be employed by an addressed recipient of a turn to demonstrate agreement with what is being said—when agreement and disagreement are implicated as relevant responding actions. In excerpt (16), which repeats excerpt (11), speaker B first asserts agreement with the emerging turn (through head nods at *your*) and then co-produces its final word:

(16)

    [SARI]
        A: You have too many white friends. You don't know
            how to be with (.) your p[eople.
  → B: [people

Here A is reenacting a complaint as a way of holding it up to ridicule and B's co-production exhibits that she is in agreement with A's assessment of this type of complaint.

So far I have described two types of action that choral co-production is used to accomplish: conjoined action for a third participant and demonstration of agreement with the current speaker. Not surprisingly, these are also the types of action that the closely related form of conditional entry—turn co-optation—can be used to accomplish. In the next two subsections I describe the role of choral co-production in opening and closing conversations and in reminiscing. A final subsection then shows that co-production can be appropriated for use in other than "cooperative" or "affiliative" action.

Openings and Closings

Co-production can be used in both openings and closings to convert a sequence of actions that ordinarily have their initiating and responding parts in adjacent turns at talk into simultaneously and chorally completed reciprocal actions. Some greetings and leave-takings can be specifically designed to achieve a choral crescendo, as in excerpts (17) and (18):

(17)

    [GL:FN:opening]
    A: ↑HI:EE[:::::::
    B: [↑HI:EE::

(18)

    [GL:FN:closing]
    A: Good luck. Nice to [↑s e e::   y o u::   ]
    B: [>Nice to< ↑see:: you::]

Turn-sharing of this sort provides a way to relax the turn-taking requirement that action accomplished in the talk must have a serial placement on top of which a sequential relationship can be built. Here actions are designed to be positioned as simultaneous—converting a serially placed [action + return action] sequence into coordinated reciprocal action. Of course, actions and action sequences accomplished without the constraints of turn-taking—that is, outside the constraints of the talk—can allow for or can be organized for "overlapping" initiating and responding actions (e.g., object transfers and handshakes). Responding actions that take place outside of the talk can be launched by reference to *recognition* of the initiating action, rather than by reference to *completion* of the initiating action (i.e., completion of the initiating action's enabling turn). Turn-sharing, as well as other types of "recognition point" (Jefferson 1973, 1983) entry furnish methods for overlapping actions within the talk—in certain conversational environments.

Reminiscing Together

Another special environment for mutually or reciprocally organized action is mutual reminiscence. At the arrowed lines in excerpt (19) (which we have already considered at some length when describing how co-productions can be elicited), each participant seems to be simultaneously a speaker and a recipient—entitled both to produce and to appreciate the known-in-common matter:

(19)

        [Chicken Dinner]
           MIC: Remember that?=
           SHA: =Yeah
  → MIC: [I kne:w you were co:ming so I ba:ked a ca:ke.
  → SHA: [You knew I you coming, so I baked a cake
  → VIV: [I knew you were coming so I (   ) ca(h)ke heheheh
           NAN: [You watch the Rascals today,
           SHA: En thez about eighteen cakes
           MIC: an Shemp's (sitting there) like [this
           SHA: [Yeah, yEAH,
                  YE(h)AH(h)
           NAN: Didju watch The Rascals tihday?

Choral co-production can provide a way to produce an action as a reciprocal reminiscence of a known-(or imagined- or created-)-in-common experience.

Openings, closings and reminiscing are not the only types of activity that can accommodate mutual or reciprocal action. For example, mutual commiseration over a shared trouble or shared type of trouble furnishes another relevant domain for co-production of action in a turn. This can be seen at the arrowed lines in excerpt (20), which I have examined in some detail earlier:

(20)

```
        [SARI]
           A:  You have too many white friends. You don't know
                how to be with (.) your p[eople.
           B:                             [people
      → A:  Why are you not proud of (0.2) [you:r [peo:ple.
      → C:                                 [you:r [peo:ple
      → B:                                        [°people°
```

Co-producing a TCU component is, then, one way that participants can establish or sustain their entitlement to co-authorship/ownership of experience and do it in a fashion that concomitantly allows them to demonstrate their appreciation of their co-participant's shared entitlement.[10]

Choral Co-Production and Turn Competition

In excerpt (21), choral co-production is used as a solution to the problem of turn competition:

(21)

```
        [SARI]
        1    A:  How close (is it).=
        2    B:  =They're all in the [sa::me area.
        3    C:                       [(          )
        4    B:  (This is [the)
        5    A:           [Oh.
        6    B:  Like you walk from one campus
        7        [you can walk right to the others]
        8    C:  [C l a r k A t l a n t a,          ]
        9        Morris [Bro:wn, M [o r e [house and Spellman=
       10 → B:         [Bro:wn,   [(   ) [house
       11    B:  =yeahs
       12    C:  they're all in this big (              ).
```

At line 1 speaker A asks how close together two colleges are situated. Both B and C respond directly to A's question at lines 2 and 3 (in part, by each producing a gesture that indicates the close proximity of the two colleges to each other). Speaker B begins to expand the answer, explaining the close proximity of a whole cluster of colleges, by describing how one can walk from one campus to the others. In the course of this description C begins her own form of explanation by listing the colleges by name. These, then, are competing formulations (in response to a third participant's query), and they are competing turns at talk. Rather than attempt to retrieve or extend her own explanatory formulation, speaker B withdraws from her line of explanation and adopts speaker C's formulation by co-producing some of the names at line 10 as speaker C continues her list.[11]

In excerpt (21), co-production provides a method for arranging the conjoined production of an action addressed to a third participant and thus furnishes one solution to competing formulations of that action. Here turn competition was transformed into turn-sharing. Yet co-production can also be employed as part of a method used to *compete* for a speaking turn, rather than as a way to share the turn. An examination of excerpt (22) will show how this method for resolving turn competition can itself be part of a course of action designed to reestablish a participant's position as explainer in order to forward his/her own competing version.

Though much might be written about the "cooperative" nature of co-production and some have even suggested that differing "styles" of speaking can be grounded in the presence or absence of this type of practice (e.g., Coates 1996), the following analysis suggests that it is important to distinguish between the cooperative form of the action (as a co-production) and the less-than-cooperative action that may result from its use in a specific sequential environment.[12] Though the use of a matching utterance may seem cooperative on the face of it, its deployment—as an entry device into another's turn—may be in the service of something that might not always be best characterized as cooperative. Excerpt (22) shows that co-production can be used as a method for gaining sole speakership. Here it is used after more directly competitive methods fail—as a subsequent attempt to achieve sole speakership. In this case, turn-sharing is a first step to sole turn occupancy.[13]

In excerpt (22) speakers B and C (who are from the South) are both engaged in explaining to A (who is from the West Coast) what students from a pair of traditionally black southern colleges are like. At this point in the explanation B is competing with C for a speaking turn they are both addressing to A—with C pursuing a description, while B attempts to produce an assessment. At first, co-production is used as a solution to the problem of conjoined participation. Speaker B cuts off her attempt at producing an assessment (*an it's just all, it's just-*) and then resumes by co-producing the terminal item of C's competing description (*woman*) at line 6:

(22)

```
      [SARI]
      1    C:  . . . Morehous:e (.) [ma::n,
      2    B:                       [Yes:
      3    C:  the epitome of [ma:nhood ]
      4    B:                  [an' it's just] a::ll
      5    C:  [dates the Spellman w[oman ]
      6 →  B:  [it's jist-          [woman] an' all that B.S.
```

However, this is only part of the action. In this case B uses co-production in another attempt at issuing her assessment of the students. Both the co-production (*woman*) and the conjunction (*and*) that follows it realize a "cooperative and additive" format, but here it is used after a more openly competitive approach has been abandoned. It seems important to distinguish between formal or format cooperation and the action being pursued through that format. Someone may come in to share a turn but use that to gain a recipient so as to continue as the explainer of record, or it may be that if a speaker loses an addressed recipient to a competing speaker, then this is a way to make another bid for speakership of an extended turn such as can be produced in explaining. Thus, co-production can be a device used for countering the loss of a speaking turn to another participant. Rather than compete openly, one can drop out and take the other's line by co-producing it—and then use that as a basis for continuing one's own line as in excerpt (22), where B finishes her once-abandoned assessment (*all that B.S.*) though it is now tied to C's utterance as an expansion of it.[14] So, one upshot here is that co-production is not just a way to conjointly accomplish an action such as explaining or storytelling but also can be part of arranging who will continue the action when there is competition to do so. Thus, it might be seen as one second-order solution to the problem of turn allocation.

In the final sections of this chapter I would like to expand the discussion of choral co-production in two ways. In the next section, I will show how this form of participation is employed in talk-in-interaction beyond conversation. And then in the subsequent section I will look beyond the "utterance matching" of choral co-production and examine the phenomenon of gestural matching.

Conjoined Participation beyond Conversation

Some forms of speech exchange, with their own forms of turn-taking and their own social arrangements, can provide an ongoing relevance for conjoined or collective participation. Some of these forms of talk-in-interaction can be organized to provide opportunities for choral co-production—and some contributions can be specifically designed to make choral co-production specially relevant. In this section, I examine choral features of teacher–student interaction and several forms of public speaker–audience interaction. In each of these, speech exchange is organized for two parties and it is the members of the collective party (students or audience members) who chorally co-produce the contributions of their party (cf. Lerner 1993; Schegloff 1995).

Whole Class Instruction

Opportunities for choral co-production can be seen in whole class instruction where the social arrangements include a turn-taking system that, in the first place, allocates speaking turns to two parties—the teacher and the students. With this arrangement, speaking turns alternate between a single-person party (the teacher) and a multiperson party (the whole class of students). Of course, this can be constantly breached, defended, and impinged upon by side involvements but nevertheless continue to organize much of the participation. When speech exchange includes the systematic possibility of more than one participant speaking for a multiple-participant party, then various procedures may be used to arrange just which participant will speak as a student (e.g., calling on students who have raised their hands). However, there is another type of solution to the multiperson-party problem here; all or many of the students, as co-incumbents of the party, can speak simultaneously as a whole class, as in excerpt (23), which comes from a third-grade language arts lesson:

(23)

    [CIRC: HUG]
    Teacher: What is the title of that chapter?
    Class: Night in the forest.

The choral co-production of an answer may be one among several methods students attempt to use in alternation (or even simultaneously) in response to a teacher's question. Excerpt (24) suggests at least one possible systematic basis for determining when a choral response is specifically called for:

(24)

    [CIRC: HUG]
    Teacher: And who did we say this book
               was written by again?
    Student: Al°ice::.° ((trails off and stops))
              (.)
    Class: Alice Dashly ((mostly in unison))

Here the teacher asks a question that is formulated as a request for a repeat of known information—information known to (or at least owned by) everyone (*we*). Also notice that one student trails off her solo response. The prosodic features of her utterance suggest that she designed the onset of her contribution to be part of a whole class response and then, finding at the first beat that she is the lone speaker, trailed off the first name.

The possibility for opportunistic choral response can be ongoing, since speech exchange can be organized for two parties over the course of a whole class instructional activity. However, a teacher can also specifically structure their contribution to elicit choral co-production, as in excerpt (25) at line 3:

(25)

    [CIRC: HUG]
    1   Teacher: Where was this book published?
    2   :
    3 → Teacher: Macmillan Publishing Company in?
    4   (.)
    5   Class: New York ((mostly in unison))
    6   Teacher: Okay,

By using a "fill in the blank" turn format as the beginning of an answer turn, the teacher can direct students (who have not yet been able to answer the original question at line 1) where to look in their currently open books for the answer. And since this format does not require an answerer to begin a new turn but only requires conditional entry into the current turn to furnish the answer to the still-relevant question, other forms of whole class instruction turn-taking are not as relevant. I am not suggesting here that students never raise their hands at this point when doing answering but only that this format is not designed as a place for that form of participation.[15]

Audience Participation

There are forms of talk-in-interaction that establish opportunities for participation in which talk is ordinarily associated with or bound to one category of participant (e.g., performer or orator) and is not, for the most part, a proper activity for the other category of participant (e.g., audience). However, speech exchange can be made a relevant part of performer/orator–audience interaction. This type of exchange can be designed as two-party talk-in-interaction with the performer/orator as one party to the talk and the audience as the other (multiperson) party to the talk, as in excerpt (26) from a partisan political rally:

(26)

> [Reagan at Bush's Orange County rally, 1992]
> Reagan: . . . really don't think thet we'll see the Democratic nominee down here
> Several: No= ((up to a dozen scattered, overlapping shouts for (0.3)))
> Audience: =NO:::::: ((large number of members mostly in unison for (2.1)))

Performers and orators can design their talk to provide a place for co-ordinated audience response (Atkinson 1984; Heritage and Greatbatch 1986), and this can be done in a fashion that makes choral co-production specially relevant. This can be seen in excerpts (27) and (28), which are both taken from the performance of an experienced storyteller at a public library. (There are both adults and children in the audience, and both join in.)

(27)

> [GL: Storyteller FN]
> ST: He lived in the woods and lived all by him
>   (.)
> Aud: self

(28)

> [GL: Storyteller FN]
> ST: He couldn't see his hand in front of his
>   (.)
> Aud: face

In these excerpts the storyteller prepares a place for audience choral co-participation by halting his turn before the projectable final word of a TCU. This is not just a shared opportunity for audience members to contribute individually, as can be the case when a performer asks for audience volunteers and then simultaneous, but competitive talk ensues. The structure of TCUs and projectivity of talk (e.g., grammatical and idiomatic structuring) provide audience members with the resources to furnish the completion of the storyteller's TCUs. And as in the case of ordinary conversation and whole class interaction, TCU terminal items are the most strongly projectable parts of a turn.

There are some forms of "talk"-in-interaction that furnish additional structure to their utterances—for example, singing a song. The systematic and recurrent voicing structure of sung utterances is one solution to the problem of vocal and verbal coordination.[16] Excerpt (29) is taken from a live recording of a novelty ballad that uses rhyming structure to enhance the projectability of the final word of each couplet, and the performers (and presumably the song's composer as well) recurrently leave it for the audience to produce the final word:

(29)

    [Roberts and Barrand: "The Ballad of the Cowpuncher" from *Live at Holsteins*]
    Duo: I am an old cowpuncher,
           I punch them cows so hard
           I have me a cowpunching bag,
           set up in my back
           (.)
    Aud: ya::rd.
    Duo: This bag is made of leather,
           and so are cows of course
           When I get tired of punching cows,
           I go and punch a
           (.)
    Aud: ho::rse.

Taken together, the recurrent melodic, precompletion pausing, and rhyming structures strongly project each next slot a chorally co-produced audience contribution is relevant and the item that goes in that place—and in unison the audience flawlessly produces the proper item in the proper place.

Gestural Matching

Schegloff (1984) points out that hand gesturing is on the whole a speaker's activity. Yet he does state that there are several sequential environments for gesturing by other-than-speaker. He reports on the practices used in three sequential environments: (1) gesturing by a nonspeaker as a way to make a move for a speaking turn, (2) gesturing in lieu of talk as a way to communicate without interrupting a current speaker, and (3) maintaining a gesturing pose after yielding to an interrupting speaker to show that one considers his/her own turn to still be in progress.

None of these "exceptions" strays very far from the original observation that hand gesturing is a speaker's activity. The current discussion briefly examines additional forms of nonspeaker hand gesturing that aim at gestural co-production— or perhaps a better term might be "gestural matching."[17] I do this in part to suggest that some of the practices that result in the choral co-production of talk may not be limited to talk but are features of social-sequential organization more broadly.

Though hand gesturing is not ordinarily itself a turn-organized activity, it can be organized in relation to turns at talk and to the actions produced in those turns at talk (see, e.g., Streeck and Hartge 1992). Ordinarily iconic gestures are "pre-positioned relative to their lexical affiliates" (Schegloff 1984:276), in effect preparing a place for the lexical affiliate. By contrast, in this section I examine gestures that are post-positioned as visible realizations of something prefigured in the talk. Here the just-prior talk prepares a place for an iconic hand gesture. It is this preparation that provides recipients of the prior talk with an enhanced opportunity both for producing and for matching the gesture. This type of sequential environment, in a sense, parallels those places in the talk that enhance the possibility of choral co-production of a TCU component.

First, I show that an iconic hand gesture can be made relevant as a form of responding action and that participants, in this case, orient to co-producing or matching the gesture that constitutes that relevant action. Then I show that gestural matching furnishes a method to a nonspeaker for assisting a speaker in a conjoined fashion—that is, I show one type of action that gestural matching can be used to accomplish.[18]

Achieving Matching Gestures

Prefiguring an action that is not yet realized in the talk provides a special opportunity for recipients to show understanding in the strongest way; they can show that they are closely following and understanding the development of what is being said by demonstrating that they can project and produce the next development. If the prefigured action lends itself to visible depiction, then gestural demonstration by a recipient can be relevant.

In excerpt (30) there is an opportunity to demonstrate recognition and understanding of *that Angela Davis look*. I will provide an analysis of the sequential slot prepared for the iconic gestures that demonstrate this recognition and understanding as I describe how the gestures by both recipients and the speaker are composed as matching two-handed gestures.

(30)

```
    [SARI]
    1    A:   . . . I have to (comb it), 'cause if I don't
    2  →      I'm gunna have that Angela Davis look,
    3           [That  [went] out [in the sixties.
    4    C:   [(((hair [gest]ure  [onset by C))
    5    B:           [Woo ]      [hoohoo
```

```
 6    B:                        [((hair gesture onset by B))
 7          (0.2)
 8          ((hair gesture onset by A))
 9          ((some laughter at apex, then matched/concerted
10          decomposition of gesture))
11    A:   No thank you
12    B:   Oh (.) but no, now you have the nineteen ninety
13          Angela look.
```

At line 2, the speaker alludes to a large "Afro" hairstyle by naming a person who is known for that hairstyle, rather than by describing its form directly. This form of reference to a hairstyle seems to initiate a sequence ([person reference + descriptive specification]) that is something like a [Puzzle + Solution] sequence. It does not present a direct description but only names as an exemplar someone who carries (or is known for) this attribute and thus can make relevant a further specification by speaker or recipients.

Both of speaker A's recipients then construct two-handed gestural depictions of the hairstyle. These gestural descriptions both specify *that Angela Davis look* and, in so doing, can be seen as demonstrating adequate recognition by recipients.[19] Notice that the onset of recipient gestures occurs at the same time as the speaker produces a next increment to her turn that refines or clarifies her prior allusion for her recipients but does not furnish a direct description.[20] In other words, A can be seen to be pursuing recognition by her recipients at just the point at which they exhibit their recognition. At the next possible completion (after the onset of both recipient gestures) the speaker then produces a matching gesture. This seems to be in response to the recipient gestures but can retain an ambiguous status for participants, since it is produced at a next place where such a gestural description could otherwise be relevant. (The slight pause after her utterance may be designed to further this latter analysis by recipients.)

The gestures are composed in the following fashion: C begins her gesture at a possible completion of the speaker's exemplar. She puts down a pencil on the way into the gesture and then moves her arms outward and upward around her head (in a large encompassing fashion) toward the apex of the gesture. The onset of B's gesture follows closely on C's but emerges from a tabletop hands-together position just as C's arms reach table level. Her onset is just at the end of C's gesture preparation (i.e., C has moved her hands from their home position to the position the gesture will begin from). B matches the upward movement of C's arms, since her gesture is begun without a preparatory move. Finally, A begins her gesture slightly after the end of her own utterance but moves toward the apex at a very quick rate and in as direct a line as possible (see Figure 9.1 where A, B, and C are arranged left to right). All have composed their gestures so that they reach the apex at virtually the same moment.[21] (Compare A's action here to that of the second speaker in excerpt (6). That speaker first uses a very quick speech tempo and then, upon catching up with the other speaker, slows down to match that other speaker's tempo.)

At this point all three participants have produced a gestural rendition of the *Angela Davis look* hairstyle by placing their arms and hands fully above their heads and to one degree or another separating their arms to depict its fullness (see Fig-

Figure 9.1. Composition

ure 9.2). The apex of each gestural pose is somewhat different from the others: B has arms forming a full circle with fingers touching, C has arms wide apart, and A has arms straight up as if indicating a goal in football. Yet it is clear and mutually appreciated that these are all depictions of *that Angela Davis look*. All three then hold this pose for a moment at the apex of the gesture, laugh, and bring their arms down in unison. They produce the decomposition of the gesture in a mutually matching fashion (see Figure 9.3). Both B and C return their hands to their home resting position at almost exactly the same moment, while A's hands segue into another gesture that is affiliated with her next TCU at line 8. This is not interactional synchrony but achieved co-production.

Accomplishing Conjoined Action

Gestural matching of a speaker's gesture by another participant can be used to participate in the production of an action in a visibly conjoined fashion with that

Figure 9.2. Apex

Figure 9.3.   Decomposition

speaker and for that speaker's addressed recipient. This procedure can provide, for example, one way to visibly assist in telling a story.

In excerpt (31), C is telling A a story about someone's drinking behavior on an occasion when both she and co-participant B were present. At one point in the story C employs a warning (*nobody light a match*) as a device to assess how much alcohol the main character was consuming. The warning is composed in a fashion that alludes to a consequence (if the warning is not heeded) but does not make explicit in the talk what the consequence will be. However, C makes that consequence visible subsequently through a two-handed iconic gesture (of the force of a flame exploding from her mouth). Just as this gesture begins, B looks toward C as she (B) matches the gesture. At the resolution of the gestures, both C and B look to their recipient, A, who throws her head back in laughter:

(31)

    [SARI]
     1   C: . . . the other night
     2   before we went out,((turns from A to B))
     3   B: Y̲eah.
     4   C: And we were like, "What's to drink here," and he was
     5   like, "Oh. I'm chasing some orange juice with some
     6   vodka" 'cause that's how ba(h)d ( ) 'cause he was
     7   outta juice. This much juice in the glass and this
     8   much vodka.
     9   B: ↑woo[o::
   10   C: [Please, [nobody light a match [(right [now)=
   11   B: [hih hih   [((lau [ghs))
   12   A: [((laughs))
   13   C: =((laughs))
   14 →   ((All are laughing. C's gesture preparation begins
   15   about (0.5) after *now* and B begins slightly after C.))
   16   C: Whoosh ((This occurs after both C and B have their arms

17   directly in front of their faces and is produced along
18   with the outward movement of the gesture.))
19   ((All laugh.))
20   B: and you know it's like (killing) that Jello you know
21   you had to see the look on his face when he was eating
22   that Jello. He was all (.) frank and stuff.

All three participants are laughing and have their arms resting on the table at line 14. A is looking up and toward C, but as they laugh C and B look down toward the table. C, while laughing, begins to move her body up from the table and simultaneously begins to move both her arms off the table in a possible gesture preparation. (This movement seems to be visible to B.) As soon as C's arms have left the table, B begins to move her head up. Both participants bring their hands up together and reach their gestural apex at about the same moment (see Figure 9.4). They are doing the same thing at the same time. Finally, B (not C) continues on with the story about the main character's behavior. Note that the use of the matching gesture furnishes an occasion for reallocation of tellership. Here, as in the discussion of co-explaining, a co-produced action is part of and sustaining of conjoined participation, and it provides an occasion to enter the telling for a story consociate. So, gestural matching includes many of the sequential features and uses of co-produced actions that are realized through the talk, but here they are realized in the hands of the participants.

Concluding Remarks

This report should again remind us that a turn at talk is an interactionally constituted social structure of conversation and should not be thought of as just an analytic template. It is necessary to develop a detailed account of a course of action to understand what part any utterance plays within it. Moreover, producing an utterance is not equivalent to gaining and producing a turn. Choral co-production of a TCU shows us that there are other forms of participation in conversation in addition to taking and being given a full turn at talk.

Figure 9.4. Apex

Speakers who do get a turn at talk are entitled by the socially sustained practices for turn-taking to produce at least one TCU to its first possible completion. But this is not an unconditional entitlement. And yet, although other participants can enter a current speaker's turn, they cannot (or at least in practice ordinarily do not) do so without restraint or countermeasure or both. Rather, entry is regularly enough based on forwarding the action of the turn or sequence and thus is a conditional entry. Further, a review of the instances of choral co-production in this chapter will reveal that many of the speakers are co-producing reenacted speech. Whatever else may be relevant in establishing opportunities for co-production, reenacting speech of another person, place, or moment seems to systematically weaken or relax a speaker's sole entitlement to voice that speech, thus enhancing the opportunity for conditional entry into the turn space by another speaker.

Choral co-production can be used to initiate or continue conjoined action, thus providing another vehicle for broadening the units of participation in conversation from individual participants to broader social entities, or it can be used to exhibit understanding, affiliation, and agreement with a current speaker. Choral co-production also furnishes a way to construct mutual participation in activities that included both a shared entitlement to voice an utterance and reciprocal recipiency such as can occur when reminiscing together. It is easy to assert, as some investigators have done, that actions such as these are outside the purview of turn-taking practices that have as their main result one-at-a-time speaking. However, that assertion seems inappropriate to me in the case of choral co-production. Here it is precisely the practices and products of turn-taking that furnish the resources for sharing a moment of speaking together.

Finally, co-production, as a feature of the organization of social interaction, does not seem to be limited to talk but can be accomplished through gestural matching. Gestural-matching practices employ the social situatedness of the body to accomplish social action. This reveals one way the body-in-action is available as a situated social resource and demonstrates that recognizable actions composed of body behaviors can be organized along the same lines as similar actions carried out through speech.

NOTES

I would like to thank Sandy Thompson and Barbara Fox for their thoughtful comments and kind patience. Earlier reports of this research were presented at the International Conference on Perspectives and Current Work on Ethnomethodology and Conversation Analysis, Urbino, Italy, 1994, and at the Annual Meeting of the Speech Communication Association, San Diego, CA, 1996.

1. Not all of these reports make clear whether the simultaneous speech occurs within a single conversation. There seems to be a tendency on the part of some discourse investigators to consider all speech that occurs in the same gathering in an undifferentiated manner. This ignores the real possibility of momentary conversational schism in multiparty interaction (Egbert 1997). Incipient simultaneous conversations (e.g., two speakers addressing two different recipients in a gathering of four or more persons) cannot be treated

analytically in the same fashion as simultaneous speech within a single conversation, as turn-taking practices only organize speaking turns within single conversations.

2. Accomplishing the choral co-production of a TCU component does not seem to require that the second speaker's utterance match the current speaker's utterance word for word. Rather, second speakers must demonstrate in the placement and delivery of their contribution that that is what they are aiming at—as B does in the following instance. (Here both B and C are addressing their remarks to A.)

```
[SARI]
    A:  (              ) ((A looks to C.))
    B:  =It was a nice cake, [you kno:w
    C:                            [You, you just have to
        e:x::p[erience them
→ B:          [perience that
```

3. In the following excerpt, speaker C can be seen to adjust her terminal item completion (through the use of a sound stretch) to match the onset of the current speaker's terminal item:

```
[SARI]
    B:  . . .I choose to wear my hair relaxed
        because that is a convenient style [for me,
    A:                                      [It's convenient.=
    B:  =but [that has nothing to do [with [self ha[te.
    A:       [(      )              [    [     [
→ C:                                     [s:::= [self  [hate.
```

However, in this case there does not seem to be any matching of rhythm or tempo. C's utterance is slower with each word discretely formed. Her contribution is realized as a separate, distinct utterance that is timed to be delivered at the point where B's terminal item is due. It does not seem to be designed to either co-opt B's completion or match its design features exactly.

4. Though I will, for the most part, examine instances of choral co-production that are successful, it is important to point out that not all projections of a possible turn-constructional component turn out to have been correct. Sometimes an attempt at co-production can misfire. For example, in the following instance speaker A aims at a possible precompletion place and attempts a rendition of a projectable terminal item—however, this turns out to be a misprojection of the turn position and of the formulation that speaker B actually produces:

```
[SARI]    ((dreadlocks-indicating gesture at them))
    B:  . . . Oh, but no. Now you got the nineteen
        ninety Angela look an' she got like
        them (re[al kanky) and dreaded look
→ A:           [Dr:ea::ds
```

In this case B seems to assimilate A's misfired rendition into her own turn through a form of colligation (Jefferson 1986), thus rehabilitating A's completion. (See Lerner 1994 for a fuller description of this sort of assimilation.)

5. An additional enhancing feature in this instance may be the slight retarding of the word's articulation that is realized through the first syllable's special accentuation, thereby producing a slight retardation of the turn's progress toward completion. Retardation of a turn's progressivity toward completion is one systematic locus of recipient entry (Jefferson 1983; Lerner 1996a).

6. Carole Edelsky's (1993) notion of "collaborative floor" might come to mind here. Edelsky states: "The floor is defined as the acknowledged what's-going-on within a psychological time/space." I would prefer to speak of "what's-going-on" in terms of action and sequences of actions. Action sequences have their own describable organization, and this can influence turn-taking within a sequence of action. For Edelsky, a "collaborative floor" occurs when no single participant establishes "what's-going-on"—that is, when several people are "on the same wavelength." What she refers to as "collaborative floor" seems to me to gloss a range of sequence-specific organizational features in the organization of action sequences and the opportunities to participate within them that specific action sequences furnish at each moment. Doing reminiscing is a recognizable and specifiable form of action that is constituted, in part, by a shared entitlement to the source events and reciprocal recipiency. It is this specific type of sequence of actions and the opportunities to participate within it that furnish the basis for choral co-production here and not the fact that the course of action is being co-constructed, since "co-construction" is a generic property of sequence organization, as well as other forms of organization that structure talk-in-interaction.

7. Actions such as these provide a sequential opportunity for co-production, but it is an opportunity that can be passed up. It should come as no surprise that actions which elicit conditional entry into the speaker's turn space would operate in a somewhat different fashion from actions that operate across distinct turns.

8. See excerpt (1) for an instance where two children chorally co-tell elements of a story to an adult and Maynard (1986:267–268) for an instance in which several children use choral co-production in conjoined disagreement with another child.

9. Differing opportunities to participate are furnished to participants differentiated by their relationship to the talk—what Goffman (1981) would call their "footing" as hearers of an utterance. Is the co-production contributed by an addressed recipient of the current turn or another participant? Is the co-production itself addressed to the current speaker, to that speaker's addressed recipient, or to someone else? In short, the action a co-produced utterance accomplishes is, in part, understood by participants by reference to its directionality of address, given the context of the footing established by the directionality of address of the ongoing turn. Does it sustain, reverse, or shift the footing established by that prior utterance? The consequentiality of directionality for organizing opportunities to participate has also been noted for anticipatory completion (Lerner 1987, 1996a) and overlap management (Schegloff 1995). In order to glimpse the import of this matter, let me just mention that the directionality of address of an anticipatory completion relative to the directionality of address of the co-opted turn-in-progress is consequential in establishing whether or not that action will launch a small sequence.

10. It is my impression that shared laughter is similarly organized for this type of reciprocal appreciation with laughers searching out another participant to establish mutual gaze, so as to both see the other laughing and present one's own laughing face to the other—thus resulting in an occasion of mutual or reciprocal laughing together (cf. Jefferson 1979).

11. See excerpt (14) for another instance in which an explainer loses a recipient to another speaker and then uses co-production to continue as an explainer in a conjoined fashion.

12. Investigators, such as Jennifer Coates (1996), have linked "cooperative" simultaneous speech to a particular category of participant (women friends). However, as Marjorie Goodwin's (1995) investigation of the games of African-American girls has led her to state, "Strong claims about female cooperative language styles fall apart under close scrutiny." Further, readers will have noticed that a number of the excerpts I present contain choral co-productions by African-American women (though I suspect this is noticeable more from the content of their talk than its organization). My aim in this chapter is to describe how an interactional practice is accomplished and to lay out some of the systematic uses it is put to in conversation and other forms of talk-in-interaction. This can provide a technical basis for grounding claims about the distribution of conversational practices across various "communities of practice." That type of investigation might tell us something about the character of those collectivities but not necessarily about the structures and practices of talk-in-interaction. In saying this, I am not saying that membership categorization cannot be consequential for the organization of interaction; I am just saying that formal or informal distributional claims cannot furnish a demonstration of consequentiality. See Garcia (1998) for an empirical analysis of an apparent gender difference in the distribution of an interactional practice.

13. This maneuver might be profitably compared to Jefferson's (1984) description of the recipiency token *yeah* that recipients can use as a device to launch a shift from recipiency to active speakership. In that case, recipient action is the first step to speakership.

14. See Lerner (1992) for an analysis of how story consociates can take over as storytellers by assisting the current teller and Lerner (1989) for another method for winning turn competition by first dropping out and then restarting in the course of a competitor's utterance.

15. It seems to me that these technical observations might be applied directly to classroom management. There are times when a teacher might make good use of establishing a place for a chorally co-produced response from the class. For example, it could be made a relevant form for response during a "noisy moment" in a whole class lesson. It can be used in this way as a device to quiet the class (i.e., to defend the whole class turn-taking system). This may seem counter-intuitive, since choral co-production produces even more "noise" in that it is made up of many or all students talking at once. However, one way to get all the students to be quiet at once is to get them first to speak at once—as one. In this way they will all finish at the same time and thus come to be not speaking at once.

16. Songs furnish just the social-productional form that is specifically designed for choral co-production, as both the text and delivery are prespecified; moreover, such verbal coordination can be used to coordinate other forms of collective action, as in the case of sea chanties, which were used to coordinate work on early sailing ships. There are also fully scripted forms of audience participation that do not include singing but do seem to include a shared prosodic form (i.e., a shared tempo and accent structure)—for example, the recitation of the "Pledge of Allegiance."

17. Over the years, a number of researchers have reported on the phenomenon of "interactional synchrony" (see Davis 1982 for an important collection of papers on this topic). Roughly, this concerns the cyclic, patterned co-actions of co-participants. Researchers in this tradition have found that the micromomentary changes of bodies, gestures, and vocal behavior can be quite precisely synchronized between speaker and recipient. I would like to distinguish the "achieved synchrony" described in this report from that type of seemingly unintended, unconscious, and unrecognized synchronization. Participants can construct closely synchronized hand gestures as a feature of the recognizable actions they are seeably engaged in producing and not merely as a mainly unrecognizable orchestration for such actions. Also, gestural matching is not limited to the hands. For an example see the discussion of head nods following excerpt 8.

18. Gestural matching can also be used by a recipient to match a speaker's gesture as part of a method for exhibiting agreement with that speaker (e.g., a recipient strikes the palm of his left hand with his right fist, just as a speaker produces the same gesture to illustrate the impact of a recent earthquake). However, I cannot provide a full analysis of this type of action in the space of this chapter.

19. The following is another instance of this type of sequence of actions in which the first action is an unresolved reference and the second action resolves the reference as a recognitional reference (Sacks and Schegloff 1979). Here the sequence is completed in the talk, rather than through gesture:

```
        MIC:  I hate thet fuckin' guy who does those c'mmercials
                that assho[le
→  SHA:              [Weh Al[an: °uh:° .tch Alan Hammil?
→  VIV:                    [Oh Alan::::
```

Michael's descriptive person reference strongly prepares a place for candidate names; responding with a name can be a way to demonstrate recognition when a prior recognitional person reference has not included naming. In this case both Shane and Vivian launch name searches in response to *thet fuckin' guy* . . . Michael may be employing a descriptive person reference here as an alternative to an explicit name search—leaving it to his co-participants to supply the name he is unable to produce. In addition, see the discussion of the inadequate reference in excerpt (13).

20. This may be especially important here since Davis, as the participants go on to discuss, has more recently changed her "look," so which hairstyle is being invoked may not be entirely clear to the recipients.

21. There could be no clearer example of what William H. McNeill (1995) calls "muscular bonding," but here it is accomplished without the practiced structures of ritual dance or military drill that he describes. Moreover, it is members' methods for accomplishing the structuring and sequencing of ordinary occasions of social life that furnish the mundane resources that are called upon to achieve, for example, practiced close order drill.

REFERENCES

Atkinson, J. Maxwell. 1984. Public speaking and audience responses: some techniques for inviting applause. In J. Maxwell Atkinson and John Heritage (eds.), *Structures of Social Action: Studies in Conversation Analysis*, 370–409. Cambridge: Cambridge University Press.
Coates, Jennifer. 1996. *Women Talking: Conversation between Women Friends*. Oxford: Basil Blackwell.
Davis, Martha. 1982. *Interactional Rhythms: Periodicity in Communicative Behavior*. New York: Human Sciences Press.
Edelsky, Carole. 1993. Who's got the floor? In D. Tannen (ed.), *Gender and Conversational Interaction*, 189–227. New York: Oxford University Press.
Egbert, Maria. 1997. Schisming: The collaborative transformation from a single conversation to multiple conversations. *Research on Language and Social Interaction* 30:1–51.
Erickson, Frederick. 1992. They know all the lines: Rhythmic organization and contextualization in a conversational listing activity. In Peter Auer and Aldo di Luzio (eds.), *The Contextualization of Language*, 365–397. Amsterdam: John Benjamins.
Ford, Cecilia E., Barbara A. Fox, and Sandra A. Thompson. 1996. Practices in the construction of turns: The "TCU" revisited. *Pragmatics* 6(3): 427–454.

Ford, Cecilia E., and Sandra A. Thompson. 1996. Interactional units in conversation: Syntactic, intonational, and pragmatic resources for the management of turns. In Elinor Ochs, Emanuel A. Schegloff, and Sandra A. Thompson (eds.), *Interaction and Grammar*, 134–184. Cambridge: Cambridge University Press.

Garcia, Angela. 1998. The relevance of interactional and institutional contexts for the study of gender differences: A demonstrative study. *Symbolic Interaction* 21(1): 35–58.

Goffman, Erving (ed.). 1981. *Forms of Talk*. Philadelphia: University of Pennsylvania Press.

Goodwin, Charles, and Marjorie Harness Goodwin. 1987. Concurrent operations on talk: Notes on the interactive organization of assessments. *IPRA Papers in Pragmatics* 1(1): 1–54.

Goodwin, Marjorie Harness. 1995. Games of stance: Conflict and footing in hopscotch. Paper presented at the LSA Linguistic Institute, Conversation Symposium, Albuquerque, NM, July 1995.

Heritage, John, and David Greatbatch. 1986. Generating applause: A study of rhetoric and response at party political conferences. *American Journal of Sociology* 92(1): 110–157.

James, Deborah, and Sandra Clarke. 1993. Women, men, and interruptions: A critical review. In D. Tannen (ed.), *Gender and Conversational Interaction*, 231–280. New York: Oxford University Press.

Jefferson, Gail. 1973. A case of precision timing in ordinary conversation: Overlapped tag-positioned address terms in closing sequences. *Semiotica* 9: 47–96.

Jefferson, Gail. 1979. A technique for inviting laughter and its subsequent acceptance/declination. In G. Psathas (ed.), *Everyday Language: Studies in Ethnomethodology*, 79–96. New York: Irvington.

Jefferson, Gail. 1983. Two explorations of the organization of overlapping talk in conversation: (a) Notes on some orderlinesses of overlap onset and (b) On a failed hypothesis: "Conjunctionals" as overlap-vulnerable; with an appended glossary of transcript symbols. *Tilburg Papers in Language and Literature* 28:1–33.

Jefferson, Gail. 1984. Notes on a systematic deployment of the acknowledgement tokens 'Yeah' and 'Mm hm'. *Papers in Linguistics* 17:197–216.

Jefferson, Gail. 1986. Colligation as a device for minimizing repair or diagreement. Paper presented at the Talk and Social Structure Conference, Santa Barbara, CA, March 1986.

Jefferson, Gail, and Emanuel A. Schegloff. 1975. Sketch: Some orderly aspects of overlap onset in natural conversation. Paper presented at the Annual Meeting of the American Anthropological Association, San Francisco, November 1975.

Johnstone, Barbara (ed.). 1994. *Repetition in Discourse: Interdisciplinary Perspectives*. Norwood, NJ: Ablex.

Lerner, Gene H. 1987. Collaborative turn sequences: Sentence construction and social action. PhD diss., University of California, Irvine.

Lerner, Gene H. 1989. Notes on overlap management in conversation: The case of delayed completion. *Western Journal of Speech Communication* 53:167–177.

Lerner, Gene H. 1991. On the syntax of sentences-in-progress. *Language in Society* 20:441–458.

Lerner, Gene H. 1992. Assisted storytelling: Deploying shared knowledge as a practical matter. *Qualitative Sociology* 15(3): 247–271.

Lerner, Gene H. 1993. Collectivities in action: Establishing the relevance of conjoined participation in conversation. *TEXT* 13(2): 213–245.

Lerner, Gene H. 1994. Responsive list construction: A conversational resource for accomplishing multifaceted social action. *Journal of Language and Social Psychology* 13(1): 20–33.

Lerner, Gene H. 1996a. Finding "face" in the preference structures of talk-in-interaction. *Social Psychology Quarterly* 59(4): 303–321.

Lerner, Gene H. 1996b. On the "semi-permeable" character of grammatical units in conversation: Conditional entry into the turn space of another speaker. In Elinor Ochs, Emanuel A. Schegloff, and Sandra A. Thompson (eds.), *Interaction and Grammar*, 238–276. Cambridge: Cambridge University Press.

Lerner, Gene H., and Tomoyo Takagi. 1999. On the place of linguistic resources in the organization of talk-in interaction: A co-investigation of English and Japanese grammatical practices. *Journal of Pragmatics* 31(1): 49–75.

Maynard, Douglas W. 1986. Offering and soliciting collaboration in multi-party disputes among children (and other humans). *Human Studies* 9:261–285.

McNeill, William H. 1995. *Keeping Together in Time: Dance and Drill in Human History*. Cambridge, MA: Harvard University Press.

Sacks, Harvey, and Emanuel A. Schegloff. 1979. Two preferences in the organization of reference to persons in conversation and their interaction. In G. Psathas (ed.), *Everyday Language: Studies in Ethnomethodology*, 15–21. New York: Irvington.

Sacks, Harvey, Emanuel A. Schegloff, and Gail Jefferson. 1974. A simplest systematics for the organization of turn-taking in conversation. *Language* 50(4): 696–735.

Schegloff, Emanuel A. 1984. On some gestures' relation to talk. In J. Maxwell Atkinson and John Heritage (eds.), *Structures of Social Action: Studies in Conversation Analysis*, 266–296. Cambridge: Cambridge University Press.

Schegloff, Emanuel A. 1987. Recycled turn beginnings: A precise repair mechanism in conversation's turn-taking organisation. In Graham Button and John R. E. Lee (eds.), *Talk and Social Organisation*, 70–85. Clevedon, England: Multilingual Matters.

Schegloff, Emanuel A. 1995. Parties and talking together: two ways in which numbers are significant in talk-in-interaction. In Paul ten Have and George Psathas (eds.), *Situated Order: Studies in the Social Organization of Talk and Embodied Activities*, 31–42. Washington, DC: University Press of America.

Schegloff, Emanuel A. 2000. Overlapping talk and the organization of turn taking for conversation. *Language in Society* 29(1): 1–63.

Schegloff, Emanuel A., and Harvey Sacks. 1973. Opening up closings. *Semiotica* 7:289–327.

Streeck, Jürgen, and Ulrike Hartge. 1992. Previews: Gestures at the transition place. In Peter Auer and Aldo di Luzio (eds.), *The Contextualization of Language*, 135–157. Amsterdam: John Benjamins.

Tannen, Deborah. 1989. *Talking Voices: Repetition, Dialogue, and Imagery in Conversational Discourse*. Cambridge: Cambridge University Press.

10

Some Linguistic Aspects of Closure Cut-Off

ROBERT JASPERSON

This chapter studies some phonetic and phonological aspects of an especially common form of cut-off in English, a form that I term here "closure cut-off." Cut-off is one of several techniques for initiating same-turn repair, and the particular variety of cut-off that involves an articulatory closure—for example, a glottal stop—is especially common. The general notion of cut-off derives from research on repair in CA as well as in other fields. Conventionally transcribed with a dash or hyphen, cut-off has been described as a "non-lexical perturbation" in speech (Schegloff, Jefferson, and Sacks 1977), whose action is perceived as "abrupt" (e.g., Goodwin 1981; Atkinson and Heritage 1984; Schegloff 1992; Nakatani and Hirschberg 1993; Sparks 1994). Its articulation has been described as typically involving glottal or other stop closure (e.g., Hockett 1967; Jefferson 1974; Schegloff 1979; Goodwin 1981; Sparks 1994). These descriptions relate to the form, or phonetics, of cut-off—how it sounds and how it is articulated. Beyond its form, cut-off has been described functionally, that is, with respect to what the form does in relation to other linguistic elements. Cut-off may interrupt a word or sound in progress (Sacks, Schegloff, and Jefferson 1974; Schegloff, Jefferson, and Sacks 1977; Goodwin 1981), or it may stop a "next sound due" from occurring when due (Schegloff 1979)—these descriptions concern phonological function. Last, what may then be called its pragmatic or interactional function is the initiation of same-turn repair: cut-off is one of several types of "repair initiators" that indicate the possible occurrence of a repair of some aspect of the speaker's current turn (e.g., Schegloff, Jefferson, and Sacks 1977; Schegloff 1984a).

In this study, I focus on the most common form of cut-off, namely, closure cut-off. I initially undertook this study in order to understand how closure cut-off is achieved linguistically. As I engaged in the analysis of talk-in-interaction, I was led to ask, What phonetic and phonological characteristics of this repair initiator make it interactionally real? And as I engaged at the same time in the analysis of speech, I was led to ask, How can closure cut-off exist as a device that interrupts speech when it involves the very same articulators and many of the same articulations that produce speech? This study addresses these questions. In addition, the linguistic exploration led to two unexpected results. First, if attention is paid to phonetic detail,[1] it is possible to specify closure cut-off independently of repair. This is an interesting result because it helps explain how repair may be initiated but then "canceled" (cf. Schegloff 1984b). Second, attention to phonetic detail also furnishes support for a claim I make about a design feature of closure cut-off, namely, that it enables soonest possible repair.

The next section provides background on repair initiation and same-turn repair and motivates the current focus on closure cut-off (hereafter referred to as "cut-off" when the reference is unproblematic). Following a section on methodology, I begin the analysis of cut-off with a consideration of its basic phonetic characteristics. This relatively form-based part of the chapter yields several interesting findings that become directly relevant for the phonology of cut-off, which is the subject of the second part of the chapter. There I propose first a repair-independent specification of cut-off that is based directly on Schegloff (1979). To preview: cut-off is a phonetically conditioned oral and/or glottal closure that prevents a "next sound due" from occurring when due. I then document a contrasting form of cut-off, what I will refer to as "pulmonic cut-off," in view of which I make the claim mentioned previously about a "design feature" of closure cut-off. A glossary of phonetic and phonological terms appears at the end of this chapter.

Background and Motivation

For students of talk-in-interaction, a linguistic study of cut-off will be motivated by the larger endeavor to understand same-turn repair. The purpose of this section is to provide some background on same-turn repair and to motivate the study of one form of its initiation, closure cut-off.

"Repair," generally, refers to a rather vast set of practices for dealing with troubles that arise in the course of speaking, hearing, and understanding talk-in-interaction. The practices of "same-turn" repair, specifically, deal with troubles as they arise in the course of the current speaker's ongoing turn. The excerpt of conversation in example (1) illustrates a striking range of the phenomenon. In this conversation, the two speakers, B and K, have been discussing the rapid residential and commercial development of the local area, a topic that seems quite disturbing to K, a lifelong resident of the area, though less so to B, who is visiting for the first time. With the question in line 1, B effects a transition to perhaps a more neutral topic:

(1)

    PA7CR
```
 1  B:  What part o% (0.6) Where do you
 2      li:ve. (N://::.)
 3  K:  Uhm (1.2) .hhh When I% <WELL I grew
 4      up in the% <mountains, an' no:w hh
 5      I live <we live uhm hh down
 6      in uhm (0.5) Martin Acr:es
 7      it's off of: Broadwa:y?
 8      Do you [know where Broadway i:s,
 9  B:         [((shakes head)) →
10  K:  (O:h.=Ok[ay.=So it's) kind of thee=
11  B:  →       [°(No::.).
12  K:  =uh:. (2.2) north, (3.0) north central,
13      (0.6) °part of town?
```

Let us examine first a case of same-turn repair that is initiated with cut-off. In line 1, B begins a question with *What part o[f]*, but suddenly cuts the utterance off. (This particular cut-off is notated with a percent sign, a convention unique to this chapter that will be explained when we consider the phonetics of cut-off.) After the cut-off and a significant pause, B replaces the utterance with a different formulation of the question. Given that B is a first-time visitor, formulating the question as a request for information about a specific part of the locale could be problematic. The more general formulation, *Where do you live?*, is more appropriate in this situation. This is a case of same-turn repair because the repair addresses trouble with some aspect of the speaker's ongoing turn.

Another common way of initiating same-turn repair is with *uhm* (and its relative *uh*). Repairs initiated with *uhm* are often referred to as "word-search" repairs, though they are not limited to cognitive "searches" for particular words. K's response to B's question in fact starts out with an *uhm* (line 3), which in this context initiates repair on the whole of the projected turn itself,[2] indicating trouble that arises from, among other possibilities, how to formulate an answer that this visitor might understand. We may compare this repair to the two initiated by the *uhm*s in lines 5 and 6. In the first, an appropriate complement to *live*—for example, a relational *east of here* or a locative *in town*—is not ready to be uttered when it is "due," that is, following utterance of *live*. The repair resolves this most immediate problem with provision of *down in*. The second *uhm*-initiated repair deals with new trouble that arises from the unavailability of the word or phrase that complements *down in*. Here the perceived trouble may be as much that B is ignorant of local place names as it is that K cannot immediately find a best complement to *down in*. K's *uhm* may well be alerting B to prepare for some local name with which he may not be familiar. The name Martin Acres, that of a neighborhood within the locale, may be entirely available to K but not so for B.

These repairs do not exhaust the formal or functional variation exhibited by the phenomenon of same-turn repair.[3] But these examples should be sufficient to get a sense for what same-turn repair is. And they should be sufficient, moreover, to suggest that the very presence of a repair itself, apart from its effect on the linguistic makeup of an utterance, can be interactionally significant as well. For example, B's repair of his question in line 1 shows that he may not be able to understand a response that is too specific. K's repair in line 6 displays sensitivity to his lack of familiarity while providing a specific place name nonetheless. The practices of same-turn repair stand not only as a resource for changing (correcting, enhancing, abandoning) the content of an utterance but also as a resource for presenting speakers and recipients in interactionally significant ways (cf. also Goodwin 1981, 1987).

The next point about same-turn repair provides key motivation for this study: specific repair initiators indicate something about the nature of the subsequent repair (Schegloff, Jefferson, and Sacks 1977; Levelt 1983). With respect to the two repair initiators we examined previously, cut-off and *uhm*, it has been noticed that they tend to be positioned differently with respect to the turn's trouble source (Schegloff 1979). *Uhm* (and *uh*) commonly initiates repair on projected talk that has yet to be produced, be it a whole turn or an element thereof, such as a name. Cut-off, in contrast, initiates repair that commonly addresses some trouble with the turn-so-far, trouble with the whole turn produced to that point or trouble with some element thereof. Cut-off—especially when it disrupts completion of a word—is commonly positioned after its trouble source (cf. also Brédart 1991). For example, B's repair in line 1 resolves some trouble with the question produced to the point of cutting off. A similar repair occurs in line 3, where K cuts off the beginning of her response, *When I*, and replaces it with a new utterance, *WELL I* . . .[4] The occurrence of cut-off in the speaker's emerging turn routinely indicates the possible occurrence of repair on some aspect of the turn-so-far.[5] Thus, how a repair is initiated can give an initial, on-the-spot indication of which part of the turn will be operated on by the repair, and this is why an account of same-turn repair will involve an account of the various techniques used to initiate it.

To summarize so far, we have looked at some same-turn repairs and seen how the direction of the repair can be indicated by the particular initiation technique deployed. This is motivation for the importance of an account of repair initiation for the larger endeavor of understanding repair. This study focuses on one especially common form of repair initiation, closure cut-off.

Methodology

The findings presented here derive from a study of same-turn repair in which I explore specifically repair initiated by closure cut-off (Jasperson 1998). I worked with a corpus of five videotapings (about two hours) of natural, co-present conversational interaction, whose participants speak fairly "standard" varieties of American English. I first examined transcripts of the videotapings for hyphens (representing cut-off) in the context of repair initiation. As expected, the vast majority of hyphens corresponded to glottal or other stop closures (e.g., [k] or [t]). Having confirmed that cut-off typically involves some articulatory closure, I then listened to the videotapings for all occurrences of closure cut-off that initiated repair. This yielded a collection of approximately 650 cases of closure cut-off, which is the basis for the findings presented here.

It should be noted that those cut-offs transcribed with a hyphen but which did not involve audible glottal or other stop closure are not comprehensively studied here, although two sorts of "closureless" cut-offs do figure in this study (viz., cut-off in certain fricative contexts and "pulmonic cut-off"). Conversely, there was a handful of cut-offs that did involve audible articulatory closure but were not transcribed originally with a hyphen. These latter cases do figure in the collection of 650.

As for the phonetic and phonological analysis itself, my judgments about the data depend partly on the fact that English is my native language and I thus have practical knowledge of cut-off. But I also made use of certain instruments and techniques, especially in the phonetic analysis. I used a program called SoundEdit on a Macintosh platform for both acoustic analysis and auditory analysis. The articulatory analysis made use of articulatory modeling, a technique for determining how a sound is produced. Although this technique requires some practice, it consists simply in reproducing the target sound and observing (feeling) which articulators are involved and how they are used.

Phonetic Aspects of Closure Cut-Off

This section examines and documents certain basic aspects of the phonetic form of closure cut-off, with an emphasis primarily on its articulation and hearing, or audition. In particular, we will be considering how the articulation and audition of cut-off is to some extent contextually conditioned by its phonetic environment, and we will examine some ways in which cut-off is "opportunistic." The results of this section will be directly relevant for the understanding of cut-off's phonological function.

The most apparent observation regarding the form of cut-off is that it can be articulated in phonetically distinct ways. The following subsections give an impressionistic sketch of the ways in which cut-off is articulated according to phonetic environment. What all of these ways of articulating cut-off have in common is that the stream of air that passes through the vocal tract is interrupted or blocked by a closure articulation. The articulation may involve a glottal stop, an oral stop, (e.g., [t] or[k]), or both, depending on the phonetic environment in which the cut-off occurs. We will begin by looking at vowel environments.

Vowel Environments and Interruption Glottalization

In the environment of a vowel, cut-off is commonly articulated with glottal closure. I term this form of closure cut-off "glottal cut-off." In vowel and other relatively sonorant environments (sounds that, like vowels, can be loud or lengthened, such as [l] or [m]), glottal cut-off produces "interruption glottalization" (Nakatani and Hirschberg 1993). When interruption glottalization is auditorily salient, and in certain types of situations it is not, its very brief effect might be described as "hollow-pitched." The cut-off articulation in the first syllable of *sister* in example (2) is especially salient and has this auditory quality, as indicated by the use of the percent sign (instead of the conventional hyphen)[6]:

(2)

    ML2CC
    1 M: . . . and to my sih%   ← glottalized vowel, [I]
    2   <my nie̯ce in
    3   William an' Mary:,

Acoustically, interruption glottalization consists in an irregularity of frequency and a rapid decrease in amplitude. This is represented in the waveform in Figure 10.1.

The waveform in the figure begins at the end of [s] in *sih* in line 1 and ends in the middle of *my* in line 2. The line with inverted arrows in Figure 10.1 represents the extent of the glottalization (approximately sixty-four msecs). The rapid decrease in amplitude is clearly visible from the change in width of the waveform. Less visible is the change in the fundamental-frequency structure of the vowel, a change that actually begins before the amplitude decrease. Both acoustic events are probably responsible for the special auditory quality of sonorant cut-offs.[7]

In the examples that appear in this chapter, a percent sign is used to transcribe those cut-offs that have salient interruption glottalization. Such cut-offs will be referred to as "glottalized," meaning that they are attended by noticeable interruption glottalization. A hyphen, however, is used to transcribe cut-offs that have either no interruption glottalization (because the cut-off is not achieved glottally) or relatively unnoticeable interruption glottalization (due to low acoustic energy, as may be the case at the ends of words). Such cut-offs might be described auditorily as "soft."

Interestingly, in many cases of glottalized cut-off, glottal closure does not result in complete blockage of the airstream. In example (3), two glottalized cut-offs occur. The first involves only partial blockage; the second involves complete blockage:

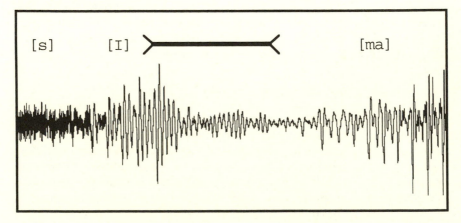

Figure 10.1. Amplitude against time for ML2CC.

(3)

    PA5GM
    1 B: An' uh:::, suh%   ← partial blockage
    2   <tha:t's what they'r%   ← complete blockage
    3   (.) they were a:ngry
    4   abou::t

In line 1, a token of the conjunction *so* is cut off early in its production (thus transcribed *suh*). Interruption glottalization begins in the vowel and persists to the beginning of the dental articulation for *that's* (line 2). Close inspection of the waveform and careful, isolated listening indicate that the airstream is never fully blocked; it enjoys only partial blockage. The glottalized cut-off in line 2, however, involves complete blockage. In general, it seems to be only the more rapid resumptions that involve partial blockage. The resumption of speech[8] after the cut-off in line 1 is quite rapid (as indicated by the <), whereas the resumption of speech after the cut-off in line 2 is not quite as fast.[9] But differences in achieved blockage notwithstanding, the auditory quality of partial glottal blockage is practically indistinguishable from complete glottal blockage. Interruption glottalization is produced under both conditions—and cut-off is heard in both. Partial versus complete blockage, then, is a matter of phonetic detail. But the significance of this phonetic detail will be appreciated later in this chapter when we consider cut-off's design.

    So far I have indicated that cut-off in the context of a vowel is commonly done with glottal closure. Importantly, however, there is a vowel cut-off technique that does not involve, at least not at first, glottal closure. I refer to this phenomenon as "opportunistic closure cut-off."[10] Opportunistic closure cut-off uses the stop closure of the first articulation of the resumption as the cut-off articulation.[11] The repair in example (4) illustrates this:

(4)

    ML2BX
    1 M: =[['Cause who*k-   ← opportunistic closure cut-off
    2   <-Ka:ren might have access,

In line 1, the speaker cuts off before recognizable completion of the pronoun *who*. I have transcribed the cut-off with **k-* to indicate that the articulation that accomplishes the cut-off is a velar closure. This velar closure has the same place of articulation as the first sound of the resumption, namely, the velar consonant that begins *Karen* in line 2. We will see that opportunistic closure cut-off occurs in other phonetic environments as well.

    It should be mentioned that there seems to be a use of opportunistic closure cut-off that in fact involves a glottal stop, though it may be equivocal as to whether the glottal stop is done in the first place as a regular glottal cut-off or as an opportunistic closure cut-off. First, some background: In English, glottal stops are regularly used in fluent speech to assist in making prominent and/or distinct the first syllables of vowel-begun words. This is referred to as "epenthesis" and is shown in example (5):

(5)

    SA2DO
    1 S: I know she married for -ey
    2   thi:rd ti:m:e,   ↑
    3 A: Mhm,   epenthetic glottal stop
    4 S: t! A ma:::n (0.6) who . . .

The glottal articulation that initiates *ey* (a stressed version of the indefinite article *a*) helps to distinguish it from the preceding word and contributes to the prosodic prominence of the phrase *ey third time*. Now, this epenthetic glottal stop is not heard as a cut-off following *for*, largely because *ey* is a projectable continuation of the turn-so-far and the transition between the words is sufficiently short (these matters are examined further when we consider the phonology of cut-off). However, cut-off can emerge under slightly different conditions, as shown in example (6):

(6)

    AD30
    1 M: They're a hi:gh a:rch spr//ing.
    2 C: Hi:gh arch spring.
    3 G: [[O:h just across the back end?
    4 C: [[-A:ny-<-a:ny high arch spring.
                ↑↑↑
             opportunistic closure cut-off/epenthetic glottal stop

Near the beginning of line 4, C cuts off upon completion of *Any* with a glottal closure and then immediately resumes with a recycling of the word. A cut-off emerges in this case because of a brief but noticeable silence before the resumption and the presence of the recycled element. The cut-off in this situation could be analyzed as opportunistic closure cut-off, since the first articulation of the resumption is analyzable as an epenthetic glottal stop, the same sound that begins the first occurrence of *Any*. In this way, a glottal stop cut-off can be consistent with its being also an opportunistic closure cut-off.

In sum, cut-off in the environment of a vowel may be accomplished in one of two ways. It is very commonly accomplished with glottal closure, with partial or complete blockage of the airstream. But it may also be accomplished in the form of an opportunistic closure cut-off, whereby a first stop articulation of the resumption is used as the cut-off closure.

Stop Environments

In the environment of an oral stop, a consonantal sound such as [p], [b], [t], [d], [k], or [g], the cut-off articulation coincides with the stop that is currently in progress. In other words, the closure that marks the onset of cut-off is "organic" to the word itself.

(7)

> AD15
> 1 G: There's twi:ns that-   ← organic stop cut-off
> 2   (0.8) twi:ns that
> 3   live over there,

In line 1 in example (7), the speaker cuts off with the alveolar articulation specified by the last consonant of *that*. The alveolar is organic to the normal articulation of the word. Cut-off in oral stop environments differs from non-cut-off situations where the stop is either fluently released into the next sound or quietly released into silence, as at the end of an utterance.

Cut-off closures organic to the host word are documented in examples (8), (9), (10), (11), and (12) for a range of places of articulation:

(8)

> SA2CO
> 1 S: Because usually the
> 2   kind of bo:dies are b-   ← bilabial (of *built?*)
> 3   <ar:e the >spindly< . . .

(9)

> SA4EY
> 1 S: I kno:w th-   ← dental stop, a variant of the dental fricative
> 2   (0.3) -the Lew::

(10)

> ML1CA
> 1 L: He's d-   ← alveolar
> 2   <he's totally different.

(11)

> ML5F
> 1 M: The larD-   ← alveopalatal (of *large*)
> 2   <by and large,

(12)

> PA2CL
> 1 J: It's a g-   ←velar
> 2   <I think it's a
> 3   grea::t. -a:ngle:

Voiceless counterparts to the preceding stops (such as [p], [t], and [k])occur in the corpus, except in the case of the dental stop.

When oral closure achieves blockage of the airstream, glottal closure usually occurs as well, probably so as to allow the oral articulators to prepare for the resumption of speech.[12] This generally seems to be the case with immediate resumptions, that is, post-cut-off resumptions of speech that occur without a significant pause.[13] Without the benefit of glottal closure, words begun immediately after the cut-off could be ill-formed, beginning as they would with the stop articulation of the cut-off (though there seems to be some latitude in the case of fricatives (e.g., [v] and [s]) and possibly laterals, (e.g., [l]), as discussed in "Approximant Environments"). Conceivably, though, glottal closure need not assist oral stop cut-off if the resumption begins with an oral stop that is identical with, close to, or anterior to the cut-off closure, since some movement between places of articulation is possible without the release of air. Based on the articulatory modeling I have done, however, even when resumption begins with the identical closure, a glottal assist feels—to me—more "natural." In sum, oral stop cut-off is assisted by glottal closure in most, if not practically all, situations.

On occasion, syllable-final oral stops are distinctly colored by interruption glottalization. This happens when the glottis begins closing sufficiently before oral closure is effected, as in example (13):

(13)

    PA4DG
    1 B: [My bro:ther:]:
    2   w'z æ w'z at%   ← glottal and oral stop closure
    3   <u>has</u> been living
    4   in Sy:racu::se 'n',

The cut-off articulation at the end of line 2 is accomplished by both oral and glottal closure, as evidenced by interruption glottalization that noticeably affects the quality of the vowel before completion of the alveolar closure.

Nasal Stop Environments

In the environment of a nasal stop, a consonantal sound such as [m] or [n], glottal closure alone typically achieves cut-off, as illustrated in example (14):

(14)

    PA2CC
    1 B: Or it's n%   ← glottal cut-off, [n]
    2   (.) <u>the</u> no:rthern
    3   accent is really
    4   loud to me.

In line 1, the speaker glottally cuts off a possible token of *not* during its first sound.

There is a variant technique for nasal cut-off that involves first a closing of the velum (the part of the palate at the back of the mouth) and then nasal blockage of the airstream, which produces a genuine, though brief, oral stop. This less frequent course of events is illustrated in example (15):

(15)

> PA5DL
> 1 B: . . . they're mb-   ← velum closure, glottal closure
> 2   (0.2) m
> 3   <I think they're::-
> 4   (0.9)
> 5   they ca:n be: (.) much more
> 6   expre:ssive . . .

In line 1, the speaker cuts off at the onset of a word that might have become a token of *much* or *more*, words that do appear in line 5. Just before labial closure (transcribed *mb*), there is brief nasalization on the final vocalic, [er], of *they're*. Then, as labial closure is achieved, the velum also closes, resulting in the briefly voiced bilabial stop (hence the *b*). Following all this, glottal closure occurs.

Fricative Environments

Closure cut-off in the environment of a fricative, a sound such as [f], [v], [s], [z], or the "sh"-sound, [ʃ], is much less salient than cut-off in other phonetic environments, and it may be articulatorily problematic as well.

   Alveolar (e.g., [s]) and alveopalatal (e.g., [ʃ]) fricatives can and do host glottal cut-off, as illustrated in examples (16) and (17):

(16)

> SA2EV
> 1 S: Just the hi:s-   ← [s]
> 2   (0.1) -y'kno:w,

In line 1, the speaker glottally cuts off what is projectably a token of *history* during the alveolar fricative.

(17)

> ML2GL
> 1 M: For the who:::le
> 2   sh[o o :(m a s h).]
> 3 L: [For the who::le] sh-   ← [ʃ]
> 4   (0.1) shmee::r.

In line 3, the alveopalatal fricative [ʃ] is cut off glottally just after it is begun.

   Although closure cut-off can occur in alveolar and alveopalatal fricative environments, it is also not uncommon to find cases of repair that begin after closureless self-interruptions in these environments, as illustrated in example (18):

(18)

> PA4FY
> 1 P: A:n'- (.) -the thing that s   ← no audible closure

2   <We: didn't like dri:ving
3   through the Sou:th.

The utterance in line 1 is interrupted during a word (possibly *struck*) and is immediately followed by the repairing utterance, *We didn't like* . . . No glottal closure is
audible at the point of interruption. It is not clear to me at this time whether a case
such as this is the result of practical difficulty—the speaker was not able to achieve
audible closure cut-off—or closure cut-off is absent by practical design. In any
event, there is a definite perceptual difference between alveolar (and alveopalatal)
fricatives that are cut off and those that are terminated without glottal (or other
stop closure) cut-off. Appendix A to this chapter contains an account of the auditory and acoustic differences between cut-off and non-cut-off alveolar fricatives.

   Alveolar and alveopalatal fricatives also host opportunistic closure cut-off, as
illustrated in example (19):

(19)

   SA25AQ
   1 A: [. . . Y'know the children jis']
   2   have ey .hh rea:l- <-uh: s*k-   ← opportunistic
   3   <-good sense of themse:lves . . .

In line 2, a possible but brief token of *sense*, transcribed *s*, is cut off with velar closure, transcribed **k-*. Just after the cut-off, voicing begins (line 3) as the closure
releases into *good* (which replaces the cut-off word-beginning *s*).

   A variant form of opportunistic closure cut-off was also observed in the case
of alveolar and alveopalatal fricatives. If the resumption is to begin with the same
fricative sound that hosts the cut-off, then homorganic stop closure—that is, a stop
closure with the same place of articulation as the fricative—can be employed to
achieve blockage of the airstream. Example (20) involves cutting off the beginning
of a word that is projectably the pronoun *she*, resulting in the sound transcribed
sh*T-:

(20)

   AD27
   1 C: . . . he's afraid sh*T-   ← homorganic opportunistic [T]
   2   <-Tshe'll get it'n'
   3   do somp'n' to it.

This cut-off involves alveopalatal stop closure (notated *T-*) even though the word
she does not contain such a stop. Use of homorganic closure may be motivated by
a preference for maximal audibility, since fricatives that are cut off with a homorganic stop seem to be more salient than those that rely on glottal closure. This greater
salience may have to do with the fact that the airstream is forced through a rapidly
constricting space (between the articulators).

   The environment of dental frication—[f], [v], [θ], and [δ]—may present challenges for cut-off, with respect to both its audition and its articulation. This is sug-

gested by the fact that in the data I have examined no repair is audibly initiated by glottal cut-off in the environment of dental frication.[14] By way of illustration, let us look at several cases of repair that *might have* enjoyed some form of closure cut-off under different phonetic circumstances:

(21)

> ML2G
> 1 M: I have to cut back an' no:t gi:v:e   ← [f]
> 2   (1.1) -an' no:t- (.) respo::nd
> 3   >kind of like every time . . .

In line 1 of example (21), the dental fricative of *give* ([v]) is stretched and gets devoiced (to [f]), but no glottal (or other closure) cut-off is audible. In this repair, *respond* replaces the phrase begun with *give*. This repair patterns like so many repairs initiated with closure cut-off, whereby the resumption first recycles some part of the turn-so-far and then replaces or inserts an element, as for example in lines 3–5 of example (15), where following a recycle of *they*, the modal element *can* is inserted. In example (22), too, no closure cut-off is audible:

(22)

> ML3X
> 1 L: See: that's why I'm:
> 2 M: =A:ll u[n:<depa:rtments don't.
> 3 L: [I don'think they've   ← [v]
> 4   <I: do]n'think the unive:rsity
> 5   has thought it through enti:rely . . .

In line 3, the final dental fricative of *they've* ends without a closure cut-off. In this repair, *they* is replaced by *the university*. In example (23), it is important to know that the speaker is talking about his experience with racial issues in the southern United States. The relevant race terms are "white southerners," "black southerners," and "white nonsoutherners," who get referred to respectively as *whites who lived there, blacks,* and *white outsiders.*

(23)

> PA5HQ
> 1 B: I felt like (.) -if uh:::,
> 2   (0.7) .h that- (0.5) -blacks
> 3   were alot mo:re acce:pting of
> 4   ou- (0.1) of whi:te outsiders
> 5   than they wer::e of (0.3)
> 6   .h thuh:: people with   ← [θ]
> 7   (0.1) thuh whites who
> 8   li:ved there.

In line 6, the dental fricative of *with* ([θ]) terminates without closure cut-off (although the segment may be slightly overbrief). The effect of the repair is the replacement of the phrase begun *the people with* with *the whites who lived there.*[15] The preceding three examples belong to a corpus-exhaustive collection of seventeen cases of repair that begin in the environment of dental frication but which do not enjoy closure cut-off (though some do enjoy a significant pause, e.g., example [21]). This suggests that closure cut-off is difficult to achieve in the environment of dental frication, though at present this must remain only a suggestion, since it is always possible that the absence of closure cut-off is a matter of practical design, not practical, phonetic difficulty.

Fricatives in general may be difficult to cut off glottally for the reason that when a fricative is produced, the glottis is maximally open to allow the airflow necessary to achieve sufficient audibility (*p.c.* Alan Bell). If the glottis is to close completely from this wide-open position, it will take some time. This length of time may be too great in certain contexts to stop the flow of air expediently; for example, simply checking the lungs from further collapse might achieve stoppage in the same amount of time (cf. discussion of pulmonic cut-off in "Some Phonological Considerations"). Homorganic stop closures are therefore a reasonable alternative to glottal cut-off for alveolar and alveopalatal contexts. Homorganic stop closure in the case of dental fricatives did not occur in the corpus, and given the low intensity of dental frication, it might be that closure cut-off is simply not practical.[16]

In sum, fricatives, especially dental fricatives, may present special difficulties for achieving closure cut-off. Glottal cut-off is possible in alveolar and alveopalatal fricative environments, and opportunistic closure cut-off occurs as well. Closure cut-off in dental environments does not occur in the corpus.

Approximant Environments

The articulation of cut-off in the environment of a central approximant, a sound such as [r], [w], or the "y"-sound, [j], can be and is done in the same manner as vowels, both with and without noticeable interruption glottalization. As it happens, though, no central approximants enjoy opportunistic closure cut-off in the corpus. As for [h], which is classed as an approximant, no case of closure cut-off occurs in the corpus. There was, however, an instance of cut-off during aspiration from a velar release, which suggests that it is possible for [h] sounds to host glottal cut-off.

Cut-off in the environment of the lateral approximant, [l], occurs less commonly in the corpus. Syllabic laterals clearly pattern like other approximants in hosting glottal cut-off. As for cut-off in nonsyllabic environments, I have been able to examine only two cases. One is illustrated in example (24), in which the beginning of a possible token of *little* is cut off probably by an alveolar closure, transcribed (l*t)-. As indicated by the parentheses around *l*t*, however, the hearing is not certain (due to excessive noise from an automobile engine):

(24)

    SA25BD
    1 A: We have h(h)(h) another (l*t)-   ← [l], opportunistic
    2   (0.1) new little boy named
    3   uh:m (0.4) Rei:lly. .hh

If the transcribed hearing is correct, the cut-off articulation, an alveolar stop on-set, and the first articulation of the repair, an alveolar nasal, are homorganic, and so this is the same technique of opportunistic closure cut-off observed in the case of fricatives. The other nonsyllabic lateral is given in example (25):

(25)

> PA5AI
> 1 P: And this is like L-   ← devoiced [l], glottal cut-off
> 2   (0.6) Li:ttle Rock
> 3   or something.

The cut-off *L-* lacks voicing; it consists of lateral airstream coming off the aspirated release of the velar in *like*. The airstream does, however, seem to be blocked glottally, but because voicing has not yet begun, this case leaves open the question as to how (regularly voiced) nonsyllabic laterals can be cut off. It is likely that they pattern as the other approximants.

Summary of Phonetics

Closure cut-off is articulated by oral and/or glottal closure that blocks the flow of air through the vocal tract. A full range of English oral stops is evident: bilabial, dental, alveolar, alveopalatal, and velar. When a glottal stop is deployed, the blockage may be full or partial. Partial blockage occurs in the case of rapid resumptions, for which interruption glottalization alone is sufficient to display the articulation of cut-off. Glottalized cut-offs were contrasted with cut-offs that are auditorily soft. Oral stop cut-offs are typically organic to the lexical makeup of the word. Oral stop and glottal closures can work together, probably to allow the oral articulators to prepare for resumption noiselessly. On occasion, glottal cut-off may be perceived to co-occur with oral stop closure organic to the word (since interruption glottalization can occur during the oral stop closing). Nasals and central approximants are usually cut off in the same manner as vowels, and probably laterals similarly. Fricatives, especially dentals, may be problematic for closure cut-off.

I documented in addition several forms of opportunistic closure cut-off, which is accomplished articulatorily by an oral stop identical to or homorganic with the first articulation of the resumption.

Last, each way of articulating cut-off is to some extent conditioned by the phonetic environment in which the cut-off occurs. Roughly, if the speaker knows (in some sense) that the first articulation of the resumption will be a stop, opportunistic closure cut-off can be articulated. If the first articulation is not yet known and if the immediate environment is a vowel, nasal, or approximant, then glottal cut-off is done. If the immediate environment is an alveolar or alveopalatal fricative, glottal cut-off can be tried. If the environment is a dental fricative, glottal cut-off may not be practical.

The results of the foregoing phonetic analysis bear directly on the phonology of cut-off considered in the next section. Specifically, the articulatory form of cut-off is relevant for its general specification, and the phenomena of opportunistic closure cut-off and both complete and partial blockage in glottal cut-off figure as evidence for a design feature of cut-off.

Some Phonological Considerations

Having examined certain aspects of the phonetic form closure cut-off, we are now in a position to examine its phonology, that is, what that phonetic form most immediately accomplishes in talk. Here we will consider two such aspects of closure cut-off. The first concerns the way in which closure cut-off interrupts talk. Since this is central to cut-off, I regard this as its specification. The second aspect concerns the way in which closure cut-off enables talk to resume. I treat this as a design feature of closure cut-off. To get to this point, however, it will be necessary to consider a distinct form of cut-off, pulmonic cut-off, which I have so far mentioned only in passing.

A Specification of Closure Cut-Off

My purpose in this section is to propose a specification of cut-off. The basic claim is that the cut-off articulation stops the projected occurrence of the next sound. This claim derives directly from Schegloff (1979).

A specification may be approached beginning with the recognition that cut-off is not a context-free device. It is not, for instance, analogous to the flash of a light to signal an official stop to the ongoing turn. Cut-off employs the same articulators and many of the same articulations as "normal," fluent speech and is therefore sensitive to its immediate articulatory environment. So how then does cut-off mesh with the other speech practices that accomplish talk but at the same time distinguish itself from them?

It is especially the practices of fluent articulatory closures to which cut-off must be most sensitive. How, in particular, are the stop closures of cut-off distinguished from the normal stop closures in speech that are not related to repair initiation? What distinguishes an oral stop that is organic to the fluent articulation of a word from oral-stop cut-off that might occur within or adjacent to that word?

Let us explore these questions with the following examples of cut-off. In example (26), C is trying to get M to acknowledge a type of automobile suspension spring:

(26)

```
        AD22
        1  C:  Dju know what (        [ ) I'm ta:lkin'=
        2  M:                         [Yea::h,
        3  C:  =a[bou:t,
        4  M:    [I think-                          ← overlong stop closure
        5     (.) I know whatchu mea:n,
```

In M's turn in lines 4 and 5—*I think I know whatchu mean*—there is a cut-off at the end of *think*. M's talk is stopped only briefly, as indicated by the micropause notation at the beginning of line 5, but it is sufficient to achieve cut-off. The cut-off that occurs at the end of *think*, what I have termed "word-offset cut-off" elsewhere (Jasperson 1998), is achieved by velar stop closure. This velar closure, however, is also organic to *think* itself. Given this, there must be some component in addition to the articulatory event of the velar closing that accomplishes the cut-off. That component clearly involves the temporal character of the closure. To accomplish this cut-off, the closure must be sustained for a period of time beyond which release of the velar closure is not projected, as either the last sound of the same word or the first sound of a next. Had the closure released any earlier into the next sound (the first sound of *I*), a cut-off would not be recognizable.[17] Time, then, seems to be a key component of the phonology of cut-off.

Example (27), seen at the outset in example (1), shows stopless lexical contexts that permit cut-offs to occur in very short periods of time. K's talk is part of a sequence through which she laments the rapid development in and around the area in which she grew up. In her response to B's question, the talk's dispreferredness is created largely through K's use of repair-related devices (cf. Fox and Jasperson 1995):

(27)

```
PA7CO
1 B:   Where do you li:ve. (N://::.)
2 K:   Uhm (1.2) .hhh When I%          ← brief glottal closing
3      <WELL I grew up in the%         ← extremely brief
4      <mountains, an' no:w hh
5      I live <we live uhm hh
6      down in uhm . . .
```

At the end of line 2, K cuts off to begin a new utterance. This cut-off is accomplished by a brief glottal closing that produces interruption glottalization sufficient to stop, by effectively "blotting out," normal articulation of the last part of *I*.[18] At the end of line 3, K does an extremely brief glottal cut-off, producing a kind of halting effect between *the* and *mountains*. This is achieved in the same way, with glottalization effectively blotting out the normal character of the last part of *the*.[19] These cut-offs are accomplished in a much shorter period of time than the organic stop cut-off of *think* in the previous excerpt. The reason that cut-off is nonetheless achieved is because no closure has been projected at the point when *I* and *the* are cut off, whereas closure is normally present at the point when *think* hosts cut-off, thus requiring its stop closure to be held longer (long enough to overcome interpretations of a normal closure).

The duration of the closures that participate in accomplishing cut-off will always depend on the lexical makeup of the talk, the tempo of the interaction, and no doubt other grammatical aspects. The preceding examples present relatively straightforward cases of cut-off. Analyzing cut-off in vowel environments will, for instance, be complicated by the presence of the epenthetic glottal releases noted earlier that regularly occur in English at the beginning of stressed, vowel-initial syllables.

In any event, there must be a temporal component to the articulation of cut-off that makes it a special phonological device distinct from the articulation of stop closures per se. It is this temporal aspect that Schegloff references when he describes cut-off as a technique for stopping "a 'next sound due' from occurring when it is due" (1979:273). In other words, the cut-off articulation stops the progress of the talk in such a way that whatever next bit of talk was expectably or projectably to occur—the next sound due—does not occur when it would have.

In practice, the next sound due may not occur next, or ever. Let us look at several illustrations of the phonology of cut-off in the context of specific repairs. In example (28) the speaker is describing his experiences as a political canvasser. He cuts off at the end of line 1 during a word that likely would have been *what*. The repair replaces the phrase begun with *what*:

(28)

```
    PA3HM
    1  B:   'N' going house to hou:se 'n' wha%      ←
    2        <ho:w they respo:nded tuh:, (0.5)
    3        to you kno:ckin' on (your) door:
    4        an' askin' them for money,
```

The cut-off stops the occurrence of some next sound—projectably the voiceless alveolar stop of *what* ([t]). The next sound due in this case never occurs as such because the repair redirects the talk.

When cut-off occurs at the very end, or offset, of a word, the next sound that is stopped is the beginning of the next projected word (or, on occasion, the aspirated release of a final stop consonant). The repair in example (29), in which the speaker is relating an incident at a racetrack, involves the insertion of a clause:

(29)

```
    AD10b
    1  M:   So b(o:y) when
    2        Kee:g'n come in he-                      ←
    3        (0.4) you know how he:'s
    4        gotta  temper anyway,
    5        he j's::: °wa:::::h
    6        sc//reamed 'is damn
    7        e:ngine yihknow:
    8  C:   Mm
```

In line 2, M cuts off just as the word *he* is recognizably complete (in its context). In this case, the next sound due could have been the beginning of the adverbial *just*, which eventually does get uttered in line 5 (transcribed *j's:::*) after the insertion.

A specification of cut-off can now be proposed. This specification combines the articulatory characteristics of cut-off described in the previous section with the temporal characteristics described here. This specification is based directly on Schegloff (1979):

Closure cut-off

Contextually conditioned oral and/or glottal closure that stops a "next sound due" from occurring when due.

As discussed, the particular identity of the closure employed—the various oral and/or glottal closures—is conditioned by phonetic context. The "next sound due" is the next bit of talk, that next articulation that projectably would have occurred had repair not been initiated. The fate of that next sound is determined by the nature of the repair; with replacement repairs, for example, it may occur eventually or not at all.

A theoretically significant feature of this specification is that it is stated independently of repair itself. Cut-off initiates repair, but it is recognizable and specifiable independently of the operation of any repair. And this is how it is possible for repair to be initiated but then canceled (Schegloff 1984b). A case of cancellation appeared (but was not examined) in example (1) and in example (27), the relevant portion of which is repeated again in example (30):

(30)

```
        PA7CO
    1 K:  Uhm (1.2) .hhh When I%
    2        <WELL I grew up in the%        ← repair initiation
    3        <mountains, an' no:w hh...      ← repair canceled
```

The speaker cuts off toward the end of *the* in line 2, but then continues immediately with *mountains*, without repair.

In this subsection, we have examined the way in which cut-off brings talk to a halt. Following Schegloff, I proposed that cut-off halts talk by stopping a next sound due. The remaining two subsections explore further the form and function of cut-off, with an eye to the way in which cut-off enables talk to resume.

A Talk-Stopping Alternative to Closure Cut-Off

One thing that may be noticed about the form of closure cut-off is that it is not the only way of stopping a next sound due. There is at least one other articulatory technique—what I have termed earlier "pulmonic cut-off"—that is functionally similar to closure cut-off insofar as it stops a next sound due (and insofar as it routinely initiates repair). Here I want to consider this technique insofar as it contrasts with closure cut-off. Then, in the next subsection, I will bring this consideration to bear on the matter of the design of closure cut-off.

We have seen that the way closure cut-off stops a next sound due is by blocking the flow of air with oral and/or glottal closure. Pulmonic cut-off, in contrast, does not stop the flow of air by blocking it. Rather, this technique consists in stopping the flow of air by removing its source: it stops the chest cavity from generating the pulmonic pressure that pushes the air out of the lungs. When the chest cavity is held from further collapse, airflow subsides as pulmonic and external air pressures equalize. Pulmonic cut-off is just another way of stopping the flow of air. But

it is distinct from closure cut-off because instead of blocking the flow of air, it removes its source.[20] Pulmonic cut-off stops a next sound due by removing the airflow altogether.

Pulmonic cut-off probably occurs in a variety of contexts. Those that struck
me as especially relevant for understanding cut-off involve situations where production of a word-in-progress is terminated before its recognizable completion.
These situations, I feel, are ones in which closure cut-off *might* otherwise be found.
Pulmonic cut-off initiates premature termination of words-in-progress in two distinct contexts: one is in abandoning a unit-in-progress, and the other is in recycling. In the corpus, moreover, this happens only in the context of overlapping talk.

In example (31), speakers P and M are telling C about a go-cart driver (M is
the referent of *Mike* in line 1). M abandons an overlapped turn in line 4 with a
pulmonic cut-off. (I have not altered the hyphen that was originally transcribed.)

(31)

        AD13; simplified[21]
        1 P: M[ike said 'e usetuh:]::=
        2 C: [W e:l l you r'meh%]
        3 P: =race go[carts] an'e=
        4 M: [He use-]   ← pulmonic cut-off
        5 P: =got barred from the gok-
        6   (0.3) -cart track
        7   be//cause he ra:n little
        8   kids (h)off the tra::ck,
        9 M: Over in Ti:ffen.

M begins his line-4 turn in overlap but shortly thereafter abandons it during articulation of the auxiliary, *used*. In this case the next sound due that would have
occurred is an alveolar stop ([t]). The pulmonic cut-off appears to result in an
overlengthening of the alveolar fricative that hosts it. Now, it seems that closure
cut-off might have been a practical alternative to the pulmonic cut-off, as suggested
by the presence of the closure cut-off at the end of C's terminated turn in line 2, a
turn that similarly begins and ends in overlap. (The interactional difference between M's abandoned turn and C's cut-off turn might have to do with the fact that
M's brief contribution is assumed by P, who is telling the same story; M's terminated turn is part of what constructs him as a co-teller in the activity. C's talk,
however, is not of this story and is "put on hold" until M and P's story sequence is
completed, whereupon C rebegins his talk (not shown) with the same phrasing,
Well you remember . . . .)

Another case of turn abandonment is given in example (32), where S is assessing the treatment of a professional dancer. A abandons an overlapping turn in
line 6 with a pulmonic cut-off:

(32)

        SA3AI
        1 S: . . . but anyhow they're k- <kee:ping
        2   her kind of at a:rm's di:stance.

```
3 A:   =Mhm
4 S:   W[ell there's alotta fe%]
5 A:     [Maybe s h e   p r e f ]e:rs tha:t,
6        y'kno:[w,=°maybe she prefer]          ← pulmonic cut-off
7 S:          [We::ll , = or I t]hink
8        the other, she's a threa:t
9        to everybody.
```

In line 6, A's overlapped talk is abandoned just before completing *prefers*. The next sound projectably due is the alveolar third-person marker, *-s*. The pulmonic cut-off in this case causes the second syllable of *prefer* to "die out"; there is a drop in volume and pitch, consistent with the fading of pulmonic pressure. Elsewhere in this excerpt, too, a closure cut-off is employed by S (line 4) in the face of overlapping talk, though the sequence is quite different from the preceding case since S is not heard as taking up the same talk as that begun in the cut-off turn.

The other sort of overlap context in which pulmonic cut-off prematurely terminates words-in-progress involves the recycling of the terminated element. In example (33), a pulmonic cut-off occurs preceding the micropause in line 7:

(33)

```
   E1DS
   1 C:   No b- <Bob<Bo<Bo [<Bo<Bo<Bo<°Bo<Bo
   2 B:                   [La:ter I: -I: said
   3        it wa[s ok]a::y and the:n he=
   4 C:        [Bob!]
   5        =(sort'a) [mellowed o u : t.]
   6 C:             [Tha tha:t's someth]ing=
   7 C:   =[[I no:ticed about the Ge:rm (.) the Ge:rman]=
   8 H:    [ [Right.=He didn'wanna do:it anymo:re because]
   9 C:   =students in my- <in my phy:sics classes . . .
```

In line 7, C recycles the beginning of the phrase *the German* (*students*). The pulmonic cut-off engenders an overlong [m] that may have just the beginnings of the alveolar nasal. There is no closure cut-off, nor is there the fluent transition into the recycling that occurs in other varieties of recycling (cp. the recycling in lines 1, 2, and 6). A similar situation occurs in example (34). L is explaining to M the results of a meeting about a proposed restructuring of salary-increase categories at their institute:

(34)

```
   ML3GK
   1 L:   The:n they had the straight one thousand
   2        do:llars which would (0.4) k:i:nd of make
   3        everybody ha:ppy because they were a:ll
   4        equal: in amou:nthh,
   5 M:   These were choi:ces.
   6        (0.5)
```

```
 7  L:   No. =These were
 8       th[ree::      di:fferent-]
 9  M:      [Oh three things they] did at o:nce.=
10  L:   =salar                              ←
11       (.) Three different things they did.
```

L terminates production of *salary* in line 10 with a pulmonic cut-off initiated during the lateral approximant ([l]) and then resumes in line 11 with a (partial) recycle of M's overlapping talk. Like the previous cases, this pulmonic cut-off engenders a fading of the second syllable of *salary*.

There is much about pulmonic cut-off to explore. In the preceding examples, the pulmonic cut-off is brief. After the flow of air has subsided, expiration or inspiration may resume. Interactionally, overlap may be in some way relevant for the use of pulmonic cut-off as opposed to closure cut-off. Further, pulmonic cut-off might differ from the way in which vocalization ceases at the ends of utterances. Typically, when vocalization ceases, the articulators disengage the airstream without a pulmonic cut-off, and the chest either continues its collapse or begins immediately to expand. Why pulmonic cut-off might exist in contrast to this typical way of ceasing vocalization is not clear.

In sum, pulmonic cut-off seems to be an articulatory technique whose phonological function—like that of closure cut-off—can be described as stopping a next sound due. However, this technique is phonetically distinct from closure cut-off, and it is probably interactionally distinct as well. Pulmonic cut-off stops a next sound due by removing the source of the airflow, whereas closure cut-off accomplishes this by blocking the flow of air.

A Design Feature of Closure Cut-Off

Having examined both the articulatory form of closure cut-off and a cut-off technique that contrasts with closure cut-off at least in form and (possibly) in interactional function, we are now in a position to appreciate a feature of the design of closure cut-off. This feature has to do with the way in which closure cut-off enables post-cut-off speech to start. Namely, closure cut-off enables soonest possible starts, or in the terminology of this study, *closure cut-off enables soonest possible resumptions*. This is evidenced in three ways:

1. Closure cut-off is opportunistic. It can employ articulators most convenient to the task of both stopping the next sound due and starting the resumption. This is evidenced by opportunistic closure cut-off of vowels, fricatives, and possibly laterals.
2. Closure cut-off blocks the flow of air instead of waiting for it to subside. Blocking the flow of air glottally allows the oral articulators to position for resumption without nonlexical vocalization occurring. In the case of pulmonic cut-off, however, resumption articulators would have to wait until the airflow has subsided; otherwise the resumption could be ill-formed.

3. In some cases of glottal cut-off, resumption occurs even *before* the flow of air has had a chance to be completely blocked. These are the glottal cut-offs with partial, as opposed to complete, blockage of the airstream.

These points are offered as evidence that closure cut-off enables soonest possible resumption. And this is significant for repair, since the ability to resume as soon as possible after cut-off means that the repairing talk can begin as soon as possible. Other things being equal, soonest possible resumption is tantamount to soonest possible repair. In short, a design feature of closure cut-off is that it enables soonest possible repair.

Closure cut-off's speed-oriented design helps explain what seems to me to be part of the phenomenology of cut-off, which is that when closure cut-off occurs, it often seems to have occurred as soon as possible. The reasoning is simply that when cut-off is used to facilitate soonest possible repair, which I am suggesting closure cut-off is designed to enable, then the initiation of the repair itself, that is, the cut-off, presumably is done as soon as possible as well. Or, from the perspective of the design metaphor, if speed is a sufficiently important property to "build into" a repair initiator, then speed in general must be an important aspect of doing repair. And so, once the decision to repair is made, it is initiated as soon as possible.[22]

These remarks on cut-off's speed-oriented design should be tempered, however. Even though closure cut-off is designed to allow soonest possible repair, it does not follow that a given repair will be launched as soon as possible. Closure cut-off can and does occur, for example, without the speaker necessarily knowing at the time of cut-off how the repair should be accomplished (though just such a practical contingency is covered by the "as-possible" condition in the "as-soon-as-possible" clause). Thus, while closure cut-off is "built for speed," it is not always so deployed. Indeed, *some* forms of closure cut-off appear not to display an immediate concern with speed. The cut-offs I have in mind are those that occur upon the normal, unhurried completion words, such as with *think-* in example (26) and *he-* in example (29). The articulation of such cut-offs surely requires careful timing so as not to occur too early or too late. And that would seem to be a luxury if speed were an overriding concern.

Summary of Phonology

Closure cut-off is a contextually conditioned articulatory technique for stopping a next sound due from occurring as projected, or when due. By way of consideration of pulmonic cut-off, a technique similar to closure cut-off in phonological function but distinct in articulatory form and possibly interactional function, I argued that a design feature of closure cut-off is that it enables soonest possible resumption of speech after cut-off and therewith soonest possible repair. This, I suggested, helps explain how the initiator can seem to have occurred as soon as possible. Last, I pointed out that while closure cut-off may allow soonest possible repair, it is not always so deployed.

Conclusion

An account of the techniques of repair initiation will be an important component of the larger endeavor to understand repair. This study is intended as a contribution toward an account of one repair initiation technique, closure cut-off. I identified some of the basic phonetic and phonological characteristics that make this repair initiator interactionally real. I also sketched an account of the relationship of cut-off to other speech practices. It is hoped that the attention to linguistic detail has resulted in a deeper understanding of this otherwise innocuous element of talk-in-interaction.

We examined articulatory and auditory characteristics of closure cut-off and uncovered certain opportunistic forms as well as phonetic contexts that may resist repair initiation by this technique. We learned in addition that the particular form closure cut-off takes seems to be conditioned partly by phonetic context. We then considered how closure cut-off functions in relation to the "normal" practices of articulating fluent speech and proposed a specification of closure cut-off that derives from Schegloff (1979), namely, that closure cut-off is a contextually conditioned oral and/or glottal closure that stops a next sound due from occurring when due. This is significant in part because it allows that cut-off exists and is recognizable independently of the operation of repair. In view of the phonetics of cut-off and of a briefly considered pulmonic technique for stopping a next sound due, I suggested that a design feature of closure cut-off is that it allows soonest possible resumptions of speech and therewith soonest possible repair.

This study should motivate further research into other forms of cut-off, such as the pulmonic cut-off that could only be treated in passing, or the nature of cut-off in fricative environments. There is also room for systematic phonological analysis of the durational requirements of closure cut-off: how long does closure have to be held to achieve cut-off in a given phonological context?

Appendix A: Acoustic Information for Alveolar Fricative Offsets

Figure 10.2 gives a waveform (amplitude against time, upper tier) and a corresponding frequency spectrum (frequency against time, lower tier) for six alveolar fricative vocalizations uttered in isolation by this author. The durations of the original vocalizations were greater than 400 msecs, longer than any normal fricative. In the figure, only the last approximately 240 msecs of these vocalizations are shown. The horizontal axis of the frequency spectrum has gridlines at 2,000-Hz intervals; the fricative energy is mostly located between the 4,000-Hz gridline and the 8,000-Hz gridline, as would be expected. Three occurrences of normal fricative offsets (without closure/glottal cut-off) and three occurrences of fricatives with glottal cut-off offsets are given as indicated under the spectrogram.

What distinguishes these sounds perceptually is that in relation to the normal offsets, the glottal cut-off offsets seem to enjoy a slight increase in frequency of the "hissing sound" just before the fricative ends. Acoustically, there is no such increase in frequency; however, the normal offsets lose energy at the higher frequencies (in

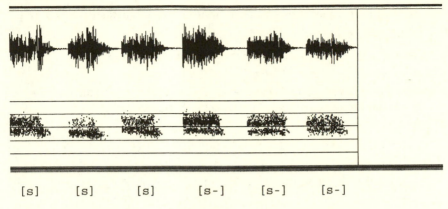

[s]   [s]   [s]   [s-]   [s-]   [s-]

Figure 10.2. Acoustic information for six alveolar fricatives.

the vicinity of 7,000 Hz) somewhat earlier than their closure cut-off counterparts. Specifically, normal offsets lose most of their higher frequency energy in the neighborhood of 35 to 55 msecs before the lower frequency energy dissipates (in the vicinity of 5,000 Hz), whereas the closure cut-off offsets lose that energy much later, at approximately 20 to 30 msecs before the lower frequencies dissipate.

Appendix B: Glossary of Phonetic and Phonological Terms

Readers who may be less familiar with the phonetic and phonological terms used in this chapter may find the following glossary helpful.

acoustic Refers to the physically measurable properties of sound.

alveolar A sound articulated with the front of the tongue and the alveolar ridge, which lies behind the upper front teeth. Examples are the [d] in *dog* and the [s] in *sack*.

alveopalatal A sound articulated with the body of the tongue and the frontal region of the roof of the mouth, for example, the "sh" sound in *she* that is phonetically transcribed [ʃ].

amplitude The acoustic energy of a sound; the perceptual correlate is loudness.

approximant A sound whereby the articulators approach each other but not so much that frication is produced. Approximants in English are either central as in the [r] sound or in the [j] sound (e.g., that begins *yes*), with the flow of air over the center of the tongue, or lateral as in [l], with airflow over the side or sides of the tongue.

articulation The gesture of two or more articulators.

articulator Any of the speech organs that participate in the articulation of a speech sound. The tip of the tongue, the upper teeth, the soft palate, and the vocal cords are examples of articulators.

aspiration The "puff of air" that can occur when an articulation is released.

auditory Refers to the perceived quality of sound.

bilabial A sound articulated with the upper and lower lips, for example, the [p] and the [m] sounds in *Pam.*

dental A sound articulated with the upper teeth, for example, the [f] in *fan* or the 'th' sound in *theory*, which is phonetically transcribed as [(].

frication The turbulence and its resulting noise that is produced when the airstream is forced through a constriction in the vocal tract.

fricative A consonantal sound in which the articulators are sufficiently close to each other that the airflow is turbulent, for example, the [s] in *see* or the [ʃ] in *she.*

fundamental frequency The frequency of vibration of the vocal cords; the perceptual correlate is pitch.

glottal An articulation that involves a closing of the glottis, the space between the vocal cords.

glottalization An effect on the airstream caused by a certain positioning or action of the vocal cords, and its perceived quality.

homorganic Two sounds are homorganic if they involve the same place of articulation, for example, [s] and [t].

laryngealization A type of voice quality, also called creaky voice, that is produced by a certain way of holding the vocal cords during voiced sounds.

lateral An articulation that involves flow of air around the side or sides of the tongue, for example, the occurrences of [l] in *little.*

nasal stop A consonantal articulation that involves complete oral closure but allows air to flow through the nasal cavity by lowering the velum, for example, the [n] in *nose.*

oral stop A consonantal articulation that involves complete blockage of the flow of air through the vocal tract, for example, the occurrences of [p] in *people.* Oral stops are usually referred to as "stops."

phonetics Phonetics is concerned with the physiological *articulation* of speech—how sounds are produced by the speech organs—as well as with the *acoustic*, physically measurable properties of sounds. The acoustic properties of sounds may be further described in perceptual, or *auditory*, terms, such as "loud" and "hissing."

phonology Phonology is concerned with how the particular sounds of a language pattern or function in that language. While phonetics concerns the formal (physical and physiological) aspects of sounds, phonology concerns how those sounds relate to other linguistic elements (such as other sounds) in the language.

sonorant/sonority The loudness of a sound relative to that of other sounds in the same linguistic context.

stop Usually refers to an oral stop, though nasals consonants such as [n] and [m] may technically be considered stops.

syllabic Refers to a single sound that can be a syllable by itself, for example, the [l] that forms the second syllable of *little*.

velar A sound articulated with the back of the tongue and the velum, for example, the [g] in *dog* or the [k] in *sack*.

velum The part of the palate at the back of the mouth. This can also be opened to allow air to flow through the nasal cavity (e.g., for nasal stops).

voiced Refers to a sound that involves vibration of the vocal cords, for example, the [d] and [z] in *dozen*. The voiced/voiceless distinction is used primarily for consonants, since vowels are naturally voiced.

voiceless Refers to a sound that does not involve vocal cord vibration, for example, [t] and [s].

NOTES

This study benefited greatly from comments on earlier drafts by Cecilia Ford, Barbara Fox, and Sandra Thompson, who deserve my sincere thanks. The errors and shortcomings remain my own. I would like to express my gratitude also to Charles Goodwin for use of the "Auto Discussion" materials and to Barbara Fox for use of the "Housemates" materials. Last, I wish to thank Alan Bell, Susanna Cumming, Barbara Fox, Cecilia Ford, Charles Goodwin, Makoto Hayashi, Dan Jurafsky, Emanuel Schegloff, Maria Thomas-Ruzic, and Sandra Thompson for their input in shaping my understanding of repair and cut-off.

1. Work by John Local and John Kelly (e.g., Local and Kelly 1986) demonstrates the value of detailed phonetic analysis for the study of talk-in-interaction.

2. In using the term "projected," I am referring to the normative, temporal, and context-dependent property of interactional objects such that some earlier part of the object (e.g., the beginning of a turn at talk or the beginning of a word) provides information as to the general character of the object as a whole. From an understanding of the global character of the object as a whole, which may in fact get modified through time, it is possible to make judgments about what it will take to complete that object.

3. Of the same-turn repairs not examined, there are several initiated by pause, such as the long pause after *north* in line 12. There is, in addition, a repair that has no dedicated "initiator" at all, namely, the repair that alternates *I live* to *we live*. And there is even a case of cut-off that does not result in repair of any linguistic aspect of the turn. This is the very brief cut-off of *the* in line 4; here the turn is continued without change from its projected course (that is, *mountains* is an expectable and recognizable continuation of *I grew up in the*). This is a good example of repair being initiated but then "canceled" (Schegloff 1984b).

4. These particular cut-off-initiated repairs happen to address some trouble with the whole turn-so-far, but as will be seen in many of the examples in this chapter, cut-off-initiated repair commonly addresses trouble that arises from some already-produced word or phrase or even some aspect of its delivery (e.g., its intonation).

5. There are classes of orderly exceptions to this statement (Jasperson 1998).

6. Certain transcription notations employed in this chapter may differ from those given in the appendix that appears at the end of this volume. They are given here:

(.)   "Micropause" indicates a brief pause in the range of from approximately 90 to 120 msecs.

<   "Left push" indicates extremely rapid transition from cut-off to resumption, in the range from approximately 50 to 90 msecs.

%   Percent sign indicates closure cut-off with salient interruption glottalization.

-              Hyphen indicates closure cut-off without (salient) interruption glottalization. (The one exception to this usage is indicated at the relevant point in the text.)

*   Asterisk following a segment indicates that the segment is not fully articulated due to the cut-off; this notation is used in conjunction with a hyphen.

-word   A hyphen that precedes a word indicates that a glottal or oral stop is released into the beginning of the word.

7. Interruption glottalization differs acoustically from laryngealization, or "creaky voice," at least in having less "spiky" fundamental pitch peaks and possibly less regular peaks (except when at the speaker's fundamental frequency floor). In addition, the articulation of interruption glottalization does not seem to be sustainable, whereas laryngealization is. These differences are no doubt due to different activities of the larynx, possibly in that interruption glottalization is a product of a rapidly closing glottis, whereas laryngealization is a product of a specially tightened glottis that is held comparatively constantly.

8. I use the terms "resumption" and "resume" to refer to the (re)beginning of speech after it has been cut off.

9. In the first cut-off, the dental articulation begins approximately seventy msecs after the beginning of the interruption glottalization, whereas the dental in the second cut-off begins approximately one hundred msecs later.

10. I thank Alan Bell for suggesting this term.

11. A precondition for the use of opportunistic closure cut-off is that the identity of the first sound of the resumption is available to the speaker, and that may not always be the case.

12. This or a similar sequence of events may attend the fluent production of syllable-final voiceless stops that follow vowels in some varieties of English (cf. Ladefoged 1982).

13. A significant post-cut-off pause typically does not develop until roughly 0.2 seconds (Jasperson 1998).

14. There are seventeen cases of repair in the corpus that are initiated in the environment of a dental fricative. There is one case of repair that is initiated by closure cut-off at the beginning of what is either the definite article *the* or the complementizer *that*. However, the cut-off articulation is a type of dental stop, which commonly begins these items (*personal communication* Alan Bell). The case appears in example (8) in the text.

15. In this case it is worth noting that absence of cut-off could make an interpretation of the utterance problematic. That is, to the extent that the presence of a repair is not appreciated, we get the result . . . *blacks were alot more accepting of white outsiders than they were of thuh people with thuh whites who lived there*, which is bizarre in its conversational context. Rhythmic differences between line 6 and lines 7 and 8, however, recommend against this interpretation, along with the possibility that *with* is truncated and followed by the brief pause. In any event, the listener does seem to appreciate the presence of the repair, since she gives an understanding nod.

16. It remains possible that glottal closure be used "privately" as a means to avoid nonlexical vocalizations while articulators prepare for the resumption of speech. But such closures will not be interactionally real as closure cut-off.

17. In the example, the time from completion of velar closure at the offset of *think* to the beginning of the vowel of the next word, *I*, is approximately 145 msecs. If even 30 msecs is spliced out of this part of the audio signal, the cut-off seems to disappear.

18. Duration of the interruption glottalization is approximately sixty msecs.

19. Duration of the interruption glottalization is approximately twenty-five msecs.

20. There may be articulatory components to this technique in addition to the pulmonic action, such as the glottis opening (larynx dropping) during voiced sounds.

21. I have omitted talk by a co-present child whose participation is peripheral.

22. On this basis, it is possible to derive what Willem Levelt (1983) refers to as the Main Interruption Rule, originally stated by S. Nooteboom (1980): "Stop the flow of speech immediately upon detecting the occasion of repair" (Levelt 1983:56).

REFERENCES

Atkinson, J. Maxwell, and John Heritage (eds.). 1984. *Structures of Social Action: Studies in Conversation Analysis.* Cambridge: Cambridge University Press.

Brédart, Serge. 1991. Word interruption in self-repairing. *Journal of Psycholinguistic Research* 20:123–138.

Fox, Barbara, and Robert Jasperson. 1995. A syntactic exploration of repair in English conversation. In Phillip Davis (ed.), *Alternative Linguistics: Descriptive and Theoretical Modes*, 77–134. Amsterdam: John Benjamins.

Goodwin, Charles. 1981. *Conversational Organization: Interactions Between Speakers and Hearers.* New York: Academic Press.

Goodwin, Charles. 1987. Forgetfulness as an interactional resource. *Social Psychology Quarterly* 50(2): 115–131.

Hockett, Charles. 1967. *Where the Tongue Slips, There Slip I: To Honor Roman Jakobson*, 910–936. The Hague: Mouton.

Jasperson, Robert. 1998. Repair after cut-off: Explorations in the grammar of focused repair of the turn-constructional unit-so-far. Ph.D. diss., University of Colorado at Boulder.

Jefferson, Gail. 1974. Error correction as an interactional resource. *Language in Society* 2(1): 181–199.

Ladefoged, Peter. 1982. *A Course in Phonetics.* 2nd ed. New York: Harcourt Brace Jovanovich.

Levelt, Willem. 1983. Monitoring and self-repair in speech. *Cognition* 14:41–104.

Local, John, and John Kelly. 1986. Projection and 'silences': Notes on phonetic and conversational structure. *Human Studies* 9:185–204.

Nakatani, Christine, and Julia Hirschberg. 1993. A speech-first model for repair detection and correction. *Proceedings of the Association of Computational Linguistics:* 46–53.

Nooteboom, S. 1980. Speaking and unspeaking: Detection and correction of phonological and lexical errors in spontaneous speech. In Victoria Fromkin (ed.), *Errors in Linguistic Performance*, pp. 87–95. New York: Academic Press.

Sacks, Harvey, Emanuel A. Schegloff, and Gail Jefferson. 1974. A simplest systematics for the organization of turn-taking in conversation. *Language* 50(4): 696–735.

Schegloff, Emanuel A. 1979. The relevance of repair to a syntax-for-conversation. In *Syntax and Semantics*, vol. 12: *Discourse and Syntax*, edited by Talmy Givón, 261–286. New York: Academic Press.

Schegloff, Emanuel. 1984a. On some gestures' relation to talk. In J. Maxwell Atkinson and John Heritage (eds.), *Structures of Social Action: Studies in Conversation Analysis*, 266–296. Cambridge: Cambridge University Press.

Schegloff, Emanuel. 1984b. SOC 144/244B lectures, Winter Term. Lecture transcripts, University of California, Los Angeles.

Schegloff, Emanuel. 1992. Repair after next turn: The last structurally provided defense of intersubjectivity in conversation. *American Journal of Sociology* 97(5): 1295–1345.

Schegloff, Emanuel A., Gail Jefferson, and Harvey Sacks. 1977. The preference for self-correction in the organization of repair in conversation. *Language* 53(2): 361–382.

Sparks, Randall. 1994. The structure of self-repair in English conversation. Ph.D. diss., University of Colorado at Boulder.

INDEX